Mastering the ACI Dealing Certificate

In an increasingly competitive world, we believe it's quality of thinking that will give you the edge – an idea that opens new doors, a technique that solves a problem, or an insight that simply makes sense of it all. The more you know, the smarter and faster you can go.

That's why we work with the best minds in business and finance to bring cutting-edge thinking and best learning practice to a global market.

Under a range of leading imprints, including Financial Times Prentice Hall, we create world-class print publications and electronic products bringing our readers knowledge, skills and understanding which can be applied whether studying or at work.

To find out more about our business publications, or tell us about the books you'd like to find, you can visit us at
www.business-minds.com

For other Pearson Education publications, visit
www.pearsoned-ema.com

market editions

Mastering the ACI Dealing Certificate

a practical guide to the ACI Education level 1 syllabus and examination

PHIL PARKER ACIB

FT Prentice Hall
FINANCIAL TIMES

An imprint of Pearson Education

London • New York • Toronto • Sydney • Tokyo • Singapore
Hong Kong • Cape Town • Madrid • Paris • Amsterdam • Munich • Milan

PEARSON EDUCATION LIMITED

Head Office:
Edinburgh Gate
Harlow CM20 2JE
Tel: +44 (0)1279 623623
Fax: +44 (0)1279 431059
Website: www.financialminds.com

London Office:
128 Long Acre
London WC2E 9AN
Tel: +44 (0)20 7447 2000
Fax: +44 (0)20 7447 2170

First published in Great Britain in 2003

© Philip Parker 2003

The right of Philip Parker to be identified as Author of this Work has been asserted by him in accordance with the Copyright, Designs and Patents Act 1988.

ISBN 0 273 66107 8

British Library Cataloguing in Publication Data
A CIP catalogue record for this book can be obtained from the British Library.

All rights reserved; no part of this publication may be reproduced, stored in a retrieval system, or transmitted in any form or by any means, electronic, mechanical, photocopying, recording, or otherwise without either the prior written permission of the Publishers or a licence permitting restricted copying in the United Kingdom issued by the Copyright Licensing Agency Ltd, 90 Tottenham Court Road, London W1T 4LP. This book may not be lent, resold, hired out or otherwise disposed of by way of trade in any form of binding or cover other than that in which it is published, without the prior consent of the Publishers.

This publication is designed to provide accurate and authoritative information in regard to the subject matter covered. It is sold with the understanding that neither the authors nor the Publisher is engaged in rendering legal, investing, or any other professional service. If legal advice or other expert assistance is required, the service of a competent professional person should be sought.

The Publisher and contributors make no representation, express or implied, with regard to the accuracy of the information contained in this book and cannot accept any responsibility or liability for any errors or omissions that it may contain.

Information in this book is correct at the time of going to press but is subject to change without notice. Information in this book has been produced in good faith as supporting documentation for candidates proposing to sit the **ACI Dealing Certificate** whose syllabus and examination format is subject to change without notice. See the website www.aciforex.com for further information.

ACI Certificate examination texts and certain Multiple choice question formats are © **ACI - The Financial Markets Association**. They are reproduced here with their permission.

10 9 8 7 6 5 4 3 2 1

Typeset by Pantek Arts Ltd, Maidstone, Kent
Printed and bound in Great Britain by Bell & Bain Ltd, Glasgow

The Publishers' policy is to use paper manufactured from sustainable forests.

Dedication

Dedicated to my wife Carole, son Robert and daughter Juliette.
My thanks go to David Kingston for proof reading the difficult bits.

About the Author

Philip Parker, before forming Lywood David International Limited, the UK training and consultancy company, worked in and around Lloyds Bank Group dealing operations for the whole of his banking career spanning 25 years. He spent ten years as a foreign exchange and money market dealer in Lloyds Bank International (LBI) in London, trading the major world currencies. There then followed three years during which he acted in an audit/consultancy role, regularly visiting and reporting on the overseas dealing operations of LBI which at that time spread from North, Central and South America to the Far East financial market centres of Tokyo and Hong Kong. At this time Philip was also involved in redrafting the bank's Treasury rule book. In the early 1980s, based back in London, Philip was given special responsibility for developing computer-based dealer rate information and decision support systems for use in the dealing environment.

It was at this time that Philip first became involved in training by developing and presenting week-long Treasury seminars for international branch managers of the Lloyds Bank Group to advise them on best practices in managing and controlling dealing operations. Such seminars ran in the UK, Europe, the USA and the Far East. From 1988, as Senior Manager Training Services within the Treasury Division of Lloyds Bank plc, Philip was responsible for the specialized treasury training of Treasury Division personnel worldwide, also making his services available to other operating divisions of the Group in the UK and abroad for training and the dissemination of treasury product knowledge.

In 1992 Philip left the bank and formed Lywood David International Limited. Over the last ten years he has undertaken extensive training and consultancy commissions in western, central and eastern Europe – working in the emerging markets on behalf of the Know How Fund and PHARE in the mid-1990s and elsewhere across the globe. He also continues to present a range of open training courses in London and overseas locations. The company's training courses towards the ACI qualifications are popular with management and participants alike – many candidates eventually gaining distinctions and passes with merit. These courses have also been presented in overseas financial centres on behalf of local ACI/Forex Clubs and in-house for a number of financial institutions and banking schools.

About the Author

Through another group company, Multimedia TradeWind Limited, working with software developers Tradewind Design, Philip designs and markets interactive computer-based training products developed using the latest multimedia technology. The PC software products developed are WINDEAL – a range of Windows-based dealing room simulations covering the foreign exchange and money markets – and WINFOREX – the unique PC-based study aid aimed at candidates for ACI Education qualifications. These products frequently feature on the company's courses and have been sold to individuals and financial institutions across the globe.

CONTENTS

Foreword	xiii
The Aim of This Book	xv
List of Abbreviations	xviii
Recognized ISO Currency Codes	xxi

1 How to Use This Book — 1
Introduction — 2
The ACI Dealing Certificate examination — 3
Prometric electronic delivery examination — 5

2 Introduction to the International Money Markets, the Foreign Exchange Markets and Their Associated Derivative Markets — 11
Setting the scene — 12
Foreign exchange market — 14
Market participants — 15
Foreign exchange derivatives — 19
Basic market concepts — 19

SYLLABUS PART 1

3 Topic 1 · Background — 25
Pre-Second World War — 26
Post-Second World War — 27
ACI – The Financial Markets Association — 36

4 Topic 2 · Basic Interest Rate Calculations — 39
Topic 3 · Money Market Products — 39
Introduction — 41
The cash market — 42
LIBOR — 57
Yield curves — 59
Position keeping — 64
Negotiable financial instruments — 66
Repos — 87

Contents

5 Topic 4 (part) · Money Market Derivatives — 99
Introduction — 100
Derivation of forward/forward interest rates — 101
Financial futures — 105
Forward rate agreements — 127
Longer-term interest rate derivatives – interest rate swaps — 141

6 Topic 5 · Spot Foreign Exchange — 157
Introduction — 158
Spot date — 159
Target — 160
Currencies traded — 162
Market makers/market users — 163
Spot rate — 164
Spot rate spread — 164
Spot rate calculations — 174
Cross currency calculations — 177
Interbank dealing methods — 184
Rates information — 188
Position keeping — 189

7 Topic 6 · Forward Foreign Exchange — 197
Introduction — 198
Forward FX transactions — 200
Premium/discount — 205
Forward rate quotation terminology — 207
Forward exchange price calculations — 209
Outright forward cross currency calculations — 211
Corporate FX business — 224
Interbank forward exchange operations — 228
Other forward exchange calculations — 232
Interest arbitrage — 247

8 Topic 4 (part) · FX Derivatives — 255
Introduction — 256
Currency options — 256
Terminology and definitions — 264
Hedging currency option positions — 268

9 Topic 8 · The Role of Settlements 279
Introduction 280
The treasury division 281
Treasury division support functions 284

10 Topic 9 · The Risk Environment 293
Introduction 294
Risks in cash markets 294
Risks in financial instruments 298
Risks in financial futures 299
Risks in FRAs 300
Risks in interest rate swaps 301
Risks in spot foreign exchange 303
Risks in forward foreign exchange 308
Risks in exchange traded currency options 311
Risks in over the counter options 312
Capital adequacy 313

SYLLABUS PART 2
11 Topic 10 · The Model Code 319
Introduction 320
Chapter I – Business hours and time zone related 321
Chapter II – Personal conduct issues 324
Chapter III – Back office, payments and confirmations 327
Chapter IV – Disputes, differences, mediation and compliance 328
Chapter V – Authorization, documentation and telephone taping 332
Chapter VI – Brokers and brokerage 334
Chapter VII – Dealing practice 336
Chapter VIII – Dealing practice for specific transactions 339
Chapter IX – General risk management principles for dealing business 340
Chapter X – Additional guidelines for dealing with corporate/commercial clients 341
Chapter XI – Market terminology 342
Appendices 1–7 343

Contents

12 Approaching the Examination — 347
Preparation for the examination — 348
The ACI Dealing Certificate examination — 351
ACI Dealing Certificate examination techniques — 353
Specific points to remember — 354

Appendices — 361
I ACI Formulae Sheets — 363
II Glossary of Terms and Dealing Jargon — 369

Index — 395

FOREWORD

A. E. Moore CBE, *Deputy Chairman, Lloyds TSB Group plc*

When the foreign exchange markets returned to life in the 1950s, available textbooks on the subject still contained examples of calculations showing at what point it was profitable to ship gold between London and New York to limit fluctuations in currency exchange rates.

We have come a long way from the Gold Standard concept, living through phases where the authorities dominated the markets, to periods characterized by wild swings in exchange and money rates driven by changing economic realities and speculative movements. The present climate is more orderly, including the creation of the Euro to unify many European currencies, but, paradoxically, exchange and money market operations have become infinitely more complex.

The range of products and instruments traded has changed beyond recognition. In the beginning there was spot and forward foreign exchange with the forward rate determined by interest rate differentials (except when it was the other way round!) and cash deposits with perhaps certificates of deposit to give liquidity. Then came futures, options and all the other derivatives such as swaps and FRAs.

The most striking feature of the last 25 years has indeed been the explosion of products designed to allow the management of risk, as opposed to dealing in the underlying cash product, be it an interest rate or an exchange rate risk. The key activity in most dealing rooms now resembles an inverted pyramid, with a small volume of traditional cash products supporting a vast amount of trading in derivatives. Some of this may be to hedge the risks on the underlying cash business of the institution, but it is just as likely to be a vehicle for the taking of risk, without the problem of inflating the balance sheet – derivative instruments are so much more convenient and capital efficient!

The history of the market continues, nevertheless, to be littered with examples of losses incurred by imprudent behaviour compounded by lack of management control. Constant enhancement of reporting mechanisms never quite seems to close the door, partly because the reporting is in itself

Foreword

open to fraud. Management needs to have at least sufficient skills to understand the activities of traders, ask the right questions and test the answers for credibility. Traders and management have to have a full appreciation of the instruments in which they deal, in particular, for example, the nature of embedded options.

Mastering the ACI Dealing Certificate is therefore a welcome addition to the range of available educational literature: it provides an excellent overview of today's markets written in terms that strip away the spurious mystery that sometimes appears to cloud the activities of a dealing room. With its future companion volumes on the ACI Settlements Certificate and the ACI Diploma it will, I am sure, feature prominently on the shelves of the next generation of ACI members and examination candidates. Its author combines a practical experience of dealing activity with a proven ability to convert that knowledge into a training environment for those attracted by today's fast-moving and constantly developing money and exchange markets.

THE AIM OF THIS BOOK

The *ACI Dealing Certificate* is a foundation programme that allows candidates to acquire the basic knowledge and skills utilized within the foreign exchange and money markets together with their associated derivatives. Candidates should also be able to apply the Model Code as it stands today. As such, it demonstrates the skills required for participation in the market, and the ability to use and manipulate the fundamental mathematics used in the markets.

The programme is designed for anyone whose effectiveness would be enhanced by explanations of the market, its products and operation, and is a precursor to the ACI Diploma. In particular, the qualification is designed for the following groups:

- new entrants and junior dealers (0–18 months' experience) in the dealing room;
- middle office and operations personnel;
- auditors and compliance officers.

The *ACI Dealing Certificate* aims to test candidates' knowledge and the application of that knowledge in the core products of the market place and their interrelationships.

(Reproduced in part from the official syllabus on www.aciforex.com.)

If you are a dealer, settlements specialist or anyone involved in foreign exchange, treasury or capital markets operations and you are thinking about taking ACI – The Financial Markets Association – Dealing Certificate, Settlements Certificate or Diploma examinations, then this series of books has been designed just for you.

This book looks at the Level 1 ACI Dealing Certificate syllabus and examination. Other volumes are planned for the Level 1 ACI Settlements Certificate and the Level 2 ACI Diploma.

The intention is that each book will contain all the information necessary for you, the candidate, to select the correct qualification, review the examination syllabus and identify any personal training needs in areas specific to the examination chosen.

The Aim of This Book

The aim of this volume is to introduce you to the topics of the *ACI Dealing Certificate* examination syllabus, the style of questions and the ACI marking methodology, and provide hints in approaching the multiple choice format questions and selecting the correct answers in the examination.

The principal objective is to ensure that at the end of the day *you* are confident in your approach to your chosen examination.

THE ACI DEALING CERTIFICATE SYLLABUS

The *ACI Dealing Certificate* was introduced in late 1999 as a straight replacement for the previously titled Level 1 examination: Introduction to Foreign Exchange and Money Markets. The marking methodology was amended in January 2001 to include a minimum mark requirement per topic.

In simple terms the syllabus covers all the market activities of a bank's treasury dealing room requiring you to be familiar with the various separate dealing functions found in such an operation plus coverage of the Model Code published by the ACI in June 2000.

The latest *ACI Dealing Certificate* syllabus may be found on the ACI website at www.aciforex.com. The syllabus topics are explained at the start of each chapter of this book.

DIFFERENCES FROM PREVIOUS INTRODUCTORY SYLLABUS

On reviewing the latest *ACI Dealing Certificate* syllabus the opening paragraphs note the changes from the previous Level 1 examination. Anyone who ever looked at the old Introduction to Foreign Exchange and Money Markets syllabus will notice two main differences.

First, there is wider coverage of and greater emphasis placed on derivatives. The old "Intro" examination included only FRAs – now interest rate swaps, futures and options all feature alongside traditional cash market operations (now also including repos) in the 50 multiple choice questions of Part 1 chosen from the general topic headings.

The second big difference is that, with the consolidation of the five separate Codes of Conduct drawn up by regulators in the principal global financial market centres into the Model Code (published by ACI in June 2000), Part 2 of the examination now comprises 30 multiple choice questions based on the Model Code.

The ordering of topics has also changed in the examination but this book seeks to order them in a logical sequence, focusing first on cash market products, their quotation, dealing techniques and risks followed by their associated derivatives (split by underlying market, i.e. interest rate or foreign

The Aim of This Book

exchange derivatives) including input on position keeping as appropriate. Later chapters address the ancillary – though no less important – topics such as the role of settlements and risk before the chapter on the Model Code. A final chapter includes suggestions on the candidate's approach to revision and the *ACI Dealing Certificate* examination itself. Appendices include the ACI dealing formulae (available in the examination) and a glossary of terms.

LIST OF ABBREVIATIONS

ACI	The Financial Markets Association
API	application program interface
ATM	at the money
BA	bankers' acceptance
BBA	British Bankers Association
BBAIRS	British Bankers Association Interest Rate Swaps
BBAISR	British Bankers Association Interest Settlement Rate
BIS	Bank for International Settlements
bp	basis point
CAD	Capital Adequacy Directive
CBOT	Chicago Board of Trade
CD	Certificate of Deposit
CFD	Contract for Difference
CGO	Central Gilts Office
CHAPS	Clearing House Automated Payments System
CHIPS	Clearing House Interbank Payment System
CME	Chicago Mercantile Exchange
CMO	Central Moneymarkets Office
CP	Commercial Paper
CRE	credit risk equivalent
CREST	CrestCo – UK and international settlement system for shares, UK government bonds and corporate securities
CTD	Cheapest to Deliver
DTB	Deutsche Termine Borse
DVP	delivery versus payment
EBA	European Banking Association
EBS	Electronic Broking Services
EC	European Community (now the European Union (EU))
ECP	Euro Commercial Paper
ECU	European Currency Unit – now replaced by euro (EUR)
EDSP	Exchange Delivery Settlement Price
EEC	European Economic Community (now EU)
EMI	European Monetary Institute

List of Abbreviations

EMS	European Monetary System
EMU	Economic and Monetary Union
ERM	Exchange Rate Mechanism
EUR	euro
EURIBOR	Euro Interbank Offered Rate
FATF	Financial Action Task Force
FIFO	first in first out
FOX	forward with optional exit
FRA	Forward Rate Agreement
FRABBA	FRA British Bankers Association standard terms
FRN	Floating Rate Note
FV	future value
FX	foreign exchange
GC	general collateral
GMRA	Global Master Repurchase Agreement
HIC	hold in custody
IBRD	International Bank for Reconstruction and Development
ICCH	International Commodities Clearing House
IFEMA	International Foreign Exchange Master Agreement
IMF	International Monetary Fund
IMM	International Monetary Market
IMRO	Investment Managers Regulatory Organization
IRS	interest rate swap
ISDA	International Swaps and Derivatives Association
ISIN	International Securities Issue Number
ISMA	International Securities Market Association
ISO	International Standards Organization
ISV	independent software vendor
ITM	in the money
LCH	London Clearing House
LIBID	London Interbank Bid Rate
LIBOR	London Interbank Offered Rate
LICOM	London Interbank Currency Options Market
LIFFE	London International Financial Futures and Options Exchange
LIFO	last in first out
LTOM	London Traded Options Market
MATIF	Marche a Terme des Instruments Financiers
MtM	mark to market
NIP	non-investment product
OECD	Organization for Economic Cooperation and Development
OTC	over the counter

List of Abbreviations

OTM	out of the money
PFE	potential future exposure
PIBOR	Paris Interbank Offered Rate
PPS	LCH Protected Payments System
PSA	Public Securities Association
PV	present value
RoR	rate of return
SDR	special drawing right
SPAN	Standard Portfolio Analysis of Risk
SRO	self-regulatory organization
SSI	Standard Settlement Instructions
STIR	short-term interest rate
SWIFT	Society for Worldwide Interbank Financial Telecommunications
TARGET	Trans-European Automated Real-Time Gross Settlement Express Transfer System
T-bill	Treasury bill
TBMA	The Bond Market Association
T-bond	Treasury bond
TIBOR	Tokyo Interbank Offered Rate
T-note	Treasury note
TTC	Tender to Contract
VaR	value at risk
WI	when issued
XEU	European Currency Unit (ECU) – now replaced by euro (EUR)

RECOGNIZED ISO CURRENCY CODES

SWIFT currency codes for the currencies of the 66 affiliated members of ACI (from Model Code Appendix 6)

Americas
Argentina	ARS
Bahamas	BSD
Bermuda	BMD
Brazil	BRL
Canada	CAD
Mexico	MXN
Panama	PAB
USA	USD

Asia Pacific
Australia	AUD
China	CNY
Hong Kong	HKD
India	INR
Indonesia	IDR
Japan	JPY
Korea (Republic of)	KRW
Macau	MOP
Malaysia	MYR
New Zealand	NZD
Pakistan	PNR
Philippines	PHP
Singapore	SGD
Sri Lanka	LKR
Thailand	THB

Europe
Austria	EUR
Belgium	EUR
Channel Islands	GBP

Croatia	HRN
Cyprus	CYP
Czech Republic	CZK
Denmark	DKK
Finland	EUR
France	EUR
Georgia	GEL
Germany	EUR
Greece	EUR
Hungary	HUF
Iceland	ISN
Ireland	EUR
Israel	ILS
Italy	EUR
Luxembourg	EUR
Macedonia	MKD
Malta	MTL
Monaco	EUR
Netherlands	EUR
Norway	NOK
Poland	PLN
Portugal	EUR
Romania	ROL
Slovakia	SKK
Slovenia	SIT
Spain	EUR
Sweden	SEK
Switzerland	CHF
United Kingdom	GBP
Yugoslavia	YUN

Middle East and Africa

Bahrain	BHD
Egypt	EGP
Jordan	JOD
Kenya	KES
Kuwait	KWD
Lebanon	LBP
Mauritius	MUR
South Africa	ZAR
Tunisia	TND
United Arab Emirates	AED

How to Use This Book

Introduction

The ACI Dealing Certificate examination

Prometric electronic delivery examination

INTRODUCTION

As an ACI candidate you may use this book in association with any other textbooks, hard copy or PC-based distance learning products you are currently using. Where appropriate, suggestions are made for additional reading material.

The intention of this book is to highlight syllabus subject matter which is *vital* for you, the candidate, when you approach the ACI Dealing Certificate examination. We would love to be able to read the examiners' mind, but sadly our crystal ball is in for service at the moment. Not every aspect of every topic can be covered in this book but those issues in markets and products on which the examiners have concentrated in the past are discussed with highlighted *Notes* and *Hints* on how to approach certain question types to give you confidence when sitting the examination. You should, however, bear in mind that this book may not contain every aspect of the subject matter of the ACI Dealing Certificate qualification.

Chapter 2 sets the scene and defines various elements which go across all the markets/products involved in the foreign exchange, interest rate and derivative markets covered by the syllabus.

The remaining chapters dealing with the official syllabus are arranged to align exactly with the ACI Dealing Certificate syllabus topics and the text includes information where these differ from the question baskets of the Prometric delivered examination.

Each syllabus topic chapter contains an introduction to the topic subject matter, important market and financial instrument learning points with worked examples of product pricing and dealing calculations. There are also examples of the types of question which can be asked and *Hints* on how to deal with each generic type.

These *Hint* headings indicate issues of which you should take particular note and refer to issues where it is known that candidates have experienced problems in the past or where questions can be worded in such a way as perhaps to be confusing when first encountered.

Each chapter ends with a brief list of other textbooks on the relevant syllabus topic and reference to any related publications together with recommendations of websites worth a visit.

The final chapter of the book is on overall revision and examination techniques – particularly bearing in mind the multiple choice question types chosen for delivery in the Prometric examination.

There are also two appendices:

- *Appendix I* is a copy of the ACI formulae sheets – made available to candidates on-screen and in hard copy during the ACI Dealing Certificate examination.
- *Appendix II* is a glossary of dealing terms which will assist candidates in their preparations for the ACI Dealing Certificate.

THE ACI DEALING CERTIFICATE EXAMINATION

Format

The examination consists of a single paper of two hours duration. There is a total of 80 multiple choice questions out of which 30 questions relate to the Model Code. Candidates will be required to pass the Model Code section of this examination.

In addition to an overall pass mark of 50 percent for Part 1, the minimum pass levels for each topic in the ACI Dealing Certificate have been set by the Board of Education as follows:

Risk Management & Control	1 correct out of 4	25.0%
Foreign Exchange	3 correct out of 7	42.8%
Foreign Exchange Calculations	3 correct out of 8	37.5%
Money Markets	3 correct out of 7	42.8%
Money Markets Calculations	2 correct out of 6	33.3%
Derivatives	3 correct out of 7	42.8%
Repo Market	2 correct out of 6	33.3%
Market Conv. & Env.	2 correct out of 5	40.0%
Total	19 correct out of 50	38.0%

However, to *pass* a candidate must have 25 correct answers out of 50 (50 percent overall), *plus*...

The Model Code	15 correct out of 30	50.0%

The examination is a single electronically delivered paper divided into two parts. The first part covers topics 1 to 9 of the syllabus and consists of 50 multiple choice questions. The second part covering section 10 of the syllabus (the Model Code and market practice) consists of 30 multiple choice questions.

Notes

- Topic titles do not exactly align with examination question basket titles.
- The topic title of questions in Part 1 of the examination is *not* separately identified to the candidate on the Prometric screen in the examination.
- After the first 50 multiple choice questions making up Part 1 of the examination have been completed (all topics intermingled), the 30 Model Code multiple choice questions of Part 2 appear in a block.

Pass marks

Candidates are required to achieve a *minimum* pass mark in each topic (see above) as well as 50 percent overall in Part 1 *plus* 50 percent of Part 2 to gain a *pass*.

Provided the minimum pass marks per topic are achieved, a *pass with merit* is awarded at 65 percent and a *distinction* at 75 percent overall.

ACI formulae

A formulae sheet is available on-screen during the Prometric delivered examination and in hard copy in the examination centre. This is contained in Appendix I of this book.

Hint

As we have been advised that in some Prometric test centres candidates have encountered problems with availability of hard copy formulae sheets you are strongly recommended to download the official ACI formulae sheets from the ACI website and take the sheets with you to the examination centre (just in case!).

Calculators

Some questions will require the use of a basic calculator. This will be provided on-screen (MS Windows Calculator) or, alternatively, candidates may take into the examination a calculator of their choice.

Dictionaries

If your first language is not English you are permitted to take a standard dictionary (your language/English) into the Prometric examination. The language dictionary used may not be a specialized dictionary, e.g. *not* a dictionary of business terms. Prometric centre invigilators will check the dictionaries to ensure that no written information or notes exist which could be used by the candidate during the examination.

How to Use This Book

PROMETRIC ELECTRONIC DELIVERY EXAMINATION

The following screen shots are repeated from the www.aciforex.com website ACI Dealing Certificate interactive demonstration (see Figure 1.1 et seq.) and are included here with ACI permission.

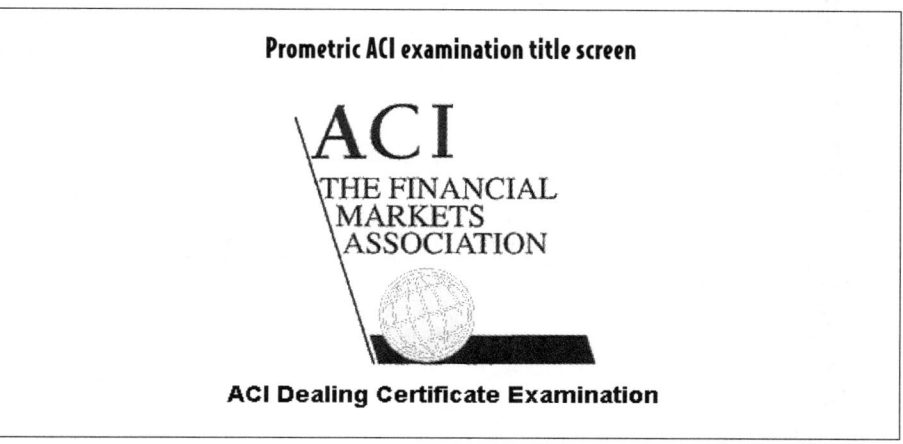

Fig 1.1

Survey

On commencing the Prometric examination you will be prompted to input additional information, including the training method you followed (see Figure 1.2). The survey input screen should include all training companies and distance learning products. Please select the method followed by you.

> *If you have only used this book for your preparation please select* **Lywood David International Limited** *as the training company used.*

Hint

Mastering the ACI Dealing Certificate

Fig 1.2

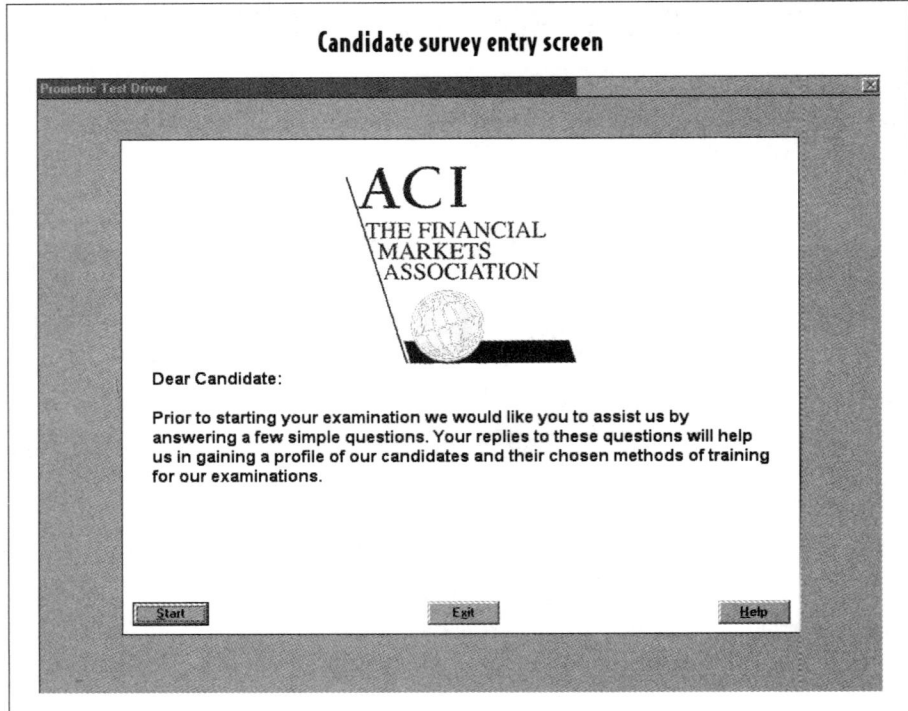

Candidate survey entry screen

Multiple choice screen display

A typical Prometric screen based examination question looks like that shown in Figure 1.3 (ACI Dealing Certificate example).

A – B – C – D Correct answer selection

There are four answers to each multiple choice question of which only one is correct. You are prompted to select the best answer by clicking on the appropriate Windows radio button alongside one of the four choices available. When the question has been answered the next question in the sequence can be displayed by clicking the *Next* button.

Next

You do not have to answer a question immediately. You may pass to the next question by clicking on the *Next* button and the passed question will be highlighted on the *Item Review* screen (see below) at the end of the test identified as being incomplete.

How to Use This Book

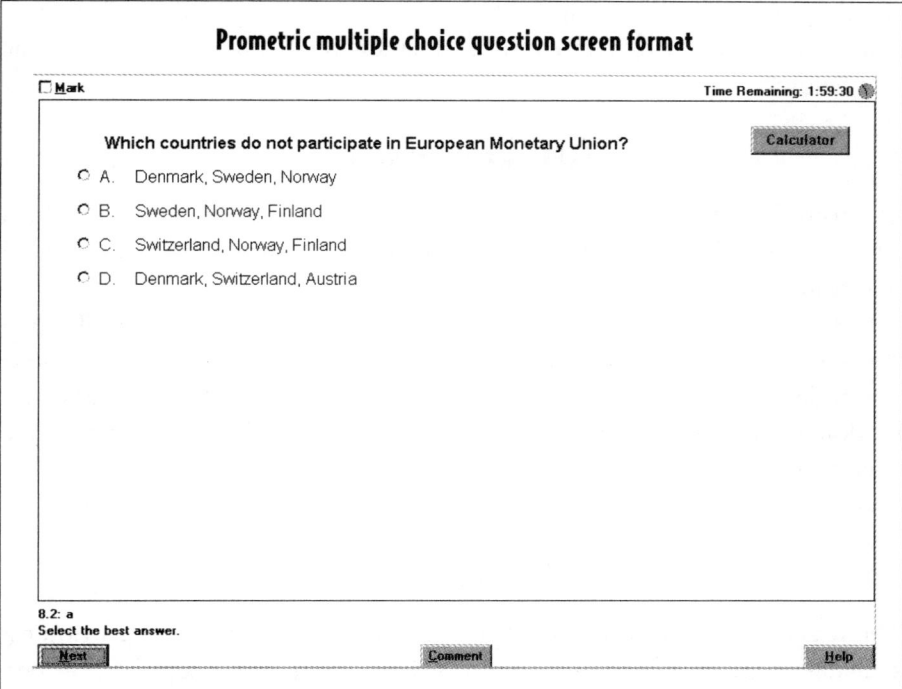

Fig 1.3

Change

You may change your choice of answer at any time. There is an opportunity to review all questions/answers at the end of the examination (via the *Item Review* screen). Only when your allotted time has expired are the answers taken as firm by the system.

Mark

You may *Mark* any question, whether an answer is already selected or not. This is done by selecting the checkbox in the top left-hand corner – perhaps for revision later during the examination time. This mark will be identified on the *Item Review* screen.

Clock/time remaining

Time remaining is displayed in the top right-hand corner of the screen.

Help

The additional facility buttons available on each Prometric screen should be self-explanatory. Access buttons for the MS Windows *Calculator* and the on-screen *ACI Formulae* listings are displayed. There is a *Help* button

Mastering the ACI Dealing Certificate

which gives access to a Help facility dealing with the use of the Prometric system (not in question content or correct answer!) and a *Comment* button (see below).

Item Review screen

On completion of all 80 questions (ACI Dealing Certificate), the *Item Review* screen is displayed (in the demo screen shown there were only 25 questions – see Figure 1.4).

The ACI Dealing Certificate examination screen will indicate all 80 questions and their status. *Mark*ed questions are highlighted and incomplete questions are identified. You may review any question and its answer either by double clicking on the item or by completing the *Review Item* box and clicking the button alongside.

Once you are happy with your examination you must click on *End*.

Results screen

The *Results* screen will then be displayed (see Figure 1.5) and if a printer is available in the examination room this will print out a hard copy of your performance including your result with topic by topic scores and confirmation

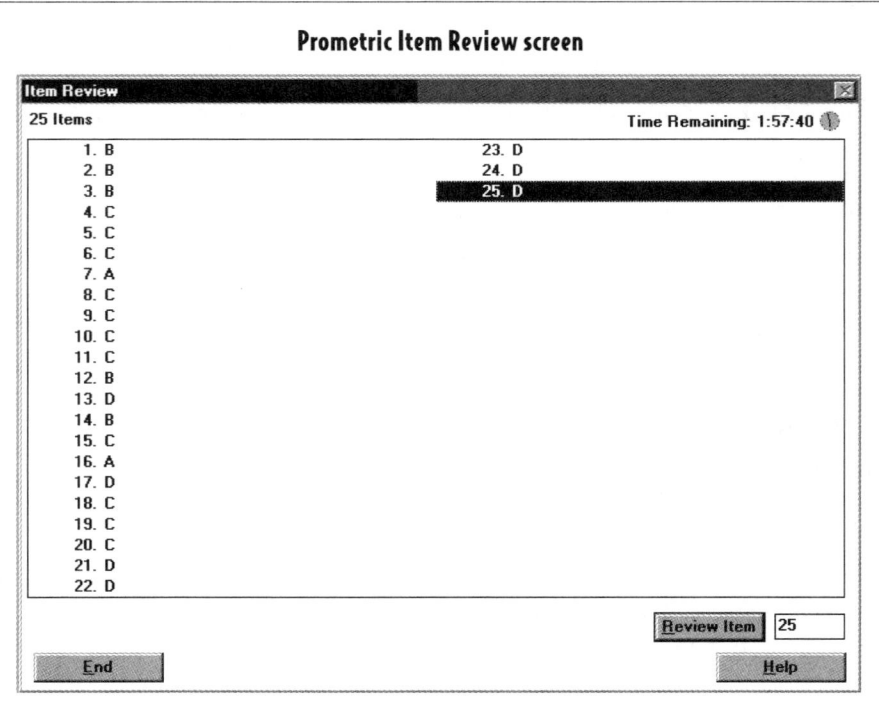

Fig 1.4

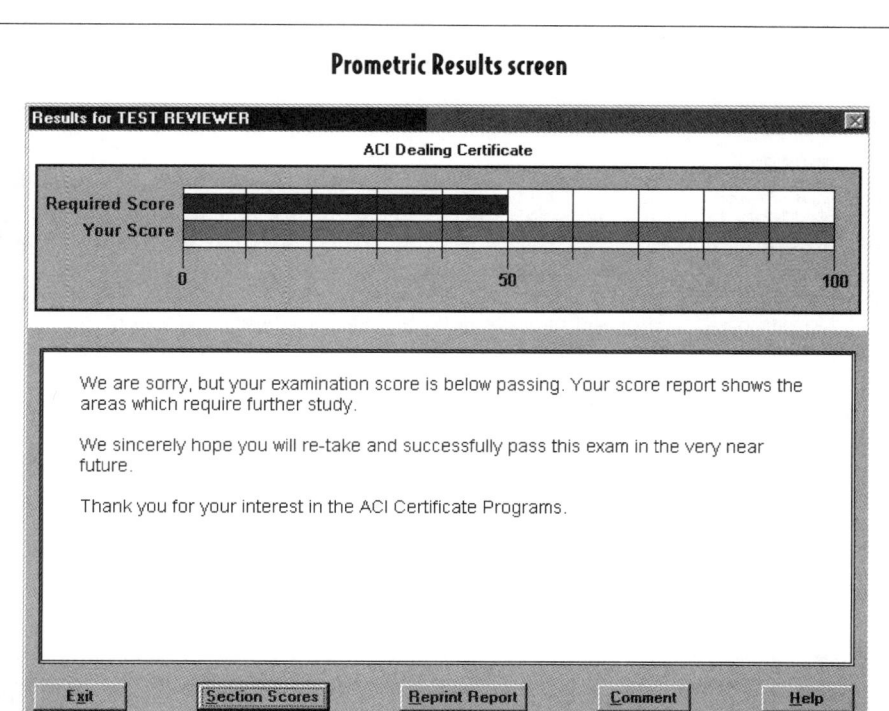

Fig 1.5

of pass or fail. To produce an additional printed report there is a *Reprint Report* button. Clicking on the *Section Scores* button displays your results topic by topic (see Figure 1.6 overleaf).

> Although there are ten separate topics in the syllabus the report is produced under only nine headings (Background questions, if included, could appear in any of the Part 1 question baskets).

Note

Comments

On any screen you are able to make a comment about the PC environment, the overall examination, the individual question or the Prometric test centre (see Figure 1.7).

TAG

We would also encourage you to pass on any comments on the examination separately to TAG – the Trainers Action Group in London (e-mail: tag@lywood-david.co.uk), which is in regular contact with ACI Education on such issues.

Mastering the ACI Dealing Certificate

Fig 1.6

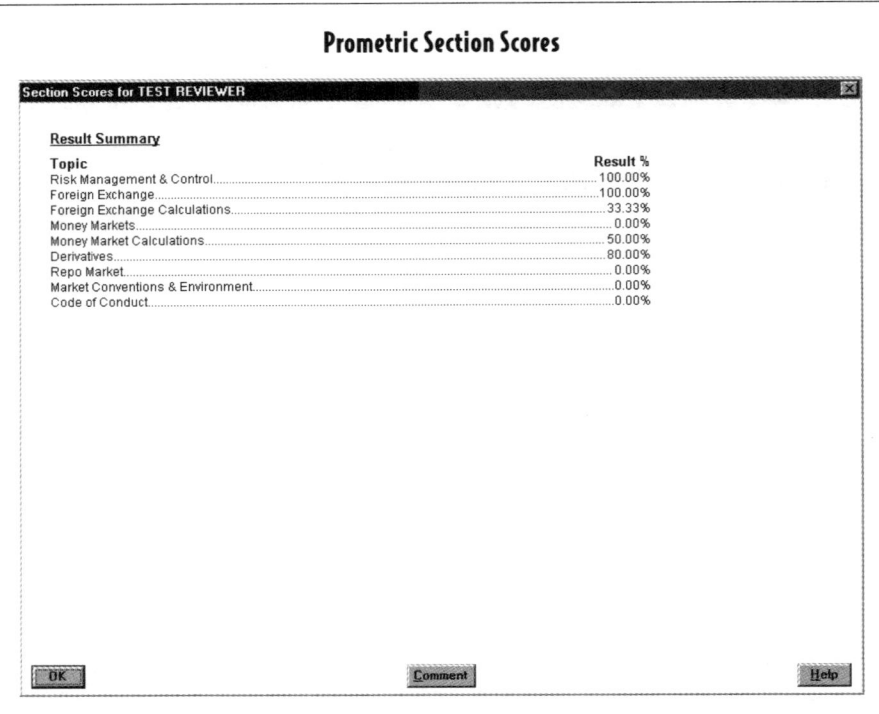

Fig 1.7

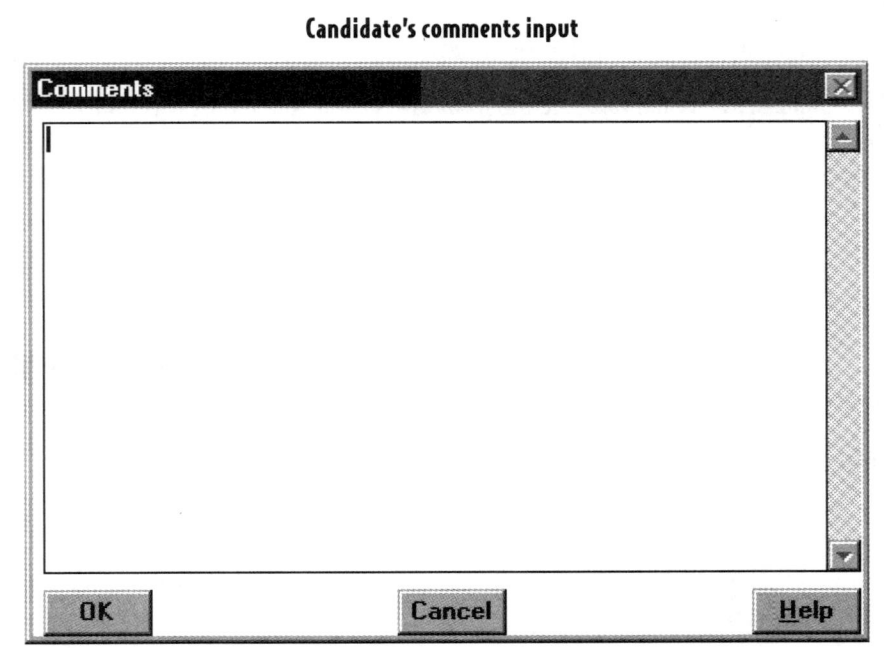

Introduction to the International Money Markets, the Foreign Exchange Markets and Their Associated Derivative Markets

Setting the scene

Foreign exchange market

Market participants

Foreign exchange derivatives

Basic market concepts

SETTING THE SCENE

This chapter attempts to set the scene in respect of the markets and products covered by the ACI Dealing Certificate syllabus and introduce some basic concepts (such as market making and market using) which go across more than one of the syllabus topics.

Money market

In simple terms "money market" encompasses all interbank and other wholesale market transactions which involve the loan or deposit of a currency for an agreed period or for repayment after an agreed period of notice at an agreed rate of interest.

To differentiate between the money market and the capital market, money market transactions will in most currencies cover loans/deposits for periods with maturities up to one year, whereas the term capital market tends to refer to substantially longer-dated debt.

Domestic currency money markets

Regardless of size and overall market involvement, all banks will require a presence in their local domestic currency money market. The actual size and sophistication of products available in domestic currency money markets differs dramatically from centre to centre.

Money market products listed in the syllabus can be found in the major financial centres such as London, New York and Tokyo. However, varieties of these products, sometimes with local differences in quoting, pricing or settlement will be found in most domestic markets around the world. Domestic markets are controlled and transactions monitored by the local regulatory authority, typically the central bank, which in most instances will act as "lender of last resort".

Eurocurrencies

Currencies merit the prefix "euro" where the particular currency dealt is not the local domestic currency of the country in which the deposit is placed (although the funds concerned never leave that currency's clearing system). The eurocurrency markets consist of international and other commercial banks in a number of financial centres, which perform the wholesale function of matching the supply of and demand for currencies on a loan/deposit basis between interbank and other market participants.

The prime example of the use of the prefix "euro" is of course the eurodollar market, the first of the eurocurrency markets to develop during the 1960s, and by dint of the continuing US balance of payments deficit and the acceptance of the dollar as the universal "hard" currency, by far the most widely dealt and still therefore the most liquid eurocurrency market.

Eurocurrency operations are not confined to such deposits placed in, or funds owned by market participants in the European financial centres, though certain other trading areas have adopted similar prefixes – the "Asia-dollar" market is a good example of this in the Far Eastern money market centres.

Unlike the control exercised over a domestic currency money market by the currency's local regulatory authority, there is no "lender of last resort" in the eurocurrency markets, and in some instances, due to exchange control regulations, no access to domestic market funds is even available to the eurocurrency operator.

Interest rate derivatives

Interest rate derivatives "derive their value" from the underlying cash markets in interest rates. Here we are talking about exchange traded financial futures, STIR and bond contracts and options and OTC products such as forward rate agreements and interest rate swaps. The price of a derivative closely follows the price of the underlying asset or liability in the cash markets.

Derivatives are described as "off balance sheet" because, unlike the cash markets, there is no exchange of the principal amount of the asset or liability involved. The derivative is traded merely as the notional equivalent of an actual transaction which will take place sometime in the future. The value of the derivative at any time is its comparison with the actual cash market transaction.

Market centres

The principal global market centres for the foreign exchange, money and associated derivative markets are located in London, New York and Tokyo.

BIS survey, April 2001

Every three years the BIS and central banks around the world's financial centres conduct a survey on values and volumes being transacted in the foreign exchange and OTC derivative markets. The triennial April 2001 figures quoted here are therefore compared with those of April 1998.

OTC interest rate derivatives volumes and values

In the OTC derivatives market, average daily turnover in April 2001 amounted to USD 575 billion, exceeding that in April 1998 by 53 percent.

Forward rate agreements

Trading in FRAs witnessed a fairly strong and broad-based expansion (up by 74 percent to USD 129 billion) following slower growth in the previous reporting period. By contrast activity in interest rate options, a much smaller segment of the OTC interest rate market, contracted by 19 percent to USD 29 billion, with much of the decline occurring in the Japanese yen segment.

The vast majority of the outstanding amounts and growth is accounted for by interest rate derivatives. Interest rate derivatives grew by 85 percent to USD 489 billion.

Interest rate swaps

According to the BIS survey there was tremendous buoyancy in the longer-term interest rate derivatives markets, led by interest rate swaps with daily turnover rising by 114 percent to USD 331 billion. Dollar-denominated IRS grew even faster than in the previous survey period with turnover up by 178 percent to USD 100 billion. Euro-denominated interest rate swaps turnover also expanded rapidly, by 104 percent to USD 173 billion, while Japanese yen denominated IRS expanded by 14 percent only, to USD 16 billion.

FOREIGN EXCHANGE MARKET

In simple terms "foreign exchange" encompasses all transactions which involve the exchange of one currency for another on an agreed value date at an agreed rate of exchange. In reality there are various alternative deals which can be effected in the foreign exchange market: spot, short date and outright forwards and foreign exchange swaps. Each deal type will be explained in more detail in later sections of this book.

ISO 4217 standard

Market terminology in recent years has tended towards standardization (vital in the correct interpretation of computer-generated and readable advices, payment orders, etc.). In all foreign exchange and money market dealings expressed in written form, currencies should always be abbreviated using their International Standards Organization (ISO) codes. These

ISO codes should be used in most computer systems in financial institutions and lists should be freely available in in-house rule books and instruction manuals issued by organizations such as SWIFT (Society for Worldwide Interbank Financial Telecommunications).

> *Candidates should be aware of how these ISO codes are typically constructed. As a general rule they are made up of two letters for the country and one for the currency abbreviation, i.e. United States (US) dollar (D) = USD, Japanese (JP) yen (Y) = JPY. In the examination you can expect the majority of questions to involve the world's major currencies although one or two currency codes where mistakes are often made can and do feature, e.g. SAR (Saudi Arabian riyal) and ZAR (South African rand). (See List of Abbreviations and Recognised ISO Currency Codes, pp. xviii–xxii.)*

Currency pairs

In foreign exchange market quotations there are perforce two currencies involved. These two currencies are frequently described as a "currency pair". One currency in any quoted currency pair remains constant and is referred to as the base currency (or the *certain* currency in Bank of England terminology). The second currency is the quoted or countercurrency (or the *uncertain* currency in Bank of England terminology). The exchange rate is quoted as the number of units of the *uncertain* currency to be exchanged for one unit of the *certain* currency.

While no hard and fast rule exists it is usual practice for currency pairs to be identified by their ISO codes with the first mentioned currency (before the forward slash) being the base or certain currency in any foreign exchange quotation, e.g. USD/JPY, EUR/USD, GBP/JPY.

MARKET PARTICIPANTS

Central banks

Every country has a central bank or monetary authority. Some are completely under government control, some have joint shareholding and a modicum of independence while a few are totally independent of their national government. It is typically the central monetary authority's role to control and ensure the smooth operation of the foreign exchange and money markets in their local currency, with the institutions of the major centres collaborating in times of market turbulence.

Trading banks

Every financial centre has its range of trading banks. These are the principal commercial banks – those institutions that are frequently household names in their own country. These banks are trading in the international interbank markets on a regular basis and act as market makers in a variety of markets and products.

Commercial banks

There are many sizes and structures of commercial banks. Under this heading we mean those institutions which, rather than acting as market makers in the interbank market, are happy to quote their own customers dealing rates for transactions in various markets and products and then, acting as market users, contact their correspondent banks to cover such transactions, perhaps preferring to make a small margin per deal rather than run a risk position.

Investment (merchant) banks

Investment banks are major operators in the world's financial markets. Through their fund management businesses they are constantly seeking opportunities to improve investment returns and use the foreign exchange and money markets and associated products to this end.

Multinational corporations

There are many worldwide commercial enterprises which have over the years grown into operations spanning many different industries and countries. Many of these are able to operate in similar fashion to banks in the markets and some have even diversified into the financial services industry using foreign exchange and money market activities to add value to their other commercial operations.

International trading companies

Many of these companies are similar in size to the multinational corporations already described. The difference is in their market involvement. These international trading companies involve themselves in the financial markets merely to support their mainstream commercial activities, i.e. entering the markets only when it is necessary to repatriate foreign currency earnings or provide foreign currency cover for their ongoing business.

Private clients

Here we are not talking about personal travel facilities (sometimes termed foreign money) where the bid–offer spread is extremely wide, but transactions effected by high net worth individuals (some in multi-million currency units) switching currencies in their constant search for the best return on global investments.

Hedge funds

Take private client business further and the centrally managed so-called hedge funds (George Soros et al.) are able to enter the foreign exchange and money markets with consolidated amounts far in excess of those available individually. These managed funds have over recent years caused high market activity and have on occasions been blamed for periods of speculation and currency unrest.

Traditional/voice brokers

Brokers in the foreign exchange and money markets and associated treasury derivative markets are intermediaries *only*. They are frequently referred to these days as traditional or "voice" brokers (to differentiate them from electronic matching systems fulfilling the same function). There are several large broking institutions with worldwide presence. All such institutions are authorized by the local central bank or regulatory authority.

These brokers do not operate on their own account, merely on-quoting their client institutions' bid and offer prices to all market participants with the express intention of achieving the finest (closest) spread between bid and offer in an attempt to encourage participants to deal through their offices, thereby earning a commission on each transaction closed.

Electronic matching systems

Electronic matching systems such as Reuters 2000/2 and EBS now provide dealers with a further alternative to close exchange transactions. The market penetration of these electronic matching systems has increased dramatically in recent years and their scope has become more diverse. A wide range of currency pairs and products are now available via these means.

BIS Basel survey, April 2001

Every three years the BIS and central banks around the world's financial centres conduct a survey on values and volumes being transacted in the foreign exchange and OTC derivative markets. As with money market derivative figures quoted earlier, the April 2001 figures are compared with those of April 1998.

Foreign exchange

Results of the April 2001 triennial central banks survey (BIS and 48 central banks from around the world's financial markets) were published in October 2001. These showed a marked decline in the values and volumes of foreign exchange business being traded globally.

The introduction of the euro, the growing share of electronic broking in the spot interbank market and consolidation in the banking industry appear to have been the main factors driving the fall in foreign exchange turnover.

The survey identified the following salient points in foreign exchange transaction values in the international markets:

- Total average daily turnover: USD 1210 billion, down 19 percent from the previous survey (USD 1490 billion in 1998). Average daily turnover in the spot foreign exchange market fell from USD 568 billion to USD 387 billion.
- Forward exchange business transacted fell 8.7 percent from USD 862 billion to USD 787 billion, but in percentage of overall foreign exchange turnover forward exchange business (outrights and foreign exchange swaps) grew from 57.8 to 65 percent. Interbank trading volumes in foreign exchange swaps actually dropped by 11 percent.
- Since the previous survey the main impact of the introduction of the euro appears to have been through the elimination of intra-EMS trading. The euro appeared on one side of 38 percent of all foreign exchange transactions – higher than the deutschmark's share (30 percent) but lower than that of all euro constituents taken together (53 percent) in 1998.
- The US dollar's share of foreign exchange markets rose from 87 percent to 90 percent and the Japanese yen increased slightly to 22.7 percent in 2001 (20.2 percent in 1998). Sterling too increased its market share from 11 percent to 13.2 percent.
- Emerging market business continued to grow with over USD 67.5 billion per day reported (up to 4.5 percent from 3.1 percent in 1998). The main emerging market currency pairs traded were USD/ZAR, USD/MXP and USD/KRW.
- While overall volumes are down, the distribution of foreign exchange business around the major financial centres is little changed from 1998. London (USD 504 billion) leads the way with 31.1 percent, followed by New York (USD 254 billion) 15.7 percent and Tokyo (USD 147 billion) 9.1 percent. Singapore (USD 101 billion) 6.2 percent and Germany (USD 88 billion) 5.4 percent are the next most active centres.

FOREIGN EXCHANGE DERIVATIVES

Similar to money market derivatives, foreign exchange derivatives "derive their value" from the underlying cash markets in foreign exchange. Here we are talking about exchange traded financial futures and options and OTC products such as margin trading, n-d-fs (non-deliverable forwards), currency (and interest rate) swaps and currency options. The price of a derivative closely follows the price of the underlying cash market.

Derivatives are described as "off balance sheet" because the derivative is traded merely as the notional equivalent of an actual transaction which will take place sometime in the future. The value of the derivative at any time is its comparison with the actual cash market transaction.

OTC foreign exchange derivatives volumes and values

Daily turnover in currency options, by far the largest group of non-traditional foreign exchange products, dropped substantially by 31 percent to USD 60 billion. Much of the decline was concentrated in the USD/JPY currency pair (48 percent down from 1998).

Foreign exchange margin trading figures and non-deliverable forwards turnover are not available in the BIS survey.

Turnover in currency (and interest rate) swaps, a relatively small segment of the overall OTC derivatives market, also contracted by 30 percent to USD 7 billion.

BASIC MARKET CONCEPTS

Whether you are involved in the foreign exchange or the interest rate markets (money markets and derivatives) you need to know the market conventions regarding market making and market using.

Market making

In the majority of OTC markets (interbank wholesale markets) it is the custom for the calling counterparty (market user) to ask the market maker for his two-way price (to buy/sell in foreign exchange markets and to borrow/lend in interest rate markets – though some interest rate/discount rate based short-term securities can also be "bought" and "sold" in these markets). The logic is the same regardless of market concerned. The market maker dictates the two-way price and gets the "benefit of the spread".

Market making examples

A bank dealer quoting his corporate customer or incoming calling bank counterparties will always be market maker, but when looking to cover any transactions himself he may call a broker or another bank and take the role of market user (see Figure 2.1).

Fig 2.1

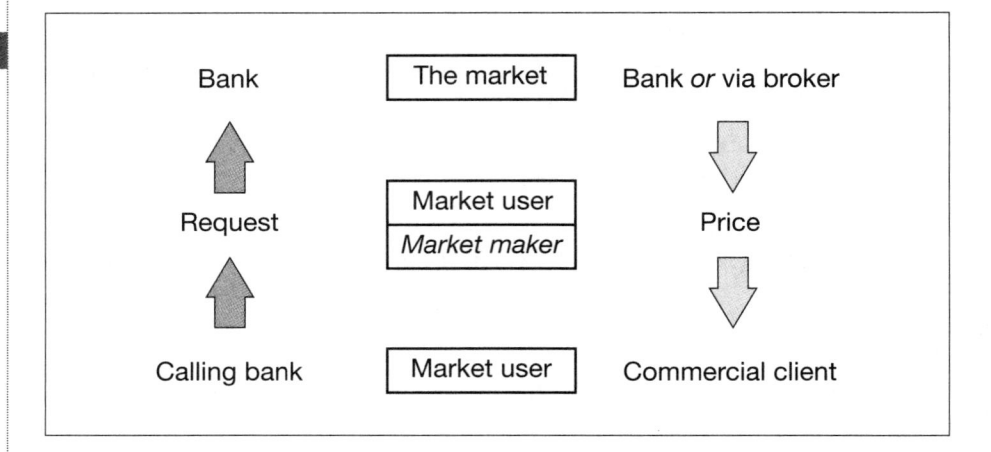

```
Bank              The market         Bank or via broker

  ↑                                         ↓
Request         Market user               Price
                Market maker
  ↑                                         ↓

Calling bank     Market user        Commercial client
```

Quotation methods

Foreign exchange bid–offer for base currency

Remember BOB!

- *Spot foreign exchange*: bid–offer for the base currency (currency movement on the *spot* date).
- *Forward foreign exchange*: bid–offer for the base currency (currency movement on the *forward* date). (See Chapter 7.)

Care!

Some dealers in London, when using the terms bid and offer (particularly in forward foreign exchange quotations/transactions) may refer to the quoted or counter-currency, i.e. offer–bid. This practice dates from the time when sterling was a reserve currency and *all* other currencies were quoted to a sterling base, so reference was always made to the foreign currency movement. Dealing sides and calculations are unaffected. *ACI Dealing Certificate* examination questions should always make it clear in which manner any rate quotation is being made.

London money market quotation

- *Money market*: offer–bid for the cash (high–low in interest rate terms).
- *Financial instruments* (such as T-bills, CDs): bid–offer for the security (still high–low in interest rate terms).
- *OTC interest rate derivatives*:
  – such as FRAs: offer–bid (still high–low in interest rate terms);
  – such as interest rate swaps: receive–pay (for the fixed rate).

International money market quotation

- *Money market*: bid–offer for the cash (low–high in interest rate terms).
- *Financial instruments* (such as BAs): offer–bid for the security (still low–high in interest rate terms).
- *OTC interest rate derivatives*: – such as FRAs: bid–offer (still low–high in interest rate terms);
  – such as interest rate swaps: pay–receive (for the fixed rate).

> **Hint**
> *The market maker always gets the benefit of the spread. Therefore, regardless of how the quotation is expressed, as a market user you must always lend to the lower rate and borrow at the higher rate.*

> **Note**
> Wherever it is useful the market making/market using concept and quotation methods are repeated as appropriate to the market and products being described within each chapter of this book.

FOR FURTHER READING

Bank of England (2001) *The UK Foreign Exchange Market and Over-the-Counter Derivatives Markets in April 2001* (Results Summary). Bank of England (October).

Bank for International Settlements (2001) *Central Bank Survey of Foreign Exchange and Derivatives Market Activity in April 2001* (Preliminary Global Data). Basel: BIS (October).

Fitch, Thomas (1990) *Dictionary of Banking Terms*. Barrows.

Geisst, Charles R. (1993) *A Guide to Financial Institutions*. Macmillan.

WEBSITES WORTH A VISIT

Bank of England, London: www.bankofengland.co.uk
Bank for International Settlements, Basel: www.bis.org
European Central Bank, Frankfurt: www.ecb.int
Federal Reserve Bank of New York, New York: www.federalreserve.gov

SYLLABUS PART 1

3	Topic 1 · Background
4	Topic 2 · Basic Interest Rate Calculations
	Topic 3 · Money Market Products
5	Topic 4 (part) · Money Market Derivatives
6	Topic 5 · Spot Foreign Exchange
7	Topic 6 · Forward Foreign Exchange
8	Topic 4 (part) · FX Derivatives
9	Topic 8 · The Role of Settlements
10	Topic 9 · The Risk Environment

Topic 1 · Background

Pre-Second World War

Post-Second World War

ACI – The Financial Markets Association

Mastering the ACI Dealing Certificate

> ### Overall objective
>
> *To explain the historical context within which markets currently operate, and for candidates to list the significant market features. In addition, this section will include an outline of the role played by ACI and the National ACI Associations.*
>
> *At the end of this section, candidates will be able to:*
>
> - *explain the evolution of the foreign exchange and money markets, and why they exist;*
> - *explain the operation of ACI and the National ACI Associations.*

Note — There is no separate Background question basket in the ACI Dealing Certificate examination. Multiple choice questions relating to this topic could be generated under any of the financial markets and products question baskets (see later chapters).

The background topic is always a difficult one to approach. There is a wealth of information about the history of the markets available from many different sources. You should be familiar with why and how various markets developed and have a reasonable grasp of significant events and dates in the financial markets.

In respect of the Background (History) topic, a brief résumé of some market benchmark dates and other relevant information with which you should familiarize yourself is included here together with a suggested additional reading list.

Hint — *In the syllabus this section has been extended to include details of ACI – the Financial Markets Association – and the national associations. While there are several details regarding the ACI at the end of this chapter further information on this subject is best gleaned from the www.aciforex.com website, your local ACI Association and the Model Code (see Chapter 11).*

PRE-SECOND WORLD WAR

Gresham's law

If coins of the same metal, but of varying weight and quality, circulate together at the same nominal value, the worse coins will tend to drive out the better from circulation, but the better will never drive out the worse. (After Thomas Gresham, the Elizabethan knight and founder of the Royal Exchange)

The Gold Standard

From the reorganization of England's coinage in 1816 up to the passing of the Gold Standard Act (see below), any individual in Great Britain could take standard gold bullion to the Mint and, provided the quantity was sufficient, demand sovereigns in exchange at the Mint price of £3 17s. 10d. (pre-decimal pounds, shillings and old pence – equivalent to approximately GBP 3.89 in today's currency) an ounce, free of all charges for coining (this charge was called "seigneurage"). Similarly Bank of England notes were freely exchangeable at the Bank for gold coins (sovereigns).

Similar practices in other countries and the general principles of settling international indebtedness between countries by gold transfers were common place in the early years of the twentieth century.

Gold Standard Act 1925

Following the devastation of European countries and their economies during and immediately following the First World War, Great Britain was keen to restore stability and convertibility of the currency. The UK Gold Standard Act was passed in 1925 with this intention.

The Act laid down that holders of legal tender notes could demand gold in exchange on presentation of bank notes at the Bank of England, Head Office and the Bank should deliver gold bullion at the price of £3 17s. 10d. per troy ounce of standard gold in the form of bars containing approximately 400 troy ounces. Thus the individual exchangeability of notes for gold coins was replaced by the need for surrender of larger values of legal tender to the Bank of England in exchange for gold bars.

Abandonment of the Gold Standard 1931

The Gold Standard was abandoned in the UK in September 1931 when the British government released the Bank of England from its obligation to convert legal tender into gold at the option of the holder.

POST-SECOND WORLD WAR

Bretton Woods agreement 1944

In July 1944 at the International Monetary and Financial Conference held at Bretton Woods, the world's finance ministers agreed to set up the International Monetary Fund (IMF) and the World Bank (IBRD). It was the

IMF which was commissioned to oversee the system of fixed parities between the world's currencies and the US dollar.

Sterling devaluation 1949

In September 1949 Sterling was devalued by 30.5 percent against the US dollar from the level agreed at Bretton Woods to a new parity band of 2.78–2.82. This was accompanied by devaluations of several other European and worldwide currencies.

Creation of the European Economic Community (EEC)

The EEC (now retitled the EU – European Union) came into being on 1 January 1958. The Treaty of Rome was signed by the six original member states, namely France, Germany, Italy, the Netherlands, Belgium and Luxembourg.

European revaluations 1961

Germany and the Netherlands revalued their currencies upwards against the US dollar by 5.00 percent. These realignments resulted in the modern foreign exchange market's first bank collapse with the failure of the Frankfurt-based bank Hugo Stinnes.

US Regulation Q

Regulation Q was introduced by the US in the 1960s and restricted the payment of interest on domestic US dollar demand deposits (current or chequeing accounts). Deposit interest rate ceilings under this Regulation were abolished in 1986.

US "Edge Act"

Prior to deregulation in the mid-1980s inter-state banking used to be tightly controlled in the United States of America. Many states' banking legislation did not even allow multi-branch banking within their jurisdiction. Banks financing international commerce and chartered by the Federal Reserve Act, which set up subsidiary operations outside their US state of domicile, were known as Edge Act corporations (after the US senator who introduced the legislation). They frequently had a title including the descriptive word "International".

Sterling devaluation 1967

After weeks of pressure in the markets and heavy Bank of England intervention at the old fixed parity, on 18 November 1967 sterling was devalued against the US dollar by 14.3 percent from USD 2.80 to USD 2.40. This was the end of an era when sterling had been the world's reserve currency. The famous line, "The pound in your pocket will not be devalued", was coined by Harold Wilson, UK Prime Minister, on announcing the devaluation.

Smithsonian Agreement 1971

In May 1971 Germany and the Netherlands let their currencies float. In December that year the Group of Ten met at the Smithsonian Institute in Washington DC to agree on several issues to attempt to calm the volatility in the exchange markets at that time:

1. The US increased the official price of gold to USD 38.00 per ounce.
2. There was a realignment of currencies including a devaluation of the US dollar.
3. Currencies were permitted to fluctuate within a $2\frac{1}{4}$ percent band on either side of their new "fixed" parities against the US dollar "pending the outcome of discussions on the working of the international monetary system", thereby paving the way to the later freely floating exchange rate environment.

The US crisis programme August 1971

The US announced various measures over the weekend of 14 August 1971:

- a 90-day freeze on wages and prices;
- a cut in federal spending of USD 4.7 billion accompanied by tax reductions to stimulate the economy;
- a 10 percent surcharge on imports subject to duties;
- a 10 percent cut in foreign economic aid; and
- the suspension of the convertibility of the US dollar into gold or other reserve assets.

An immediate consequence was the closing for a restricted period of the foreign exchange markets in almost all countries of the western world.

The "Snake in the Tunnel" 1972

The Smithsonian Agreement allowed limited floating of exchange rates, and the European Snake ($2\frac{1}{4}$ percent fluctuation bands between EC currencies) in the Tunnel (the Smithsonian parities) was introduced in March 1972, with the official start in April that year.

> **Question**
>
> A typical ACI Dealing Certificate question might be:
>
> In which year was the Smithsonian Agreement drawn up?
>
> A: 1979
> B: 1944
> C: 1982
> D: 1971
>
> **Correct answer**
> D: The Smithsonian Agreement was formulated in 1971 and heralded the era of floating exchange rates.

Sterling and the Snake

Sterling joined the Snake on 1 May 1972 and left it on 23 June the same year after the UK government lost USD 2.5 billion of reserves in six days trying to defend the parity.

Two-tier currencies

Postwar Belgium had lived with a convertible and a financial franc for many years, but in 1971 during dramatic exchange market activity in the major European currencies, the French government introduced a two-tier French franc. In later years Italy (1973) and then Spain also experimented with this method of exchange control to curb speculative currency dealing and the flight of capital.

Arab–Israeli War

In October 1973, as a result of the Arab–Israeli War, an oil embargo was imposed by the Arab oil-producing nations. The oil price was raised initially in October and then quadrupled again in December.

Bankhaus I.D. Herstatt, Cologne

In June 1974, following months of rumour and speculation concerning this private German bank, the Bundesbank closed Bankhaus I. D. Herstatt, Cologne. The 12 noon European time closure (before NY banking hours) resulted in problems of non-payment of US dollars in settlement of foreign exchange deals for that value date. This factor dramatically changed the attitudes of trading banks to foreign exchange dealing and delivery risk.

LBI Lugano

Following the discovery of unauthorized forward exchange contracts in the Lugano branch of Lloyds Bank International in late 1974, where the dealer kept transactions out of the bank's official accounting records and handled confirmations etc. himself, losses of GBP 33 million were announced. The then governor of the Bank of England, Lord O'Brien, published the O'Brien letter, the forerunner of today's Model Code, following the fiasco. This included recommendations for controls such as the division of duties (dealers and back office), forward transactions based on current spot exchange rates and regular audits of dealing rooms.

A typical ACI Dealing Certificate question might be:

What was the Snake in the Tunnel?

A: The forerunner of the ERM
B: A chartist's view of a volatile trend
C: A nickname for Jaques Delors
D: An early form of derivative market

Correct answer
A: The Smithsonian Agreement allowed limited floating of exchange rates, and the European Snake ($2\frac{1}{4}$ percent fluctuation bands between EC currencies) in the Tunnel (the Smithsonian parities) was introduced in March 1972. It was therefore a forerunner of the ERM.

European Community expansion 1973

In January 1973 the United Kingdom, Ireland and Denmark joined the European Economic Community bringing the number of participating countries to nine.

Creation of the ERM

The Exchange Rate Mechanism (ERM) was created within the European Monetary System (EMS) in March 1979. The founding members of the ERM were the then nine countries within the European Economic Community except the United Kingdom, although sterling has always been a member currency within the EMS and was a weighted constituent part of the European Currency Unit (ECU, ISO currency code = XEU) until its replacement by the euro in January 1999.

Irish punt 1979

In March 1979, in readiness for the creation of the ERM, Ireland broke the Irish punt's traditional link with and imposed exchange controls against sterling.

3 May 1979

Margaret Thatcher and the Conservative party won the General Election in the United Kingdom and UK exchange controls were removed "at a stroke".

Federal Reserve Bank chairmanship 1979

In July 1979 Paul Volker was appointed Chairman of the Federal Reserve Bank resulting in a dramatic change in US monetary policy. Over coming months US dollar interest rates rose steeply, culminating with six months US dollar domestic interest rates rising to above 20 percent in 1980.

ERM realignment 1979

In September 1979 the Deutsche mark was revalued against the Danish krone by 5 percent and against all other EMS currencies by 2 percent.

Swiss National Bank 1979

During 1979, to dissuade speculative hoarding of Swiss francs (the safe haven currency), the Swiss National Bank imposed punitive rates of interest on nostro balances held by foreign banking institutions. This resulted in levels of negative interest rates (minus 250 percent p.a. for short date deposits) unseen before.

Gold price 1980

In January 1980 the price of gold on the international market rose to USD 850.00 per ounce.

European Community expansion 1981

In January 1981 Greece joined the European Economic Community, bringing the number of participating countries to ten.

The Plaza Accord 1985

The Group of Seven (G7) countries meeting in the Plaza Hotel in New York over a weekend in September 1985 made an announcement concerning their resolve to bring down the value of the US dollar. This announcement, without a single exchange deal being done, led to a dramatic fall in the value of the US dollar (approaching 9 percent against the major international currencies) at the market opening on the Monday morning.

European Community expansion 1986

In January 1986 Portugal and Spain joined the European Economic Community, bringing the number of participating countries to 12.

The Louvre Accord 1987

The Louvre Accord was the joint statement made following the meeting of the Group of Six (G6) finance ministers and central bank governors at the Louvre in Paris in February 1987. This announcement referred back to the Plaza Accord (1985), recognized the progress made since that concerted effort to control exchange rates and stated that further substantial exchange rate shifts could damage growth. The agreement was in the main to cooperate closely to foster stability in exchange rates around current levels.

Sterling and the ERM 1990–92

Sterling entered the ERM in October 1990. The announcement that sterling would participate in the ERM from Monday 8 October 1990 was made by John Major, then UK Chancellor of the Exchequer (Finance Minister), on Friday 5 October at 4.30 p.m. The official mid rate for sterling was set at XEU 0.696904.

Black Wednesday 1992

On Wednesday 16 September 1992 sterling left the ERM after several weeks of intense speculative pressure and a huge support operation on the part of the Bank of England. The date was initially referred to as Black Wednesday – since termed "white" by many commentators as the currency's departure from the ERM is now seen as the catalyst for the later improving economic situation.

European Community expansion 1995

In January 1995 Austria, Finland and Sweden joined the European Economic Community, bringing the number of participating countries to the current total membership of 15.

Economic and Monetary Union (Treaty of Maastricht 1993)

The EU (then entitled the EEC) originally set a target date of 1980 for EMU – Economic and Monetary Union – among its member states.

The Community's policy leading towards the single currency was developed within the Delors Plan ratified by EU nations in the Treaty of Maastricht of 1993. The Delors Plan ensured that the economic and monetary policies of the member states of the Union were harmonized prior to the introduction of the euro – the EU's single currency. There were four stages of EMU as defined under the Delors Plan:

- *First stage* (1 July 1990 to 31 December 1993): free movement of capital between member states was introduced, together with closer coordination of economic policies and closer cooperation between central banks.
- *Second stage* (1 January 1994 to 31 December 1998): the convergence process for the economic and monetary policies of the member states (to ensure stability of prices and sound public finances) took place.
- *Third stage* (from 1 January 1999): the European Central Bank was established and all participating countries' exchange rates were irrevocably fixed against the euro.

Eleven EU nations participated in the euro from that date – Germany, France, Italy, Belgium, Luxembourg, the Netherlands, the Republic of Ireland, Spain, Portugal, Austria and Finland. Greece became the twelfth nation to join the euro in January 2001 (EC Council Decision, 19 June 2000).

- *Fourth stage* (from 1 January 2002): introduction of euro notes and coins in the 12 participating countries, with initially a dual circulation period for euro and legacy currencies. Each country set its own period for this stage with a final withdrawal date of 28 February 2002.

Three member states have not adopted the single currency, either because they decided not to – under the protocols annexed to the EC Treaty granting them the option (United Kingdom and Denmark) – or because they failed to meet the convergence criteria laid down by the Treaty of Maastricht (Sweden).

Collapse of Barings Bank 1995

In March 1995 unauthorized position taking and overtrading in the SIMEX and Osaka futures markets by Nick Leeson, the trader in Barings Bank, Singapore branch, who then as the general manager of the back office succeeded in concealing resultant losses from his local and head office management, generated losses in excess of GBP 800 million. The division of duties concept (non-compliance with which was LBI Lugano's downfall over 20 years previously) was not implemented within the bank and an almost complete lack of senior management understanding and basic controls resulted in this loss effectively bankrupting the bank. It was eventually sold to ING for GBP 1.00.

Allfirst Maryland 2002

In February 2002 Allied Irish Banks Dublin reported losses of approaching USD 850 million resulting from foreign exchange and currency options activities of a single dealer in their small US-based subsidiary over a number of years. At the time of writing the story is still unfolding but it seems that it is yet another example of poor controls over dealing activities which had supposedly been very profitable.

Question

A typical ACI Dealing Certificate question might be:

When was the Exchange Rate Mechanism (ERM) of the European Monetary System (EMS) created?

A: January 1971
B: September 1992
C: March 1979
D: March 1974

Correct answer
C: The ERM was created in March 1979. The founding members were the then nine countries within the European Economic Community (EEC) except the United Kingdom.

ACI – THE FINANCIAL MARKETS ASSOCIATION

> **Note**
> The following information has been obtained from official ACI sources including the website www.aciforex.com and features in Appendix 6 of the Model Code – see Chapter 11.

Mission statement

To be regarded within the business community, authorities, media and financial services industry as the leading association representing the interests of the international financial markets, and to actively promote the educational and professional interests of the markets and the industry.

Charter of the ACI

Article I

ACI – The Financial Markets Association – is a non-commercial organization based on mutual recognition of professionalism by traders of financial instruments, with the objective of the development of the profession, without discrimination of any sort.

Article II

Members undertake to maintain the professional level of competence and the ethical standards of loyalty that are indispensable in the development of international relations, and render mutual assistance so far as possible.

Article III

The national Associations that have been formed in various countries are groups linked by affiliation to ACI.

Article IV

The affiliated Associations are united by the moral ties of their common membership of the profession and by the common desire to give the best possible service within it, particularly by the establishment of personal and friendly relations between all those who are so engaged.

Article V

The national Associations and their members will do all in their power to maintain the highest possible standards in the profession by constantly setting an example of propriety and best ethical behaviour in business under all circumstances.

Article VI

Each national Association will be fully autonomous in designing and managing its national scope of business, but commits itself and its members to behave in line with the ACI Code of Conduct, the current Charter and Statutes.

Article VII

Education is a key objective of ACI. It will seek to ensure that programmes that reflect the constantly changing nature of the industry are made available to both new entrants to the profession and seasoned professionals.

ACI Code of Conduct

In 1975 the first ACI Code of Conduct covering foreign exchange and euro-currency dealing was published. There followed similar publications by the markets in New York (1980), London (1990), Singapore (1991) and Tokyo (1995).

The Model Code

The ACI published the Model Code consolidating the many different worldwide financial market centre codes in June 2000 and it is the document on which Part 2 of the ACI Dealing Certificate is based. A downloadable Adobe pdf file version of the Model Code is available on the website www.aciforex.com or in hard copy from ACI Secretariat Paris.

KEY POINTS FOR ACI DEALING CERTIFICATE MULTIPLE CHOICE QUESTIONS

Even though there is no separate question basket in the examination, Background questions could appear in any of the financial products question baskets. You are advised to read as much about the origins of the markets, recent history and significant current issues in the markets as you can.

> *Administration-wise the examination questions are updated approximately twice a year, so any questions relating to "current" issues could be as much as six months out of date.*

Hint

FOR FURTHER READING

ACI (2000) *The Model Code*. ACI – The Financial Markets Association.
RIIA (1976) *International Monetary Relations, Volume II*. Oxford University Press for the Royal Institute for International Affairs.
Sykes, Ernest (1937) *Banking and Currency*. Butterworths.
[Various] (1991) *The Foreign Exchange Manual*. Woodhead Faulkner.
Vaitilingham, Romesh (1996) *Guide to Using the Financial Pages*. FT Pitman.
Walmsley, Julian (1983) *The Foreign Exchange Handbook*. Wiley Interscience.
Walmsley, Julian (1996) *International Money and Foreign Exchange Markets – An Introduction*. Wiley.

WEBSITES WORTH A VISIT

ACI – The Financial Markets Association: www.aciforex.com
Bank of England: www.bankofengland.co.uk
Bank for International Settlements (BIS): www.bis.org
Federal Reserve Bank of New York: www.federalreserve.gov

Topic 2 · Basic Interest Rate Calculations
Topic 3 · Money Market Products

Introduction

The cash market

LIBOR

Yield curves

Position keeping

Negotiable financial instruments

Repos

TOPIC 2 · BASIC INTEREST RATE CALCULATIONS

Overall objective

To provide a basic knowledge of the mathematics of interest rates and the calculations that form the basis for evaluation of short-term investment opportunities. This will include explanations of the underlying rationales for different yield curve shapes.

At the end of this section, candidates will be able to:

- calculate simple interest rates on different day bases;
- demonstrate the principles of the time value of money, present and future value, discounting and compounding;
- calculate broken dates through interpolation;
- explain the difference between money market basis and bond market basis;
- calculate the yield on money market instruments on both a true yield and discount to yield basis;
- construct a yield curve and explain the possible causes of its shape;
- manipulate core formulae correctly.

Note

There are 6 (calculation) multiple choice questions on Topic 2 Money Market Calculations in the ACI Dealing Certificate out of which candidates are required to gain a minimum of 33.33 percent to pass (2 out of 6).

TOPIC 3 · MONEY MARKET PRODUCTS

Overall objective

To list the differences and similarities between the major products and key interest rates in the money markets in order to calculate how they satisfy the varying requirements of borrowers and investors.

At the end of this section, candidates will be able to:

- explain the main features of a broad range of money market products, e.g. cash deposits, treasury bills, etc.;
- calculate the yields on key instruments;
- explain the rationale for differing returns from differing products;

- list the advantages and disadvantages of the products;
- explain the interrelationship between the products;
- list the different types of repos;
- explain the terminology of the repo market, why they are used and the main characteristics of repos.

Note

There are 7 (textual) multiple choice questions on Topic 3 Money Market Products in the ACI Dealing Certificate out of which candidates are required to gain a minimum of 42.80 percent to pass (3 out of 7). While repos only feature in the last two bullet points of the Topic 3 Money Market Products syllabus above, there are 6 multiple choice questions on the repos topic in the ACI Dealing Certificate out of which candidates are required to gain a minimum of 33.33 percent to pass (2 out of 6).

Note

The logical progression followed here is to discuss the cash market, pricing/quotation methods and associated calculations, followed by the most frequently encountered financial instruments and their pricing/quotation methods (many relying on the ACI formulae provided). We then move on to the topic of repos.

INTRODUCTION

Just like in a dealing room with separate desks manned by specialist dealers concentrating on different aspects of the bank's market involvement, so too is the ACI Dealing Certificate similarly structured with syllabus topics comprising the cash market and a range of money market instruments and interest rate risk management activities.

Money makes the world go round. Cash is king. There are many similar hackneyed phrases but it is true to say that even in this age of derivatives the cash settled markets demand to be understood by all associated with the full range of financial markets.

The syllabus requires candidates to be familiar with the cash markets and the financial instruments traded on a daily basis on a bank's money market desk in the major financial centres. Definitions of products and differing pricing and dealing methods for loans/deposits, certificates of deposit (CDs), Treasury bills, bankers' acceptances (BAs) and commercial paper feature in the syllabus.

Another topic introduced to Level 1 in 1999 is found here – the repo market, only meriting two bullet points under Topic 3 but a separate examination question basket accounting for six questions in the examination.

Once the subject of the problematical separate Calculations paper in the old-style handwritten exam, calculations are now approached very differently in multiple choice format. Candidates must still, however, be comfortable in manipulating data in standard money market formulae to be able to identify the correct calculation result. Everything from simple interest to more complex interest arbitrage calculations have to be attempted under this heading with the help of a calculator of your choice or the standard MS Windows Calculator and an on-screen listing of recommended formulae (hard copy should also be available in the examination).

Also you will find *position keeping* issues relating to the cash market and financial instruments covered in this chapter.

THE CASH MARKET

When we use the words "money market" we are describing cash-based transactions involving the lending and borrowing of funds which are paid away/received on the start date and repaid on a fixed date or determinable maturity (notice money). In the interbank "professional" market these are typically unsecured loans between principals.

Retail and wholesale definitions

Most financial centres' regulators seeking to provide protection for the general public in their contacts with the "professional" market participants have some form of definition for retail and wholesale operations. Smaller retail transactions are usually covered by some form of depositor protection scheme – in the UK this is one of the issues under legislation included with the Financial Services Act 1986. Investors with larger amounts are deemed to be "professional" themselves and so these amounts are not subject to the same level of insurance. In the UK the FSA defines retail money market transactions as less than GBP 100 000 (or equivalent in foreign currency), or rather the wording of the London Code of Conduct is "wholesale transactions…are not usually less than GBP 100,000."

Call and notice deposits

In the interbank markets amounts of currency may be placed or accepted by a bank for an indeterminate period, subject to an agreed contractual term of notice of repayment/withdrawal of funds. This can vary from call to pre-agreed periods of notice.

Call account money is immediately recallable and will be repaid by the account holding institution with value the same day on receipt of such a notice in accordance with any conditions attached. In the sterling markets in London, call money is recallable value the same day up to 12 noon while in other centres and time zones differing conditions and cut-off times for interbank payments may determine the flexibility of this call money description.

Notice accounts are repayable after the pre-agreed period of notice. While various periods can be agreed the majority of such funds tend to be placed at short notice in the interbank money markets. The most frequently dealt notice periods are repayable on the first available business day in that currency after advice of notice (one day's notice) or on spot value date (two days' notice). There are other popular short-period notice accounts such as seven days and one month notice loans/deposits. In retail areas, though, three months and even one year notice deposits are frequently encountered and these periods too can sometimes be seen in the interbank market.

> **Question**
>
> A typical ACI Dealing Certificate question might be:
>
> You work for Major Bank, London. It is 1 p.m. on a Wednesday. You have a call account (liability) in your books in sterling and the depositor calls and requests repayment. When will payment be effected?
>
> A: Value today
> B: Value tomorrow
> C: Value spot
> D: Value next Monday
>
> **Correct answer**
> B: Sterling is a value same day market and up to 12 noon money on call is repayable value today. After 12 noon the balances will only be repaid (without penalty) value tomorrow.

Interest variation

It is important to remember that the deposit acceptor bank also retains the right to alter the rate of interest on any call or notice account, always subject to the appropriate period of notice before the amendment of rate becomes effective.

Interest on call and notice accounts is payable on withdrawal of the full balance but any other frequency of payment or capitalization of interest amounts prior to full repayment can be agreed between the parties at the time of dealing. Many banks for ease and synchronization of administrative functions repay or capitalize interest on call and notice accounts monthly (end of month) or an appropriate accounting date basis.

Fixed date operations

If money market operations are described as fixed date loans/deposits the money is committed for the fixed period agreed at the time of dealing. The rate will apply for the full fixed term and is not able to be changed once the deal is agreed.

The periods for which fixed deposits and loans may be agreed can be as short as one day and go out to five and even ten years in the major currencies. Overnight – from today until tomorrow – and tom/next – tomorrow against the next day (spot date) – are examples of the shortest periods able to be traded in the market. Interest is paid together with the repayment of the principal amount at maturity of such fixed loans and deposits.

A fixed deposit is non-negotiable. It cannot be cancelled or repayment requested by the depositor before the originally agreed maturity date without severe penalties being imposed by the deposit acceptor.

Interest payment

The payment of interest on fixed deposits and loans up to one year's duration occurs at maturity along with repayment of the principal amount invested. If the deposit/loan is for a longer period than 12 months then interest is payable annually on the anniversary and at final maturity.

> **Question**
>
> A typical ACI Dealing Certificate question might be:
>
> Interest on an 18-month money market deposit will be paid:
>
> A: Semi-annually
> B: At maturity
> C: After one year and at maturity
> D: Quarterly
>
> **Correct answer**
> C: Fixed money market loans placed and deposits accepted for periods in excess of one year pay interest on the anniversary and at final maturity.

London money market quotation

Market maker quotes:

- *Money market*: offer–bid for the cash (high–low in interest rate terms).

Topic 2 · Basic Calculations/Topic 3 · Money Market Products

International money market quotation

Market maker quotes:

- *Money market*: bid–offer for the cash (low–high in interest rate terms).

> **Care!**
>
> The London market switches round the rates quoted elsewhere. Dealing logic and calculations are unaffected. *ACI Dealing Certificate* examination questions should always make it clear in which manner any rate quotation is being made.

Rate selection

A favourite examination question type is to provide you with two separate two-way money market interest rate price quotations, tell you what you are trying to achieve and ask you to select the best rate of those available, i.e. you are market user.

Dealing logic dictates that if you are told you are a *lender* then you are looking for the best overall return and must select the *highest* interest rate of the two *bid* sides of the two-way prices. If the quote is made in London terms then the rule is select the *highest* on the right. If the quote is made in international terms then the rule is select the *highest* on the left.

If you are told you are a *borrower* then you are looking for the lowest cost of funds and must select the *lowest* interest rate of the two *offered* sides of the two-way prices. If the quote is made in London terms then the rule is select the *lowest* on the left. If the quote is made in international terms then the rule is select the *lowest* on the right.

> **Question**
>
> A typical ACI Dealing Certificate question might be:
>
> You are looking to borrow six months USD in the London market. Bank A quotes you $3\frac{7}{8} - 3\frac{3}{4}$ and Bank B quotes $3\frac{13}{16} - 3\frac{11}{16}$. Which bank is quoting you the best rate and at which rate will you deal?
>
> A: Bank B $3\frac{13}{16}$ %
>
> B: Bank A $3\frac{7}{8}$ %
>
> C: Bank A $3\frac{3}{4}$ %
>
> D: Bank B $3\frac{11}{16}$ %
>
> **Correct answer**
>
> A: As a borrower you are looking to raise funds as cheaply as possible. Both banks are quoting offer–bid for cash, high–low in interest rates. You will therefore deal with Bank B who is offering cash at $3\frac{13}{16}$ percent – the lowest rate on the left-hand sides of the two banks' prices.

This type of question also crops up under any of the financial instruments and will be discussed again later in this chapter.

Days and dates

Bank of England and FSA terminology refers to short dates as transactions with a maturity of up to one month. Fixed date (standard period) transactions have a maturity of one month and beyond. A typical set of standard period money market rates in any of the major currencies would be: 1, 2, 3, 6 and 12 months. In some currencies with less liquidity in the longer periods a set of rates quoted may only be for one to six months.

> **Note**
>
> The following rules for maturity days and dates also apply to forward value dates for foreign exchange transactions (Chapter 7).

Standard period maturity dates

In eurocurrency money market operations the standard period maturity dates are calculated based on the benchmark spot date. The standard period maturity value date will normally be the same date in the appropriate forward month. For example, the three months maturity date from dealing date Monday 19 April 200X (spot date Wednesday 21 April 200X) is Thursday 21 July 200X (a three-month period April to July 200X of 91 days), the six months forward value date is Friday 21 October 200X (a six-month period of 184 days), etc.

As spot date is affected by weekends and other non-business days in the financial centres where the currency will be settled, so too are the standard period maturity dates. If a holiday or other financial centre closure affects any such period the maturity date moves forward to the next working day. For example, the one-month forward value date from dealing date Monday 19 April 200X (spot date Wednesday 21 April 200X) is Monday, 23 May 200X – 21 May is a Saturday and the one month end date therefore moves on to the next business day giving a one month period in this instance of 32 days.

There is always an exception to every rule. In the case of money market maturity dates, there are two exceptions.

Calendar month standard periods

No fixed period maturity date is ever quoted further forward than its standard period calendar month. In other words, the one month date from June must always be a date in July. When, for example, at the end of the month of March 200X the last business day was the last calendar date – Thursday 31 March – but in the four month standard period the same date in July was in fact a Sunday, then the maturity date for the four month period is moved backward to the last business date in that month, i.e. Friday 29 July 200X. The maturity date never crosses a month end "threshold".

End/end

If the last business day in the current month is not the last calendar date in the month (due to a weekend or holiday), for standard period maturity date calculation purposes this date is deemed to be the month end, and all other standard period maturity dates are then also the last business dates in the appropriate forward months. This rule is termed the "end/end" rule.

An example of this rule coming into play, again in 200X, was in April when the last business day was Friday 29 April. Standard forward period dates from this spot date were: one month – Tuesday 31 May (a one-month period of 32 days); two months – Thursday 30 June (a two-month period of 62 days); three months – Friday 29 July (a three-month period of 91 days); and six months – Monday 31 October 200X (a six-month period of 185 days). Each month's final business date is treated as the month end due to the "end/end" procedures.

Question

A typical ACI Dealing Certificate question might be:

If the maturity date for a eurodollar transaction falls on a Saturday, which also happens to be the last day of the month, when will the transaction be settled?

A: On the Saturday
B: On last working day of the month
C: On the following Monday
D: On the next working day

Correct answer
B: Here "end/end" comes into play. The maturity date never crosses a month end threshold so the date moves back to the last working day of the month in question (the day before – Friday, the last working day in the month, if this is a good value date).

Value dates for domestic GBP markets quoted in London

Sterling interest rates for fixed date transactions in the London sterling money market are based on a value same day market and run from value today (up to 12 noon) rather than spot date, though the end/end rules still apply to fixing the maturity dates where appropriate. In some other financial centres the local currency is similarly quoted on a value same day basis.

Quotation methods (fractions and decimals)

Interest rates can be quoted in fractions, decimals or (particularly the more modern derivative products) in basis points (1 basis point or $bp = 0.01$ percent). Fractions tend traditionally to be halves, quarters, eighths, sixteenths, thirty-seconds and, for some sterling money markets, even sixty-fourths $\left(\frac{1}{64}\right)$. The decimal equivalent of $\frac{1}{64}$ (one sixty-fourth) is 0.015625. Other decimal equivalents are shown in Table 4.1.

$\frac{1}{32}$	0.03125	$\frac{9}{32}$	0.28125	$\frac{17}{32}$	0.53125	$\frac{25}{32}$	0.78125
$\frac{1}{16}$	0.0625	$\frac{5}{16}$	0.3125	$\frac{9}{16}$	0.5625	$\frac{13}{16}$	0.8125
$\frac{3}{32}$	0.09375	$\frac{11}{32}$	0.34375	$\frac{19}{32}$	0.59375	$\frac{27}{32}$	0.84375
$\frac{1}{8}$	0.125	$\frac{3}{8}$	0.375	$\frac{5}{8}$	0.625	$\frac{7}{8}$	0.875
$\frac{5}{32}$	0.15625	$\frac{13}{32}$	0.40625	$\frac{21}{32}$	0.65625	$\frac{29}{32}$	0.90625
$\frac{3}{16}$	0.1875	$\frac{7}{16}$	0.4375	$\frac{11}{16}$	0.6875	$\frac{15}{16}$	0.9375
$\frac{7}{32}$	0.21875	$\frac{15}{32}$	0.46875	$\frac{23}{32}$	0.71875	$\frac{31}{32}$	0.96875
$\frac{1}{4}$	0.25	$\frac{1}{2}$	0.5	$\frac{3}{4}$	0.75	1.0	1.0

Table 4.1 Fraction to decimal table (minimum $\frac{1}{32}$)

Simple interest formula

The simple interest formula shown in Figure 4.1 with the interest rate entered as an integer permits interest on a loan or deposit to be calculated.

This interest is calculated on the principal amount invested at the interest rate agreed for the actual number of days the investment is made divided

Fig 4.1

$$\text{interest} = \frac{\text{principal} \times \text{rate} \times \text{days}}{360^* \times 100}$$

*365 in case of sterling

by the interest day basis × 100 (the asterisk (*) against the denominator depends on the interest day basis – explained below).

> **Hint**
>
> *This simple interest formula is not included on the ACI formulae sheet discussed later in this chapter. It is assumed that candidates know this basic formula.*

Day basis

The simple interest formula in Figure 4.1 varies depending on the various alternative interest day bases found in the financial markets. In the money markets and other financial instrument markets there are various different interest bases quoted. These bases differ from country to country and sometimes within a country from instrument to instrument. It is a case of learning the standard versions and remembering the exceptions to each rule.

Money market – actual/360

Interest on US domestic and eurocurrency money market cash and financial products is calculated on an *actual/360* day count basis. This basis is frequently referred to as the *money market* basis.

Sterling money market – actual/365

All cash and financial products in sterling are quoted on an *actual/365* day count basis. There are other currencies where interest is also calculated on this basis. Examples are (not an exhaustive list): Australian dollars (AUD), New Zealand dollars (NZD), Hong Kong dollars (HKD) and Singapore dollars (SGD).

> **Care!**
>
> In some countries different day count bases are used in domestic and eurocurrency transactions and even for different products within the domestic market.

Actual/actual

There is a further day count basis referred to as *actual/actual* where standard years are calculated as *actual/365* but leap years are calculated as *actual/366*. Typically government bond markets (including euro-zone government bond issues) use this day count basis.

Actual

For all the above bases the term "actual" refers to the actual number of days in any period for which interest is being calculated, i.e. an overnight deal is one day whereas a one month transaction may vary from 27 to

Mastering the ACI Dealing Certificate

around 35 actual elapsed days depending on the calendar dates/holidays involved. This is sometimes referred to as the *tenor*, particularly when bills of exchange transactions are being described.

> **Hint**
>
> *For convenience, in the* ACI Dealing Certificate *examination many questions will advise you to consider 30-day months in calculations.*

Bond basis (Eurobonds)

In the international markets eurobond interest is calculated on a 30/360 (360/360) day count basis, i.e. each month is assessed as 30 days. This is referred to as the *bond basis* and is used for commercially issued bonds in the euromarkets (i.e. corporate bonds issued in a currency which is a foreign currency in the chosen financial market centre).

> **Hint**
>
> *Bonds are* not *included in the* ACI Dealing Certificate *syllabus but questions on the differing day count bases are frequently set in the examination.*

> **Question**
>
> A typical ACI Dealing Certificate question might be:
>
> Which of the following currencies/products is quoted on an actual/360 basis for the calculation of interest?
>
> A: GBP T-bills
> B: EUR deposits
> C: JPY government securities
> D: USD eurobonds
>
> **Correct answer**
> B: Of those listed euro deposits are the only currency/product quoted on an actual no. of days/360 day basis for interest calculation.

ACI formulae

There are many different formulae available and in use around bank dealing rooms to calculate prices and dealing outcomes. Each dealer will have his favourite. The formulae in this and other chapters which are included in the ACI formulae sheet (see Appendix I – made available in the examination) are identified with the notation <ACI preferred>.

> *While interest rates in ACI Dealing Certificate examination questions are quoted as integers as in the market, when using the ACI formulae remember that these have to be input as decimals, i.e. rather than inputting an interest rate of 5.00 percent as 5.00 and dividing by 100, for <ACI preferred> formulae this interest rate has to be entered as 0.05.*

Hint

Conversion between different bases
To bond from money market

To calculate an interest rate on bond (360/360) day count basis from an actual/360 money market day count basis (365/360) interest rate:

$$\text{interest rate on bond basis} = \text{rate on money market basis} \times \frac{\text{days on money market basis}}{\text{money market year basis}} \times \frac{\text{bond year basis}}{\text{days on bond basis}}$$

<ACI preferred>

Question

A typical ACI Dealing Certificate question might be:

What is the equivalent of a money market yield of 6.00 percent in terms of a eurobond coupon rate?

A: 6.00%
B: 6.0833%
C: 5.9178%
D: 5.875%

Correct answer

B: On a bond basis interest is payable for five days less in the year (360 divided by 360 rather than 365 divided by 360), therefore the equivalent coupon rate must be higher. Through the formula it can be calculated as 6.0833 percent.

Proof

To convert from a money market yield of 6.00 percent to a bond basis interest rate:

$$0.06 \times \frac{365}{360} \times \frac{360}{360} = 0.0608333 = 6.0833\%$$

Mastering the ACI Dealing Certificate

> **Hint**
>
> *The equivalent bond basis interest rate converted from a money market day count basis will always be a higher number as the day count basis means that interest is payable for five days less in the year (360 divided by 360 rather than 365 divided by 360).*

To money market from bond

To calculate an interest rate on a 365/360 money market day basis from a bond (360/360) day basis interest rate:

$$\text{interest rate on money market basis} = \text{rate on bond basis} \times \frac{\text{days on bond basis}}{\text{bond year basis}} \times \frac{\text{money market year basis}}{\text{days on money market basis}}$$

<ACI preferred>

Proof

To convert from a bond basis interest rate of 6.50 percent to a money market yield:

$$0.065 \times \frac{360}{360} \times \frac{360}{365} = 0.064109 = 6.4109\%$$

> **Hint**
>
> *The equivalent money market interest rate converted from a bond basis will always be a lower number as the day count basis means that interest is payable for five days more in the year (365 divided by 360 rather than 360 divided by 360).*

Topic 2 · Basic Calculations/Topic 3 · Money Market Products

> **Question**
>
> A typical ACI Dealing Certificate question might be:
> Which of the following rates represents the best yield?
> A: Semi-annual money market yield of 4.50%
> B: Semi-annual bond yield of 4.50%
> C: Annual bond yield of 4.50%
> D: Annual money market rate of 4.50%
>
> **Correct answer**
> A: The more frequently interest is paid gives the best return. Here with the same numerical rate quoted on each basis a semi-annual rate provides the best return and money market (actual/360) is always better than bond basis (30/360), paying five days more interest per full year.

> **Hint**
>
> In an examination question where you are given identical bond basis (360/360) and money market basis (365/360) rates and are being asked to select the interest rate giving you the better return, this will always be the money market rate (effectively paying five days more interest over a full year).

Annual and semi-annual interest rates

These days many percentage per annum rates are recalculated on a semi-annual basis. This is often the case in interest rate swap quotations.

Interest rates will always give a better return the more compounding periods there are. A semi-annual interest rate means that the two compounding interest periods will improve the return when recalculated on an annual basis.

The converse is that when an annual interest rate has to be converted into a semi-annual one then the rate will be numerically lower but the one compounding date will ensure the return is the same overall.

To annual from semi-annual interest formula

To calculate the effective annual interest rate:

$$\text{annual rate} = \left(1 + \left(\frac{\text{semi-annual rate}}{2}\right)\right)^2 - 1$$

<ACI preferred>

Mastering the ACI Dealing Certificate

Question

A typical ACI Dealing Certificate question might be:

A semi-annual CHF rate is 5 percent. What is the effective annual yield?

A: 4.939%
B: 4.945%
C: 5.0000%
D: 5.0625%

Correct answer

D: Using the annual from semi-annual formula the answer 5.0625 percent can be calculated.

Proof

To convert from an annual interest rate of 5.00 percent to a semi-annual rate:

$$\left(1 + \left(\frac{0.050}{2}\right)\right)^2 - 1 = 0.050625 = 5.0625\%$$

Hint

A semi-annual rate will always equate to a numerically higher equivalent annual rate: the more frequently interest is payable the more attractive the investment.

Semi-annual from annual interest formula

To calculate the effective semi-annual interest rate:

$$\text{semi-annual rate} = \left(\sqrt{(1 + \text{annual rate})} - 1\right) \times 2$$

<ACI preferred>

Question

A typical ACI Dealing Certificate question might be:

An annual DKK rate is 5 percent. What is the effective semi-annual yield?

A: 4.939%
B: 4.945%
C: 5.0000%
D: 5.0625%

Correct answer

A: Using the semi-annual from annual formula the answer 4.939 percent can be calculated.

Proof

To convert from an annual interest rate of 5.00 percent to a semi-annual rate:

$$\left(\sqrt{(1 + 0.050)} - 1\right) \times 2 = 0.049390 = \mathbf{4.9390\%}$$

> **Hint**
> *An annual rate will always equate to a numerically lower equivalent semi-annual rate.*

> **Note**
> These conversions between annual and semi-annual yields really only apply between interest rates on similar bases, strictly speaking only actual/actual or 365/365.

> **Hint**
> *When rates of interest quoted on the two bases are identical, semi-annual yield rates will* always *provide a better return than an equivalent annual rate.*

Time value of money

Money, as with any commodity, has value. The time value of money is a concept which permits any sum of money due on a forward date to be given an equivalent value today. That value today is the amount which, if invested at current interest rates for the interim period, would accumulate (including interest) the originally identified amount.

Today's value is known as the *Present Value (PV)*. The *Future Value* is known as *FV* and the rate to be used to achieve the PV from the FV is the *discount rate* applicable to the appropriate interim period. The discount rate is also referred to as the *required rate of return (RoR)*.

Discount rate

The discount rate can be expressed as a percentage, e.g. 10 percent, or a decimal (0.10) and frequently the rate will be expressed as [1 + rate], here 1.10. The discount rate can also be expressed as a discount factor, e.g. 10 percent = [1 ÷ 1.10] or 0.9091.

Within a one-year time horizon (remember an interest rate or discount rate is *percent per annum*) PV invested at a rate of *r* will grow to FV. The effect of interest rates on the PV will depend on whether simple or compound formulae are used.

Mastering the ACI Dealing Certificate

Present value formula

$$\text{Present value} = \frac{\text{future value}}{(1 + \text{annual interest rate})^n}$$

Where n is the number of compounding periods.

Care!

This formula is *not* provided on the ACI formulae sheet distributed during the examinations. Questions are, however, frequently included in the *ACI Dealing Certificate* needing this calculation.

Question

A typical ACI Dealing Certificate question might be:

Given a two-year interest rate of 5.00 percent, what is the present value of a debt of GBP 1,000,000 in exactly two years' time?

A: GBP 1,092,970.52
B: GBP 1,000,000.00
C: GBP 900,000.00
D: GBP 907,029.48

Correct answer
D: Using the PV formula this can be calculated to be $1,000,000/(1 + 0.05)^2$ = GBP 907,029.48.

Proof

To calculate the present value of a debt of GBP 1,000,000 in exactly two years' time given a discount rate of 5.00 percent:

$$\frac{1,000,000.00}{(1 + 0.050)^2} = \text{GBP } 907,029.48$$

Future value formula

$$\text{Future value} = \text{present value} \times (1 + \text{annual interest rate})^n$$

Where n is the number of compounding periods.

Care!

This formula is *not* provided on the ACI formulae sheet distributed during the examinations.

Proof

To calculate the future value of GBP 907,029.48 invested at 5.00 percent for two years:

$$907{,}029.48 \times (1 + 0.050)^2 = \text{GBP } 1{,}000{,}000 \text{ (rounded)}$$

LIBOR

LIBOR (London Interbank Offered Rate) is the money market "benchmark" interest rate. Any rates quoted as an offer at any time during the day can be so described. The term LIBOR, however, takes on a more significant meaning at 11 o'clock each day when the official market fixing takes place.

BBA LIBOR

LIBOR has been in existence for many years. In 1995 LIBOR was officially redefined by the British Bankers Association (BBA) as "the rate of interest at which deposits are perceived to be generally available in the London interbank market".

BBA LIBOR offered rates per period for the major currencies are obtained from 16 reference banks in London selected by the BBA on the basis of private nominations and discussions with advisory panels of senior market practitioners. These banks are selected to reflect the balance of the market in terms of country of origin and type of institution and on the basis of reputation, scale of market activity and perceived expertise in the currency. The BBA, having discarded the four highest and four lowest rates, calculates BBA LIBOR by arriving at an arithmetically averaged rate (rounded up to the nearest $\frac{1}{16}$ percent). The resultant interest rate is broadcast to the world by Reuters, Bloomberg and other rates/news vendors as the day's benchmark interest rate – BBA LIBOR.

BBA Euro LIBOR

BBA Euro LIBOR will be fixed on any day on which the TARGET (Euro clearing) system is open, i.e. including UK bank holidays. Both LIFFE (London International Financial Futures and Options Exchange) and the DTB (Deutsche Termine Bourse) use BBA Euro LIBOR as the futures benchmark comparitor rate in preference to any other Euro fixings (e.g. EBA's EURIBOR – see below).

EURIBOR

The European Banking Association (EBA) fixes a similar daily benchmark rate by reference to a panel of 57 banks. These are a majority of banks in the euro zone, other EU countries and a smaller number of non-EU international banks. Because of the wider spread of reference banks (some perhaps with a lesser credit rating or market standing than for the BBA Euro LIBOR fixing), EURIBOR is typically always higher than EUR LIBOR.

BBA LIBOR uses

BBA LIBOR is used for many different purposes in the market. It is the reference rate for all commercial roll-over loans due for re-rating that day (see below). It is the comparitor rate used for settling FRAs. When the day is a LIFFE futures market delivery date (i.e. for value the third Wednesday of a quarter month) the appropriate LIBOR rate forms the basis for the Exchange Delivery Settlement Price (EDSP) of LIFFE short-term interest rate contracts.

The LIBOR rate is the rate used for the floating rate side of the majority of interest rate swaps under ISDA (International Swaps and Derivatives Association) terms. The LIBOR rate is the reference rate for single period interest rate options and the longer-term caps, floors and collar products.

There are similar fixing rates in other centres: TIBOR in Tokyo, SIBOR in Singapore. The fixing and use of these reference rates may vary from centre to centre subject to local market rules and conventions.

Commercial lending

Commercial lending can take a variety of forms with committed lines and uncommitted lines of credit being made available to a bank's corporate customers. Perhaps the most frequently encountered corporate lending "product" is the roll-over loan introduced in the late 1960s.

Roll-over loan

Where a corporate borrower is seeking longer-term finance for capital projects but the lender (the bank) is unhappy about the interest rate exposure on such long-term fixed lending, a roll-over loan meets both parties' requirements and effectively exports the interest rate risk to the borrower.

An example of a roll-over loan is a three-year (36 months) lending arrangement with an agreement to alter the fixed rate of interest payable by the corporate customer in line with current short-term interest rates on a regular basis (typically three or six months fixed). The customer knows the interest rate payable on the current period and at the end of the period will pay the interest due at that rate and be advised of the rate of interest for the new roll-over period. The interest rate is always a market rate, i.e. LIBOR based (or equivalent), with any additional margin a reflection of the creditworthiness of the borrower as assessed by the bank. Such loans are re-rated and rolled in accordance with the descriptions of days and dates already discussed.

Roll-over loan example

An example of a three-year loan with interest rate reset (LIBOR) every six months is illustrated in Figure 4.2.

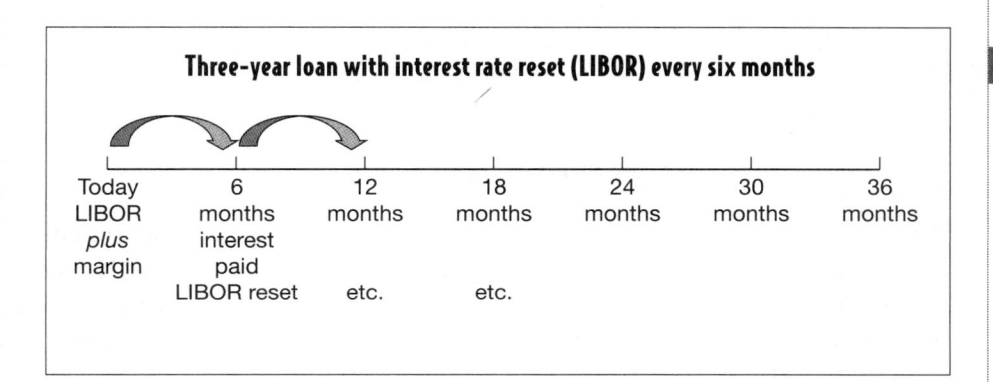

Three-year loan with interest rate reset (LIBOR) every six months

Fig 4.2

| Today | 6 months | 12 months | 18 months | 24 months | 30 months | 36 months |

Today: LIBOR plus margin
6 months: interest paid, LIBOR reset
12 months: etc.
18 months: etc.

YIELD CURVES

The shape of a yield curve is one of many pointers as to current market sentiment in respect of the anticipated level of future interest rates. Some textbooks will suggest that longer period rates are usually higher than short rates to allow for the time and inflation risks in longer-term investment. But the shape of the money market yield curve up to 12 months at any time more significantly identifies the current market sentiment that over time interest rates are going to rise or fall. There are four basic shapes to yield curves: positive, negative, flat and humped. Examples of each follow.

Positive yield curve

A positive yield curve (see Figure 4.3) tends to suggest that over time rates will rise, the maxim being: "If you believe rates are going higher then borrow as much as you can now in what will soon appear to be a cheap interest rate environment." The demand for money is greater in the longer term, therefore the price (the rate of interest) is higher.

Fig 4.3

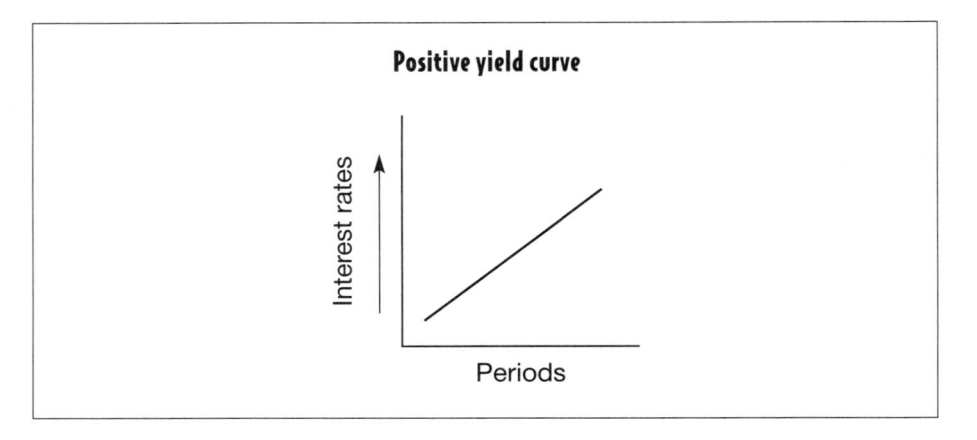

Positive yield curve

[Graph: Interest rates vs Periods, upward sloping line]

Negative yield curve

A negative yield curve (see Figure 4.4) identifies the market's sentiment that over time interest rates are going to fall, the maxim being: "If you believe rates are going lower then borrow only on short term rather than lock into longer-term rates which may indeed be cheaper tomorrow." Demand for short-term money exceeds supply. Alongside this, the professional market is looking to lend long now at higher rates than anticipated in the future (supply exceeding demand).

Fig 4.4

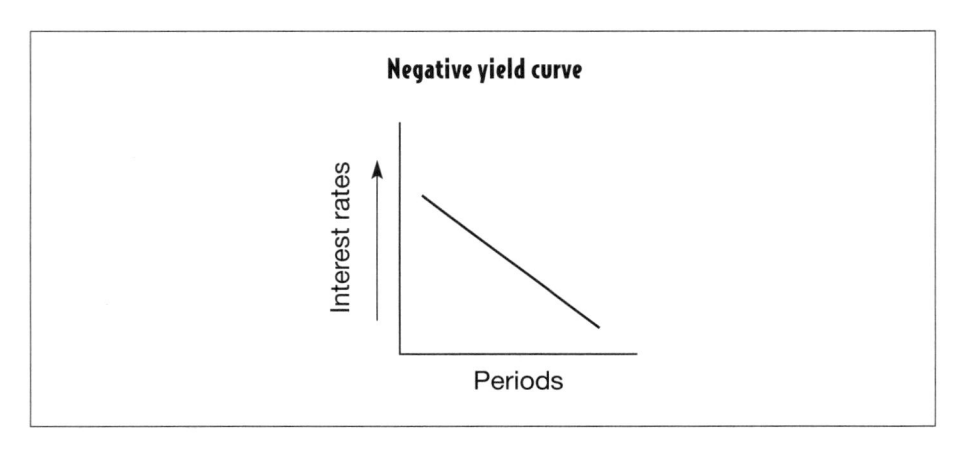

Negative yield curve

[Graph: Interest rates vs Periods, downward sloping line]

Other yield curve shapes

Flat

A flat yield curve (see Figure 4.5) suggests either the market is happy with current interest rate levels or that the market does not know where rates are going. It could also be an interim shape as the yield curve is switching from positive to negative or vice versa.

Flat yield curve

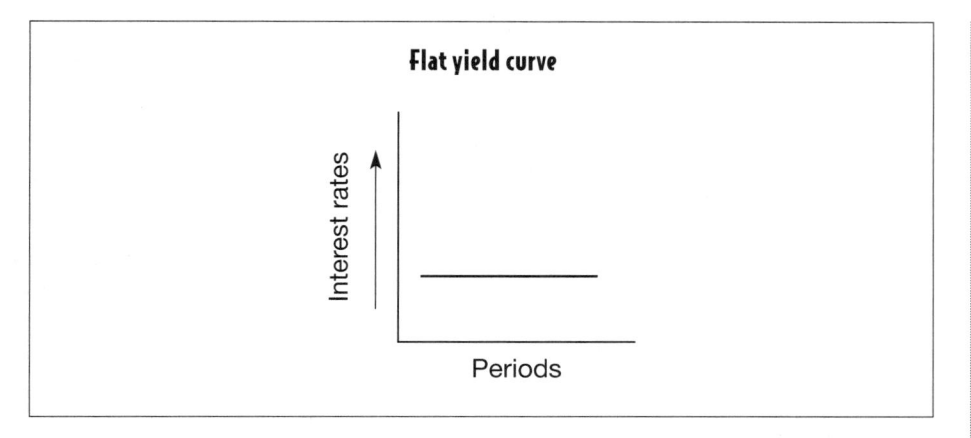

Fig 4.5

Spiked or humped

Some textbooks may state that a spiked or humped shape (see Figure 4.6) means that in the short term the market expects rates to rise but that they will fall in the longer term. A perhaps more realistic reason is that there is an unusual date, a reserve requirement or a turn of the year factor sometime in the future which is causing rates to be quoted higher than they should be and once that date is dissipated over a longer period the yield curve returns to its correct level.

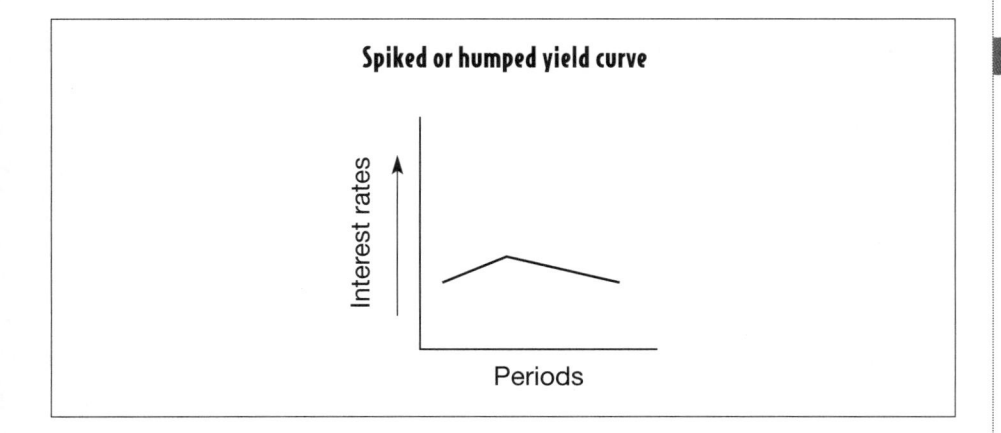

Spiked or humped yield curve

Fig 4.6

Extraordinary days – Thursday/Friday US dollars

Older generations of dealer will recall there was such a spike on a weekly basis in US dollars in the eurodollar market until the CHIPS payments system was introduced in New York. Clearing house funds were good funds (cleared) value tomorrow whereas federal funds were good funds (cleared) value today. The interbank eurodollar market settled in clearing house funds.

As an example of the Thursday/Friday anomaly, USD interest rates based on settling clearing house funds (good funds value next day) would be 6 percent per day Monday/Tuesday, Tuesday/Wednesday and Wednesday/Thursday because the cleared funds were available the next day for the same overnight period and rate. But, because clearing house funds on a Thursday were good funds on a Friday and could be applied for three days over the weekend, the Thursday/Friday eurodollar interbank interest rate would be three times the daily rate (6% × 3 = 18%). Similarly, clearing house funds on a Friday were not good funds until the Monday and so the Friday/Monday (weekend) interbank eurodollar interest rate would be one third of the daily rate (6%/3 = 2%).

Extraordinary days – "ultimo" Swiss francs

Until a few years ago a similar "extraordinary" day occurred every month end in Swiss francs. This was due to the window dressing required for Swiss National Bank minimum reserve returns at this date each month. With Swiss franc rates traditionally low (around 1 percent) the turn of the month ("ultimo" in market terminology) was always much higher, sometimes fluctuating between 30 and 50 percent. The whole market seemed not to care about daily rates and all efforts were concentrated on the correct estimate of the level of the turn. Eventually the Swiss National Bank decided to alter the minimum reserve requirements and this monthly speculative event disappeared.

Question

A typical ACI Dealing Certificate question might be:

What do you call a yield curve where shorter rates are higher than longer rates?

A: Inverted
B: Convex
C: Parabolic
D: Flat

Correct answer
A: A yield curve where shorter-term interest rates are higher than longer-term rates is described as inverted or negative.

Interpolated (broken date) interest rates

To calculate an interest rate for a non-standard period from spot (or today) a rough approximation can be reached by averaging the daily products of the two standard period interest rates falling either side of the broken date maturity (see Figure 4.7).

Calculating interim period interest rates by straight line interpolation

Yield curve

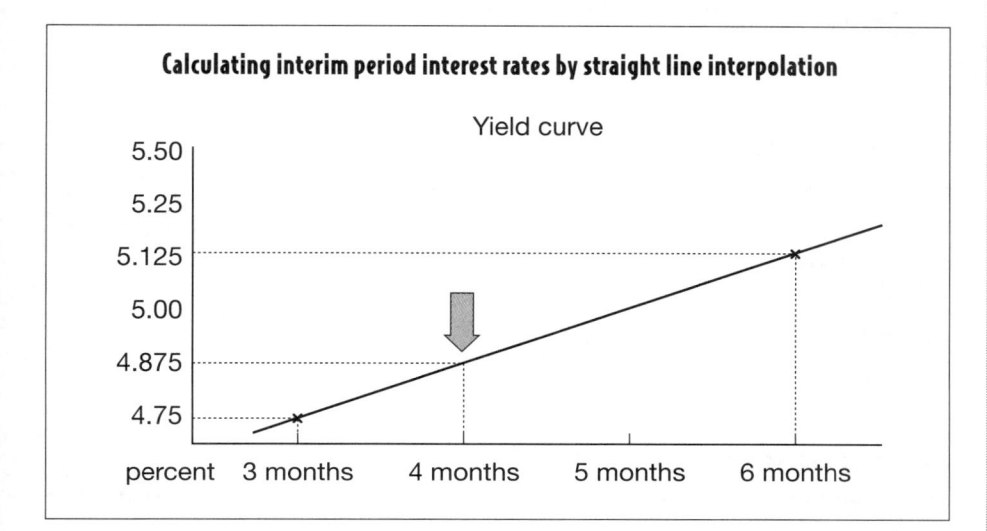

Fig 4.7

This is referred to as "straight line interpolation" and is based on the concept that the rise or fall in a yield curve between two periods can be assumed to be steady, implying that any interest rate required for an interim period from spot can be plotted. For example, to plot a four months rate (120 days) when the yield curve rises from 4.75 percent in the three months (90 days) to 5.125 percent in the six months (180 days) the difference of 0.375 over 90 days can be divided by the number of months between the fixed periods (3), so for an additional one month (30 days, but 120 in total) the rate will be 4.875 (90 days 4.75 plus 0.125).

This method is not appropriate should there be a particularly steep yield curve (positive or negative). In such instances the accurate method to calculate broken date deposit rates is to identify the rates for the periods falling either side of the broken date and then adjust the near date rate (actual number of days) by the forward/forward interest rate for the balance of the broken date period (from the near date standard period maturity date to the broken date, again counted in days).

Care!

Mastering the ACI Dealing Certificate

Hint

The forward/forward interest rate formula appears in Chapter 5. In the ACI Dealing Certificate examination the questions will typically request such a rate to be calculated "using straight line interpolation".

Question

A typical ACI Dealing Certificate question might be:

If a 90-day SGD interest rate is 5.25 percent and a 180-day SGD interest rate is 6.30 percent, what is the 126-day SGD rate using straight line interpolation?

A: 5.66
B: 5.68
C: 5.67
D: 5.69

Correct answer
C: If 90 days is quoted at 5.25 and 180 days is quoted at 6.30 then the difference between the two rates of 1.05 for 90 days is equivalent to an increase of 0.011666 per day. For a 126-day rate there is an additional 36 days at 0.011666 = 0.41999 plus the 90-day rate of 5.25 making an interpolated SGD rate of 5.67 percent (rounded).

POSITION KEEPING

The way dealers refer to money market positions differs from market to market and even from dealer to dealer. It is important that all involved with any dealing position are aware of the jargon being used. Money market cash dealers tend to talk about the cash movement of funds, i.e. a dealer stating his position is long five million in the six months typically means he has accepted deposits in excess of loans granted in that period. His liabilities exceed his assets in that period – he is cash long.

Dealers tend to keep separate records per financial instrument traded (see later in this chapter). All cash associated with the purchase and/or sale of such instruments will be recorded in the dealer's cashflow and under the appropriate maturity period. The records will also include an average position or holding interest rate and possibly a current market interest rate for marking to market purposes.

> **Question**
>
> A typical ACI Dealing Certificate question might be:
>
> If you have lent EUR 10 million for six months (182 days) at 6 percent and borrowed back 7 million at 5.8125 percent, what is the average rate (breakeven) of the remaining uncovered EUR 3 million position?
>
> A: 6.5%
> B: 5.5625%
> C: 6.5625%
> D: 6.4375%
>
> **Correct answer**
>
> D: 0.1875 percent margin made on the 7 million funding (0.1875 × 7 = 1.3125) is rolled in to make the breakeven on the balance = (1.3125/3) 6.4375 percent.

> **Hint**
>
> *The ACI Dealing Certificate examination frequently includes similar position keeping questions on other aspects of money market/financial instrument trading.*

Position average rates

Position keeping is a vital part of a money market dealer's activities. Examination questions can be set for money market positions. A sequence of deals are presented and you must average the rate of interest on assets or liabilities. The more complicated question type will involve long and short positions, i.e. a weighted average is required.

Mismatching

Where a dealer is covering in a different period from that originally requiring funding, e.g. running a position with three months liabilities funding a six months asset, this is referred to as a *mismatch* or *gap* position.

> **Hint**
>
> ACI Dealing Certificate *examination questions seeking the breakeven rate of a mismatch position (which can be calculated using the forward/forward formula discussed in Chapter 5) frequently occur.*

These mismatch positions are described using the number of months from spot to the start of the gap to the number of months from spot to the end of the period. For example, in January a mismatch position from March to July would be described as 2s v. 5s (said "twos fives"). Similar terminology is used to describe forward/forward periods in foreign exchange and short-term derivatives (FRAs) – see Chapters 5 and 7.

Mastering the ACI Dealing Certificate

> **Question**
>
> A typical ACI Dealing Certificate question might be:
>
> What does the term "mismatched" in respect of money market maturities mean?
>
> A: You have borrowed forward/forward against a long futures position
> B: Your assets and liabilities are not traded for exactly matching dates
> C: You have borrowed cash against securities
> D: You have short date deposits accepted surplus to requirements
>
> **Correct answer**
>
> B: The usual meaning of the term "mismatched" is that you have consciously taken liabilities for different periods from the assets they are funding, perhaps in anticipation of a general change in the level of interest rates.

Interest profit and loss

Profit and loss on money market activities is calculated on an interest accrual basis. Typically in active money market banks this is done in arrears on a daily basis. Alternatively this will be done on a regular (monthly) reporting date.

Where interest accrued on foreign currency money market operations is involved the net of receivable/payable in foreign currency will give rise to an open exchange position against local currency (the P&L balance sheet currency) and will be accounted for and reported accordingly.

Deal date accounting issues

Most active money market banks will have strict rules requiring that all transactions are entered into the bank's general ledger on deal date. Where the effective dates of transactions are in the future (i.e. from spot value for foreign currency money market transactions) this will mean that interim committed/suspense account entries will have to be raised on deal date to be reversed against live balance sheet accounts on effective date.

Deal date accounting entries ensure that all transactions are accurately reflected in the bank's accounting records and feature immediately in all risk management reportage.

NEGOTIABLE FINANCIAL INSTRUMENTS

There are several cash-settled financial instruments which can be bought in the primary and traded in the secondary markets (with liquidity in certain of the markets greater than others). These instruments provide a depositor who perhaps needs the facility to re-acquire his funds prior to the pre-agreed maturity date with a readily available market in which to deal. There is a range of these cash-settled negotiable financial instruments available in the major centres' markets. These notes concentrate on the UK and the US markets and instruments available.

Treasury Bills

Short-term government debt is issued in many different jurisdictions in the form of Treasury Bills (T-Bills) of varying tenor (maturity). Here we discuss aspects relating to the UK and US markets.

> *T-Bills are low risk instruments (the credit risk is on the government of the country) and you would therefore expect them to have a comparatively lower rate of return than other financial instruments issued by commercial banks/companies.*

Hint

UK Treasury Bills

UK Treasury Bills are issued at weekly tenders, held by the Debt Management Office (DMO) on the last business day of each week (i.e. usually Fridays). Treasury Bills can be issued with maturities of 1 month (approximately 28 days), 3 months (approximately 91 days), 6 months (approximately 182 days) and 12 months (up to 364 days). The DMO announces the size of the following week's tender and maturity of bills on offer at the preceding week's tender.

Tenders are held on a competitive bid yield basis. All bids must be received before 11.00 a.m. on the day of tender. Bills are allotted to those bids that are at, or below, the yield deemed by the DMO to be the highest accepted yield. Bids at the highest accepted yield may only receive a proportion of the nominal amount of bills bid for.

Information following each weekly tender is published on the DMO's website: www.dmo.gov.uk.

UK Treasury Bills in the secondary market

Once "in circulation" Treasury bills can be bought and sold in the secondary market, where they are traded as discount operations with the appropriate tenor discount rate being applied to the face value of the T-Bills.

There is a highly liquid secondary market and holders of T-Bills are able to rediscount them at any time prior to maturity. The price paid/received is then the face value *less* the discount amount.

London money market quotation

The secondary market – market maker quotes:
- *T-Bill*s: bid–offer for the securities (high–low in interest/discount rate terms).

Mastering the ACI Dealing Certificate

International money market quotation

The secondary market – market maker quotes:

- *T-Bill*s: offer–bid for the securities (low–high in interest/discount rate terms).

Care!
> Here the market terminology refers to the securities being traded. The London market switches round the rates quoted elsewhere. Dealing logic and calculations are unaffected. ACI Dealing Certificate examination questions should always make it clear in which manner any rate quotation is being made.

UK T-Bill rates

In the secondary market T-Bills in London will be quoted high–low in line with standard London market terminology and will be referred to as bid–offer (for the T-Bills).

A T-Bill rate is a *pure discount* rate which is applied to the face value to achieve the discount amount which is then subtracted from the face value to calculate the price to be paid on purchase.

The market maker in London is in effect quoting "buy–sell" rates for T-Bills as a two-way price and the dealing terminology relates to the movement of the securities.

Question
> A typical ACI Dealing Certificate question might be:
>
> You are a buyer of three months GBP eligible bills in the London market. Bank A quotes you $7\frac{1}{16} - 6\frac{15}{16}$ and Bank B quotes $7 - 6\frac{7}{8}$. Which bank is quoting you the best rate and at which rate will you deal?
>
> A: Bank B 7.00 %
>
> B: Bank A $6\frac{15}{16}$ %
>
> C: Bank A $7\frac{1}{16}$ %
>
> D: Bank B $6\frac{7}{8}$ %
>
> Correct answer
>
> B: As a buyer of eligible bills you are looking to buy at the cheapest price (to lend funds at as high a rate achievable as possible). You will therefore deal with Bank A who is offering bills (i.e. bidding for cash against securities) at $6\frac{15}{16}$ percent.

US Treasury Bills

US Treasury Bills (T-Bills) are US dollar denominated bearer instruments with three-, six- and 12-month maturities. Three- and six-month bills are issued and auctioned weekly with 12-month bills available once a month.

In the United States there is also a market which trades T-Bills before issue. This market, similar to the grey market in bonds, is called the "When Issued" or WI market. The WI market trades such bills after auction but before settlement takes place.

US Treasury Bill rates

The rate quoted for T-Bills is a pure discount rate. As market participants buy and sell T-Bills, terminology also relates to the movement of the securities which in the US market is quoted offer–bid (for the T-Bills) in line with other market quotations. The two-way discount rate quote will be made low–high, i.e. 3.75–4.00 percent.

Pure discount operations

All US T-Bills are discount securities. In the secondary market they are traded as *pure discount* operations with the appropriate tenor discount rate being applied to the face value of the T-Bills. There is a highly liquid secondary market with the possibility of trading blocks of USD 50 to USD 100 million in a single transaction without difficulty. Holders of bills are able to rediscount them at any time prior to maturity. The price paid/received is then the face value *less* the discount amount.

> *There are many variations on the pure discount formulae which can be used to calculate the price of T-Bills quoted on a pure discount basis.* **Hint**

Pure discount: discount amount

To calculate the discount amount (a pure discount rate is applied to face value):

$$\text{amount of discount} = \text{face value} \times \text{discount rate} \times \frac{\text{days}}{\text{day base}}$$

<ACI preferred>

Pure discount: secondary market proceeds

To calculate the price (secondary market proceeds) – the face value *less* the discount amount is the price:

$$\text{secondary market proceeds} = \text{face value} \times \left(1 - \left(\text{discount rate} \times \frac{\text{days}}{\text{day base}}\right)\right)$$

<ACI preferred>

Hint

This formula can be used in calculations involving UK/US Treasury bills, bills of exchange, bankers' acceptances, UK eligible bills and US domestic commercial paper, plus the occasionally encountered discount certificates of deposit (CDs).

Question

A typical ACI Dealing Certificate question might be:

You buy 90-day US T-bills at a rate of 5.91 percent. The face amount is USD 10,000,000. What would you expect to pay for them?

A: USD 10,097,750.00
B: USD 9,900,000.00
C: USD 9,852,250.00
D: USD 9,854,273.97

Correct answer
C: US T-bills are quoted on an actual/360 day basis and traded at a discount. The price paid will be the face value adjusted down by the discount amount which is calculated using the discount rate of 5.91 percent applied to the face value of USD 10,000,000. Here the price is USD 9,852,250.00 (10,000,000 less the discount amount of 147,750).

Proof

To calculate the price of a US T-bill offered at a discount rate of 5.91 percent:

$$10{,}000{,}000.00 \times \left(1 - \left(0.05910 \times \tfrac{90}{360}\right)\right) = \text{USD } 9{,}852{,}250.00$$

<ACI preferred>

> In some countries, including Australia, the Czech and Slovak Republics and Poland, Treasury bills are redeemed at face value, but in the secondary market prior to maturity they are priced on a yield basis. The formula used for such instruments is that used for UK commercial paper and eurocommercial paper to be found later in this chapter.

Care!

Commercial bills of exchange

The UK Bills of Exchange Act 1882 defines a bill of exchange as "...an unconditional order in writing, addressed by one person to another, signed by the person giving it, requiring the person to whom it is addressed to pay on demand or at a fixed or determinable future time a sum certain in money to or to the order of a specified person, or to bearer."

Bills have provided a source of finance for the commercial sector for centuries. The London discount market has its origins in the coffee houses of seventeenth-century London where the entrepreneurs of the day met to socialize and transact business, including the discounting of bills of exchange.

Today many financial markets regard such bills once they have been guaranteed (accepted) by a bank to be a highly sought after tradable instrument and are referred to as bankers' acceptances.

Bankers' acceptances

To obtain finance against a bill of exchange, the instrument (the bill of exchange) has to be discounted. The practice of a bank accepting (endorsing) a bill evidences the bank's undertaking or guarantee to pay the bill on maturity, thereby creating an instrument which can be sold to raise the necessary finance.

Bankers' acceptances (BAs) are normally generated from facilities granted under documentary credits or clean acceptance credits, and secondary markets in which acceptances may be rediscounted are found in various worldwide financial centres.

Bills of exchange, when discounted, are "pure discount" operations with the appropriate tenor discount rate being applied to the face value of the bills. The price paid is then the face value *less* the discount amount.

UK eligible bills

In the United Kingdom the business of accepting bills of exchange (within certain criteria) creates a category of negotiable instrument called an *eligible bill*. These instruments are correctly described as being "eligible for re-discount at the Bank of England" – in other words they are as good as cash.

To be defined as an eligible bill certain conditions have been laid down by the Bank of England. The bill must have been issued by a corporate company in respect of a self-liquidating trade transaction with an initial maximum tenor of 187 days. Additionally it must have been accepted payable (guaranteed) by a bank whose name appears on the Bank of England's list of eligible acceptors. There are approximately 150 banks with this status in London.

Up to 1996 the Bank of England's preferred method of supplying funds to the London money markets in its daily open market operations was the re-discount, outright purchase or sale and repurchase agreements (repos) involving such eligible bills. These transactions were almost exclusively effected with institutions known collectively as discount houses. With a broadening of the gilts market in London over recent years, the Bank's open market operations have subtly changed.

UK eligible bills settlement

UK eligible bills along with a range of other short-term sterling money market securities traded in London are in the process of complete dematerialization. While bills of exchange can still be physically signed, issued by companies and transferred, the majority of transactions are electronically settled (transfer of title) across the Central Moneymarkets Office (CMO), originally set up by the Bank of England but now managed by CrestCo.

London money market quotation

The secondary market – market maker quotes:

- *Eligible bills*: bid–offer for the securities (high–low in interest/discount rate terms).

Care!

Here the market terminology refers to the securities being traded. The London market switches round the rates quoted elsewhere. Dealing logic and calculations are unaffected. ACI Dealing Certificate examination questions should always make it clear in which manner any rate quotation is being made.

Discount formulae: pure discount

There are many different variations on formulae to calculate discount amounts, discounted prices to be paid, secondary market proceeds, conversions from discount to yield rates, etc. in the financial markets. Formulae used in connection with the financial instruments which are the subject of the ACI Dealing Certificate are included here. Where these are the formulae made available on the ACI formulae sheet this is indicated <ACI preferred>.

Pure discount: discount amount

To calculate the discount amount (a pure discount rate is applied to face value):

$$\text{amount of discount} = \text{face value} \times \text{discount rate} \times \frac{\text{days}}{\text{day base}}$$

<ACI preferred>

Pure discount: secondary market proceeds

To calculate the price (secondary market proceeds) – the face value *less* the discount amount is the price:

$$\text{secondary market proceeds} = \text{face value} \times \left(1 - \left(\text{discount rate} \times \frac{\text{days}}{\text{day base}}\right)\right)$$

<ACI preferred>

Hint

This formula can be used in calculations involving UK/US Treasury bills, bills of exchange, bankers' acceptances, UK eligible bills and US domestic commercial paper, plus the occasionally encountered discount certificates of deposit (CDs).

Note

All <ACI preferred> formulae require discount/interest rates to be input as decimals, i.e. an interest rate of 5.00 percent is input as 0.05.

Mastering the ACI Dealing Certificate

Question

A typical ACI Dealing Certificate question might be:

You buy 90-day eligible bills offered at a discount rate of 5.00 percent. The face amount is GBP 10,000,000. What would you expect to pay for them?

A: GBP 10,097,750.00
B: GBP 10,000,000.00
C: GBP 9,875,000.00
D: GBP 9,876,712.33

Correct answer
D: Eligible bills in the UK are quoted on an actual/365 day basis and traded as a pure discount instrument. The price paid will be the face value adjusted down by the discount amount which is calculated using the discount rate of 5.00 percent applied to the face value of GBP 10,000,000. Here the price is GBP 9,876,712.33 (10,000,000 less the discount amount of 123,287.67).

Proof

To calculate the price of UK eligible bills GBP 10,000,000 face value, offered at a discount rate of 5.00 percent:

$$10,000,000.00 \times \left(1 - \left(0.0500 \times \frac{90}{365}\right)\right) = \text{GBP } 9,876,712.33$$

<ACI preferred>

Pure discount: discount rate knowing discount amount

To calculate the discount (pure discount) rate knowing the discount amount:

$$\text{discount rate} = \left(\frac{\text{discount amount} \times 360^*}{\text{face value} \times \text{days}}\right)$$

365 in case of sterling

This formula (not included in the ACI formulae sheet) can be used to confirm the accuracy of the calculation of the discount amount and price in the sample examination question above.

Hint

This formula can be used in calculations involving UK/US Treasury bills, bills of exchange, bankers' acceptances, UK eligible bills and US domestic commercial paper, plus the occasionally encountered discount certificates of deposit (CDs).

> This formula is *not* made available to candidates in the ACI Dealing Certificate examination.

Note

Proof

To calculate the discount rate knowing the face value and the 90-day GBP discount amount of GBP 123,287.67 (10,000,000 − 9,876,712.33):

$$\frac{123{,}287.67 \times 365}{10{,}000{,}000.00 \times 90} = 0.04999 = 5.00\% \ (rounded)$$

Pure discount: discount rate knowing price

To calculate the discount (pure discount) rate knowing the price:

$$\text{discount rate} = 1 - \left(\frac{\text{price}}{\text{face value}}\right) \times \frac{360^*}{\text{days}}$$

*365 in case of sterling

This formula (not included in the ACI formulae sheet) can be used to confirm the accuracy of the calculation of the discount amount and price in the sample examination question above.

Proof

To calculate the pure discount rate knowing the price of GBP 9,876,712.33 to be paid for 90-day GBP eligible bills face value GBP 10,000,000.00

$$1 - \left(\frac{9{,}876{,}712.33}{10{,}000{,}000.00}\right) \times \frac{365}{90} = 0.04999 = 5.00\% \ (rounded)$$

This formula can be used to confirm the accuracy of the calculation of the discount amount and price in the sample examination question above.

> *This formula can be used in calculations involving UK/US Treasury bills, bills of exchange, bankers' acceptances, UK eligible bills and US domestic commercial paper, plus the occasionally encountered discount certificates of deposit (CDs).*

Hint

> This formula is *not* made available to candidates in the ACI Dealing Certificate examination.

Note

Discount v. yield rates

A financial instrument such as a UK or US T-bill or bill of exchange is a pure discount operation. This means that at final maturity the instrument will be worth its face value. On issue and when the instrument trades at any time before the final maturity it will be priced lower than face value by an amount calculated at current discount, market rates. Where an instrument is quoted and traded on a pure discount, applying a discount rate to the face value gives you the discount amount which is in effect interest in advance.

So that it may be compared to a simple interest rate (yield) a discount rate must be converted onto the same basis as the yield rate. This is done using the discount to yield formula. A discount rate will always appear numerically to be lower than its equivalent yield rate. This is because the return (the interest or discount amount earned) is the result of applying the discount rate to the face or maturity value – a larger amount than the price paid for the instrument. To achieve the same return on the amount invested (the price) a numerically higher rate of return must be achieved.

Care!

As already noted, in some countries, including Australia, the Czech and Slovak Republics and Poland, Treasury bills are redeemed at face value, but in the secondary market prior to maturity they are priced on a yield basis. In the case of these instruments therefore the rate at which the instrument trades is already a yield rate.

Pure discount: equivalent yield from discount rate

To calculate the interest rate (yield) p.a. knowing the discount (pure discount) rate:

$$\text{true yield} = \frac{\text{discount rate}}{\left(1 - \left(\text{discount rate} \times \frac{\text{days}}{\text{day base}}\right)\right)}$$

<ACI preferred>

Hint

This formula can be used in calculations involving UK/US Treasury bills, bills of exchange, bankers' acceptances, UK eligible bills and US domestic commercial paper, plus the occasionally encountered discount certificates of deposit (CDs).

Topic 2 · Basic Calculations/Topic 3 · Money Market Products

> **Question**
>
> A typical ACI Dealing Certificate question might be:
>
> If GBP eligible bills are being quoted in the three months (92 days) at $6\frac{7}{8}$ percent, what is the equivalent true yield per annum?
>
> A: 6.53(46)%
> B: 6.88(54)%
> C: 6.875%
> D: 6.99(62)%
>
> **Correct answer**
> D: Using the discount to yield formula to calculate the equivalent yield and remembering that GBP is quoted on an actual/365 day basis the equivalent true yield rate is 6.99(6236) percent.

Proof

To calculate the yield knowing the 92-day GBP discount rate of 6.875 p.a.:

$$\frac{0.06875}{\left(1 - \left(0.06875 \times \frac{92}{365}\right)\right)} = 0.069962 = 7.00\% \text{ (rounded)}$$

<ACI preferred>

Pure discount: discount rate from yield

To calculate the discount (pure discount) rate knowing the interest rate (yield) p.a.:

$$\text{discount rate} = \frac{360^* \times \text{yield}}{360^* + (\text{yield} \times \text{days})}$$

365 in the case of sterling

> **Hint**
>
> This formula can be used in calculations involving UK/US Treasury bills, bills of exchange, bankers' acceptances, UK eligible bills and US domestic commercial paper, plus the occasionally encountered discount certificates of deposit (CDs).

> **Note**
>
> This formula is *not* made available to candidates in the *ACI Dealing Certificate* examination.

Proof

To check the above GBP yield calculation (0.069962 percent) in discount rate terms:

$$\frac{365 \times 0.069962}{365 + (0.069962 \times 92)} = 0.0687496 = 6.875\% \ (rounded)$$

This formula (not included in the ACI formulae sheet) can be used to confirm the accuracy of the calculation of the yield from the discount rate in the sample examination question above.

London certificates of deposit

A certificate of deposit (CD) is a negotiable interest bearing certificate, payable to bearer and issued by a bank as a receipt for a deposit placed. Most major international banks in London issue CDs in sterling, US dollars and a variety of other currencies including euros and SDRs (special drawing rights). Periods of issue vary between a minimum of three months and a maximum of five years and the certificates are issued at par and bear a simple interest rate.

CDs issued for periods longer than 12 months will pay interest annually on the anniversary of issue and at final maturity and tend to be considered in the capital markets topic – not the subject matter of the ACI Dealing Certificate.

UK CDs

UK CDs along with a range of other short-term sterling money market securities traded in London are in the process of complete dematerialization. While CDs can still be produced in security printed hard copy if requested by the purchaser, the majority of transactions are electronically settled (transfer of title) across the Central Moneymarkets Office (CMO), originally set up by the Bank of England and now managed by CrestCo.

US certificates of deposit

There is a significant short-term market in certificates of deposit in the United States. CDs are issued by banks for maturities ranging from as short as 14 days out to five and seven years. Also, CDs in the US markets tend to be a retail investment instrument whereas in the European markets they are only bought and sold by wholesale market participants.

Simple interest bearing CDs

CDs are in the main interest bearing, though a variation on a theme is the floating rate CD or floating rate note, where the instrument is issued for three to five years but the interest rate is adjusted in line with prevailing market interest rates – usually by reference to a benchmark interest rate such as LIBOR. The major percentage of secondary market turnover in interest bearing CDs is, however, in maturities up to six months.

Discount CDs

You may occasionally come across discount CDs. These are based on the pure discount formula for pricing (similar to UK and US T-bills). The Bank of England market guidelines publication allows for these instruments and states that "discounted CDs are bought and sold on a discount per annum basis or on a yield to maturity basis". As already stated the true cost or yield is always higher than the discount rate.

CD issuance

Certificates of deposit issued by banks and building societies in the primary market in the UK are eligible liabilities to the issuer – liable to prudential liquidity requirements.

There is a benefit to the issuer who is able to issue CDs (accepting money on deposit) at rates which are marginally lower than "clean" deposits. The better the name (credit rating) the greater the margin below the LIBID rate. In London the CD issuing banks are graded, with the best referred to as "prime name" CDs, the next as interbank CDs (ICDs). There are screens available on rates information systems such as Reuters illustrating the difference in prices for the various grades of CD and the cash markets (LIBOR – LIBID rates).

Purchasing liquidity

London CDs are negotiable. The buyer of a CD is buying liquidity – obtaining a fixed period interest rate while retaining the ability to cash in the CD at a date before maturity if funds are needed. To do this the buyer (holder) of a CD will deal in the secondary CD market. The price he receives will reflect interest accruals to date and a factor relating to the level of interest rates at the time of sale against those applying at issue of the CD.

Trading CDs

Whether in the UK or the US wholesale markets, the value of a certificate of deposit when traded in the secondary market is calculated from a uniform agreed formula which takes into consideration accruals to date and interest rates prevailing from that date to final maturity.

In other words there is an appreciation or depreciation element involved in trading CDs as well as an interest accrual. The actual yield achieved in holding a CD can be considerably enhanced (or worsened) depending on the level of interest rates when it was issued against when it is traded.

London money market quotation

The secondary market – market maker quotes:

- Certificates of deposit: bid–offer for the securities (high–low in interest rate terms).

International money market quotation

The secondary market – market maker quotes:

- Certificates of deposit: offer–bid for the securities (low–high in interest rate terms).

Care!

Here the market terminology refers to the CDs being traded. The London market switches round the rates quoted elsewhere. Dealing logic and calculations are unaffected. ACI Dealing Certificate examination questions should always make it clear in which manner any rate quotation is being made.

Question

A typical ACI Dealing Certificate question might be:

You are a seller of three-month GBP secondary market CDs in the London market. Bank A quotes you $6\frac{7}{8} - 6\frac{3}{4}$ and Bank B quotes $6\frac{13}{16} - 6\frac{11}{16}$. Which bank is quoting you the best rate and at which rate will you deal?

A: Bank B $6\frac{11}{16}\%$

B: Bank B $6\frac{13}{16}\%$

C: Bank A $6\frac{7}{8}\%$

D: Bank A $6\frac{3}{4}\%$

Correct answer

B: As a seller of secondary market CDs you are looking to raise funds as cheaply as possible. Both banks are quoting bid–offer for the security, high–low in interest rates. You will therefore deal with Bank B who is bidding for CDs (i.e. offering cash against securities) at $6\frac{13}{16}$ percent.

Certificates of deposit in the secondary market

A typical certificate of deposit bears a coupon rate (simple interest). This is payable by the issuer to the holder of the CD at final maturity date. Any holders of the CD during its life are entitled to interest accrued for the period they have held the instrument. This fact plus any change in current market interest rates will have to be taken into account in the secondary market sale/purchase price.

Secondary market certificates of deposit formula

The <ACI preferred> formula provided to candidates for secondary CD proceeds is in fact a two-stage formula. It initially calculates the maturity value (principal plus interest for the full issue period) and then applies the yield for the remaining period to the result of this calculation.

$$\text{maturity proceeds} = \text{face value} \times \left(1 + \left(\text{coupon rate} \times \frac{\text{days from issue to maturity}}{\text{day base}}\right)\right)$$

$$\text{secondary market proceeds} = \frac{\text{maturity proceeds}}{\left(1 + \left(\text{yield} \times \frac{\text{days left to maturity}}{\text{day base}}\right)\right)}$$

<ACI preferred>

Alternative secondary market CD formula

In the UK CDs come under Bank of England control and there is another popular formula published in the BBA's London CD market guidelines (typically the one which would have been printed on the reverse of hard copy certificates). It is a single stage formulae but you must bear in mind that it does not feature on the ACI formulae sheet and therefore will not be available in the examination.

$$\text{price} = \text{principal} \times \frac{(360^* \times 100) \; plus \; (\text{original interest rate} \times \text{original no. of days})}{(360^* \times 100) \; plus \; (\text{days remaining to maturity} \times \text{desired yield})}$$

365 in case of sterling

Both formulae result in the same correct answer.

Mastering the ACI Dealing Certificate

> **Question**
>
> A typical ACI Dealing Certificate question might be:
>
> As a market user, which of the following prices would you expect to pay for a GBP secondary CD originally issued in the amount of GBP 5 million for 184 days at $6\frac{1}{2}$ percent with 92 days to run and current 92-day CD rates quoted at $7-6\frac{7}{8}$ percent?
>
> A: GBP 5,075,876.93
> B: GBP 5,000,000.00
> C: GBP 5,074,305.41
> D: GBP 5,089,897.03
>
> **Correct answer**
> A: You are buying the CD as market user, therefore you deal on the market maker's offer of secondary market CDs (the lower rate). Using the secondary market CD formula and remembering that GBP is quoted on an actual/365 day basis the price you would pay as a market user would be GBP 5,075,876.93.

Proof

To calculate the price to be paid for the above secondary market GBP CD:

$$5{,}000{,}000.00 \times \left(1 + \left(0.065 \times \frac{184}{365}\right)\right) = 5{,}163{,}835.62$$

$$\frac{5{,}163{,}835.62}{\left(1 + \left(0.06875 \times \frac{92}{365}\right)\right)} = \text{GBP } 5{,}075{,}876.93$$

<ACI preferred>

Proof

To prove the calculation using the BBA secondary market CD formula:

$$5{,}000{,}000.00 \times \left(\frac{((365 \times 100) + (6.50 \times 184))}{(365 \times 100) + (92 \times 6.875)}\right) = \text{GBP } 5{,}075{,}876.93$$

Return on secondary CD purchased and held to maturity

To calculate the yield achieved you must first calculate the final maturity value of the CD at maturity (principal *plus* interest for the full issue period) and compare this to the secondary market price paid – the amount invested. You can then use a variation of the simple interest formula to calculate the return obtained for the instrument between purchase and final maturity:

$$\text{holding period return} = \frac{(\text{principal } plus \text{ interest}) - \text{secondary market purchase price} \times 360^* \times 100}{\text{secondary market purchase price} \times \text{no. of days}}$$

365 in case of sterling

Return on secondary CD purchased and sold prior to maturity

Take this process a stage further and you can calculate the return achieved for any period when you held a CD, i.e. the return achieved for the period between initially purchasing the secondary market CD and on-selling at a later date (prior to maturity), again in the secondary market.

Question

A typical ACI Dealing Certificate question might be:

Two months ago you bought a 90-day USD 10 million CD at 6.00 percent at issue. If now you sell this CD at 5.75 percent for the remaining 30 days what yield have you achieved for the holding period?

A: 6.0625%
B: 6.00%
C: 5.75%
D: 6.0958%

Correct answer

D: Having bought this CD at issue you have earned USD 101,596.52 (sale proceeds less purchase price USD 10,101,596.52 minus 10,000,000) for 60 days – the equivalent of a yield of 6.0958 percent for this holding period of 60 days.

Proof

First, calculate the secondary price to be paid for the above USD CD:

$$10,000,000.00 \times \left(1 \text{ } plus \text{ } \left(0.06 \times \frac{90}{360}\right)\right) = 10,150,000.00$$

$$\frac{10,150,000.00}{\left(1 \text{ } plus \text{ } \left(0.0575 \times \frac{30}{360}\right)\right)} = \text{USD } 10,101,596.52$$

<ACI preferred>

Then compare the price received with the price originally paid for the CD.

The difference between the sale proceeds and the purchase price at issue is the profit made for the holding period (60 days): (USD 10,101,596.52 less 10,000,000 = USD 101,596.52).

Then, using the standard simple interest formula (manipulated):

$$\frac{101,596.52 \times 360 \times 100}{10,000,000.00 \times 60} = 6.0957(91)\%$$

Commercial paper

Commercial paper is the generic money market term applied to short-term unsecured promissory notes, payable to bearer, which are issued in order to obtain funds by various industrial, financial and insurance companies and also by public utilities and sovereign borrowers.

Commercial paper issuance

Commercial paper consists of the issue of short-term promissory notes by commercial companies through dealer banks acting as brokers seeking investors willing to purchase the issue. Commercial paper is issued on demand according to the issuing company's funding requirements and is usually for very short-term periods – typically 14 days and one month.

UK commercial paper

UK commercial paper along with a range of other short-term sterling money market securities traded in London is in the process of complete dematerialization. While CP can still be issued in security printed hard copy the majority of transactions are electronically settled (transfer of title) across the CrestCo Central Moneymarkets Office (CMO).

UK commercial paper market

In the UK sterling and euro commercial paper (ECP) is most frequently issued and afterwards traded (with very limited liquidity) on a "discount to yield" basis. The yield rate is applied to the price paid to achieve the discount amount.

According to the FSA London Code of Conduct, UK companies must have a net worth of a minimum of GBP 25 million (the aggregate of the company's assets less the aggregate of the company's liabilities) to be able to issue commercial paper in the UK. Such CP must be issued with a minimum face value of GBP 500,000.00 and must have a maturity of less than one year but not less than seven days.

The CP issue rate tends to be expressed as the number of basis points above (or below) LIBOR, i.e. CP issued for one month at LIBOR plus 25 basis points when LIBOR is fixed at 5.00 will be rated at 5.25 percent.

CP programme dealer bank

In the UK banks agreeing commercial paper programmes with customers act as dealer banks for the CP and market the customer's paper to other wholesale investors, or alternatively effectively underwrite the issue for later onward sale to other market customers. There is no active secondary market in commercial paper, but dealing firms including banks will normally undertake to repurchase the paper at prevailing rates, thus providing limited liquidity to investors.

Discount instrument quoted on a yield: secondary market proceeds

To calculate the price (secondary market proceeds) on a financial instrument where the discount is calculated by reference to a true yield and applied to the price paid:

$$\text{secondary market proceeds} = \frac{\text{face value}}{\left(1 + \left(\text{yield} \times \frac{\text{days left to maturity}}{\text{day base}}\right)\right)}$$

<ACI preferred>

Hint

This formula can also be used for calculations involving certain countries' Treasury Bills (see earlier in chapter), sterling CP and euro commercial paper (ECP).

Question

A typical ACI Dealing Certificate question might be:

As an investor, what will you pay for one-month commercial paper with a face value of GBP 5,000,000.00 with 30 days to maturity at LIBOR plus 25 bp? One-month LIBOR today was fixed at 5.00 percent.

A: GBP 5,021,482.64
B: GBP 5,000,000.00
C: GBP 4,978,517.36
D: GBP 4,978,424.66

Correct answer
C: Sterling CP is issued "at a discount by reference to a yield". The discount instrument quoted on a true yield formula applying the rate of 5.25 percent (LIBOR 5.00 plus 0.25) gives the answer GBP 4,978,517.36.

Proof

To calculate the price to be paid for the above 30-day sterling CP GBP 5,000,000.00 at a discount to yield of 5.25 percent (LIBOR 5.00 plus 0.25):

$$\frac{5,000,000.00}{\left(1 + \left(0.0525 \times \frac{30}{365}\right)\right)} = \text{GBP } 4,978,517.36$$

<ACI preferred>

US domestic commercial paper market

US domestic commercial paper is priced and issued as a pure discount, i.e. the discount rate is applied to the face value. The same formula as used for Treasury bills and bankers' acceptances is used in US domestic CP pricing.

In the US the size of outstandings in the commercial paper market is larger than the US Treasury bill market. There is virtually no secondary market, however, as most issues are held to maturity.

In the US CP can be issued for periods ranging from two days to 270 days with the most active issues being in issues of under 30 days.

Especially in the US, to be able to "sell" its commercial paper the issuing company needs to have a rating granted by a recognized rating agency such as Standard & Poors or Moody's Investor Services.

Pure discount instrument: secondary market proceeds

$$\text{secondary market proceeds} = \text{face value} \times \left(1 - \left(\text{discount rate} \times \frac{\text{days}}{\text{day base}}\right)\right)$$

<ACI preferred>

Question

A typical ACI Dealing Certificate question might be:

What will an investor pay for one-month US domestic CP with a face value of USD 25,000,000.00 for 30 days at a rate of 4.25 percent?

A: USD 24,911,770.81
B: USD 24,911,458.33
C: USD 25,000,000.00
D: USD 24,912,671.23

Correct answer
B: US domestic CP is issued at a discount and priced using the pure discount formula already discussed for T-bills and bankers' acceptances. Here the formula produces a price of USD 24,911,458.33.

Proof

To calculate the price to be paid for the above US domestic CP USD 25,000,000.00 at a pure discount rate of 4.25 percent:

$$\text{USD } 25{,}000{,}000 \times \left(1 - \left(0.0425 \times \frac{30}{360}\right)\right) = \text{USD } 24{,}911{,}458.33$$

<ACI preferred>

Remember US domestic CP is a pure discount operation (like T-bills) whereas UK sterling CP and ECP are "discount instruments quoted on a true yield" necessitating the use of a different pricing formula.

REPOS

Government securities and repos

Syllabus topic reprise

Part 1 Topic 3 Money market products

- list the different types of repos
- explain the terminology of the repo market, why they are used, and the main characteristics of repos

Whilst Repos only feature in these two bullet points under the Money market products syllabus topic heading (repeated above) there are 6 multiple choice questions on the Topic 3 Repos topic in the ACI Dealing Certificate out of which candidates are required to gain a minimum of 33.33% to PASS (2 out of 6).

The ACI Dealing Certificate syllabus does *not* include capital market issues such as bonds but brief mention of these instruments has to be made to introduce the repos topic.

UK government securities: Gilts

UK government securities are known as gilts. Gilts are issued in sterling and euros by the British government. Gilts are registered securities with either a fixed or a floating rate of interest and with redemption either fixed (various periods up to 30 years) or on predetermined dates, at the option of the government. The majority of gilts are fixed interest securities. The interest on bonds, frequently called the coupon, is described as a "dividend" on gilts. Gilts interest calculations are based on an actual/actual day basis and the coupon is payable semi-annually. Different issues pay interest on different dates (see the *Financial Times* capital markets/bonds page on a Monday for further information).

The UK government has also in the past issued index-linked gilts with a guaranteed return over the current Retail Price Index (inflation measure) adjusted regularly. In earlier times the UK has also been able to issue non-redeemable gilts known as perpetuals. These are bonds where the government has no obligation to repay. Such instruments have certain tax advantages and are still traded in the financial markets.

US Treasury notes

Medium-term US government US dollar funding requirements are met by the issue of US Treasury notes which are registered securities with a fixed rate of interest for maturities of between two and ten years. There is a two-year note issue monthly, whereas the other years' maturities (three, four, five, seven and ten years) are issued quarterly. US Treasury notes pay interest (coupon) semi-annually and interest is calculated on an actual/actual day basis.

US Treasury bonds

Longer-term US government USD funding requirements are met by the issue of US Treasury bonds which are registered securities with a fixed rate of interest for maturities of up to 30 years. These 30-year securities are commonly termed "long bonds" in the money market.

US Treasury bonds are in the main fixed-interest securities, paying simple interest (a coupon) semi-annually on an actual/actual day basis and are traded at a price to yield the appropriate current market interest rates.

Note

> The above T-notes and T-bonds are collectively referred to as "Treasuries" in the financial press.

Repos – sale and repurchase agreements

A repo is the sale and commitment to repurchase securities at a fixed price or at the same price but with a repo rate of interest applied and paid (set at time of dealing) at a later date. This mechanism is used by money market and bond traders as a form of collateralized financing.

Reverse repos

A reverse repo is a repo operation looked at from the viewpoint of a borrower of securities/lender of funds.

> **Question**
>
> A typical ACI Dealing Certificate question might be:
>
> If Bank A sells securities to Bank B and at the same time commits to repurchase equivalent securities on a specified future date (or at call), on payment of a rate of interest on the cash countervalue, Bank A has dealt a:
>
> A: Buy/sell back
> B: Repo
> C: Reverse repo
> D: Forward rate agreement
>
> Correct answer
> B: The above describes a repo transaction.

Repo example

Figure 4.8 is a graphic portrayal of a sale and repurchase agreement (repo). **Counterparty A** (in bold type) is entering into a repo selling and buying securities while ***Counterparty B*** (bold italics) is entering into a reverse repo buying and selling securities.

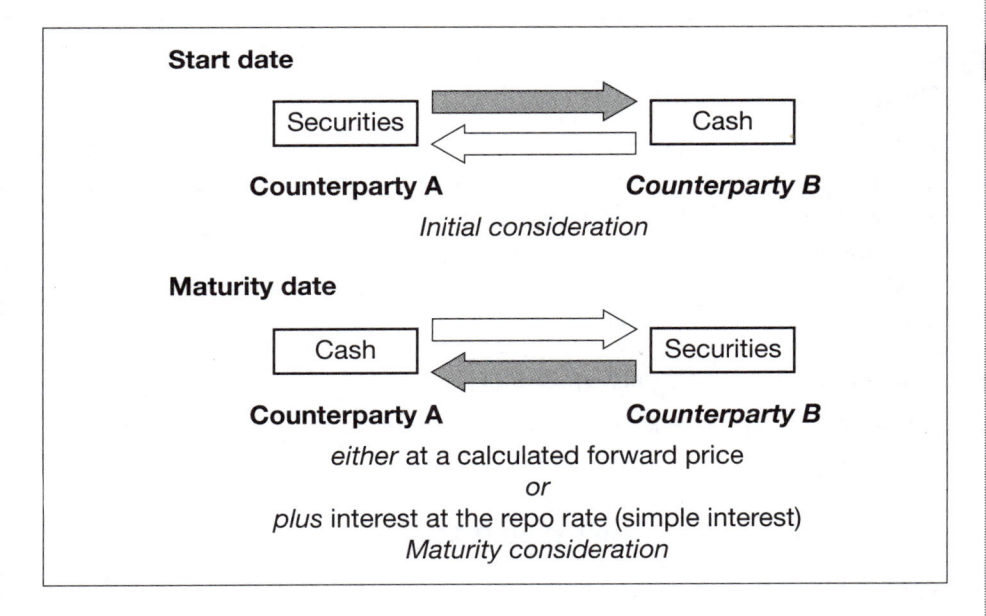

Start date

Securities → Cash
Counterparty A   ***Counterparty B***
Initial consideration

Maturity date

Cash ← Securities
Counterparty A   ***Counterparty B***
either at a calculated forward price
or
plus interest at the repo rate (simple interest)
Maturity consideration

Fig 4.8

London money market quotation

Market maker quotes:

- *Repos*: bid–offer for the securities (high–low in interest rate terms), in effect "reverse repo–repo" quote by the market maker.

International money market quotation

Market maker quotes:

- *Repos*: offer–bid for the securities (low–high in interest rate terms), in effect a "repo–reverse repo" quote by the market maker.

> **Care!** Here the market terminology refers to the collateral changing hands. The London market switches round the rates quoted elsewhere. Dealing logic and calculations are unaffected. ACI Dealing Certificate examination questions should always make it clear in which manner any rate quotation is being made.

UK gilt repo rates

As noted above gilt repos in London will be quoted high–low in line with standard London market terminology and will be referred to as bid–offer (for the collateral).

A repo rate is a simple interest rate which is applied to the initial consideration paid on the start date of the repo to the repoing party (cash in) and paid on the maturity date of the repo (or as otherwise agreed).

Gilt repos

Since 1996 all UK financial institutions have been able to trade gilts on a repo basis. Gilt repos can be transacted in the form of either "classic repo" or "sell/buy backs". Classic repos have over the years become the main instrument in the international and gilt repo markets. Sell/buy backs are, however, still common in the international market and predominate in some European repo markets.

> **Hint** *There is a* Gilt Repo Code of Best Practice *published by the Bank of England which provides much further useful information on this topic.*

US repo markets

Apart from interbank repo transactions, central banks may frequently use repos when they wish to alter the supply of cash to the commercial banks in the money market, thereby influencing the level of interest rates.

Different methods are used in different markets. Several markets use the repo method and this is the primary means used by the Federal Reserve Bank (Fed) in the United States. These repos can be undertaken to satisfy daily market demand and be effected for the Fed's own account or can be undertaken on behalf of other central banks who hold US dollars as part of their currency reserves.

System repos

Where the market is short of cash the Federal Reserve Bank will announce repos (to supply funds to the banks). Such an injection of cash is frequently only needed as a short-term smoothing measure and in such instances the Federal Reserve Bank will use repurchase agreements (repos).

Customer repos

Where the Federal Reserve Bank effects repos specifically on behalf of other central banks who hold US dollar securities as part of their currency reserves, these transactions are referred to as "customer repos".

Matched sales

Where the market is long of cash the Federal Reserve Bank will instigate reverse repos (to drain surplus cash from the banks). These transactions are also referred to as system reverse repos in the US markets.

Such operations effected by the central bank are always described from the commercial bank's point of view.

Classic repo

In contrast to secured deposits, *legal title* to collateral in a classic repo is transferred to the buyer. This allows the buyer to sell on securities he has bought through reverse repo. Transfer of legal title also gives the buyer of collateral the *rights of close-out and set-off* in the event of repo counterparty default, i.e. the collateral can be sold immediately to recoup the cash. In a secured deposit the disposal of collateral must wait upon the implementation of bankruptcy proceedings.

GMRA

Classic repos are subject to a bilateral agreement signed by the parties to such repos. This agreement is the TBMA/ISMA Global Master Repurchase Agreement (GMRA). TBMA is The Bond Market Association (previously known as the PSA – Public Securities Association) and ISMA is the International Securities Market Association.

Legal title

While legal title to collateral is transferred in repo, the risk and return on the collateral remains with the seller. Thus a default on the collateral (however unthinkable in respect of government debt) in a Classic Repo would require the seller to supply new collateral.

Because of the fixed price of the repurchase (i.e. in cash driven transactions the same as the initial consideration *plus* repo interest), any fall in the price of the collateral is automatically a loss to the seller and any rise in the price of the collateral is automatically a gain.

Because the seller in a classic repo retains the risk and return on the collateral, he can lend securities from his portfolio without affecting the trading, liquidity, investment or tax objectives for which he originally acquired them.

Coupon payment/interest accruing

Any coupon payment/interest accruing on collateral during a classic repo is either returned to the seller (repoer) or effected automatically in the case of gilts (through the Central Gilts Office(CGO). Interest paid (coupon) during the term of repo traded as a buy/sell back is paid to the new owner of the security.

> **Question**
>
> A typical ACI Dealing Certificate question might be:
>
> Coupon payments made during the life of a buy/sell back are:
>
> A: Paid to the original owner of the bond
> B: Paid to the new owner of the bond for onward transmission to the original owner
> C: Not paid
> D: Paid to the new owner of the bond
>
> **Correct answer**
> D: Coupon payments made during the life of a buy/sell back are paid to the new owner of the bond.

UK gilt repo settlement

As with the bond market gilts, repos are settled across the Central Gilts Office (CGO). Gilts are exchanged in repo transactions with the cash settlement based on the bond's dirty price (see below).

Margin (haircut)

In many financial centres, margin payments may be agreed at the time of agreeing a repo. The margin payments are intended to compensate for any loss or gain in the value of the securities which are the subject of the repo. Either the repoing out institution or the recipient of securities (reverse repo) may seek initial margin and the TBMA/ISMA terms and conditions already referred to permit further variation margin calls to be made during the period of any repo. Such a margin is referred to as a "haircut".

> **Question**
>
> A typical ACI Dealing Certificate question might be:
>
> In respect of repo transactions what is meant by the term "flat basis"?
>
> A: A repo effected under a gilt-edged stock lending agreement
> B: A repo on which the initial margin is zero
> C: A repo on an index-linked gilt
> D: A repo with no fixed maturity date
>
> Correct answer
>
> B: According to the Bank of England Gilt Repo Code of Best Practice, a repo on which the initial margin is zero is described as being on a "flat basis".

Equivalent securities

An essential feature of repos is that the buyer only has to return equivalent securities. This typically means that different security numbers of the same issue may be returned at maturity.

Clean price

A bond's clean price is the price quoted on the trader's rates service screen (e.g. Bloomberg's) and in the press. This price is expressed as currency units per 100 (100 being the par/redemption value of the bond). In the case of gilts, for example, this could be 98.50 meaning GBP 98.50 per GBP 100 face value.

Bond prices are an arithmetic calculation of the sum of the present values of all future cash flows on the bond (regular interim interest/coupon/dividend payments and repayment of principal at final maturity).

As bonds are typically fixed income securities they may be priced below, at or above par value. Bond prices below the par value indicate that current interest rates are higher than the bond coupon, meaning that an investor, to achieve current interest rates overall, must buy at a discount. Bond prices above the par value indicate that current interest rates must be lower than the bond coupon, meaning an investor, to achieve current interest rates overall, is prepared to pay a premium. The relationship of current interest rates v. fixed income bonds means that when interest rates are rising the price of a bond falls and when interest rates are falling the price of a bond rises.

Dirty price

In addition to the clean price (the sum of the PV of all future cashflows) the current holder of a bond is due the interest earned from the last coupon payment date to the trade (sale) date. Adding this accrued interest (at the bond coupon rate) to the clean price achieves the "dirty price" of the bond.

Initial consideration

The initial consideration in a repo transaction is the dirty price of the bond. In cash-driven transactions (in the ACI Dealing Certificate) the repo rate of interest is payable on this initial consideration amount by the cash borrower.

Question

> A typical ACI Dealing Certificate question might be:
>
> A dealer repos GBP 10 million UK gilts Treasury 5.50 percent 2009 with a clean price of 95.00 and 54 days accrued interest at a one-month repo rate of 5.25 percent. What is the initial consideration (rounded) paid across to him?
>
> A: GBP 9,581,000
> B: GBP 10,000,000
> C: GBP 10,081,369.86
> D: GBP 9,500,000
>
> **Correct answer**
> A: The initial consideration (rounded) paid across is the dirty price (clean price of GBP 9 500 000 plus 54 days accrued interest (5.50 percent on GBP 10 000 000 = 81,369.86). As this is a cash-driven trade there is no margin (haircut) and the final consideration is rounded to the nearest 1,000.00, i.e. GBP 9,581,000.

Proof

The initial consideration on the repo is the "dirty price". The "dirty price' is the clean price plus accrued interest since the last dividend date.

The clean price of the above GBP gilt repo is 10,000,000 × 95.00 = GBP 9,500,000.00.

The question mentions 54 days' accrued interest. Gilts pay simple interest on the nominal value of the holding at the coupon rate – here 5.50 percent on an actual/actual day basis:

$$\frac{10{,}000{,}000.00 \times 5.50 \times 54}{365 \times 100} = \text{GBP } 81{,}369.86$$

The "dirty price" is therefore GBP 9,500,000.00 plus 81,369.86 = GBP 9,581,369.86. This is the initial consideration on this gilt repo transaction.

Repo terminology

Cash and carry arbitrage Cash and carry arbitrage is a round trip buying the bond, repoing the bond to finance the original purchase and selling the future (hopefully) to a profit.

Cash-driven trade According to the Bank of England Code of Best Practice, where the principal reason for entering into a repo transaction is to generate cash balances then this is described as a "cash-driven trade" and typically no margin or haircut is involved.

Cheapest to deliver (CTD) The expression "cheapest to deliver" refers to the bonds closest to the notional underlying bond in a deliverable futures contract.

Cross currency repo A cross currency repo is a repo where the cash loan and collateral are denominated in different currencies.

Dollar repo A repo where the collateral repaid at maturity can differ from that originally delivered at the start date is described as a dollar repo.

Double indemnity (repo) A classic repo is described as having unique "double indemnity" status because of counterparty credit considerations and the fact that it is supported by a standard legal agreement.

Equivalent securities If as a repo buyer you are required to return "equivalent securities" at maturity, you must deliver the same security as you took initially but not the same sequentially numbered securities (ISIN) as originally delivered to you.

Flat basis According to the Bank of England Gilt Repo Code of Best Practice, a repo on which the initial margin is zero is described as being on a "flat basis".

Flex repo A flex repo is a repo with a pre-agreed repayment schedule across the life of the repo.

General collateral According to the Bank of England Gilt Repo Code of Best Practice, a general collateral repo trade is one whose principal aim is the borrowing or lending of money secured against most issues of gilts.

HIC (hold in custody) An HIC repo is where the security remains with the custodian who is arranging repos on instructions from the owner.

Icing This is the practice of holding gilts in reserve at the request of other parties who expect to need them in repo operations. This is subject to "open challenge" by other third parties who may also want the securities.

Matched Book trading Matched book trading means that the repo trader makes two-way prices for repo transactions as a market maker.

Special collateral When a bond goes "special" it means that demand for bonds in the repo market exceeds supply. Typically the cheapest to deliver (CTD) bond against a bond futures contract will attract this status in reverse repo transactions.

Substitution In repo terminology "substitution" is when the seller substitutes one type of collateral for another.

Term repo According to the Bank of England Gilt Repo Code of Best Practice, a term repo is a repo trade (of a maturity over one day) with a fixed end or maturity date.

KEY POINTS FOR ACI DEALING CERTIFICATE MULTIPLE CHOICE QUESTIONS

- Many multiple choice financial instrument pricing questions will include *wrong* answers which have been calculated using the incorrect formula, e.g. pure discount rather than discount instrument quoted on a true yield.
- Where there are two answers which are "too close to call" this probably indicates the wrong day count base is being used in one of the answers, e.g. actual/365 rather than actual/360.
- Remember the different pricing methods used for UK and US commercial paper.

FOR FURTHER READING

Money market products and basic interest rate calculations

BBA (1986) *Sterling Commercial Paper – Market Guidelines*. British Bankers Association (December).

BBA (1990) *Certificates of Deposit on the London Market – Market Guidelines*. British Bankers Association (November).

Kohn, Meir (1991) *Money, Banking and Financial Markets*. Dryden Press.

Reuters Financial Training (1999) *An Introduction to Foreign Exchange and Money Markets*. Wiley.

Steiner, Robert (1998) *Mastering Financial Calculations*. Prentice Hall.

Stigum, Marcia (1981) *Money Market Calculations*. Irwin.

Repos

Bank of England (1998) *Gilt Repo Code of Best Practice*. Bank of England (August).

BIS (1999) *Implications of Repo Markets for Central Markets*. Basel: Bank for International Settlements (March).

Reuters Financial Training (1999) *An Introduction to Bond Markets*. Wiley.

Steiner, Robert (1999) *Mastering Repo Markets*. Prentice Hall.

TBMA/ISMA Global Master Repurchase Agreement published jointly by the Bond Market Association and the Public Securities Association.

WEBSITES WORTH A VISIT

Bank of England, London: www.bankofengland.co.uk
The Bond Market Association: www.bondmarkets.com
British Bankers Association (BBA): www.bba.org.com

Topic 4 (part) · Money Market Derivatives

5

Introduction

Derivation of forward/forward interest rates

Financial futures

Forward rate agreements

Longer-term interest rate derivatives – interest rate swaps

Mastering the ACI Dealing Certificate

> **Overall objective**
>
> To explain the derivation of forward rates, the use of interest rate protection products and the mechanics of their trading.
>
> At the end of this section, candidates will be able to:
>
> - list the driving forces behind the development of the derivatives markets;
> - explain the derivation of forward/forward interest rates, forward rate agreements (FRAs) and short-term interest rate futures;
> - explain the basics of options and their main characteristics;*
> - explain the concept of interest rate swaps (IRSs) and their main characteristics;
> - describe the trading practices in the derivatives markets.

Note
There are 7 multiple choice questions on Topic 4 Interest Rate Swaps, Forward Rate Agreements, Futures and Options products in the ACI Dealing Certificate out of which candidates are required to gain a minimum of 42.80 percent to pass (3 out of 7).

INTRODUCTION

Balance sheet constraints have been much in evidence in recent years in the majority of banks involved in the foreign exchange and currency money markets. There has been a continuing expansion in the use of financial instruments which give the banks risk management flexibility without increasing balance sheet footings.

During the 1980s and early 1990s there was a proliferation of "off balance sheet" products enabling banks and their customers to hedge most financial exposure against adverse rate movements (either exchange or interest rate).

These products, having grown out of real concern over cash market exposures, have matured and also been embraced by trading banks and financial institutions as a means to take a view on market movements. The ACI Dealing Certificate is structured with this topic relating to a range of derivatives on both underlying interest rate and foreign exchange markets.

Following on from Topics 2 and 3 relating solely to money markets it makes sense to deal here solely with those derivatives tracking the underlying cash interest rate markets, leaving those based on foreign exchange market rates until those markets themselves have been discussed (Topics 5 and 6). Before discussing these interest rate derivatives and their development, however, an understanding of the derivation of forward/forward interest rates is required by the syllabus and begins the learning points covered in this chapter.

After that we concentrate on those derivatives, although any reference to currency options (indicated * above) will be left until after the subject of foreign exchange has been discussed.

It is also logical to deal with each of the interest rate derivatives to be discussed in order of maturity. This chapter starts therefore with the shorter-term instruments, first describing *financial futures* (short-term interest rate contracts) and then moving on to *forward rate agreements* (FRAs). The *interest rate swap* (IRS) product and its uses in both longer-term hedging and trading as featured in the syllabus is also discussed towards the end of the chapter.

You will also find *position keeping* questions relating to short-term interest rate derivatives included here.

DERIVATION OF FORWARD/FORWARD INTEREST RATES

So far in Chapter 4 we have only discussed interest rates and yield curves for cash deposits/loans commencing from spot date (or today in GBP). It is also possible to deal for deposit periods commencing on one forward date and maturing on a further forward date. You must therefore be able to calculate an interest rate for such a period described as "forward/forward". Similarly an interest rate for such a period commencing in the future is known as a forward/forward interest rate.

Pricing along the yield curve

To manage interest rate risk effectively for periods beginning on a forward date the dealer must be able to calculate a price (an interest rate) "along the

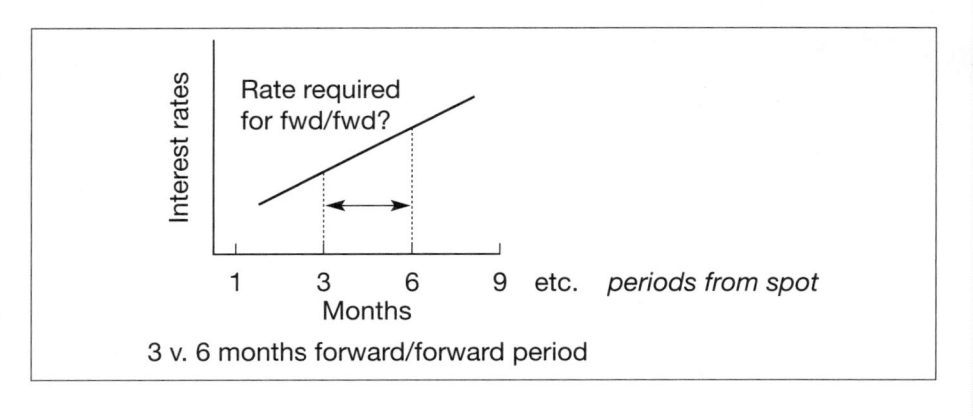

Fig 5.1

3 v. 6 months forward/forward period

yield curve" (see Figure 5.1). This forward/forward interest rate can be calculated by reference to the cash market rates for maturities from spot to the standard period maturities either side of the desired forward/forward period.

Example of forward/forward

As an example let's look at a three-month loan/deposit against a six-month deposit/loan reverse position. From these transactions we can calculate the correct interest rate for the forward period starting three months from spot and maturing six months from spot (see Figure 5.2). There is nothing extraordinary about this calculation which merely has to take into consideration the fact that interest is payable on the maturing shorter period transaction before the settlement of the interest on the longer period transaction. This interest has to be funded/laid off in the market to ensure all cash flows net out.

Fig 5.2

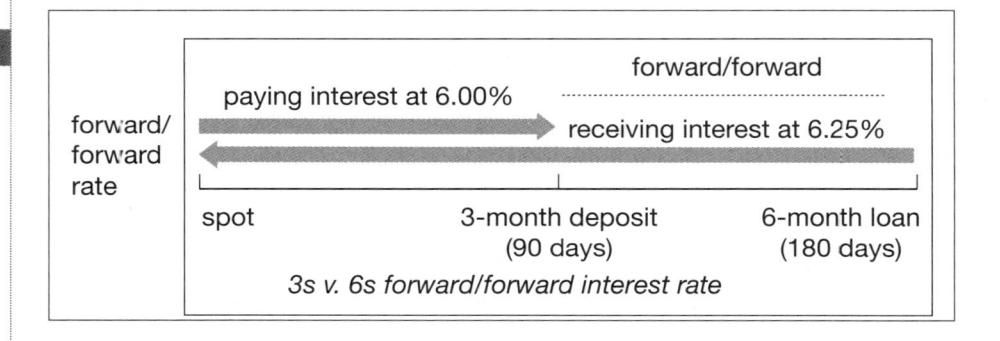

forward/forward rate

paying interest at 6.00%
receiving interest at 6.25%

spot | 3-month deposit (90 days) | 6-month loan (180 days)

3s v. 6s forward/forward interest rate

There are several formulae you can use to calculate the forward/forward rate. This is the formula included in the ACI formulae sheet: <ACI preferred>.

$$\text{forward/forward rate} = \left[\frac{\left(1 + \left(\text{interest rate for longer period} \times \frac{\text{days in longer period}}{\text{day base}}\right)\right)}{\left(1 + \left(\text{interest rate for shorter period} \times \frac{\text{days in shorter period}}{\text{day base}}\right)\right)} - 1 \right] \times \left(\frac{\text{day base}}{\text{days difference}}\right)$$

<ACI preferred>

Calculation

This forward/forward interest rate is calculated using the forward/forward formula:

$$\left[\frac{\left(1 + \left(0.0625 \times \frac{180}{360}\right)\right)}{\left(1 + \left(0.060 \times \frac{90}{360}\right)\right)} - 1\right] \times \left(\frac{360}{(180 - 90)}\right) = 0.064039\%$$

<ACI preferred>

In this example the forward/forward interest rate is calculated to be 6.4039 percent.

> **Question**
>
> A typical ACI Dealing Certificate question might be:
>
> Using the following rates – three months EUR: 3.50 percent. 90 days; six months EUR: 3.75 percent 180 days – what is the rate for an EUR deposit which runs from three to six months?
>
> A: 3.965%
> B: 3.625%
> C: 3.285%
> D: 3.835%
>
> **Correct answer**
> A: Here the forward/forward interest formula must be used to calculate the correct result as 3.965 percent.

Broken date interest rates

The forward/forward formula can also figure in the calculation of accurate broken date interest rates. Where there is a steep yield curve (positive or negative) the straight line interpolation method (see Chapter 4) is not accurate enough. For example, required to calculate a two-and-a-half month broken date rate in such circumstances the two-month rate (60 days) is adjusted by the extra number of days at the calculated 2s v. 3s forward/forward interest rate. The logic is that merely taking an average of two-month and three-month rates (the straight line method) is too inaccurate in a steep yield curve as the three-month (90 day) rate used already includes the first 60 days – the two-month rate. This is included here for information purposes. Questions in the ACI Dealing Certificate tend always to advise the use of the straight line interpolation method.

Basis for all hedging

The forward/forward interest rate is a vital element in any hedging strategies undertaken by dealers. Before a dealer can even decide whether or not to hedge he must be aware of any current forward/forward mismatch positions and their "breakeven" rates. These are calculated using the forward/forward formula.

The hedging instruments themselves (such as financial futures and FRAs, the subject matter of this chapter) also rely on the forward/forward formula for their pricing.

Descriptions of positions

Forward/forward positions are described using the number of months from spot to the start of the forward/forward period to the number of months from spot to the end of the period. For example, in January a forward/forward position from March to June would be described as 2s v. 5s (said "twos'/fives'). Similar terminology is used to describe forward/forward periods for FRAs (see later in this chapter).

> **Question**
>
> A typical ACI Dealing Certificate question might be:
>
> Your dealer has taken a three-month SGD deposit as funding for a seven-month SGD loan. How would you describe the position created?
>
> A: Short SGD 3s v. 4s
> B: Long SGD 3s v. 7s
> C: Short SGD 3s v. 7s
> D: Short SGD 4s v. 7s
>
> **Correct answer**
> C: Here the position created is described as being short SGD 3s v. 7s forward/forward.

> **Hint**
>
> *Questions asking for forward/forward period descriptions and seeking the breakeven rate of such positions (which can be calculated using the forward/forward formula already discussed above) occur frequently in the ACI Dealing Certificate examination.*

Topic 4 (part)· Money Market Derivatives

FINANCIAL FUTURES

A futures contract is an agreement to buy or sell a standard amount of a specified commodity, currency or financial instrument at a fixed price on a fixed future date. Futures contracts are traded either electronically or by open outcry on recognized exchanges by dealers who are members of that exchange.

Futures represent an agreement to buy or sell (go long or short) the underlying commodity, currency or financial instrument at a price agreed on any day up to a predefined last trading date. As futures contracts are all standardized they are readily traded until this last trading date.

Background

International Monetary Market

After approaching one hundred years of trading agricultural and commodity futures, in the late 1970s the Chicago Mercantile Exchange (CME) started trading financial futures through the International Monetary Market (IMM). Futures contracts based on underlying financial markets/instruments in foreign currencies and interest rates were introduced. With the liberalization of the foreign exchange markets earlier in that decade business expanded swiftly and other centres soon started examining the possibilities to create similar markets.

LIFFE

The London International Financial Futures Exchange opened in London in 1982. LIFFE started operations in the Royal Exchange building opposite the Bank of England in the City of London and after several years of rapid expansion outgrew that location and moved to new premises at Cannon Bridge towards the end of 1991. LIFFE, by now merged with the London Traded Options Market (LTOM), continued to trade financial futures, options on futures, stock options and the Footsie (Financial Times Stock Exchange 100 index) on an open outcry basis until mid-2000. LIFFE merged with EURONEXT in 2001 and full information on the Euronext/Liffe exchanges may be found on the websites www.liffe.com and www.euronext.com.

> **Question**
>
> A typical ACI Dealing Certificate question might be:
>
> Which of the following is a recognized financial futures exchange in the international markets?
>
> A: MATIF
> B: TARGET
> C: CMO
> D: CREST
>
> **Correct answer**
>
> A: MATIF (Marché à Terme des Instruments Financiers) is the futures exchange in Paris. The others are initials relating to totally unconnected organizations: TARGET is the pan European central banks EUR payment system; CMO the Central Moneymarkets Office developed by the Bank of England; and CREST is the stock market settlements system for UK share transactions.

Open outcry v. screen-based trading

Futures started life back in the nineteenth century being traded by open outcry on the floor of a recognized exchange such as the IMM in Chicago. In some financial centres, dealers in trading pits continue to trade in this way using voice and hand signals to indicate their market orders/requirements. These markets include the IMM (CME) Chicago, the Chicago Board of Trade (CBOT) and the Singapore International Monetary Exchange (SIMEX).

In recent years, with more and more systems sophistication becoming available through the latest IT developments, some exchanges have moved to screen-based electronic trading systems promising more efficient, accurate and cost-effective trade execution.

In May 1998, LIFFE began development of an electronic trading platform capable of replacing open outcry trading. The system, called LIFFE Connect, was designed by LIFFE in conjunction with customers and selected independent software vendors to handle all London traded futures and options contracts, the first of which, individual equity options, were migrated off the floor and onto the screens in November 1998. Since mid-2000 all LIFFE's futures and options contracts have been traded electronically on LIFFE Connect.

LIFFE Trading Host

At the heart of LIFFE Connect is the LIFFE Trading Host where all orders are received and matched. The Host also performs price reporting and dissemination, displaying all transacted prices together with the aggregate size of all bids and offers above and below the market, updated on a real-time basis.

LIFFE members are able to access the Trading Host using front-end software developed either by themselves or by an independent software vendor (ISV), who has developed customized trading front-ends for LIFFE Connect which are capable of "talking" to the Host system via the LIFFE API (Application Program Interface) which is a common software protocol.

Futures contracts

Futures contracts are designed to meet the needs of the market. If contracts prove not to be popular with traders they can be withdrawn. An example is the eurodollar contract which was traded on LIFFE between the market's opening and 1996 when the exchange decided to expand its involvement in longer-term bond contracts and ceased trading the eurodollar contract. The latter was (and continues to be) well served by the International Monetary Market (IMM) of the Chicago Mercantile Exchange and Singapore International Monetary Exchange (SIMEX).

Delivery dates

Typically financial futures contracts coincide with the four quarter dates, namely March, June, September and December. Certain contracts on some exchanges (not the subject matter of the ACI Dealing Certificate syllabus) are available with more frequent delivery dates. The current nearest dates are known as the *front months* with delivery months in later years described in a colour code, red, blue, green and gold, indicating that futures prices can be available for periods five years from date – though the market liquidity will not be too great in the distant months.

Uses of financial futures

Financial futures have increased in popularity over recent years because they can provide protection, or "insurance cover" to the risk-averse bank dealer/corporate treasurer/investor wishing to reduce his exposure to currency and interest rate risk. Financial futures may be used in risk management strategies to protect the capital value of equity and fixed-interest portfolios in a rising interest rate environment. In a similar way, yields on short-term investments can be protected during periods of falling interest rates.

Futures allow portfolio managers to adjust the sensitivity of a portfolio, by changing the asset distribution without having to trade in the underlying cash market – a process which could prove expensive and which may move the market in an adverse direction. Banks and corporations can employ financial futures to establish borrowing costs in advance, thereby providing a sound and more certain basis upon which to make strategic business decisions. To summarize, futures afford market participants greater control of the risks inherent in an uncertain financial environment.

Reasons to use financial futures

There are three main reasons for using financial futures:

- *Hedging*. A hedge is a temporary substitute for a known future requirement. Essentially it involves taking a futures position that is equal and opposite to an existing or anticipated position in the cash market. Thus an adverse price movement in the cash position will be offset to a greater or lesser extent by a favourable price move in the futures.
- *Trading*. Trading is buying and selling futures with the aim of making a profit. It allows an investor to take a view on the cash market's direction without having to buy or sell the underlying financial instrument. In doing so the trader accepts the market risks which the hedger is seeking to avoid and thus trading is a vital and necessary part of any futures marketplace. Traders help to improve both volume and liquidity, thereby making the hedging process more precise and reliable.
- *Arbitrage*. Arbitrage involves using futures to profit, at minimal risk, from price discrepancies either between different futures contracts or between futures and the underlying cash instrument. These anomalies can never be expected to last for very long as arbitrageurs will quickly move into the market and redress the prevailing imbalance by buying the cheap instrument or contract and selling the more expensive one.

The role of the London Clearing House

The London Clearing House (LCH) was formerly known as the International Commodities Clearing House (ICCH). Open outcry exchanges insist that all trades are entered by both parties independently within 30 minutes of dealing. Once the system has matched all trades entered the Clearing House assumes the role of second party to all trades, becoming buyer to each seller and seller to each buyer. This eliminates much of the credit risk for the exchange's clearing members as well as facilitating the process of entering into and closing out transactions. Once the trades have been agreed between the Clearing House and the clearing member (normally early the next day), the Clearing House will effectively issue the guarantee of performance.

In the same way as before under open outcry rules, once a futures trade has been matched within LIFFE Connect the London Clearing House stands between the parties to every trade, thereby guaranteeing their performance.

Costs involved in financial futures

Initial margin

To safeguard its exposure the Clearing House requires its members to deposit a margin or minimum security deposit so as to ensure performance under the terms of the futures contract. The level of initial margin is standardized per contract and is set by the Clearing House. Clearing members pay this margin on all contracts and claim this back from other brokers and their customers. Customers will frequently have an account relationship with their broker/clearing member for the settlement of margins. Another popular way is to lodge securities (Treasury bills) with the broker/clearing member to cover initial and variation margin calls. Initial margin is returned to the investor when the futures position is closed out.

The level of all contracts' initial margins can be adjusted at short notice in times of high market volatility to dissuade speculative position taking.

SPAN

*S*tandard *P*ortfolio *AN*alysis of Risk (SPAN) is the margining system adopted by the LCH for LIFFE. The major New York and Chicago exchanges also use this system.

> *You should refer to the LIFFE, CME or other exchange websites or publicity literature for current initial margin requirements on all exchange-traded contracts.*

Hint

Variation margin

Additionally each clearing member's net open position is revalued (marked to market) daily at the market's official closing price. Any difference between the value at the closing price and the original value, or, for an ongoing outstanding contract, the previous day's revaluation, must be paid to or will be received from the Clearing House by the clearing member as variation margin. Individual clients of the clearing member will be called for margin or their accounts adjusted following this revaluation process by 10.00 a.m. the day following. Variation margin is a zero sum with one trader's profits netting off against another's losses on marking to market all individual positions on a daily basis.

Commission

Dealing commission on futures trades is negotiable between member and customer and depends on the level of service required and the volume of business undertaken. Commission is normally charged on a "round trip" basis meaning that the fee covers opening and closing the futures position.

> **Question**
>
> A typical ACI Dealing Certificate question might be:
>
> How is the variation margin on a futures contract normally calculated?
>
> A: A fixed margin per contract
> B: Revaluation against the closing price on exchange
> C: Revaluation against LIBOR fixing
> D: Revaluation against a weighted average price
>
> Correct answer
> B: The variation margin on a futures contract represents the profit or loss on the position revalued against the daily closing price on the electronic trading platform/in the trading pit.

Fungibility

With a small number of exceptions the exact terms of a financial futures contract are specific to a particular exchange. Where more than one exchange across different time zones quote identical contract specifications they frequently offer fungibility, i.e. positions opened in one time zone (e.g. SIMEX in Singapore) can be closed in another (e.g. IMM in Chicago). This means that initial margins paid to the first clearing house do not have to be duplicated to the second and the original position is considered squared by the second transaction with appropriate repayment of any initial margin.

Sample LIFFE short-term interest rate contract specification

> *Short sterling*: three-month sterling interest rate future (traded electronically via LIFFE Connect):
>
> | | |
> |---|---|
> | Unit of trading: | GBP 500,000 notional three-month (90 days) deposit |
> | Delivery months: | March, June, September and December |
> | Delivery date: | First business day after the last trading day |
> | Last trading day: | 11.00 a.m. third Wednesday of the delivery month |
> | Quotation: | 100 *minus* the implied interest rate |
> | Minimum price movement: | 0.01 (GBP 12.50) |
> | Contract standard: | Cash settled against EDSP |
>
> Options on this short sterling contract are also traded on LIFFE.

LIFFE short-term interest rate contract specification (foreign currency)

LIFFE offers a range of other short-term interest rate (STIR) futures and options contracts in foreign currencies. These include euroswiss futures and options, euro (EUR) futures (based on both BBA Euro LIBOR and EURIBOR – the EBA fixing) and euroyen options and futures (based on both TIBOR and LIBOR) and options.

Euro LIBOR: three-month Euro LIBOR interest rate future (traded electronically via LIFFE Connect):

Unit of trading:	EUR 1,000,000 notional three-month (90 days) deposit
Delivery months:	March, June, September and December
Delivery date:	First business day after the last trading day
Last trading day:	11.00 a.m. two business days prior to third Wednesday of the delivery month
Quotation:	100 *minus* the implied interest rate
Minimum price movement:	0.005 (EUR 12.50)
Contract standard:	Cash settled against EDSP (BBA Euro LIBOR)

LIFFE also trades a 90-day EURIBOR futures contract (EDSP = EBA Euribor) and options on both these euro contracts are also traded.

The size of each financial futures short-term interest rate contract is approximately USD 1 million or equivalent. For example, each short sterling contract is in the standard size of GBP 500,000 but for JPY contracts the size is JPY 100 million.

Pricing of STIR futures

Prices of interest rate futures such as the contracts noted above are quoted on an index basis, i.e. 100 minus the interest rate. Therefore when underlying interest rates are *falling* futures prices *rise* and vice versa (see Figure 5.3).

Fig 5.3

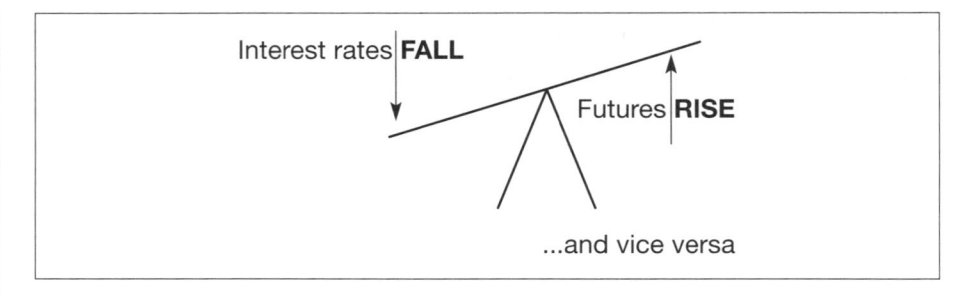

Interest rates **FALL**

Futures **RISE**

...and vice versa

Pricing example

With implied three months forward/forward interest rates (3 v. 6) at 5.00 percent, the equivalent futures price would be traded at around 95.00 (100 – 5.00). If forward/forward implied interest rates then fall to 4.00 percent, the futures price will rise to approximately 96.00.

Futures market quotation

The market quotes: bid–ask (low–high in index quote terms, i.e. 100 minus the implied interest rate).

Buying/selling rationale

This method of quotation ensures that the futures maxim *buy low/sell high* is able to be followed in these futures contracts alongside the other longer established futures contracts in commodities.

Futures prices extract from Reuters screen

LIFFE short sterling futures prices as posted during early December 200X are shown in Figure 5.4.

The Reuters style information screen in this figure shows for illustration purposes the contract month, the last traded and current bid/ask prices on LIFFE Connect (i.e. the highlighted last traded March 200Y implied fwd/fwd three-month sterling rate for March–June 200Y is 4.09 percent (100 minus 95.91)), the day's high and low, then the day's opening price and information regarding the volume traded yesterday and open interest in number of contracts outstanding (i.e. positions maintained by market users at last night's close).

Topic 4 (part)· Money Market Derivatives

Fig 5.4

SHTSTG	Last	Bid	Ask	High	Low	Open	Vol	Open Int
Z DEC 0X	9533	9533	9534	9555	9525	9552	14828	66698
H MAR 0Y	**9591**	9589	9591	9607	9578	9607	3024	36425
M JUN 0Y	9598	9597	9599	9612	9588	9612	873	24943
U SEP 0Y	9594	9595	9596	9608	9590	9608	693	31179
ZF DEC 0Y	etc.	etc.						

Financial futures price determinants

The price of money in the money markets is the interest rate payable. The money markets deal in cash, i.e. funds are delivered either value today (sterling markets) or on spot date (eurocurrency markets) for all deposits/loans effected today.

Futures prices show what market expectations are for similar cash deposits but for three-month periods in the future commencing from the quarter month delivery dates. As in the cash markets yields graphically portrayed in a yield curve provide one (by no means the only) source of information on the future course of interest rates.

Tick size/value on STIR contracts

Contract prices move in half ticks and ticks. A tick equals 0.01 percent and the monetary value of a one tick movement is easily calculable for profit and loss purposes:

This is shown in brackets alongside the minimum price movement for the two sample contracts already detailed.

$$\frac{\text{contract size}}{\text{total no. of ticks}} \times \frac{3 \text{ (90 days)}}{12 \text{ (360-day basis)}}$$

Bond futures

LIFFE also trades long-term interest rate products based on notional government bonds (not the subject matter of the ACI Dealing Certificate). These include five-year gilt contracts, long gilt (ten-year) futures and options, German government Bund futures and options, German Bobl futures and options, Italian government BTP futures and options, and Japanese government JGB futures and options.

Pricing of bond futures

Bond futures are priced on the same basis as the underlying security, i.e. a future tracking a bond price of 95.00 will be similarly quoted (95.00).

Variation margin

As already mentioned variation margin is the result of marking to market all open interest positions. At the close of business, the exchange calculates a settlement price – the closing price on the electronic platform/in the pit. This forms the basis for the calculation of any variation margin which must be settled by 10.00 a.m. the following day. On LIFFE this is effected through the LCH Protected Payments System (PPS).

Variation margin is calculated as:

> no. of ticks* × tick value (see above) × no. of contracts outstanding
> * Movement since any purchases/sales today and/or from previous settlement price

As there is a buyer for every seller, with a higher settlement price the buyer will be on a profit and the seller will be on an equal loss. The mark to market process is a zero sum.

Question

A typical ACI Dealing Certificate question might be:

I buy 25 GBP March 200X contracts at 93.71. The market moves three ticks in my favour and I decide to sell and take a profit. How much profit will I make?

A: GBP 1,875.00
B: GBP 937.50
C: GBP 75.00
D: GBP 3,000.00

Correct answer
B: Having bought 25 contracts and made a three tick profit you will make GBP 937.50, being 25 × 3 × GBP 12.50 (the tick value of a short sterling futures contract).

Short-term interest rate contract "delivery"

Unlike other commodity and certain financial futures contracts LIFFE and other exchanges' short-term interest rate contracts (such as the short sterling futures contracts) cannot be taken to delivery. Such financial futures positions are most often closed-out before delivery date. On LIFFE, if there are open interest positions still outstanding in these contracts at 11.00 a.m. on the final trading date, these are all cash settled based on the exchange delivery settlement price (EDSP).

Exchange Delivery Settlement Price

The exchange delivery settlement price for LIFFE STIR contracts is based on the British Bankers Association Interest Settlement Rate (BBAISR), which is set at 11.00 a.m. on the last trading day. The market rates for three-month sterling, eurodollar or euro deposits being offered to prime banking names between 9.30 a.m. and 11.00 a.m. on the last trading day, stated by a random sample of 16 from a list of designated banks, are collated and, having disregarded the three highest and the three lowest quotes, the settlement price is set at 100.00 minus the average of the remaining ten rates.

> The EDSP on the final contract trading date is the BBAISR's fixing rate for three-month deposits at 11.00 a.m. rounded to two decimal places, therefore there could be a small imperfection against LIBOR due to the latter being to the nearest $\frac{1}{16}$ (four decimal places). Basis risk, albeit small, is therefore in evidence should the contract be used to hedge any of the instruments noted in Chapter 4 priced in pure fractions.

Note

Bond futures delivery

Although not specifically part of the ACI Dealing Certificate syllabus it is worth mentioning here that bond futures contracts *are* deliverable. However, the bond futures are based on notional securities and so to facilitate delivery procedures each exchange lists a number of bonds which closely resemble the notional contracts and the price factor required to adjust the real bonds to match the notional futures contracts. As an example, in respect of gilt futures contracts the market is always assessing the "cheapest to deliver" (CTD) of the available five-year and long gilts listed.

An example of a list of deliverable gilts

Gilt	Price factor	Initial accrued interest
6.25% Tr 10	0.9486415	101.902174
9.00% Cn 11	1.1431026	3455.801105
9.00% Tr 12	1.1531626	2834.254144
8.00% Tr 13	1.0814990	1413.043478

Hint

There is a link back to repo transactions here with the CTD bond against the futures contract typically being traded as a "special" in the repo market.

Hedging with financial futures STIR contracts (here sterling)

The three-month short sterling contract tracks and eventually settles against three-month LIBOR. This contract can be used by lenders and borrowers in the short-term sterling cash money markets looking to protect (hedge their forward dated positions or funding/investment requirements) against rises/falls in cash market interest rates.

The contract can also be used by issuers and purchasers of short-term securities such as CDs and sterling Commercial Paper, purchasers of eligible bills, Treasury bills, short-dated gilts as well as market makers and traders in such instruments.

In addition, participants in the sterling swaps, FRA, FRN and forward foreign exchange markets may well hedge any net exposure using such short-term futures.

Long and short hedges

A *long* hedge involves buying a futures contract to protect against a fall in cash market interest rates.

The *buyer* of futures contracts buys now to sell back later at a higher price. He is therefore looking for futures prices to rise and because of the inverse nature of price v. interest rate must be concerned about falling interest rates (perhaps a fund manager hedging/guaranteeing the return on an investment).

A *short* hedge involves selling a futures contract to protect against rises in cash market interest rates.

The *seller* of futures contracts sells now to buy back later at a lower price. He is therefore looking for futures prices to fall and because of the inverse nature of price v. interest rate must be concerned about rising interest rates (perhaps a corporate treasurer hedging/protecting funding costs).

Topic 4 (part)· Money Market Derivatives

Yield curves and futures prices

Yield curves have already been explained in Chapter 4. Remembering the "time value of money" concept discussed earlier, futures markets are looking at the forward value of money somewhere out along the yield curve, specifically what money will be worth between two points on the yield curve three months apart – in market terminology the forward/forward interest rate.

As we have already seen, the forward/forward rate can be inferred (created) from current cash market rates by using money market interest rates applying to transactions which together produce the same forward/forward effect.

Futures equivalent run/"fair value"

Traders will frequently refer to the futures equivalent run. Using the forward/forward formula, the implied interest rate for the exact dates of each futures contract traded (the "fair value') can be calculated. Traders will watch the relationship of each futures contract to its "fair value" closely. In practice, with the wealth of other derivatives available in the marketplace (FRAs and interest rate swaps), arbitrage between the most closely correlated products ensures that the futures market keeps broadly in line with the theoretical fair value.

IMM dates

Given the liquidity in the Chicago Mercantile Exchange (CME) futures markets when considering arbitrage opportunities there are frequently prices being requested in the OTC FRA market matching the forward/forward period implied in the International Monetary Market (IMM) futures contracts. These are referred to as **IMM dates** in the FRA market. Futures/FRA arbitrage is discussed later in the chapter and this terminology may well appear in ACI Dealing Certificate examination questions.

Futures hedge imperfections

Futures contracts are always for a notional 90-day period commencing on the quarter month delivery date (third Wednesday of the delivery month). Standard three-month cash market periods may vary between, say, 89 and 94 days (February, holidays and weekends all affect the overall day count) so there is always a slight imperfection (a small amount of basis risk) in the futures hedge.

Hedge ratios

The above gives rise to requirements for further calculations in an attempt to match the varying day counts in the cash markets. This brings us to the concept of hedge ratios and weighted hedges. An exact hedge ratio requires the following calculation (for a short sterling contract hedge for a forward dated asset in an amount of GBP 5 million):

$$\frac{\text{hedged sum} \times \text{actual no. of days in cash market} \times \text{no. of contracts per year}}{\text{contract size} \times 365}$$

$$\frac{5{,}000{,}000 \times 91 \times 4}{500{,}000 \times 365} = 9.9726$$

Futures can only be traded in contract whole numbers. Therefore in this example 10 contracts must be sold to hedge the position – the hedge can never be perfect.

Were the amount to have been 5,250,000 or another such "odd" amount another imperfection arises. Where any amount to be hedged is not equal to an exact number of contracts another imperfection creeps into the calculation. This imperfection must also be managed, usually by over-hedging the amount.

Contract strips

Interest rate risk may need to be managed for time periods in excess of individual futures contract periods. In such cases a strip of futures may be used as a hedge. For example, to hedge a six-month risk sometime in the future, two consecutive contract months need to be bought/sold.

Stripping example

In March the trader identifies a forward dated risk where he needs to borrow GBP 1 million for six months in three months' time (see Figure 5.5).

In March the dealer has thus put a six-month hedge in place for a forward period starting in three months' time at an average equivalent fwd/fwd interest rate of 5.5 percent.

Time moves on and in June (on the dealer's day of need) the three-month cash market rate has risen to 6.00 percent. The dealer closes out both the June and September futures contracts simultaneously at the current market prices:

LIFFE short sterling   June 94.00   Sept. 93.90

Close-out of the two contracts results in a profit on the hedge of GBP 2,750.00, being GBP 1,400.00 (94.56 – 94.00 = 56 ticks on 2 June contracts) and GBP 1,350.00 (94.44 – 93.90 = 54 ticks on 2 Sept. contracts) which will have accrued in daily mark to market variation margin credits over the life of the hedge.

The dealer now takes a funding deposit of GBP 1 million at LIBOR 6.00 percent, but his overall cost of funds is reduced due to the profit (positive

Topic 4 (part)· Money Market Derivatives

Fig 5.5

LIFFE short sterling   June 94.56   Sept. 94.44

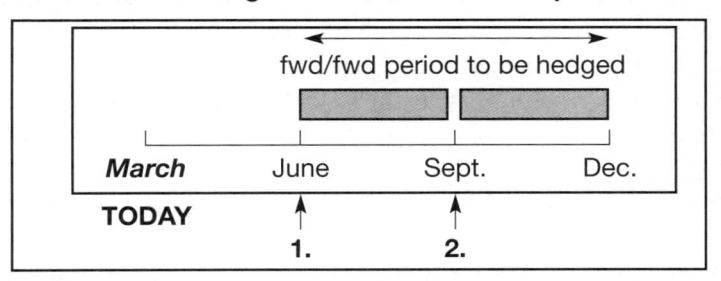

```
                    fwd/fwd period to be hedged
                    ◄─────────────────────►

    March       June        Sept.       Dec.
    TODAY        ↑           ↑
                 1.          2.
```

Futures trades required: **No. 1.** Sell **2** June short GBP contracts @ 94.56 (5.44%)

Dealt today (*March*):   **No. 2.** Sell **2** Sept. short GBP contracts @ 94.44 (5.56%)

mark to market) earned on the futures hedge. The hedge benefit of GBP 2,750.00 reduces the overall funding cost for GBP 1,000,000 for 184 days (cash market run).

GBP 2,750.00 applied to GBP 1,000,000 for 184 days:

$$\frac{2{,}750.00 \times 365 \times 100}{184 \times 1{,}000{,}000.00} = 0.5455(16)\%$$

The eventual funding cost will be 5.45 percent (LIBOR 6.00% − 0.55% (rounded)), only differing from the average hedge cost of 5.50 percent (a better rate than anticipated) due to day count imperfections.

Note

In this futures example, no account is taken of the "cost of carry" – funding the initial and any variation margin throughout the period of the futures hedge position.

Rolling/stack hedges

As we saw above a strip involves using a number of consecutive expiry contracts to hedge for a longer period than the standard futures equivalent run. A longer period can also be hedged using a *rolling hedge* (sometimes referred to as a *stack* or *stacking hedge*).

A dealer can use a larger number of contracts in the initial contract period than the cash market risk amount to be hedged. As the contracts near expiry they are closed out and replaced with contracts in the next

Mastering the ACI Dealing Certificate

consecutive contract month. One of the advantages is that liquidity is always greater in the near months whereas the use of a strip means a requirement sometimes to deal in the less liquid more distant months' contract and the hedger can ensure any calculated price is achieved.

The expression *stack* refers to the calculated requirement for contracts with a nominal value in excess of the amount to be hedged to ensure adequate coverage of the risk.

A rolling hedge may be used to hedge a period of time which is longer (a later maturity date) than the furthest forward futures contract available. A rolling hedge involves greater transaction costs due to the number of sales and purchases involved in the continuing management of the hedge.

Stack example

In June 200X the trader identifies a forward dated risk where he needs to borrow GBP 1 million for six months commencing in one year's time (see Figure 5.6).

Fig 5.6

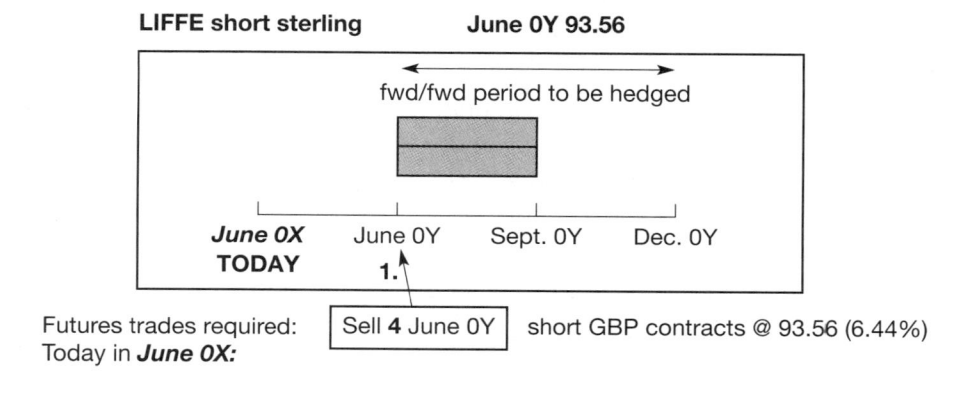

LIFFE short sterling   **June 0Y 93.56**

fwd/fwd period to be hedged

June 0X — TODAY   June 0Y   Sept. 0Y   Dec. 0Y

1.

Futures trades required: Today in **June 0X:**   Sell 4 June 0Y   short GBP contracts @ 93.56 (6.44%)

The trader sells double the number of contracts for the first month of the period to be hedged – here June 200Y – the suggestion being that covering double the amount in one contract month (half the period) is an effective hedge for the full period at risk. There are obviously flaws in this approach but sometimes where there is insufficient liquidity for the trader to cover the number of contracts needed in the further forward contract month to create a stack may be the only strategy available to him.

The stack becomes a *rolling stack* when the first contract month approaches and the position is rolled forward (buying back the June 200Y and selling the September 200Y contracts).

Stubs and tails

Where a hedge is required for a cash market broken date period shorter or longer than the futures equivalent run, the expressions *stubs* and *tails* are used to describe the "part period" either at the beginning or the end of the hedge period. To explain these terms we can look at the following examples:

Stub (at beginning)

Consider Figure 5.7 below. Stub dates are 5 September to 18 September (13 days) *plus* sales of September and December contracts (both 90 days) to hedge a 195-calendar day period from 5 September 200X to 19 March 200Y. In this case a greater number of September contracts can be sold (or bought) to offset the additional risk of the stub (broken date) period.

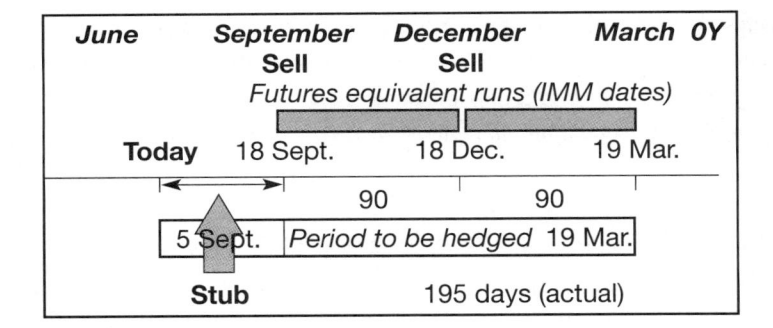

Fig 5.7

```
    June      September   December     March 0Y
                 Sell         Sell
              Futures equivalent runs (IMM dates)

    Today    18 Sept.      18 Dec.      19 Mar.
                      90            90
             5 Sept. | Period to be hedged  19 Mar.
              Stub            195 days (actual)
```

Tail (at end)

Consider Figure 5.8 below. Tail dates are 19 March to 28 March (9 days) *plus* sales of September and December contracts in September (both 90 days) to hedge a 191-calendar day period from 18 September 200X to 28 March 200Y. (200Y is not a leap year.)

Mastering the ACI Dealing Certificate

Fig 5.8

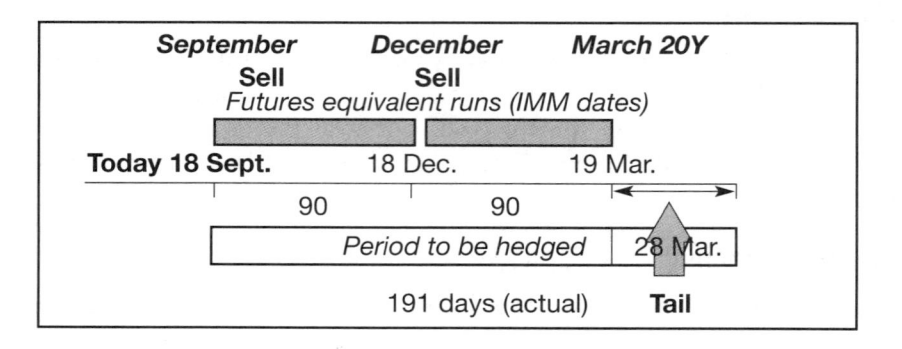

```
            September        December        March 20Y
              Sell             Sell
            Futures equivalent runs (IMM dates)

      Today 18 Sept.         18 Dec.         19 Mar.
              |        90       |       90      |←――――→|
                                                       28 Mar.
                         Period to be hedged    ↑
                         191 days (actual)      Tail
```

In this case a greater number of December contracts can be sold (or bought) to offset the additional risk of the tail (broken date) period.

Remember that futures contracts are always for 90 days regardless of the calendar period being hedged.

Hint

It is important that where a stub or tail is involved hedges are weighted accordingly. A hedge covering a tail needs to weight the tail as a fraction of the appropriate contract period whereas a stub is best treated as if it were a whole contract period with regard to weighting.

Question

A typical ACI Dealing Certificate question might be:

A trader is using only the March 0X short sterling contract to hedge the rate on a GBP loan which rolls over in March, June and December 0X. What kind of hedge is this?

A: A strip hedge
B: A stack hedge
C: A perfect hedge
D: A cross hedge

Correct answer

B: A stack or rolling hedge involves the use of a multiple number of contracts in one period to hedge a longer-term position. Here the trader will have to replace the March contracts with June contracts etc. as time goes on.

Hedge cost/income and cash market interest accruals

Most institutions have a strict rule to differentiate derivatives cost/income in respect of hedging and trading positions. Where futures are used to hedge cash market risks, banks will tend to require such cost or income to be credited to some form of profit and loss suspense account and then rebated (spread) across the period originally identified as being hedged. This will ensure that the hedge outcome is correctly reflected in the books of account.

Trading position cost/income

Where derivatives such as futures are used solely for trading purposes most banks will insist that such profits and losses impact on the trading profit and loss immediately. Indeed these profits and losses will be revalued (marked to market) on a daily basis notwithstanding the margining or other requirements and all profit and loss immediately accounted for. This requirement means that all derivatives traded must be identified as either hedge or trading positions at the outset. With sophisticated IT systems and accounting procedures and a sure understanding of risks within an institution it can sometimes be possible to permit reclassification of such derivatives.

Spread trading

Yield curve plays

While this section is primarily intended to describe the use of financial futures for hedging purposes some dealers may use the market to protect against (or trade) yield curve variations. If market sentiment is currently that over time short-term interest rates will rise there will more than likely be a positive yield curve. If the dealer believes that there will be a non-uniform shift in the yield curve, i.e. perhaps the longer-term interest rates will rise further than short-term rates and he feels he is exposed to such a move then he may take what is called a *spread* position in appropriate futures contracts. Here he would buy the near date contract and sell the far date. This is to protect his risk by offsetting any cost in running his overall position with a profit in the futures market.

If all rates do rise but the longer-term rates increase more than the shorter-term rates then, as anticipated, the yield curve will become steeper with the nearer futures contracts falling in price at a slower rate than the further forward futures contracts. The dealer may then turn his position and take his profit.

Mastering the ACI Dealing Certificate

Hint
> *Questions based on yield curve plays involving both futures and FRAs are popular examination question types in the ACI Dealing Certificate examination.*

Calendar spread trading example

If the dealer believes that longer-term (12-month) US dollar interest rates are going to rise further than shorter-term (three-month) rates then the dealer will buy a number of near dated futures contracts and sell a similar number of futures contracts in a further forward contract month.

We will assume 30-day months. The three months interest rate is quoted at 7.50 percent and the one year interest rate is quoted at 9.00 percent, with futures contracts trading today September 0X 91.66 (fwd/fwd 8.34 percent) and March 0Y at 90.13 (fwd/fwd 9.87 percent). It is anticipated that the positive yield curve will steepen (go more positive) – see Figure 5.9.

Fig 5.9

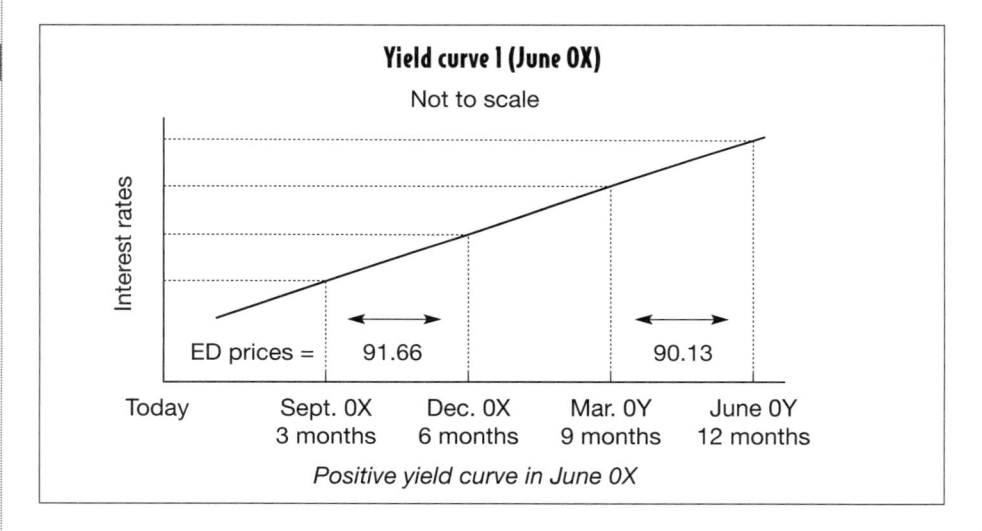

Yield curve 1 (June 0X)
Not to scale

ED prices = 91.66   90.13

Today | Sept. 0X | Dec. 0X | Mar. 0Y | June 0Y
  | 3 months | 6 months | 9 months | 12 months

Positive yield curve in June 0X

The dealer buys 10 September 0X ED contracts at 91.66 and sells 10 March 0Y ED contracts at 90.13.

Time moves on. It is now July 0X and the market has moved as anticipated. Interest rates have risen – two months US dollar cash is now 8 percent and the twelve months is 12 percent (making the five months 9.25 percent, eight months 10.50 percent and eleven months 11.50 percent – rates needed for our futures equivalent run calculations) – see Figure 5.10. Futures contracts are trading today September 0X 90.71 (fwd/fwd 9.29 percent) and March 0Y at 86.12 (fwd/fwd 13.88 percent). The anticipated steepening of the yield curve has occurred (now dramatically more positive).

Topic 4 (part): Money Market Derivatives

Fig 5.10

```
Yield curve 2 (July 0X)
     Not to scale
```

Interest rates

ED prices =   90.71   86.12

Today   Sept. 0X   Dec. 0X   Mar. 0Y   June 0Y
         2 months   5 months   8 months   11 months

More positive yield curve in July 0X

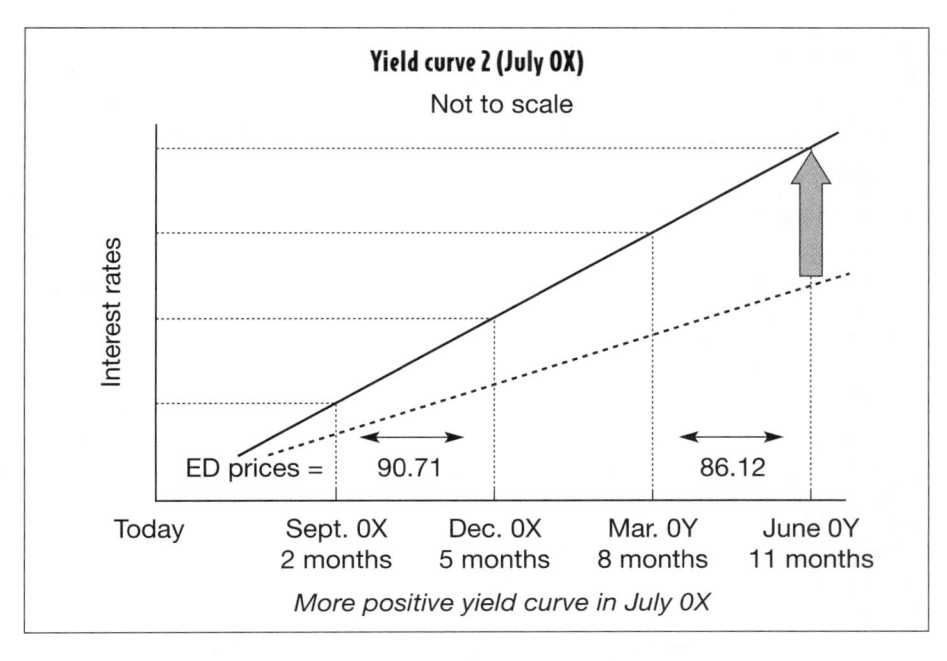

The dealer closes out his spread trade by selling 10 September 0X ED contracts at 90.71 and buying back 10 March 0Y ED contracts at 86.12.

The dealer has gained 401 ticks on the March 0Y position (90.13 – 86.12) and lost 95 ticks on the September 0X position (91.66 – 90.71). Overall the dealer has made a profit of USD 76 500.00 (306 ticks × 10 contracts × USD 25.00 per tick).

Spread trading strategies

This is not what can be called a naked position as the purchases of September 0X contracts are offset by the sales of March 0Y contracts. The dealer is merely positioning himself against a change in interest rate relationships in the future. There is clearly less risk in such a play and the futures exchange clearing house normally recognizes this by charging a lower initial margin on such a strategy. Should the dealer be anticipating a flattening of a positive yield curve then the purchases and sales entered into would be reversed. Strategies covering any eventuality can be designed – a change from positive to negative (sell the near and buy the far) or negative to positive (buy the near and sell the far, as in our example above).

> **Question**
>
> A typical ACI Dealing Certificate question might be:
>
> If you believe the short-term money market yield curve, which is currently positive, will flatten, which futures position should you take?
>
> A: Buy the far contract, sell the near contract
> B: Buy the near contract, sell the far contract
> C: Buy the near contract, buy the far contract
> D: Sell the near contract, sell the far contract
>
> **Correct answer**
> A: A flattening yield curve from a positive one means that longer-term interest rates are falling with the possibility of shorter-term interest rates moving higher. In such a situation, bearing in mind the index pricing of futures (100 minus the implied interest rate), buying the far contract and selling the near contract would put you in a position to benefit from this expected yield curve directional shift.

Position keeping in financial futures

Recording futures identified as a hedge

Financial futures interest rate contracts can be dealt either on a hedge or a trading basis. If a financial futures position is taken to hedge risks in another market (frequently the underlying cash market) it is sensible to show in dealing position and management information reportage the hedge against the risk position being hedged. This involves the generation of some form of "pseudo" cash movement in the accurate and timely cash flow reportage produced. In today's highly automated front office the ideal situation is dynamically updated cash flows, mismatch reports and on-screen mark to market evaluation.

In the majority of banks the information required will be available on one or more systems and may need manual intervention/consolidation to enable cross-instrument and market risks to be identified accurately.

Hedging profit and loss

If a financial futures position is taken as a hedging position it will be marked to market on a daily basis to reflect the variation margin calculations. However, any profit and loss will be held in some form of rebate/accrual account and then the benefit or cost will be spread (amortized) over the same period as the position originally intended to be hedged.

Trading and arbitrage

Financial futures interest rate contracts when dealt on a trading basis need to be held in portfolio in some readily accessible form so that the dealer can, as and when required, sell/buy back the contracts to close his position (and take his profit). Arbitrage – taking offsetting futures positions between different futures contracts (sometimes on different exchanges) – is closer to trading than hedging and should be similarly treated.

Various methods such as FIFO (first in first out) and LIFO (last in first out) can be specified by the dealer as individual futures positions need to be closed out during this process. Each therefore needs to be held independently, identified and valued within the portfolio.

Trading profit and loss

If a financial futures position is taken as a trading position it will be marked to market on a daily basis and any profit and loss will be taken into account immediately.

Most banks have very strict hedge/trade identification processes. The switching of futures positions between the categories can be open to abuse and should be closely monitored and controlled.

FORWARD RATE AGREEMENTS

Background

Forward rate agreements (FRAs), at first referred to as *future* rate agreements, were introduced in 1983 at the suggestion of a broking company in London as the over-the-counter answer to the futures market, which was experiencing tremendous growth since its beginnings in London in 1982. Initially all banks worked out their own terms and conditions and there were many occasions when transactions could not be completed because of differing terms between the participants, much to the frustration of all involved. The British Bankers Association responded with the publishing of standard terms and conditions in early 1984 – FRABBA.

FRABBA terms

The operation of the FRA market is governed by the British Bankers Association through their FRABBA standard terms and conditions. Under these regulations everything from currencies to be dealt, periods, terminology and market practice are covered. Banks trade with each other directly and through the brokers' market under these terms and conditions, and in the majority of cases contracts between banks and their commercial customers will also follow these standards. FRABBA terms are also included in bilateral ISDA (International Swaps and Derivatives Association) agreements.

BIS Basel triennial survey, April 2001

Trading in FRAs grew by 74 percent to USD 129 billion following slower growth in the previous reporting period. The vast majority of the outstanding amounts and growth since 1998 is accounted for by interest rate derivatives. Interest rate derivatives overall grew by 85 percent to USD 489 billion.

Forward Rate Agreements – definition

A forward rate agreement is an agreement between two counterparties, usually banks, developed to protect the parties against a future adverse movement in interest rates.

Counterparties to an FRA agree an interest rate to be applied to a notional deposit of an agreed principal amount for a specified period of time from a specified future date, known as the settlement date. An FRA can be variously compared to a forward/forward deposit without the resultant transfer of funds or a financial futures contract dealt between two parties outside a futures exchange and without any margin requirements.

Buyers and sellers of FRAs

The buyer of an FRA seeks to protect himself against a rise in interest rates, the seller seeks protection against a fall in interest rates. With an FRA you are in effect buying or selling the interest rate.

Note the buy/sell logic is the reverse of the futures market. Futures operate like a bond where buying the bond is like lending money at a rate while selling a bond is like borrowing the money at a rate. With an FRA it is the interest rate itself which is bought or sold – buying the FRA is like borrowing the money while selling is like lending.

Interest rate risk protection

An FRA is not linked to a loan or deposit transaction. It is a totally independent product providing interest rate protection. When dealing in FRAs there is no obligation for either party to enter into an eventual underlying "cash market" transaction, i.e. neither a loan nor deposit will be effected on settlement date. No physical exchange of principal amount ever takes place, the counterparties agree that on settlement date the contractual rate for the FRA is compared against a market rate benchmark (usually the appropriate LIBOR rate) and the difference is paid over by one counterparty to the other.

FRA periods

FRA contracts are quoted for periods akin to forward/forward deposit periods and are expressed as the first date of the contract period (settlement date) against the second date (maturity date). Standard periods are quoted in the market, with three-month and six-month FRAs providing the most liquid markets. These standard periods themselves are described in market terminology as for other forward/forward products – measuring the time gap between deal date and effective dates, i.e. the number of months from today (for sterling) or from spot (eurocurrencies) to the start date of the period (first number) against the number of months to the maturity date of the period (second number).

An example of a typical FRA quoted period would be three months forward against six months forward, which would be described in the market as "3 against 6 months FRA" or "3/6" or "3 × 6" – said as "threes/sixes" (see Figure 5.11).

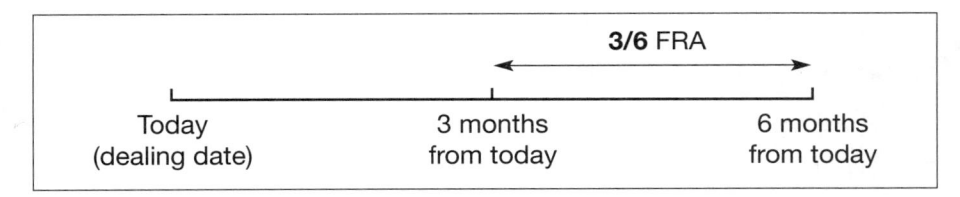

Fig 5.11

```
                        3/6 FRA
                 <------------------->
|_____|_____|
Today            3 months            6 months
(dealing date)   from today          from today
```

Note

The numbers in the description of the period do *not* relate to the calendar months numbers but to the time gaps as described above. (see Figure 5.11.)

With many FRAs being requested and priced on an over-the-counter basis (between banker and customer direct) any forward/forward period can be quoted to suit the customer's hedging requirements.

Mastering the ACI Dealing Certificate

Question

A typical ACI Dealing Certificate question might be:

In order to hedge a forward/forward mismatch money market position short of JPY for four months in three months' time (and you are concerned that interest rates will rise), you should:

A: buy a 4s/7s JPY FRA
B: sell a 4s/7s JPY FRA
C: sell a 3s/7s JPY FRA
D: buy a 3s/7s JPY FRA

Correct answer

D: Buying a 3s/7s JPY FRA enables you to hedge a short JPY position for four months commencing in three months' time. The buyer of an FRA seeks to hedge against a rise in interest rates.

FRA prices

Prices in the London market for FRAs are quoted on the same basis as money market operations as an interest rate (percentage per annum). As for money market rates the price consists of an offer and a bid, with the market spread varying according to current conditions – a typical spread for US dollar FRAs being four or five basis points (0.04 or 0.05 percent).

London money market quotation

Market maker quotes:

- *FRAs*: offer–bid for the FRA (high–low in interest rate terms).

International money market quotation

Market maker quotes:

- *FRAs*: bid–offer for the FRA (low–high in interest rate terms).

Two-way price

A bank making a market for FRAs will quote its "offer" – where it will sell FRAs – and its "bid" – where it will buy FRAs. An example of a quote in London for US dollars 3/6 months FRA might be as shown below.

Market marker's price (London)

3/6 USD FRA

Bank offers (sells FRAs) – Bank bids (buys FRAs)

5.90 – 5.85

Topic 4 (part)· Money Market Derivatives

The market maker will make a two-way price to calling counterparties as in other interbank trading markets and deal as noted above, taking the benefit of the dealing spread. As with a spot exchange operation there is no immediate profit (unless the dealer is simultaneously dealt with on his offer and bid by two counterparties). Profit is generated in a market-making bank by constant involvement in the market, trading (jobbing) and shading the dealing spreads to encourage/discourage counterparties from dealing. In a large institution many transactions can also be slotted into the bank's money market cash positions (as interest rate hedges) should this be desired.

Settlement

At fixing date of the FRA (the first date of the forward/forward contract period in the case of sterling), or, in the majority of currencies, two working days before settlement date (the fixing date), the contractual rate of the FRA is compared with LIBOR for the currency and period dealt, and any difference is settled in cash between the counterparties to the contract (see Figure 5.12).

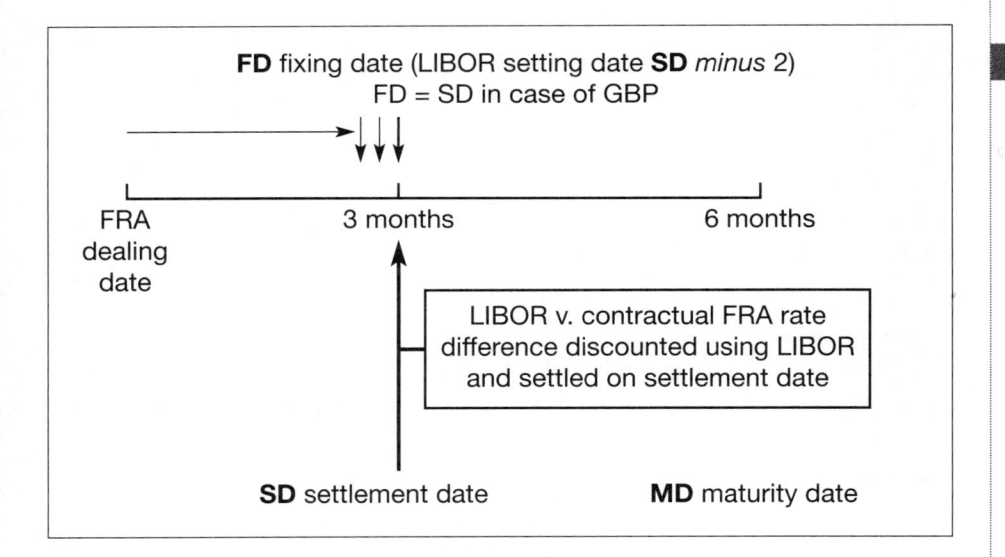

Fig 5.12

```
                FD fixing date (LIBOR setting date SD minus 2)
                        FD = SD in case of GBP
                             ↓↓↓
    |_____|_____|
   FRA             3 months              6 months
 dealing
   date
                              LIBOR v. contractual FRA rate
                              difference discounted using LIBOR
                              and settled on settlement date

                    SD settlement date     MD maturity date
```

This cash settlement takes the form of a discounted amount (discounted at the then prevailing LIBOR), as should an actual money market operation have ensued interest would not ordinarily have been settled until maturity.

FRABBA Settlement Rules

Where LIBOR on fixing date is a *higher* rate than the FRA contractual rate, the buyer of the FRA (originally wishing to protect against a rise in interest rates) receives a discounted settlement payment from the seller equal to the difference between the contractual rate of the FRA and the higher LIBOR.

Where LIBOR on fixing date is a *lower* rate than the FRA contractual rate, the seller of the FRA (originally wishing to protect against a fall in interest rates) receives a discounted settlement payment from the buyer equal to the difference between the contractual rate of the FRA and the lower LIBOR.

Contract for difference

An FRA is a contract for difference (CFD) in Bank of England terminology. It is not an option product and settlement of the difference (between the FRA contractual rate and LIBOR) must take place between the parties on the agreed FRA settlement date.

Question

A typical ACI Dealing Certificate question might be:

Today is the fixing date for a 3/6 USD FRA which you bought at 5.50 percent for which the FRABBA USD LIBOR has been set at 6.00 percent. Which of the following is true?

A: Your counterparty will pay you
B: You will pay the counterparty
C: Too little information to decide
D: There will be no exchange whatsoever

Correct answer
A: If on settlement date the USD LIBOR rate is higher than the contractual FRA rate the buyer is reimbursed with the difference. Here you (the buyer) will be reimbursed.

Trading FRAs

Trading in FRAs in the major currencies in the standard forward/forward periods is the closest trading of interest rates gets to trading spot currencies in the foreign exchange market.

Topic 4 (part)· Money Market Derivatives

FRA example

We will look at an example from the "end user's point of view" – here a corporate treasurer. Today's date is XX January 200Y.

The corporate treasurer has a six-month roll-over loan facility from another bank on which he is paying LIBOR plus $\frac{1}{2}$ percent margin. The loan in an amount of USD 10 million is next due for re-rating on XX June 200Y, having been rolled over last month (December 200X) at the rate of $6\frac{1}{2}$ percent (LIBOR 6 percent plus $\frac{1}{2}$ percent margin).

The corporate treasurer is concerned that US dollar interest rates may rise before the next roll-over date meaning that the next period cost of funds may be higher. Note he can only hedge the market rate (not the margin). He wishes to hedge this forward/forward interest rate risk and calls for an FRA price quotation.

The corporate treasurer's position is shown in Figure 5.13.

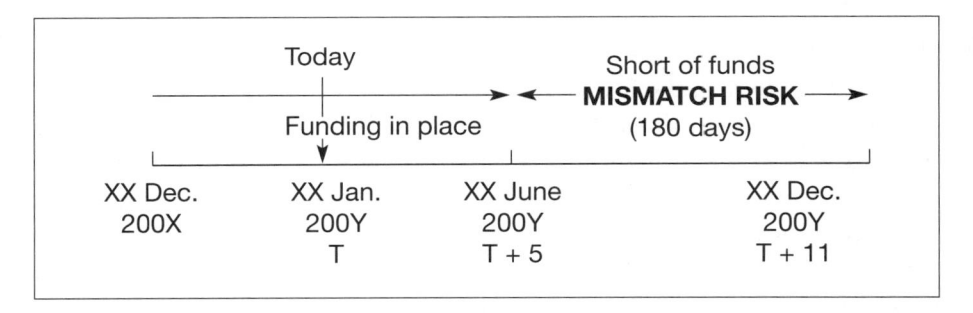

```
                Today                    Short of funds
                 |          →    ←  MISMATCH RISK  →
              Funding in place           (180 days)
                 ↓
  XX Dec.      XX Jan.        XX June              XX Dec.
  200X         200Y           200Y                 200Y
               T              T + 5                T + 11
```

Fig 5.13

The FRA required by the corporate treasurer is a 5s v. 11s period (June being today +5 months and December today +11). There is currently a positive yield curve with market sentiment favouring a US dollar interest rate rise over the next few months.

The dealing price quoted to the corporate treasurer by the dealer (London terminology = offer–bid) is:

> USD FRA 5s/11s
> 6.40 – 6.36

The corporate treasurer wants to protect against rates rising and therefore needs to buy a 5s v. 11s FRA in the amount of USD 10 million. He elects to deal and takes the bank's offer – the higher rate of the two-way price in similar fashion to dealing in the money market. The corporate treasurer buys an FRA in an amount of USD 10 million XX June to XX December 200Y (180 days) at 6.40 percent – the bank's FRA offered rate.

FRA settlement

The corporate treasurer still has the FRA outstanding. Time moves on. It is now XX June 200Y (the fixing date for the FRA traded back in January). Just after 11.00 a.m. on the fixing date the LIBOR rates will be confirmed for the current cash market periods from spot. The six months LIBOR rate will be the rate for the period originally hedged by the purchase of the FRA by the corporate treasurer. It is this rate which is compared with the original contractual rate for the FRA.

> XX June 200Y
> LIBOR 6 months: **6.875%**

Under FRABBA terms, if the current LIBOR is *higher* than the FRA contractual rate the *buyer* of the FRA is reimbursed with the discounted difference.

This is the case in this example and so the seller (the bank) will pay to the buyer (the corporate treasurer) the settlement amount equal to the interest difference calculated on the FRA notional principal, USD 10 million at 0.475 percent for 180 days.

However, as interest on loans and deposits is paid at maturity and the period originally hedged will run until XX December 200Y, rather than have to keep the FRA open and pay at that date the difference so calculated is discounted back to and paid on settlement date. For this purpose the LIBOR fixing rate is also used as the discount rate. This settles the FRA, which now ceases to exist – the forward/forward hedge is no longer valid as the period is now the straight six months cash period.

The subject of the FRA hedge, the roll-over loan from the lending bank, will also be re-rated at today's current six months LIBOR. The lending bank will contact the corporate treasurer and the new rating period XX June to XX December 200Y (assume 180 days) will attract the rate of $7\frac{3}{8}$ percent (the current LIBOR of 6.875 percent plus the margin of $\frac{1}{2}$ percent). But to offset this higher rate charged on the new roll-over period the corporate treasurer has the "profit" (better described as a benefit earned) on the hedging FRA of 0.475 (discounted), making his actual cost of funds for the new rating period 6.40 percent (LIBOR 6.875 minus 6.40 = 0.475). The protection against rising interest rates originally sought through the FRA has worked. The rate paid by the corporate treasurer is actually that hedged with the FRA, 6.40 percent.

Topic 4 (part): Money Market Derivatives

> Only the market rate (LIBOR) can be hedged. The margin of $\frac{1}{2}$ percent will still have to be included in the corporate treasurer's overall cost of funds.

Note

FRABBA settlement

When an FRA is settled the FRABBA settlement formula will be used:

$$\text{FRA settlement amount} = \text{principal} \times \frac{(\text{FRA rate} - \text{fixing rate}) \times \frac{\text{days in FRA period}}{\text{day base}}}{\left(1 + \left(\text{fixing rate} \times \frac{\text{days in FRA period}}{\text{day base}}\right)\right)}$$

<ACI preferred>

In this example:

Data: Principal: USD 10,000,000 FRA contractual rate: 6.40%
6 months LIBOR (180 days) rate: 6.875% higher

$$10{,}000{,}000.00 \times \frac{\left((0.0640 - 0.06875) \times \frac{180}{360}\right)}{\left(1 + \left(0.06875 \times \frac{180}{360}\right)\right)} = -\text{USD } 22{,}960.72 \text{ (negative)}$$

<ACI preferred>

The result is *negative* (LIBOR is higher than the FRA), therefore this sum is due to the buyer of the FRA – here the bank will pay the corporate treasurer the "difference" on settlement date.

However, if on fixing date the FRA is still outstanding and LIBOR is fixed *lower* than the FRA contractual rate at, say, 6 percent then the settlement process is as follows. Under FRABBA terms if the current LIBOR is *lower* than the FRA contractual rate the *seller* of the FRA is reimbursed with the discounted difference.

Data: Principal: USD 10,000,000 FRA contractual rate: 6.40%
6 months LIBOR (180 days) rate: 6.00% lower

$$10{,}000{,}000.00 \times \frac{\left((0.0640 - 0.060) \times \frac{180}{360}\right)}{\left(1 + \left(0.060 \times \frac{180}{360}\right)\right)} = \text{USD } 19{,}417.47 \text{ (positive)}$$

<ACI preferred>

The result is *positive* (LIBOR is lower than the FRA), therefore this sum is due to the seller of the FRA – here the corporate treasurer will pay the bank the "difference" on settlement date.

The roll-over loan will also now be rated at the lower rate of $6\frac{1}{2}$ percent (LIBOR 6 percent plus $\frac{1}{2}$ percent margin) but because the corporate treasurer has had to pay the discounted difference of 0.4 percent on the FRA to the bank the overall cost of funds will be 6.40 percent.

If an FRA is held to settlement (fixing date) whatever the LIBOR is fixed at the original interest rate hedged will be achieved.

Regardless of LIBOR being higher or lower than the FRA rate, the product therefore permits a hedger (FRA buyer) to "buy certainty" and fix an interest rate to be paid for a forward/forward period. It is the interest rate equivalent of an outright forward exchange contract.

Hint

The ACI formulae sheet including the FRA settlement formula noted above does not *include information regarding the logic in respect of the direction of payment. If you ensure you always input the FRA rate first followed by the LIBOR (fixing) then if the result is positive (FRA higher than LIBOR) the settlement amount is due to the* seller; *if the result is negative the settlement amount is due to the* buyer *(LIBOR higher than FRA).*

Question

A typical ACI Dealing Certificate question might be:

You originally purchased a three-month GBP FRA (92 days) in the amount of GBP 10 million at the contractual rate of 7 percent. Today is fixing date. If three months GBP LIBOR is fixed at $5\frac{1}{2}$ percent what will the settlement amount be?

A: GBP 37,802.01
B: GBP 37,291.25
C: GBP 38,333.33
D: GBP 37,808.22

Correct answer
B: Using the FRA settlement formula the settlement amount is calculated as GBP 37,291.25 (Actual/365). Although the question does not ask it *you* will pay the counterparty this amount on settlement date.

Unwinding FRAs

To comply with the definition of a true hedge any protection put in place via an FRA must be able to be lifted (unwound). In the above example, if in the period January to June for some reason the hedge was no longer needed (the reason for the hedge may disappear, the corporate treasurer's opinion may change, market conditions may no longer give cause for concern), the hedge could be unwound.

To unwind the hedge in our example above, the corporate treasurer would effect an equal and opposite FRA. In this case he would sell an FRA. If he sells it to the same bank, the bank and corporate treasurer can agree to cancel the two offsetting FRA transactions immediately by discounting the FRA settlement amount back to cancellation date (at the appropriate LIBOR) and paying the difference there and then – permitting the transactions to be cancelled and removed from credit line utilization records.

If this sale is effected with a different counterparty then both the original purchase and the subsequent sale would be left to settle with one difference against LIBOR payable to the corporate treasurer and the other difference against LIBOR payable by the corporate treasurer. The cost from these two offsetting transactions would equate to the cost of maintaining the hedge while it was appropriate.

FRA participants

Participants in the FRA market range from banks and financial institutions to corporate treasurers, pension fund and other investment managers, and even sovereign governments.

Uses for an FRA – in a bank

The uses of an FRA in the bank may be listed as follows:

- hedging interest rate risks in the cash book;
- hedging short-term interest rate risks in the floating side of the swaps book;
- assisting in liquidity management (bridging the gap and perhaps offsetting some of the costs between shorter-term low-yielding liquid assets and the longer-term liabilities taken in funding);
- a trading substitute for "on balance sheet" position taking (taking a view and trading interest rates);
- providing a corporate customer service (perhaps better placed first on this list for many banks).

Uses for an FRA – by a corporate treasurer

Similar uses to some of those noted under banks also apply to corporate treasurers. There are also further benefits for the budgeting/forward planning process and the provision of a means to extend the price availability (though not the liquidity) of credit to cover longer-term projects than perhaps a company's bankers will lend for.

Summary of benefits

- An FRA is a contract for difference in Bank of England terminology. There is no commitment express or implied to enter into a deposit or loan at any time. The FRA provides interest rate protection only.
- The FRA market is extremely liquid with many banks and financial institutions acting as market makers willing to quote prices in any currency and period up to around a two/two and a half year time horizon, i.e. 24 v. 30 months FRAs are feasible.
- The FRA may be tailored to suit a customer's individual requirements. FRAs offer great flexibility to banks and commercial customers alike in their efforts to hedge forward positions and manage interest rate risk over longer periods than perhaps cash markets are prepared to offer facilities.
- The FRA rate is market driven, reflecting the pricing of forward/forward periods off the cash market yield curve. The FRA market is quoted and dealt in similar fashion to the cash markets and therefore involves no steep learning curve to use the product.
- There is no upfront premium or margin to pay on entering into an FRA.
- The product complies with the true definition of a hedge in that it can be unwound if no longer required – though sometimes this may result in the FRA not being totally cost free. There is an added advantage in that, unlike cash market transactions, all FRA outstandings are "off balance sheet", offering trading opportunities to those seeking such profit-oriented involvement.
- Credit utilization is low (exposure limited to interest rate fluctuation – regularly marked to market during the life of the FRA) which suits both the bank offering the service and the corporate using the product. From a bank's point of view it is a low-risk weighted contract for difference in terms of capital adequacy requirements.

Futures and FRAs

A futures trader may refer to FRAs as "over the counter futures" while an FRA trader may refer to futures as "exchange traded FRAs". There are close similarities in both products' uses but major differences in their execution and costs. These similarities and differences have been highlighted in the two sections describing the products.

Hedging/arbitraging positions between futures and FRAs

With the inverse relationship of futures prices to interest rates the buy/sell logic is also reversed. Therefore when considering futures as a hedge (or arbitrage operation) against FRAs, to hedge a short FRA position the trader must sell futures and to hedge a long FRA position the trader must buy futures (see Figure 5.14).

Fig 5.14

FRA position	**Long** FRA	**Short** FRA
Rationale	(interest rates will **RISE**)	(interest rates will **FALL**)
Futures arbitrage	Buy futures	Sell futures
Rationale	(interest rates will **FALL**)	(interest rates will **RISE**)

Futures v. FRA hedging/arbitrage is always therefore BUY/BUY or SELL/SELL: i.e. if you are long of Futures you must buy the equivalent FRA to hedge the position; if you are short of Futures and wish to hedge/arbitrage the positon with FRAs you must sell the equivalent FRA.

Such arbitage tends to be treated as a trading position in the bank's books of account.

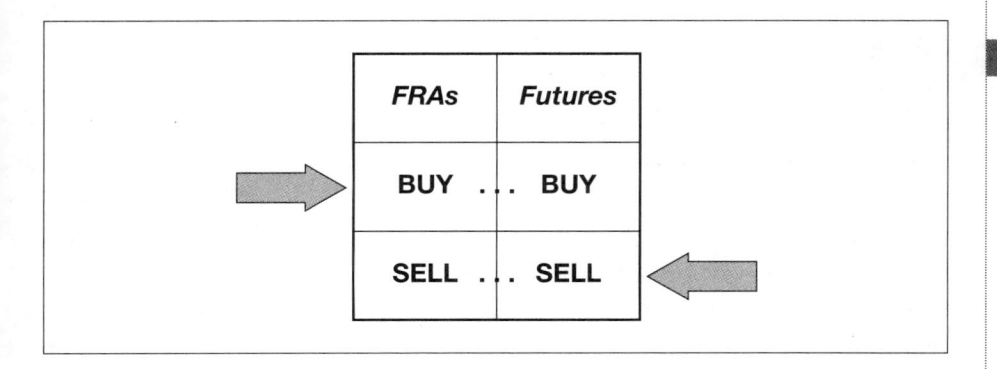

Fig 5.15

FRAs	Futures
BUY ...	BUY
SELL ...	SELL

Mastering the ACI Dealing Certificate

Question

A typical ACI Dealing Certificate question might be:

Which of the following pairs of financial instruments provide arbitrage opportunities?

A: Swap points and futures margins
B: FRAs and interest rate futures
C: Currency swaps and currency options
D: Interest rate swaps and CDs

Correct answer
B: Both FRAs and interest rate futures track forward/forward interest rates and of the instruments quoted have the closed correlation and frequently provide arbitrage opportunities.

Calendar spread trading

In the futures section of this chapter we looked at spread trading and the example on page 124 can be replicated here using FRAs with a 3 v. 6 FRA being *sold* and a 9 v. 12 FRA *purchased*. Remember FRAs are based on interest rates rather than the index prices of futures.

Hint

Questions based on yield curve plays involving both futures and FRAs are popular examination question types in the ACI Dealing Certificate *examination.*

Question

A typical ACI Dealing Certificate question might be:

There is a positive yield curve which you expect to flatten in the longer end. To take advantage of this you would:

A: Buy 3/6 FRA and sell 6/9 FRA
B: Buy 3/6 FRA and buy 6/9 FRA
C: Sell 3/6 FRA and sell 6/9 FRA
D: Sell 3/6 FRA and buy 6/9 FRA

Correct answer
A: Buying the 3/6 FRA and selling the 6/9 FRA is a yield curve strategy to take advantage of longer-term interest rates falling more sharply than shorter-date interest rates, i.e. the yield curve out to one year will flatten.

Position keeping

Hedging

FRA contracts can be dealt either on a hedge or a trading basis. If an FRA position is taken to hedge risks in another market (frequently the underlying cash market) it is sensible to show the hedge against the risk position being hedged. This involves generation of some form of "pseudo" cash movement in the accurate and timely cash flow reportage produced for the cash market positional management.

In today's highly automated front office the ideal situation is dynamically updated cash flows, mismatch reports and on-screen mark to market evaluation.

In the majority of banks the information required will be available on one or more systems and may need manual intervention/consolidation to enable cross-instrument and market risks to be identified accurately.

Trading

FRAs (like financial futures interest rate contracts) when dealt on a trading basis need to be held in portfolio in some readily accessible form so that the dealer can, as and when required, sell/buy back the contracts to close his position (and take his profit). All FRAs need to be settled individually on settlement date and remain in portfolio until that date.

If an FRA position is taken as a trading position it will be marked to market on a daily basis and any profit and loss will be taken into account immediately.

Risk management reportage

For more "bureaucratic" risk management purposes, "pseudo" cash flows, balance sheet nominal amounts per currency and consolidated broken down by asset/liability sector and period (ideally daily) should be available.

Whatever the reportage outstandings to be assessed against, any "limits" or other constraints imposed should be readily identifiable.

LONGER-TERM INTEREST RATE DERIVATIVES – INTEREST RATE SWAPS

Together with medium- and long-term bonds the interest rate swap market is the major OTC (over the counter) market available to banks, other financial institutions and commercial companies for managing their interest rate structures and the risks arising.

Background

Early development

Having grown out of back-to-back loans and parallel loans developed in the early 1970s, interest rate swaps were soon recognized by multinational corporations as a medium through which they could tap new markets for cheaper and more flexible funding.

The principal of comparative advantage drove early interest rate swaps with the swap transaction on the back of a *Triple A* rated corporation issuing fixed rate debt through the bond market. The swap enabled the issuer to convert this fixed rate funding into sub-LIBOR floating rate while the lower rated second party to the swap, perhaps better able to tap the market for LIBOR-linked funds but needing fixed-term money, was also able to achieve this objective through the interest rate swap. This type of transaction, initially arranged directly between the parties (IBM and the World Bank are the usual example quoted) but soon identified by banks as a further financial service from which to produce profit, is a popular example of the early beginnings of the market in interest rate swaps.

The product has undergone very rapid and large-scale expansion and is now firmly established as the most flexible of products for both hedging and trading interest rates. It is in daily use in both banks and commercial companies to these ends.

BIS Basel triennial survey, April 2001

The recent BIS triennial survey reported daily turnover volumes of USD 331 billion – a rise of 114 percent from the previous survey (1998).

Flexibility

Due to the market's liquidity the interest rate swap product offers a high degree of flexibility to a wide range of counterparties. Deal sizes in the major currencies are tailored by many institutions to encourage middle market commercial companies to consider interest rate swaps as a means to hedge their lower transaction size interest rate risks. Formal agreements are reasonably easy to establish using standard ISDA (International Swaps and Derivatives Association) or BBAIRS (British Bankers Association Interest Rate Swaps) terms and conditions.

Counterparty risk and capital adequacy requirements, although obviously needing to be considered due to the long-term nature of the instrument, are less substantial than straight lending providing significant leveraging opportunities.

Although the US dollar has the lion's share of total outstandings (over 66 percent), the majority of the world's trading currencies are available to the potential operator. Using specially created interest rate swap variants and currency swaps (correctly described as currency and interest rate swaps) both interest rate and exchange rate exposure can be effectively managed and reduced.

Description

An interest rate swap (IRS) is an agreement between two parties to exchange two schedules of cash flows over a predetermined period ranging from one to 25 years. These schedules represent interest payments on a liability on one side and an asset on the other and are calculated at either a fixed or a floating rate denominated in the same or two different currencies.

The actual exchange of interest payments, although perhaps on different bases, is frequently synchronized, in which case only the net amount passes between the parties. An interest rate swap exchanging 'fixed for floating' interest cash flows in the same currency is frequently described as a *plain vanilla* swap. There are many other variations and descriptions.

Plain vanilla interest rate swap

A so-called plain vanilla swap involves the exchange of fixed interest flows for floating interest flows over an agreed period. IRS traders use boxes and arrows to describe these flows and a three-year fixed v. floating (six months LIBOR) swap would be displayed, as shown in Figure 5.16 below.

Plain vanilla swap

3-year fixed interest rate

C'pty A → C'pty B

Floating interest rate (LIBOR)

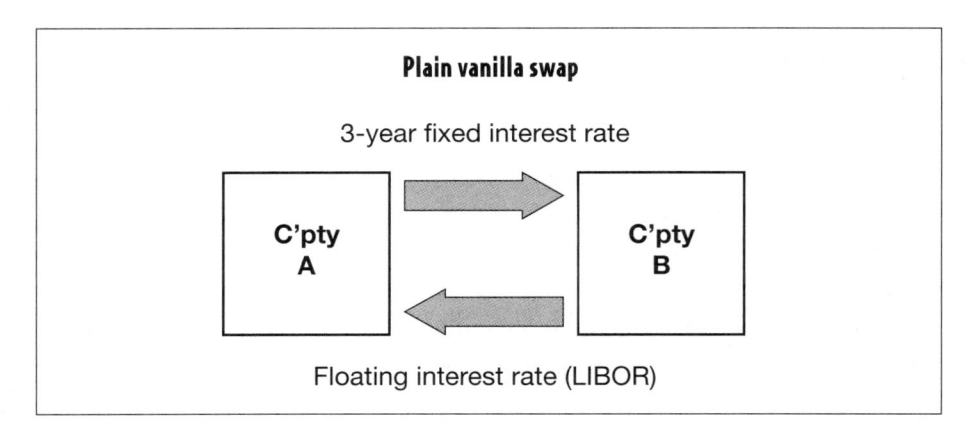

Fig 5.16

Mastering the ACI Dealing Certificate

How a swap price is quoted

In respect of plain vanilla swaps, market makers (the banks) in interest rate swaps tend to talk in terms of the fixed rate side – the other side being the appropriate current and subsequent LIBOR or other reference rates agreed.

US dollar-denominated swaps relate closely to the US Treasury markets and are frequently quoted as a bid and offer spread above the mid-point of the appropriate US Treasury bond or note rate. Banks and brokers quote these bid-offer rates on Reuters, Bloomberg's and other rates and news vendors' systems. This market-making spread in basis points (bp), either bid (for the market-using party to receive the fixed rate) or offer (for the market-using party to pay the fixed rate) has to be added to the appropriate US Treasury instrument reference rate to achieve the overall fixed rate for the swap.

In the case of sterling denominated swaps, these will be rated based on the appropriate period UK gilt prices but are usually already quoted as "all-in" rates on rates displays. In bank–commercial customer contracts a further margin to reflect the bank's credit risk on the counterparty will also be added.

London quotation

- *OTC interest rate derivatives* (such as interest rate swaps): receive–pay (high-low) swap spread or all-in price (for the fixed rate).

International market quotation

- *OTC interest rate derivatives* (such as interest rate swaps): pay–receive (low-high) swap spread or all-in price (for the fixed rate).

Question

A typical ACI Dealing Certificate question might be:

How is a USD-denominated "plain vanilla" interest rate swap frequently priced and quoted in the interbank market?

A: By reference to the floating rate side
B: As a spread above corresponding US Treasuries
C: As the differential between the fixed rate and LIBOR
D: An all-in rate for the fixed side

Correct answer
B: USD "plain vanilla" interest rate swaps are priced off the corresponding US Treasuries as a two-way dealing spread expressed in basis points (bid to pay fixed/offer to receive fixed) to be added to the mid-point of the appropriate period US Treasury bond. The floating LIBOR side is understood to be that quoted at 11.00 a.m. on the rate fixing date.

Topic 4 (part)· Money Market Derivatives

Differences from other financing methods

The main differences between an interest rate swap and a linked "back-to-back" loan and deposit transaction in the cash market are as follows.

- In respect of legality and default, an interest rate swap is one transaction rather than two so if one party fails to pay any amount due the other is no longer bound to make payments required of him.
- There is no exchange of principal at the outset nor maturity of an interest rate swap and as such swaps are deemed to be *off balance sheet* transactions.
- The interest rate swap can be "unwound" or cancelled at any time. This is effected by marking to market all the forward projections of cash-flow commitments (fixed rate) on both parties and settling the amount owing from one to the other as at the date of cancellation (NPV).

Terms and conditions

At the inception of an interest rate swap both parties agree the terms of the transaction.

- The amount of principal underlying the contract. For single currency interest rate swaps this is a notional sum as no exchange will take place and is required to serve as a reference amount in determining the cash flows to be exchanged during the life of the swap.
- The commencement and maturity dates of the swap.
- The roles of the parties to the swap, i.e. fixed rate payer and floating rate payer in the case of a plain vanilla swap.
- The fixed rate and its interest basis and payment frequency.
- The floating rate and the reference rate to be used (typically LIBOR).

> **Note**
> It is customary to draw up a master swap agreement prior to or on completion of the first swap between the parties. This frequently follows the ISDA or BBAIRS standard terms and conditions.

> **Question**
>
> A typical ACI Dealing Certificate question might be:
>
> Which of the following best describes a "plain vanilla" interest rate swap?
>
> A: A currency and interest rate swap based on paying and receiving fixed rates
>
> B: An interest rate swap not based on ISDA or BBAIRS terms
>
> C: A single currency interest rate swap in which interest flows based on fixed v. floating rates are exchanged
>
> D: An interest rate swap based on prime v. fixed rates
>
> **Correct answer**
>
> C: A so-called plain vanilla interest rate swap is a single currency IRS where the counterparties agree to exchange interest payments, one based on a fixed rate and the other on a floating rate of interest, usually LIBOR.

The swap master agreement

The swap master agreement (typically drawn up under ISDA terms and conditions) will define:

- the terms and conditions of the swap;
- the payment procedures;
- the procedures for cancellation;
- the applicable law;
- the competent legal authority in the event of dispute.

Interest calculation bases

Interest calculations differ from country to country, currency to currency and market to market. The following are the usual alternative interest payment bases used in interest rate swaps:

- *bond basis*: 30/360 (360/360) – i.e. interest calculated on a 30-day month;
- *money market*: actual no. of days/360 (over 365 in the case of sterling and certain other currencies);
- *actual/actual:* actual/365 or 366 in a leap year.

Broken date interest rate swaps

Interest rate swaps are by nature long-term interest rate risk management instruments. If the swap does not extend to an exact number of calendar years, the broken period (stub) is usually agreed to be at the near end of the swap. The first, or sometimes first few, interest periods may then differ in length from later interest periods which will be planned to achieve the final maturity date with a standard period run.

Other structures

These days whatever the structure of risk to be hedged an interest rate swap can be tailored to suit a counterparty's specific requirements. Many institutions offer a service which relies heavily on innovation to provide structured solutions using the latest in financial engineering techniques. The interest rate swap is one of the modern market's most powerful and flexible financial tools.

Question

A typical ACI Dealing Certificate question might be:

The standard documentation for interest rate swaps is:

A: IMRO
B: LICOM
C: ISDA
D: ICC500

Correct answer

C: The standard terms and conditions governing interest rate swaps are those produced by the International Swaps and Derivatives Association (ISDA). IMRO stands for Investment Managers Regulatory Organization, an SRO (self-regulatory organization) under the terms of the UK Financial Services Act. LICOM stands for London Interbank Currency Options Market, a set of standard terms and conditions for currency options, while ICC500 are the International Chamber of Commerce Trade Finance standard terms for documentary credits.

Fixing of rates

The fixed and floating rates applicable to the swap will be fixed in accordance with current market conditions either on the commencement date (value same day currencies such as GBP) or two days before commencement date (value spot currencies – the majority of cases).

Long-term fixed interest rates will reflect market conditions in the appropriate bond markets. The floating interest rates used will frequently be a recognizable reference rate such as LIBOR. The most popular LIBOR periods for the floating side of interest rate swaps are three and six months, these being the most liquid cash market periods.

Uses of interest rate swaps

Interest rate swaps can be used to transform an investment or liability into an alternative form of interest pattern or currency basis. Periods range from one to two years out to 25 years. The longer-term swaps are frequently linked to capital investments or leasing transactions where a lease contract can be viewed as a stream of interest payments on the principal, the latter being the original value of the lease object.

Example transaction

A corporate treasurer (counterparty A) has a GBP 10 million six months roll-over facility from his bank. Three years of the roll-over facility remain. The treasurer is currently paying $6\frac{1}{4}$ percent (LIBOR $5\frac{1}{4}$ plus a margin of 1 percent) but has no control over the subsequent periods' cost of funds and is concerned that interest rates will rise. He looks to change his funding from Lending Bank plc from a floating LIBOR-based rate to a fixed rate for the remaining period of the loan. He arranges a swap as follows.

Note

> The treasurer is not tied to his lending banker. He can shop around various swap market making banks for the most attractive terms and here does the swap with Swap bank plc.

The basic transaction details of the plain vanilla interest rate swap:

Notional amount:	GBP 10 million
Fixed period:	3 years from value 31 March 200X
Fixed rate payer:	Counterparty A
Fixed rate:	8% semi-annual (inclusive of margin) money market*
Floating rate payer:	Swap bank plc
Floating rate:	6 months LIBOR

*The rate is recalculated on a more frequent payment basis (here semi-annually) to enable payment synchronization and netting to be effected easily.

Interest rate swaps are frequently depicted by boxes and arrows. The boxes represent the parties to a swap and the arrows indicate the interest payment flows between them. Figure 5.17 is a graphic presentation of the above swap.

The swap has a notional principal of GBP 10 million with six monthly payments between Counterparty A and Swap bank Plc synchronized and netted. The swap is totally divorced from the loan and does not affect the

Topic 4 (part): Money Market Derivatives

Fig 5.17

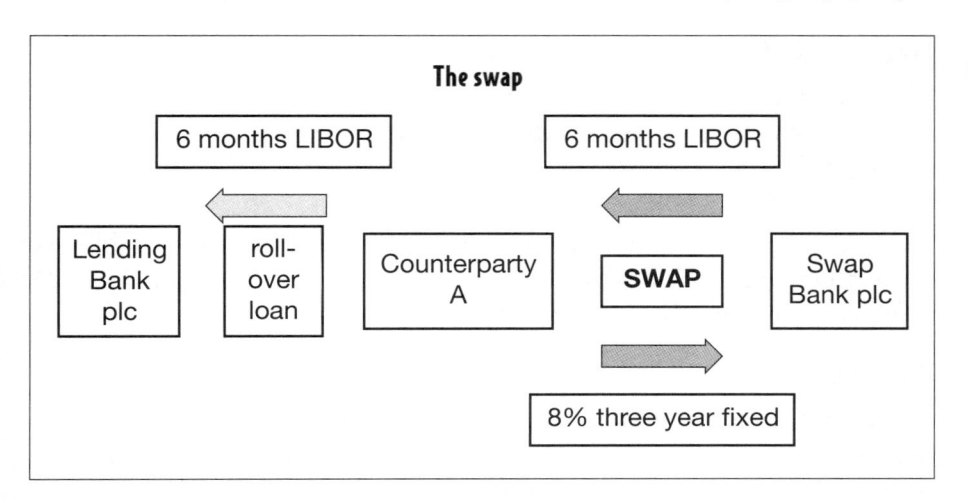

The swap

```
6 months LIBOR                    6 months LIBOR

Lending      roll-        Counterparty              Swap
Bank   <--   over   <---       A        <--- SWAP   Bank plc
plc          loan                        --->
                                    8% three year fixed
```

customer's relationship or liability towards Lending Bank plc. In this swap, every six months Counterparty A agrees to pay Swap Bank plc interest on GBP 10 million at a fixed interest rate of 8 percent and Swap Bank plc agrees to pay Counterparty A interest on GBP 10 million at the six months LIBOR agreed for each payment period over the life of the swap. The parties may agree to synchronize the payments, i.e. the fixed rate (if not already so) is calculated and agreed to be paid on a semi-annual basis (suffix s.a.).

Let us assume that the date is now 30 September 200X. Back in March 0X the six months LIBOR was fixed as 5 percent. The liabilities of the two parties under the swap on 30 September 200X are therefore:

$$\text{Counterparty A pays Swap bank plc GBP 401,095.89:} \frac{10 \text{ million} \times 183 \times 8.00}{365 \times 100}$$

$$\text{Swap bank plc pays Counterparty A GBP 250,684.93:} \frac{10 \text{ million} \times 183 \times 5.00}{365 \times 100}$$

Netting

Almost certainly Counterparty A and Swap Bank plc will have agreed to net payment exchanges and in this instance it will be Counterparty A who will pay the net amount of GBP 150,410.96 to Swap Bank plc value 30 September 200X.

Fixed v. LIBOR

The fixed rate will never differ but of course six months LIBOR will vary according to current market conditions at the start of each new rating period. As this is a GBP transaction six months LIBOR will in fact be fixed at 11.00 a.m. London time on the fixing date.

Had this been a US dollar or other eurocurrency swap this would have been done two business days prior to the interest payment date (28 September for value 30 September 200X).

Outcome

The overall effect of these transactions is that, while the corporate treasurer will continue to pay his lending banker periodic interest based on a fluctuating LIBOR basis, this cost is in fact met by the payment of LIBOR by Swap Bank plc under the terms of the swap (payments actually netted but the effect is the same). From the date of commencement of the swap the corporate treasurer is therefore paying the fixed rate of 8 percent agreed on the swap and has successfully converted his floating rate into fixed rate debt.

Currency (and interest rate) swaps

In this type of transaction the principal amounts in two different currencies are established at an agreed exchange rate at the outset. This rate of exchange will normally be at or near the prevailing spot rate for the swap commencement value date.

Whether these amounts are physically exchanged at the commencement of the currency swap depends upon the objectives of the counterparties. At final maturity the principal amounts will normally be physically exchanged at the same rate or an alternative rate agreed at the commencement of the swap. This, however, does not affect the off balance sheet nature of the transaction as forward foreign exchange transactions are contingent liabilities and themselves considered off the balance sheet.

Interest payment will be exchanged on the two currencies in accordance with the terms and conditions of the swap transaction. The most common type of currency swap is where one counterparty pays fixed in the first currency and receives the floating rate in the second currency.

Topic 4 (part): Money Market Derivatives

> **Question**
>
> A typical ACI Dealing Certificate question might be:
>
> Interest rate swaps and currency swaps can be used for many different purposes. Which of the following would *not* be an appropriate application of the instrument?
>
> A: Generating foreign currency assets from the purchase of domestic securities
> B: Covering short-term outright forward foreign exchange outstandings
> C: Hedging long-term lease contracts
> D: Arbitraging capital markets
>
> **Correct answer**
> B: Given the long-term nature of the interest rate swap and currency swap products they are not really effective for short-term covering or hedging. Swaps have been and continue to be applied against the other alternatives listed.

Currency and interest rate swaps uses

Currency and interest rate swaps, to give this type of transaction its correct name, are extremely useful in a commercial company's effort,

- *on the liability side* to protect against a rise in sterling interest rates by borrowing in a second currency
- *on the asset side* to hedge fluctuations in revenue streams due to currency/GBP exchange rate movement

to lock into current returns on any foreign currency denominated assets.

> **Question**
>
> A typical ACI Dealing Certificate question might be:
>
> Which "off balance sheet" derivative product can still involve an exchange of principal at maturity?
>
> A: A currency swap
> B: An FRA
> C: A collar
> D: A swaption
>
> **Correct answer**
> A: A currency swap – a currency and interest rate swap to give it its full title – can involve an exchange of principal at a rate of exchange (agreed at the outset) at maturity. As forward foreign exchange is a contingent item this in no way alters the off balance sheet nature of the instrument.

Uses for interest rate swaps in commerce

When a bank or commercial company is looking to fund itself in the medium term it must decide what the course of interest rates will be over the future period. What effect will those projected interest rates have on the bank/company? Can any increased funding costs be sustained?

For most companies the choice offered by their bankers will be either funding on a roll-over loan basis (floating rate) or funding on a fixed rate basis, either borrowing for as long a term as possible or by converting current floating rate debt into fixed rate via the medium of an interest rate swap.

Some companies may find it difficult to raise funds in the capital markets or on longer maturity terms than standard banking products. Using interest rate swaps linked with roll-over funding arrangements enables a company effectively to borrow over a period longer than usually available through the cash markets.

Swaps offer the opportunity to switch from one funding base to the other at any time and thus provide the bank/company with the means to modify its interest rate exposure according to its interest rate view while guaranteeing its future interest rate costs, making the budgeting process and cash flow management far easier tasks.

A bank/company can use currency (and interest rate) swaps to make its balance sheet immune to interest rate risk. In this case swaps enable the matching of fixed rate assets with fixed rate liabilities and floating rate assets with floating rate funding. A swap also enables a bank/company to make the most of any competitive advantage it may have in any financial sector.

Currency swaps allow a company to combine several loans in different currencies with different interest payment dates, amortizing schedules and interest rates into a single series of cash flows at an average interest rate.

> **Question**
>
> A typical ACI Dealing Certificate question might be:
>
> Interest rate swaps under ISDA terms can be fixed rate v. floating. Dealing in London, on which market rate is this floating rate most frequently based?
>
> A: UK clearing banks' base rate
> B: US banks' prime rate
> C: A rate agreed between bank and counterparty at re-rating dates
> D: LIBOR
>
> **Correct answer**
> D: The majority of interest rate swaps and currency swaps under ISDA terms use LIBOR three or six months as the reference rate for the floating side of the agreement.

Hedging decisions, however they are reached in a bank/company, can be made to optimize financial return and take advantage of any perceived expectations of trends and shapes of the yield curve in a particular currency or currencies.

Other structures

Most swap transactions relate to bullet maturities. However, swaps of many different profiles – amortizing, accreting and deferred starts – are readily available. Even compound operations such as swaptions (an option to enter into a swap) can be designed. The following is a list (not exhaustive) of some of the better known interest rate swap variants.

- *Deferred swap* – a swap used as a means of timing market entry, e.g. on a forward start basis, to lock into a perceived current low interest rate on a five-year loan facility, although draw down will only take place in one year's time. Where the yield curve is inverted the fixed rate payer will be able to lock into a more beneficial rate on a forward start compared to current rates. All terms, conditions and rates are agreed at the outset of a deferred swap.
- *Amortizing swap* – a swap where the balance (notional principal) reduces in accordance with repayments of a linked loan facility under a sinking fund type schedule.
- *Accreting swap* – a swap whose notional principal increases in line with the schedule of new draw downs on a linked roll-over facility.
- *Roller coaster swap* – a swap whose notional principal amount goes up and down (amortizing and accreting) in tandem with an underlying loan facility during the life of the transaction.
- *Circus swap* – a transaction which consists of both a currency swap and an interest rate swap with LIBOR-based pricing on both currencies involved.
- *Zero coupon swap* – a swap under which one counterparty makes a lump sum payment calculated on a discount basis typically (though not necessarily) at maturity instead of periodic payments over the life of the transaction.
- *Basis swap* – a swap between two floating rate indices, i.e. payments linked to six months LIBOR versus receipts based on commercial paper rates, with the intention of removing basis risk from different funding or portfolio management procedures.
- *Extendable swap* – one counterparty to the swap has the right to lengthen the transaction. This feature adds flexibility for that party who has to pay a premium (as in an option) for this privilege.

- *Putable swap* – the floating rate payer to the swap has the right to terminate the transaction prior to originally agreed maturity. For this privilege he has to accept a lower than market fixed rate.
- *Rate capped swap* – a swap where the floating rate element cannot rise above the capped rate. A front-end fee or premium is payable by the floating rate payer.

Asset-based swaps

This type of transaction is a broad category of any one of the above when combined with the purchase or sale of underlying market assets in order to diversify or limit credit, interest rate or currency risk. Through asset-based swaps synthetic assets or liabilities can be created whose characteristics would not naturally occur in the markets, e.g. fixed rate bonds combined with an interest rate swap to produce attractively priced, floating rate banking assets.

> **Question**
>
> A typical ACI Dealing Certificate question might be:
>
> Which of the following is a basis swap?
>
> A: Prime v. 3 months USD LIBOR
> B: 5 year JPY fixed v. 6 months EUR LIBOR
> C: 3 year USD fixed v. 6 months GBP LIBOR
> D: A CHF zero coupon swap
>
> **Correct answer**
> A: Prime v. 3 months USD LIBOR is an example of a basis swap.

FOR FURTHER READING

Financial futures

Wilmott, Howson and Dewynne (1995) *The Mathematics of Financial Derivatives*. Cambridge University Press.

Winstone, David (1995) *Financial Derivatives – Hedging with Futures, Forwards, Options and Swaps*. Chapman & Hall.

Forward rate agreements

BBA (1984) *FRABBA Standard Terms and Conditions*. British Bankers Association.
Walmsley, Julian (1998) *The New Financial Instruments*. Wiley.
Winstone, David (1995) *Financial Derivatives*. Chapman & Hall.

Interest rate swaps

Gup, Betnon E. and Brooks, Robert (1993) *Interest Rate Risk Management*. Probus.
Price and Henderson (1996) *Currency and Interest Rate Swaps*. Butterworths.
Petros Geroulanos, *Introduction to Swaps*. Securities Institute (services) Limited.

WEBSITES WORTH A VISIT

Financial futures

Euronext: www.euronext.com
International Money Market (CME): www.cme.com
LIFFE: www.liffe.com
MATIF: www.matif.com
EURONEXT: www.euronext.com

> **Hint**
>
> *All the world's financial futures exchanges have excellent websites and readily-available hard-copy marketing material. There is a vast amount of extremely useful information available both on the Internet and in complementary brochure form. You are advised to refer to the websites of the IMM, LIFFE, Euronext, MATIF and other leading exchanges for further information.*

Forward rate agreements

British Bankers Association: www.bba.org.com
International Swaps and Derivatives Association: www.isda.org.

Interest rate swaps

International Swaps and Derivatives Association: www.isda.org

Topic 5 · Spot Foreign Exchange

Introduction
Spot date
Target
Currencies traded
Market makers/market users
Spot rate
Spot rate spread
Spot rate calculations
Cross currency calculations
Interbank dealing methods
Rates information
Position keeping

Mastering the ACI Dealing Certificate

> **Overall objective**
>
> *To describe the trading practices in the spot market in the major currencies, to make rate selections based on market principles and to calculate cross rates.*
>
> *At the end of this section, candidates will be able to:*
>
> - *identify the main markets, their size and location;**
> - *interpret market practices successfully;*
> - *explain the difference between base currencies and quoted currencies;*
> - *calculate and use spot rates as market maker and market taker;*
> - *calculate cross rates correctly;*
> - *identify the mechanics and methods of trading;*
> - *identify the mechanics of market making;*
> - *explain the importance of liquidity.*

Note

There are 15 questions on foreign exchange (spot and forward) in the ACI Dealing Certificate – 7 textual multiple choice questions out of which candidates are required to gain a minimum of 42.80 percent to pass (3 out of 7) and 8 calculation multiple choice questions out of which candidates are required to gain a minimum of 37.50 percent to pass (3 out of 8).

INTRODUCTION

With the introduction of the euro in 1999, the spot FX desk may have lost a little of its "edge" but it is still the best example of a dynamic, information-driven market where positions taken give rise to instantly identifiable risks. The number of questions from this topic (spot and forward combined) emphasizes its importance.

The principles of market making and market using are most clearly displayed in the two-way spot exchange dealing price quoted by banks, transmitted by rates vendors' terminals and avidly reviewed and reported by the world's media.

If you can speedily and accurately identify the correct rate to deal on from varying points of view (market maker or market user as exemplified in the examiners' favoured question types) then this also stands you in good stead to understand the pricing methods of other more complex markets.

The initial bullet point of this topic (marked by an asterisk * in the objectives above) has already been addressed in Chapter 2 "Setting the scene".

Topic 5 · Spot Foreign Exchange

Remember, the examiners will strive to ask questions on the latest set of market statistics available. Those quoted in this edition date from the BIS triennial survey of April 2001 (published in October that year).

The acceptance in 2002 of the euro as the common form of physical money in 12 out of the 15 European Union countries (at the time of writing) in no way removes the need to understand the spot foreign exchange market. In Europe it may reduce the number of tradable currency pairs but, as we have seen over and over again, as long as there is one currency with an ever-changing relationship against another left in the world there will always be dealers looking to profit from this volatility and the overriding need to understand market forces will never disappear.

Major currency relationships are readily available on the rates screens of the world's banks. Some currency pairs are not so frequently traded and their rates have to be calculated from those rates freely available. To produce these cross rates the syllabus requires that you understand the basics of the quotation methods and the calculations needed.

Accurate *position keeping* is a vital aspect of all financial markets and in respect of spot dealing the syllabus treats this with such reverence that it merits its own separate topic section but not a separate question basket. However, for sake of continuity the issues are also addressed here.

SPOT DATE

The term "spot" is used in many markets. In the foreign exchange market, the spot value date is two working days forward from the deal date. These two working days may be influenced by weekends, holidays or other non-business days involving the closure of the clearing system in the financial centres of the two currencies involved in any exchange rate quotation. Foreign exchange is a cash settlement market and the transfers inwards of the currency bought and outwards of the currency sold must be able to be made on the date in question to make it a valid spot date. If a holiday or other closure affects this two-day period the spot value date moves forward to the next working day.

Spot date calculation rule

The rule for calculating the spot date is *today* + 2 business days forward in the USD/major currencies. Saturday and Sunday are not "business days" in Europe or America. When today is a Thursday, today + 2 will fall on the following Monday provided there are no financial centre holidays on that date.

Holidays and weekends (exceptions to the rule)

Care must be taken when a country has varying holiday dates between different financial centres – in Switzerland the Protestant and Catholic centres of Zurich and Lugano are an example. This also applies to domestic money market and forward foreign exchange dates.

Islamic weekend

The Middle East is another area which frequently causes problems in value dates and, indeed, each week requires a totally different technique in settlement procedures. The Islamic "weekend" is Thursday afternoon and Friday. Foreign exchange markets in the Gulf states are open over the "western weekend" and local currencies can be settled for Saturday and Sunday value dates.

The majority of such foreign exchange deals will be against the US dollar. To allow spot value dates for Middle Eastern currencies to follow the two working days practice, the settlement of US dollars on a Friday and the local currencies on the Saturday can be followed. The quoted spot rate will include the adjustment necessary for funding cost (to the Middle Eastern currency buyer) or benefit (to the Middle Eastern currency seller) of the US dollars involved over the western three-day weekend.

Processing time

Traditionally the two-day period between deal date and settlement has been used for banks and other financial institutions operating in the market to confirm the validity of the transactions, process the deals done, produce and despatch mail confirmations to each other, prepare their bookkeeping entries and, of course, make arrangements to remit the necessary currency to the counterparty to each deal on the value date.

In today's hi-tech world of electronic mail and international payment systems, these two days might seem unnecessary. However, one must not forget the time differences between the various dealing centres around the globe, necessitating the delay in order to synchronize payments in the two currencies involved in any exchange deal, and, most importantly, the ever-prudent approach of the banking fraternity in ensuring that no opportunity is missed to cross-check and confirm each and every transaction before final release of funds.

TARGET

Wherever euros are involved in a foreign exchange deal settlement the validity of any date is set by reference to the business days for the TARGET system (*Trans European Automated Real-Time Gross settlement Express Transfer system*), which is open on all weekdays during the year except Christmas Day and New Year's Day and other dates which are announced from time to time by the European Central Bank (www.ecb.int).

> **Question**
>
> A typical ACI Dealing Certificate question might be:
>
> Today is Tuesday, 30 December 200X. What is today's spot value date for dealing in GBP/USD?
>
> A: Friday 2 January 200Y
> B: Thursday 1 January 200Y
> C: Monday 5 January 200Y
> D: None of these
>
> **Correct answer**
>
> A: The rule for calculating spot date is today + 2 business days forward in the GBP and USD/major currency pairs. Today being a Tuesday the spot date would normally be a Thursday, but in this case this will be 1 January, a bank holiday in the United Kingdom, therefore spot date is Friday 2 January 200Y.

Ante-spot dates

Although spot date is the standard or benchmark value date dealt in the market, it is possible to deal for the two days prior to spot date (ante-spot). These transactions are either *outright value today* or *outright value tomorrow*.

The ability to deal prior to spot value depends of course upon the currencies involved, their geographical (time-zone) location in relation to the place of dealing, their domestic clearing system cut-off times and the short date covering possibilities available in the currencies concerned.

The rate for a value today or value tomorrow deal will be different from the spot date rate, and will be calculated by the dealer using the spot rate and the appropriate adjustment for the short dated foreign exchange swap cover required (cost or benefit of carry) to make the currency available on the date requested. The rules governing the spot rate adjustment to achieve the desired ante-spot value may be found in Chapter 7.

Short dates

Foreign exchange deals dealt for a value date anything for value up to one month from spot are termed "short date" transactions. The most frequently dealt operations are outright value today and value tomorrow requiring overnight fx swap (today against tomorrow) and tom/next fx swap (tomorrow against spot date) used both to calculate outright prices for corporate transactions and the covering of short dated cash flow requirements by dealers in the market.

CURRENCIES TRADED

The spot and forward interbank markets are well developed in certain currency pairings and less sophisticated in others. Major currencies may be assumed to be sterling, the US dollar, the euro and the principal non-EU European currencies together with the Japanese yen and other Far Eastern and Australasian currencies.

Minor currencies are those lesser traded currencies and the majority of emerging markets currencies.

Measure of value

It is the spot exchange rate which is the immediate measure of value of one currency in terms of another. There are close ties between many currencies, particularly in Europe. The Exchange Rate Mechanism (ERM) of the European Monetary System (EMS) leading up to the introduction of the euro in January 1999 is an example of such ties pre-EMU. It is still, however, each currency's rate against the euro or the US dollar that will be referred to by market commentators as the absolute measure of that currency's value, and outside EMU the majority of countries permit their domestic currency freely to float against the US unit.

For this reason – and given that the large proportion of international trade is invoiced in US dollars necessitating the most number of trade-related transactions – the "professional" interbank foreign exchange market deals primarily in foreign currencies quoted against the US dollar.

All other currency quotations, either against the euro, sterling or between other currencies (where US dollars and sterling are not involved these are frequently referred to as "cross currency" transactions), are available in local markets but sometimes may have to be calculated by using the USD/currency or EUR/currency exchange rates available.

The spot rate of a currency in the interbank market forms the basis for all other exchange rate quotations – in the case of sterling, from how a local high street branch will sell the foreign currency notes and coin you need for your summer holiday (but notice the wide spreads here) to the rate used to value a major multi-billion currency unit take-over in the international capital markets.

The spot exchange rate is also used as a benchmark rate for comparison purposes when the markets talk about forward exchange rates. In fact it is the spot rate which is the most important rate in the foreign exchange market.

MARKET MAKERS/MARKET USERS

Chapter 2 introduced the basic principals of market making and market using in the international OTC financial markets. By way of reprise, bank dealers can be both market makers to incoming calling financial institutions/corporate customers and market users when they call out to other interbank counterparties (see Figure 6.1).

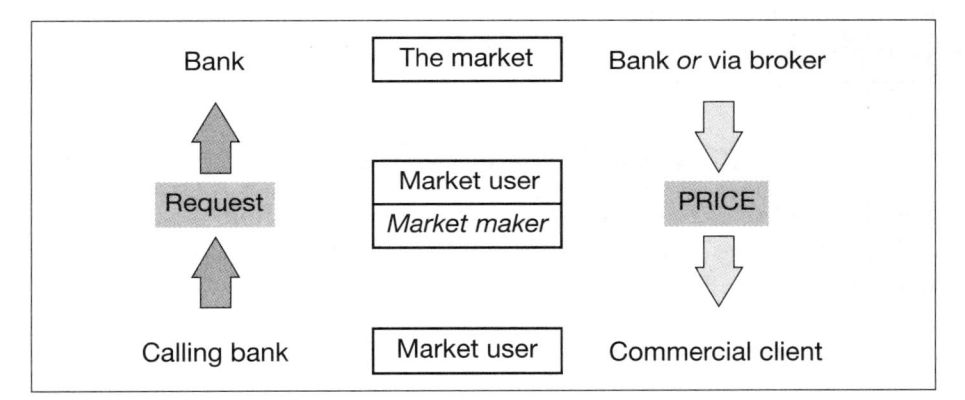

Fig 6.1

London and international foreign exchange quotation

To recap:

- *Spot foreign exchange*: bid–offer for the base currency.

Remember BOB! Bid offer for the base currency

Wherever in the world a spot rate is quoted it will always be low–high and the bid–offer terminology refers to the movement of the base currency on the spot value date.

SPOT RATE

Spot rate terminology

If we consider the situation in any of the major centres of the world quoting foreign exchange rates, market makers in each country quote their local currency against the US dollar and other foreign currencies on one of two bases – *direct* or *indirect* (reciprocal). But what is the difference and how do we know what to quote when asked to by a market user, or upon which side to deal when confronted with a market maker's spot price quotation?

Spot rate quotation

A spot rate is quoted in the interbank market as a two-way price in terms of one currency (the variable or quoted currency) against another (the base currency). As we have seen this base currency is frequently the US dollar (*direct* rate quotation).

Direct quoted currency (to a USD base)

For example, the Swiss franc spot exchange rate quotation against the US dollar indicates how many Swiss francs are equivalent to one US dollar. It is quoted to a US dollar base:

```
USD/CHF
1.66 00 – 10
```

This is how the rate might be quoted on a rates information service screen (e.g. Reuters). This rate can be expanded fully to 1.66 00–1.66 10.

SPOT RATE SPREAD

Just as in any market where a two-way price is quoted, there will be a difference between the buying and the selling price. In a fixed price market this would reflect the quoting bank's profit margin. While by definition this difference (termed the "spread") is indeed the quoting bank's profit margin, in reality rates fluctuate so quickly that it is rare indeed that the same two-way price will be quoted and/or dealt on simultaneously or twice running. As we have seen already:

Topic 5 · Spot Foreign Exchange

> USD/CHF
> 1.66 00 – 10
> means
> CHF 1.66 00 – 1.66 10 *per* USD 1

Note

A 10-point spread is used frequently in spot rate examples in this book for ease of quotation/illustration. This in no way suggests the market norm. The size of the spread will always depend upon the currency pair involved, market conditions at the time of quoting and even the creditworthiness of the market user in the eyes of the market maker.

Spot rate composition

In the interbank market a spot rate quoted on a direct basis, e.g. USD/CHF (to a USD base), is always quoted as a two way price described in dealer terms as "Big figure" and "points" (or pips):

USD/CHF 1.66 00 – 10	
1.66 "*big figure*"	00 – 10 "*points*" or "*pips*"

Within a dealing room and during telephone and other communications between dealers or dealers and brokers it is frequently the case that only the *points* or *pips* are quoted. It is assumed that someone in close contact with the market is aware of the current *big figure* of any price quotation.

The "figure"

The rate 1.66 00 or *any* spot quotation ending in "00" will frequently be quoted verbally as "one sixty-six 'the figure'". The two-way price noted above would be said "one sixty-six figure to ten" in inter-professional conversations. The term "the figure" can also be used for a rate quote of 1.65 90 – 00 or "one sixty-five ninety to 'the figure'", or when the rate quote is 1.65 95 – 05 when the rate can be quoted "ninety-five... oh five 'around the figure'", here 1.66.

In the real world, if in any doubt, there is nothing to lose and everything to gain by checking the "big figure" when points only rate quotations are made. Particularly where calculations are involved, ACI Dealing Certificate examination questions will have to stipulate foreign exchange rates in full.

"Points" or "pips"

The majority of major currency spot rates are quoted to four decimal places, where, in dealer terms, there are 10,000 "points" in a spot rate quote. Put another way, one point = $1/10\,000^{th}$ of a currency unit.

The exceptions to this rule are where the currency concerned is a relatively small unit in value, e.g. Japanese yen. In such instances the spot quote is made to two decimal places only and, again in dealer terms, there are only 100 "points" in a spot rate quote, so one point = $1/100^{th}$ of a currency unit. Such points are frequently termed "big points" by a dealer. For example:

USD/JPY
121.05 – 15

The number of decimal places is important when we come to discuss the calculation of forward exchange rates in Chapter 7, where dealing adjustments to be made to the spot rate need to be "right justified".

Alongside the USD/JPY there are several other currencies where this applies (though substantially less with the demise of the Italian lira, Greek drachma, Spanish peseta and Portuguese escudo following the introduction of the euro). The list of these currencies should be learnt although it is possible to make a reasoned judgement as to whether a currency pair should be quoted to two or four decimal places. This should mean no costly mistakes are made in the examination.

Hint

Typically, it is these same currencies (those which are quoted to two decimal places only) whose "cents" or equivalent minor units are considered too small to be included in banking transactions in the payments systems of their home countries.

Care!

Certain other currency pairs are quoted to three decimal places. These include the Czech koruna (CZK) and the Slovak koruna (SKK). These exceptions to the rule must be learnt.

Topic 5 · Spot Foreign Exchange

Note

This does not mean that an exchange rate will *never* be quoted to more than the spot exchange rate quoted number of decimal places. When markets are very quiet dealing spreads can narrow, with dealers quoting half point (or finer) spreads. Also points adjustments for transactions for value today or tomorrow (see Chapter 7 for the ante-spot rate calculation) will frequently be quoted to more than the spot exchange rate quoted number of decimal places.

Direct quoted currency (to a USD base)

Let us return to the Swiss franc spot exchange rate quotation against the US dollar:

> USD/CHF
> 1.66 00 – 10

This is how the rate might be quoted on a rates information service screen (e.g. Reuters). The rate can be expanded fully to: 1.66 00–1.66 10. This means the bank dealer quoting the rate (the *market maker*) will:

- on the left-hand side:
  – *buy* USD against CHF at 1.66 00
  – and conversely *sell* CHF against USD;

and will:

- on the right-hand side:
  – *sell* USD against CHF at 1.66 10
  – and conversely *buy* CHF against USD.

Bid and offer terminology (to a USD base)

The two-way price indicates the rates at which the bank is prepared both to buy or sell the base currency (here USD) and sell or buy the quoted or variable currency (here CHF).

In market terminology the left-hand side rate is described as the bid for US dollars (the offer of Swiss francs) and the right-hand side rate is described as the offer of US dollars (the bid for Swiss francs).

Indirect quoted currency (to a non-USD base)

The GBP/USD rate quote is traditionally referred to as "The Cable" (from its transatlantic cablegram communication beginnings):

> GBP/USD (to a non-USD base)
> 1.45 20 – 30

167

Mastering the ACI Dealing Certificate

This is how the GBP/USD rate might be quoted on a rates information service screen (e.g. Reuters). This rate can be expanded fully to: 1.45 20 – 1.45 30. This means the bank dealer quoting the rate (the *market maker*) will:

- on the left-hand side:
  – *buy* GBP against USD at 1.45 20
  – and conversely *sell* USD against GBP;

  and will:

  - on the right-hand side:
    – *sell* GBP against USD at 1.45 30
    – and conversely *buy* USD against GBP.

Indirect quoted currency – euro

While the majority of European currencies (pre-euro) were quoted on a direct basis, i.e. to a USD base similar to the Swiss franc above, since its introduction in January 1999 the euro has been similarly quoted on an indirect basis, i.e. to a euro (non-USD) base:

EUR/USD (to a non-USD base)
0.90 50 – 60

This is how the EUR/USD rate might be quoted on a rates information service screen (e.g. Reuters). This rate can be expanded fully to: 0.90 50 – 0.90 60. This means the bank dealer quoting the rate (the *market maker*) will:

- on the left-hand side:
  – *buy* EUR against USD at 0.90 50
  – and conversely *sell* USD against EUR;

  and will:

  - on the right-hand side:
    – *sell* EUR against USD at 0.90 60
    – and conversely *buy* USD against EUR.

Bid and offer terminology (to a GBP or non-USD, e.g. EUR, base)

The two-way price indicates the rates at which the bank is prepared both to buy–sell the base currency (here GBP or EUR) and sell–buy the quoted or variable currency (here USD).

Hint *Remember, in the interbank market dealers always refer to the* bid *and* offer *for the* base *currency. Remember BOB.*

Base and quoted currencies

With two currencies in any exchange rate quotation, for clarity between the market making/market using sides and to avoid unnecessary mistakes being made in fast-moving markets, dealers tend to describe currency pair transactions with reference made to only one of the two currencies involved.

This means that dealers will typically refer to and prefer to deal in "round amounts" of the base currency of any foreign exchange quote. Although sometimes regrettably not rigorously followed, a simple rule is that the base currency will normally be the currency mentioned first in any exchange rate relationship. The base currency is typically the currency appearing before the forward slash in any ISO code description, e.g. EUR/USD (base currency = EUR) or USD/JPY (base currency = USD).

Choosing the best rate as market user

In a dynamic market such as the spot foreign exchange market, rates move second by second. When acting as market user calling other banks, different exchange rates quoted can only be compared if they are obtained at precisely the same time. In the following examples as laid out in the ACI Dealing Certificate it must be assumed that all two-way dealing prices are available simultaneously – let us say that they are being shouted to you from across the dealing room by dealing colleagues each of whom at your request has made a call out to a different market-making bank.

As we have seen, a two-way price is made up of two rates (bid–offer). It will depend on your requirements as to which of any prices received best suits you. It may not always be one side of the closest two-way price quoted.

> *This is a favourite question type in the* ACI Dealing Certificate *examination.*

Hint

Market user buys base currency (USD against JPY)

In a direct quoted currency pair transaction, if you are buying the base currency (here USD) as a *market user*, you obviously want to buy it at the cheapest rate (paying the least variable currency) quoted to you by a market maker.

```
121.08 – 18
121.09 – 14
121.10 – 15
121.03 – 13
```

In this example you want to pay the least JPY for USD and have to deal on the lowest rate of those quoted on the right-hand side of the market makers' two-way prices (the market maker's offer of USD, bid for JPY) – the best USD *offer* available – here 121.13.

Market user sells base currency (USD against CHF)

In a direct quoted currency pair transaction, if you are selling the base currency (here USD) as a *market user*, you obviously want to sell it at the highest rate (receiving the most variable currency) quoted to you by a market maker.

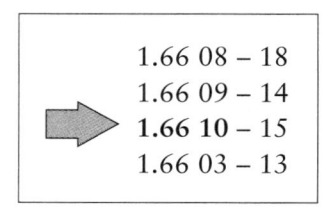

```
1.66 08 – 18
1.66 09 – 14
1.66 10 – 15
1.66 03 – 13
```

In this example you want to receive the most CHF for USD and have to deal on the highest rate of those quoted on the left-hand side of the market makers' two-way prices (the market maker's bid for USD, offer of CHF) – the best USD *bid* available – here **1.66.10**.

Market user buys variable currency (DKK against USD)

In a direct quoted currency pair transaction, if you are buying the quoted (variable) currency (the non-USD currency) as a *market user*, you obviously want to buy it at the best rate (receiving the most variable currency for the base currency units paid away) quoted to you by a market maker.

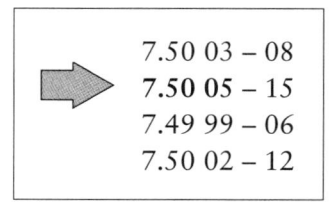

```
7.50 03 – 08
7.50 05 – 15
7.49 99 – 06
7.50 02 – 12
```

In this example you want to receive the most DKK for USD and have to deal on the highest rate of those quoted on the left-hand side of the market makers' two-way prices (the market maker's bid for USD, offer of DKK) – the best USD *bid* available – here 7.50 05.

Market user sells variable currency (SGD against USD)

In a direct quoted currency pair transaction, if you are selling the quoted (variable) currency (the non-USD currency) as a *market user*, you obviously want to sell it at the cheapest rate (paying away the least variable currency to receive the base currency units) quoted to you by a market maker.

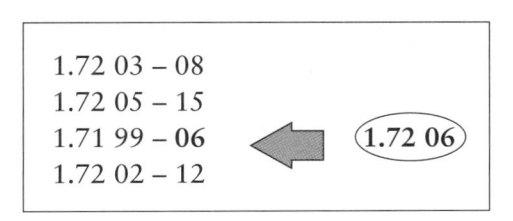

```
1.72 03 – 08
1.72 05 – 15
1.71 99 – 06      ⬅  (1.72 06)
1.72 02 – 12
```

In this example you want to pay the least SGD for USD and have to deal on the lowest rate of those quoted on the right-hand side of the market makers' two-way prices (the market maker's offer of USD, bid for SGD) – the best USD *offer* available – here 1.72 06.

The rate quote in the last example goes "around the figure" – the figure being 1.72 00.

Care!

A typical ACI Dealing Certificate question might be:

Four banks in the international market quote you spot USD/JPY. Which is the best quote for you as a buyer of JPY?

A: 121.49 – 53
B: 121.45 – 51
C: 121.50 – 57
D: 121.47 – 52

Correct answer

C: Here you are buying the variable or quoted currency (the non-USD currency) as a market user, you therefore want to receive the most JPY for USD and have to deal on the highest rate of those quoted on the left-hand side of the market makers' prices (the market maker's bid for USD, offer of JPY – here 121.50).

Question

Indirect quotation to a non-USD base

To avoid confusion, rather than repeat the above examples for an indirect quoted currency pair transaction such as GBP/USD or EUR/USD the logic is the same but the base currency will be GBP or EUR (the non-USD currency) and the variable currency in both cases the US dollar. The dealing sides as per the above sections are still appropriate bearing in mind this subtle difference.

Question

A typical ACI Dealing Certificate question might be:

Four banks offer a corporate treasurer a two-way price in the AUD/USD. From which bank will she buy AUD against USD?

A: 0.5270/75
B: 0.5272/77
C: 0.5274/79
D: 0.5268/73

Correct answer

D: The AUD is quoted against the USD on an indirect basis, i.e. to a AUD base, and the market maker's rate quote is therefore bid–offer for AUD. The cheapest rate at which the customer can buy the AUD is therefore the lowest on the offered side for AUD (the right-hand side) = 0.5273.

Euro quotes against sterling

At the time of the euro's introduction the European Monetary Institute (EMI) suggested, and market associations accepted, that the euro should be quoted in the foreign exchange market on a "certain for uncertain" basis against all currencies (i.e. euro 1 = USD x or euro 1 = GBP y).

EUR/GBP
0.62 05 – 15

The Bank of England announced in late 1998 that it would quote on this basis, EUR/GBP – a change from the traditional exchange rate quotations made against sterling where sterling has been the "certain" or base currency, e.g. GBP/USD. Wholesale market participants have adopted this method of quotation and although it would avoid confusion and misunderstanding if this method were universally accepted there is no requirement to quote on this basis.

Topic 5 · Spot Foreign Exchange

Sterling quotes against the euro

In the lead-up to January 1999 in the United Kingdom, the British Bankers Association decreed that while its members would quote rates on a EUR/GBP basis in the interbank markets, they would continue to quote GBP/EUR for commercial customers, on the basis that while the UK remains outside the euro, a change in convention was likely to cause confusion. Therefore in such circumstances in London the exchange rate for EUR against sterling may be quoted in the retail market to a GBP base.

To calculate a retail market quote on a GBP/EUR basis from the interbank EUR/GBP rate all that is required is a straightforward reciprocal calculation, i.e. 1 *divided by* the EUR/GBP rate. Care must be taken, however, in that the left-hand side of the EUR/GBP (bid for EUR/offer of GBP) will become the right-hand side of the GBP/EUR rate (offer of GBP/bid for EUR) and vice versa – see Figure 6.2.

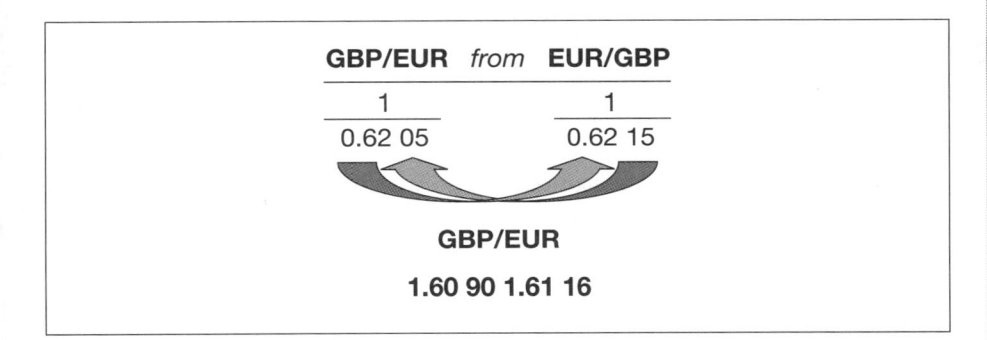

Fig 6.2

$$\text{GBP/EUR} \quad \text{from} \quad \text{EUR/GBP}$$

$$\frac{1}{0.62\ 05} \qquad \frac{1}{0.62\ 15}$$

GBP/EUR

1.60 90   1.61 16

Question

A typical ACI Dealing Certificate question might be:

You quote a corporate customer EUR/GBP 0.63 65–70. He asks to deal at the reciprocal rate of 1.57 10. What have you done?

A: You buy EUR at 1.57 10
B: You buy EUR at 0.63 70
C: You sell EUR at 1.57 10
D: You sell EUR at 0.63 65

Correct answer
A: At the reciprocal rate of 1.57 10 *you* buy EUR (1 divided by 0.63 65).

> **Hint**
>
> ACI Dealing Certificate *multiple choice questions requiring a reciprocal quote to be calculated from a single two-way price can ask how you sell or buy one or other of the currencies involved on a reciprocal basis. Be careful to choose the correct side of the quoted price before making the above calculation as you can bet that any wrongly calculated answer will be one of the multiple choice answer options!*

SPOT RATE CALCULATIONS

The ACI Dealing Certificate examination includes calculation multiple choice questions which will require cross currency quotes to be calculated from the US dollar or other based currency pair rates available on Reuters screens and from the market.

Cross currency – from one direct and one indirect quoted currency pair: condition 1

Many market making banks will quote spot exchange rates against US dollars, sterling and other major currencies (cross currency dealing) for both interbank and corporate customer deals. Where rates are available only against US dollars on rates information screen displays such as Reuters, a simple calculation is all that is required to work out the exchange rate for any currency against sterling.

In the case of UK banks where corporates require rates against sterling, the calculations below will normally be effected by the corporate dealer before any rate quote is made to the customer.

Example calculations (rates against GBP)

The Swiss franc against the US dollar is quoted as follows:

```
USD/CHF
1.66 00 – 10
```

This rate can be expanded fully to: 1.66 00 – 1.66 10.

As we have already seen the bank dealer quoting the rate (the market maker) will (on the left-hand side) buy USD against *CHF* (and conversely *sell CHF* against USD) at 1.66 00 and will (on the right-hand side) sell USD against *CHF* (and conversely *buy CHF* against USD) at 1.66 10.

Sterling against the US dollar (Cable) is quoted as follows:

GBP/USD
1.45 20 – 30

This rate can be expanded fully to: 1.45 20 – 1.45 30.

Again, this means the bank dealer quoting the rate (the market maker) will (on the left-hand side) buy GBP against *USD* (and conversely *sell USD* against GBP) at 1.45 20 and will (on the right-hand side) sell GBP against *USD* (and conversely *buy USD* against GBP) at 1.45 30.

Remember the USD/CHF exchange rate is quoted in terms of so many Swiss francs *equivalent to* USD 1 (direct quotation) and the GBP/USD exchange rate is quoted in terms of so many US dollars *equivalent to* GBP 1 (indirect/reciprocal quotation).

From this it can be seen that in terms of unit size the Swiss franc is a smaller unit than the US dollar and the US dollar is a smaller unit than the pound sterling. This can be displayed as in Figure 6.3.

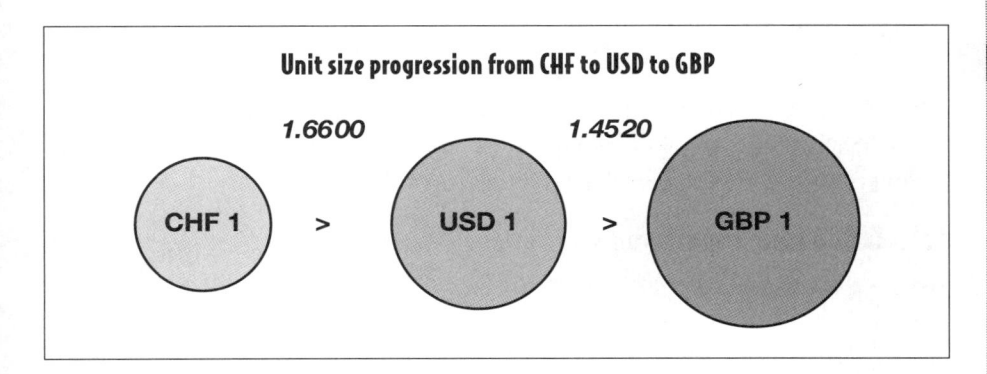

Unit size progression from CHF to USD to GBP

CHF 1 > 1.6600 USD 1 > 1.4520 GBP 1

Fig 6.3

As with the Cable quotation, since sterling is a larger unit of value, the CHF will be quoted to a GBP base i.e. so many CHF per GBP.

Cash flows

Therefore to calculate a GBP/CHF exchange rate quotation we have to use the sides of the USD/CHF and GBP/USD prices which will give us a resultant two-way price to *sell CHF* and buy GBP on one hand, and to *buy CHF* and sell GBP on the other.

This is achieved by working through the cash flows generated as if dealing through the US dollar rates and compensating the US dollar movements. The following are viewed from the quoting bank's (market maker's) point of view:

1. Bank **sells** CHF
Bank *buys* USD **	1.66 00
	multiplied by = 2.41 03 (20)
Bank *sells* USD **	1.45 20
   Bank **buys** GBP

The US dollar movement (**) nets out in the above simple cash flow leaving us with the market maker's buying rate for GBP against CHF (conversely the selling rate for CHF against GBP).

2. Bank **buys** CHF
Bank *sells* USD **	1.66 10
	multiplied by = 2.41 34 (33)
Bank *buys* USD **	1.45 30
   Bank **sells** GBP

The US dollar movement (**) nets out in the above simple cash flow leaving us with the market maker's selling rate for GBP against CHF (conversely the buying rate for CHF against GBP).

Calculation rule: condition 1

As the quotes used are so many CHF per USD and so many USD per GBP we can:

- *multiply* the two lowest rates (the two *left-hand sides*) in the original rate quotations above for the currency selling rate against sterling; and similarly
- *multiply* the two highest rates (the two *right-hand sides*) in the original quotations above for the currency buying rate against sterling.

Therefore the two-way price GBP against CHF:

2.41 03 – 2.41 34
Swiss francs
per pound sterling

> **Note**
>
> In such calculations a bank dealer may either adjust his spread to be an exact number of points (dealers favour 5 or 10 for ease of quotation) or will truncate the left-hand round up the right-hand side of any quotations so calculated. A similar approach is typically followed in the ACI Dealing Certificate examination.

> **Question**
>
> A typical ACI Dealing Certificate question might be:
>
> A client wants to sell CHF against GBP. The USD/CHF rate is 1.4915/20, the GBP/USD rate is 1.4628/33. What rate do you quote to the client?
>
> A: 2.18 24
> B: 2.18 32
> C: 2.18 17
> D: 2.18 47
>
> Correct answer
> B: Here we have a cross rate calculated from a direct quote – USD/CHF – and an indirect (non-USD base quote) – GBP/USD. Therefore multiply your offer of USD (bid for CHF) by your offer of GBP (bid for USD) – right-hand side by right-hand side to achieve the rate of 2.18 32.

CROSS CURRENCY CALCULATIONS

Cross currency rates are traditionally those exchange rate quotations which neither include the US dollar nor the pound sterling as one of the currencies. With the introduction of the euro as another major base currency we can also include any currency pairs not including the euro in this definition.

Where a price is required for such a currency quotation the rate could be expressed as changing a number of Currency 1 units to a Currency 2 base or changing a number of Currency 2 units to a Currency 1 base.

> **Hint**
>
> *The financial centre, international market convention or the customer's transaction request (or the examiner's* ACI Dealing Certificate *question wording) will dictate the method of quotation to be followed.*

Example quotation (cross currency)

Most exchange rates for cross currency transactions will be made following either international or local market convention.

When a cross rate quote is sought outside either of the countries whose currencies are involved, the rate quotation will be made according to international market conventions. These dictate a priority list of currencies and where neither the USD nor EUR are present (ranked 1 and 2) the next highest ranking currency will be taken as the base currency of the price quote.

Should the alternative quotation method be requested, however, the rate can be quoted on either basis, according to the preference of the dealing counterparties. Remember, the base currency should normally be written before the forward slash "/" in any currency pair description e.g. CHF/JPY.

For example, with USD/CHF quoted as 1.66 00 – 10 and USD/JPY quoted 121.05 – 15, the CHF/JPY rate may be quoted by a bank dealer as a *direct* quotation (to a CHF base) of:

CHF/JPY
72.88 – 72.98
Japanese yen *per* Swiss franc

Cross currency calculation methods

The above rate was possibly quoted in the international market but how do you calculate a cross rate from the two currency pair rates noted? The method of calculation of a cross currency rate is dependent upon how the individual currency pairs are quoted (i.e. direct or indirect counter currency = USD).

Cross currency – from two direct quoted currencies (both to a USD base): condition 2

The CHF/JPY cross currency rate quotation is an example. The priority order of currencies/simplicity of rate quote already mentioned determines that the Swiss franc will be the base currency of this quote (see Figure 6.4).

Where the two currencies involved are *direct* quoted currencies against the US dollar (both USD/CHF and USD/JPY are quoted to a USD base), the cross currency rate quotation will be the result of *cross dividing* the two USD-based rates.

Topic 5 · Spot Foreign Exchange

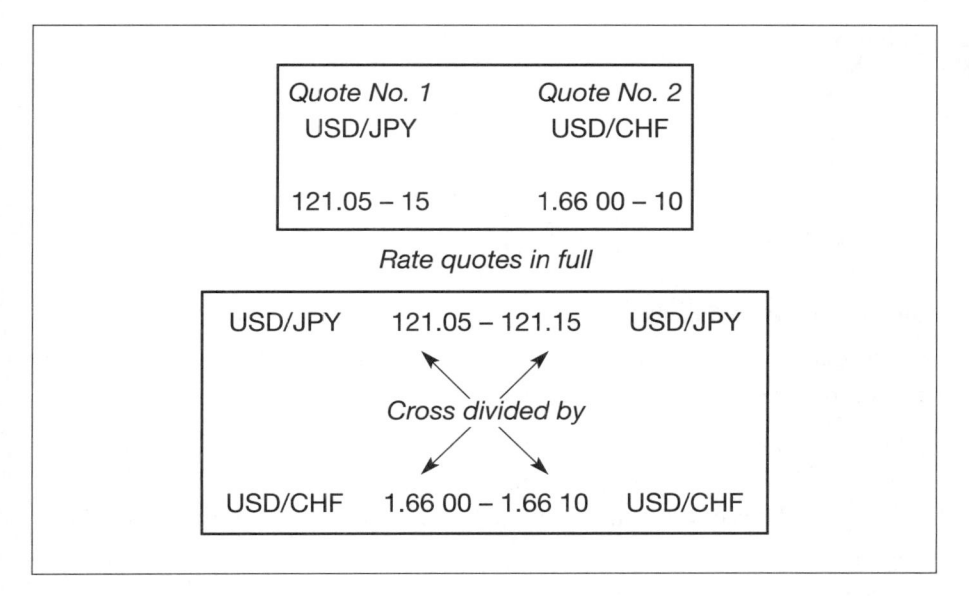

Fig 6.4

```
        Quote No. 1          Quote No. 2
        USD/JPY              USD/CHF

        121.05 – 15          1.66 00 – 10
```

Rate quotes in full

```
USD/JPY    121.05 – 121.15    USD/JPY

              Cross divided by

USD/CHF    1.66 00 – 1.66 10   USD/CHF
```

Cash flows

To see this clearly look at the actual cash flows generated by the necessary USD/CHF and USD/JPY deals against the US dollar (as we did with rates against GBP earlier).

1. Bank **sells JPY**

Bank *buys USD* **	121.05
	divided by = 72.87 (77)
Bank *sells USD* **	1.66 10

   Bank **buys CHF**

The US dollar movement (**) nets out in the above cash flow leaving us with the market maker's buying rate for CHF against JPY (conversely the selling rate for JPY against CHF).

2. Bank **buys JPY**

Bank *sells USD* **	121.15
	divided by = 72.98 (19)
Bank *buys USD* **	1.66 00

   Bank **sells CHF**

The US dollar movement (**) nets out in the above cash flow leaving us with the market maker's selling rate for CHF against JPY (conversely the buying rate for JPY against CHF).

Therefore the two-way price CHF against JPY:

> 72.88 – 72.98
> Japanese yen
> *per* Swiss franc
> (rounded)

Calculation rule: condition 2

As the quotes used are so many JPY per USD and so many CHF per USD (both direct to a USD base), we must:

- *divide* the opposing sides of the prices (the left-hand side of Quote No. 1 by the right-hand side of Quote No. 2) of the original rate quotations above for the cross currency selling rate for JPY against CHF; and similarly
- *divide* the opposing sides of the prices (the right-hand side of Quote No. 1 by the left-hand side of Quote No. 2) of the original rate quotations above for the cross currency selling rate for CHF against JPY.

With rates for the currencies against the US dollar quoted above as USD/CHF 1.66 00 – 10 and USD/JPY 121.05 – 15 the cross rate for Japanese yen to a Swiss franc base (as quoted in the interbank market) is:

> CHF/JPY
> 72.88 – 72.98 JPY *per* CHF

But should the quote be requested to a Japanese yen base this will be made as:

> JPY/CHF
> 1.3702 – 1.3721 CHF *per* JPY 100
> (rounded)

In effect, CHF 0.013702 – 0.013721 per JPY 1 (sometimes a quote in this manner may suit a customer's requirements) is then adjusted two decimal places to the right to be the equivalent of JPY 100.

Differences in size of currency unit

Either where the two currencies of any quote are similar in currency unit size or where there is a dramatic difference in size of currency units involved in a calculated cross rate, such an exchange rate can be quoted in terms of 100 units of one of the currencies. One method of quoting, is in fact the reciprocal of the other, adjusted by two decimal places.

Quotation logic

Remember spot rates are always quoted low–high. The sides of the quote therefore change depending which way any of the above calculations are effected.

> **Question**
>
> A typical ACI Dealing Certificate question might be:
>
> USD/CHF is 1.52 50/55 and USD/JPY is 120.20/25. What price would you quote to a customer who wishes to sell JPY against CHF?
>
> A: 78.79
> B: 78.82
> C: 78.81
> D: 78.85
>
> **Correct answer**
> D: To calculate a cross currency rate for CHF/JPY with both currency pairs quoted on a direct basis (to a USD base) you must cross divide the two exchange rates for the currencies against USD. Here divide USD/JPY base currency offer (where we buy JPY) of 120.25 by the USD/CHF base currency bid of 1.52 50 (where we sell CHF) – result: 78.85.

> **Hint**
>
> *Be careful not to truncate/round up in the middle of a sequence of calculations. It is always a good idea to go back to the original rates against the US dollar if you are asked to change a quotation method from direct to indirect or vice versa.*

Cross currency – from two indirect quoted currencies (both to a non-USD base): condition 3

Where the two currencies involved are both *indirect* quoted currencies against the US dollar (e.g. GBP/USD and AUD/USD), the cross currency rate quotation will similarly be the result of *cross dividing* the two rates against USD.

As an example we will look at the GBP/AUD cross currency rate quotation. The priority order of currencies/simplicity of rate quote already mentioned determines that *GBP* will be the base currency of this quote (see Figure 6.5).

Fig 6.5

```
         Quote No. 3              Quote No. 4
         GBP/USD                  AUD/USD

         1.45 20 – 30             0.52 50 – 60
```

Rate quotes in full

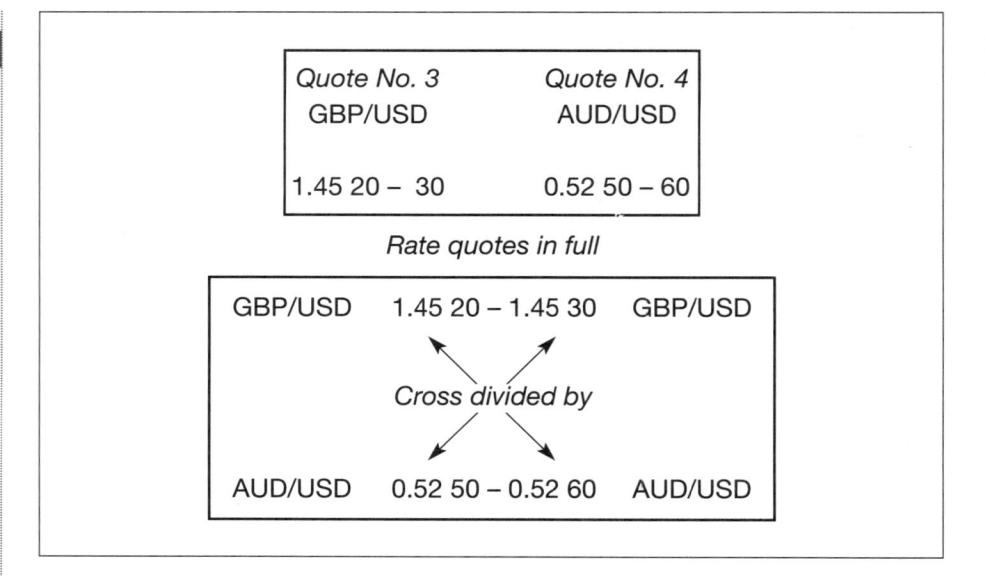

```
GBP/USD    1.45 20 – 1.45 30    GBP/USD

              Cross divided by

AUD/USD    0.52 50 – 0.52 60    AUD/USD
```

Where the two currencies involved are *indirect* quoted currencies against the US dollar (both GBP/USD and AUD/USD are quoted to a non-USD base), the cross currency rate quotation will be the result of *cross dividing* the two non-USD based rates.

Cash flows

To see this clearly look at the actual cash flows generated by the necessary GBP/USD and AUD/USD deals:

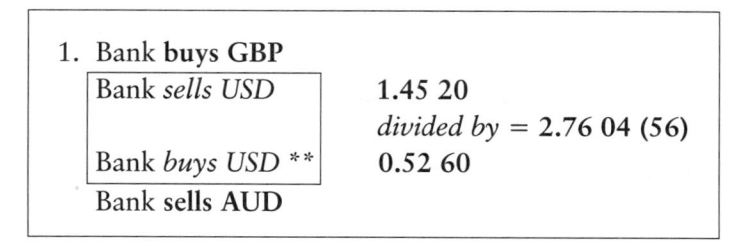

```
1. Bank buys GBP
   Bank sells USD       1.45 20
                        divided by = 2.76 04 (56)
   Bank buys USD **     0.52 60
   Bank sells AUD
```

The US dollar movement (**) nets out in the above cash flow leaving us with the market maker's buying rate for GBP against AUD (conversely the selling rate for AUD against GBP).

```
2. Bank sells GBP
   Bank buys USD **     1.45 30
                        divided by = 2.76 76 (19)
   Bank sells USD **    0.52 50
   Bank buys AUD
```

Topic 5 · Spot Foreign Exchange

The US dollar movement (**) nets out in the above cash flow leaving us with the market maker's selling rate for GBP against AUD (conversely the buying rate for AUD against GBP).

Therefore the two way price GBP against AUD:

> 2.76 05 – 2.76 76
> Australian dollars
> *per* pound sterling
> (rounded)

Cross currency calculation rules

To summarize, the method of calculation of a cross currency exchange rate is dependent upon whether the two currencies involved are:

1. one direct (to a USD base) and one indirect (to a non-USD base) quoted currency against the US dollar: **condition 1**

    multiply the same sides

    (left-hand side by left-hand side and right-hand side by right-hand side)

2. both direct quoted currencies against the US dollar (to a USD base): **condition 2**

    or

3. both indirect quoted currencies against the US dollar (to a non-USD base): **condition 3**

    cross divide opposite sides

    (left-hand side by right-hand side and right-hand side by left-hand side).

Hint

Remember there are 8 foreign exchange calculation questions (spot and forward combined) in the ACI Dealing Certificate *examination. Cross currency questions will more than likely feature prominently in respect of any spot multiple choice questions.*

Mastering the ACI Dealing Certificate

Question

> A typical ACI Dealing Certificate question might be:
>
> USD/CHF is quoted 1.5005/15 and GBP/USD as 1.6120/30. At what rate could you buy GBP and sell CHF?
>
> A: 2.4188
> B: 2.4203
> C: 2.4219
> D: 1.0742
>
> **Correct answer**
> C: USD/CHF is a direct quoted currency pair; GBP/USD is an indirect quoted currency pair. To calculate a rate for GBP against CHF you must multiply the appropriate sides of the two currency pair prices. Here, to produce a buying rate for GBP against CHF, you must multiply the left-hand side of the GBP/USD rate by the left-hand side of the USD/CHF exchange rate.

INTERBANK DEALING METHODS

Spot foreign exchange

The spot market is the most volatile and fast moving of the markets in which a foreign exchange dealer will be involved. The methods used in spot rate quotations apply equally to banks dealing with each other direct or with other counterparties, or operating through brokers in the foreign exchange market.

In any interbank dealing contact it is the bank dealer initiating the call who always requests the spot rate quotation from the bank dealer whom he has called. The calling bank is therefore the market user and the quoting bank the market maker. This is the same relationship that a corporate customer has with his bankers.

Interbank dealing conversation

A direct dealing telephone call from one bank dealer (market user) to another (market maker) can be a very short conversation.

After telephone connection is achieved to a market maker, the basic requirements are for the dealer initiating the call to identify his/her bank, request the spot rate sought, listen to the quoting bank's response and then, if appropriate (i.e. the quoted rate(s) suit the calling bank), effect the desired deal and agree all details.

Dealing conversation example

> *Calling bank*: "Hi there, High Street Bank, it's Dealing Bank London here. How's spot Cable please?"
>
> *Quoting bank*: "Hello there Dealing Bank; spot Cable – I make you 1.50 00 – 10." [said...one fifty...figure to ten]
>
> *Calling bank*: "At 10 I buy 5 million pounds sterling please."
>
> This is frequently simplified to "At 10, 5 million (please)" – the dealers appreciate that they are dealing in round amounts of sterling (the base currency) in interbank Cable quotations.
>
> *Quoting bank*: "OK, that's agreed. So to confirm: * value spot (date...) Dealing Bank buys GBP 5,000,000 at 1.50 00 10 from High Street Bank...."
>
> Once the quoting bank (market maker) has used any wording signifying acceptance of the deal requested that is the moment on contract. My word is my bond is still the market maxim.
>
> *Calling bank*: "Yes, all agreed, thanks...Sterling by CHAPS direct to me and where for your US dollars?"
>
> *Quoting bank*: "Fine, my spot dollars to my New York office please. Thanks for the deal. Goodbye."
>
> *Calling bank*: "OK. Thanks and goodbye."

The duration of such a typical spot dealing conversation over the telephone would be as long as it takes you to read the relevant passage (possibly shorter)! The actual deal takes a matter of seconds, the verbal confirmation (*) that follows takes slightly longer and is vital for three reasons:

- *first*, to ensure that both parties have understood what is being transacted;
- *second*, to ensure that full settlement (nostro payment) details are passed;

> In some financial centres in transactions between local banks – London is an example – it is not market practice for dealers to exchange settlement instructions at the time of dealing, this being effected by the back office/processing department as the first independent confirmation that the deal exists (see Chapter 9).

- *third*, to ensure the deal in full is recorded on the dealing room tape recording equipment. All dealing conversations are recorded so that they can later be referred to should any dispute arise on deal details.

Deals requested and effected over other electronic means such as the Reuters screen-based dealing system may be even more abbreviated. The important thing to remember is that both parties must be absolutely sure of all details (counterparty, purchase or sale, amount, rate, value date, payment instructions) relating to a transaction dealt in any type of conversation.

Assumptions

The above dealing conversation assumes that:

- High Street Bank has a credit limit in place with Dealing Bank plc;
- there is sufficient exposure available under this limit for High Street Bank to quote a two-way price "unqualified" by amount; and
- at this point in time High Street Bank is prepared to act as market maker and quote the spot currency rate requested.

Quoting and dealing

A quoting bank is not obliged to make a price and may decline to do so if the request does not suit him, nor is a calling bank obliged to deal when quoted. He too may decline with words such as "Thanks, nothing for me" or some other term which indicates no intention to deal. This intention or not must be made clear as promptly as possible.

Care!

> Words such as "the same" or "parity" should be avoided as a response to a price quotation as these can lead to confusion and could suggest a similar price is being quoted back to the initial market maker.

Hint

> *Dealing jargon used in the financial markets features in* ACI Dealing Certificate *examination questions. Much of the terminology used can be found in the ACI Model Code (covered in Chapter 11 and Appendix II of this book).*

Through a broker

The situation is slightly different when a bank deals through a broker. The calling bank can either be dealing with the broker "at the price" (as a market user), in other words *hitting* the bid (selling) or *taking* the offer (buying) in the market, or he can "put the broker on" by making a two-way price or merely bidding/offering to provide the broker with support for both or one side of his two-way price, or bid/offer inside the broker's current market spread (narrowing the price). In these latter cases the dealer will be acting as market maker through the broker.

Via electronic deal-matching systems

As identified in the recent BIS Basel survey a growing proportion of transactions between professional traders is effected via screen-based electronic matching systems such as Reuters 2000/2 deal matching and Electronic Broking Services (EBS) matching systems.

These systems require participants to enter into a restricted-access database their credit limits. The system then permits them to deal either as market makers inputting their bid, offer or two-way dealing prices, or as market users (aggressors) hitting a screen-based live bid (yours) or taking a similarly input live offered rate (mine).

The screen will only ever show prices which are able to be traded on by the viewer (an outcome of the credit limits held in the system) and transactions effected are instantaneously confirmed on-screen. Deal details are available electronically to both dealing parties and this information can be used to pass data to back-office deal processing systems without further (or with limited) human intervention.

Question

A typical ACI Dealing Certificate question might be:

Spot EUR/USD is quoted by the broker 0.93 00 – 10. You have an interest to sell EUR at 0.93 07 and put him on at that level. What does this make his new two-way price to the market?

A: 0.93 07 – 10
B: 0.93 00 – 07
C: 0.93 07 either way
D: 0.93 00 – 10

Correct answer

B: You want to sell EUR at 0.93 07, you put the broker on (you advise him of your offer at 07). He is currently bid 0.93 00. Your offer is an improvement on his current offer of 0.93 10, making his new price to the market 0.93 00 – 07.

For information/indication

A broker or market maker can qualify his price as being for information or indication only, meaning that there is no intention to quote a firm dealing price (see also Chapter 11 on the Model Code).

The quotation may also be qualified for or up to a specified amount. If no such qualification is made the price may be assumed by the calling bank to be at least for the minimum marketable amount – this can vary according to currency and counterparties involved, so dealers will frequently request a dealing price for a specified amount (though they will not reveal their buying/selling interest) if there may be any doubt.

"My word is my bond"

The foreign exchange market is a "my word is my bond" market. The deal is a contractual obligation once both dealers have indicated their willingness to deal at the price quoted. On the calling bank's side any words suggesting a deal ("at 10", "I buy") are a commitment to deal. On the quoting bank's side any expression including words such as "OK", "Done", "Agreed" which give the impression of accepting the transaction are deemed the moment of contract. Dealers must be very clear in expressing their intentions and signifying their agreement (or not) to deal. A single word can commit their institution to a transaction involving many millions of currency and potential risk.

Change!

A price quotation is only "good for dealing" while contact is maintained (in this instance on the phone) and a response is made quickly. Any delay may result in the quoting bank saying **"Change!"** – meaning the quoted rate is no longer firm. In such a case the calling bank will have to re-request a dealing rate. In screen-based conversations via the Reuters dealing system this function is fulfilled by the "Interrupt" button.

RATES INFORMATION

Spot exchange rates for the major currencies against the EUR or USD are dynamically updated by a wide selection of banks and are available to subscribers to electronic news/rates information services (such as Reuters and Bloomberg's), with indicative rates displayed and updated less frequently in the UK on BBC and ITV City pages on teletext.

Twenty-four hour satellite and cable TV channels ensure that wherever you are in the world these days you are not far away from information on exchange rates and other financial market data.

In addition to bank's individually input rates on Reuters and other systems, there are a range of composite rates pages which provide the latest updated rate from whatever source. This information retrieved digitally may be used in personalized rates displays and spreadsheet applications for calculation and decision support information for dealers and other market operators.

Internet

There are now many sources of dynamic spot exchange rates on the Internet – banks, brokers and specialized information providers. Some brokers even offer dealing facilities for banks and high net worth private individuals (margin traders) via this route. Much of the information available can be used in other PC-based applications (MS Excel, etc.)

Financial press reportage

The better-quality daily newspapers in most countries also give details of spot exchange rates. Some more sophisticated specialized financial newspapers (the *Financial Times* in the UK, the *Wall Street Journal* in the US) quote a range of rates and other market data for the previous trading day – market opening and closing and the day's range in respect of spot exchange rates.

POSITION KEEPING

Foreign exchange profit and loss

Spot foreign exchange profit and loss is calculated on a mark to market basis. The rate used varies from country to country and sometimes from bank to bank. The exchange rate used can be an official exchange rate (dictated by the central bank or local regulatory authority), a daily bourse fixing or a "closing rate" decided by in-house policy. The important factor is that the rate used must be a market rate independently obtained so as to avoid any problems with dealers providing favourable rates at which to assess their own profit and loss.

Dealers' profits

Sometimes, with a lower level of detail available to dealers they may make approximations of daily foreign exchange profit and loss. These will have to be at least compared and more probably agreed as reconciled with the bank's official profit and loss procedures which will rely on the mark to market principal.

Value of the quoting spread

To assess their exchange profit and loss spot dealers will frequently use the value of one point method. To see what this means we go back to basic spot rate quotations and a USD/CHF quote:

USD/CHF
1.66 00 – 10

Example to calculate the value of one point

In this example the bank dealer is quoting a 10-point spread in USD/CHF. This does not mean that the dealer will make 10 points profit each time he quotes and is dealt with, but to illustrate the value of one point we will assume that on making the above quote to a calling counterparty the dealer is sold USD 1 million on his bid for USD of 1.66 00. He then immediately sells the same amount in the market via the broker at 1.66 01 (a 1 point gross profit) – see Figure 6.6.

From the market maker's (quoting bank's) point of view the 1 point earned on the purchase and sale of USD 1 million (initial sale and covering purchase of CHF) is worth CHF 100.00.

Topic 5 · Spot Foreign Exchange

Fig 6.6

Customer **A** calls	Dealer quotes as market maker **1.66 00** – 10	
As market maker Bank dealer **BUYS** USD from **Customer A**		
+ USD 1,000,000 at **1.66 00**		– CHF 1,660,000.00
Dealer calls Broker	**Broker** quotes	1.66 01 – 11
As market user Bank dealer **SELLS** USD to **Broker Bid (Bank B)**		
– USD 1,000,000 at **1.66 01**		+ CHF 1,660,100.00
USD position *square*	CHF position	+CHF 100.00
Positive cash flow indicates a profit of **CHF100.00**		

Value of one point rule

To simplify this into a valuation rule used by dealers in their daily position keeping duties, 1 point on 1 million base currency units (here USD) = 100.00 units of variable currency (here CHF).

> **Note**
> This rule is accurate for all direct quoted currencies quoted to four decimal places (1 point = 0.0001 or 1/10 000th of a currency unit) regardless of the level of the exchange rate and is the result of simple mathematics relative to the decimal places.

For ultimate profit and loss purposes (where the local currency is not Swiss francs) the value in local currency of this CHF 100 per USD 1 million will naturally go up or down depending on the current exchange rate between the CHF and local currency.

Similarly, in other major currency pairings where exchange rates are quoted to four decimal places, for each USD 1 million traded the value of one point in currency is worth 100 of quoted currency units.

> **Note**
> In respect of the EUR/USD or "Cable" GBP/USD (indirect or non-USD based currency pairs), where the US dollar is the quoted or variable currency, the value of 1 point is USD 100.00.

Low value unit currencies

In currency pairings where exchange rates are quoted to two decimal places against the USD (1 point = 0.01 or 1/100th of a currency unit), for each USD 1 million traded the value of each point earned will be worth 10,000 units of the quoted currency. An example is USD/JPY.

Mastering the ACI Dealing Certificate

Question

A typical ACI Dealing Certificate question might be:

What is the value of 1 point movement on USD 1 million in the USD/SGD spot rate?

A: SGD 1,000
B: SGD 100
C: SGD 10,000
D: USD 100

Correct answer
B: One point on USD 1 million (the base currency) in USD/SGD is worth SGD 100 (calculated from the number of decimal places).

Hint

Based on the preceding "rule", dealers tend to talk in terms of points earned or lost per USD 1 million or multiples thereof – or other base currency – when discussing profits and losses made in spot foreign exchange trading. ACI Dealing Certificate *examination questions may also be expressed in these terms.*

Spot dealing position keeping

Regardless of any computer-based deal input methods available, a spot dealer will probably keep his open exchange position in rough format, noting down any transactions effected, by whom or via which method (colleague, corporate, broker or electronic means) as a "prompt" position check. This will be reconciled at frequent intervals against the bank's official records by the dealer's assistant/position clerk.

Dealers have different methods of maintaining these records but their purpose is the same. The record will list deals done and, most importantly, the rates of transactions with a running average (breakeven) rate for the position.

Different position keeping methods can be employed. Some dealers average all deals into a running total, constantly reworking the average price, while other dealers prefer to mark their positions to market on a regular basis, "banking" profits and losses as they go along (see example below).

Running a position/averaging the rate

Any average rate of an open exchange position includes all purchases and sales and is a weighted average arrived at through simple arithmetic. First, take a long EUR/USD position as follows:

Purchase	EUR 1 million at 0.90 00 =	USD 900,000 −
Purchase	EUR 2 million at 0.90 30 =	USD 1,806,000 −
Position Long	EUR 3 million	USD 2,706,000 −

Average rate   2,706,000 divided by 3,000,000 = **0.90 20**

The market moves higher and the dealer turns his position. He decides the rate has peaked and goes short at 0.90 80 by selling EUR 5 million:

Position Long	EUR 3 million at 0.90 20	USD 2,706,000 −
Sale	EUR 5 million at 0.90 80	USD 4,540,000 +
Position Short	EUR 2 million	USD 1,834,000 +

Average rate   1,834,000 divided by 2,000,000 = **0.91 70**

This is a "weighted" average and includes the trading profit earned by the dealer. An average rate higher than the actual market has reached is achieved.

At this point the dealer may continue to manage his position at the average rate or he can mark the position to market (revalue it at the current spot rate of 0.9080) and "bank" his profit.

Short	EUR 2 million at 0.91 70	USD 1,834,000
	EUR 2 million at 0.90 80	USD 1,816,000
Profit		USD 18,000

To check this profit figure, remembering the value of one point (noted page 191), calculate the points profit (unrealized) made on the position of EUR 2 million:

$$0.91\ 70 \text{ less } 0.90\ 80 = 90 \text{ points profit on EUR 2 million}$$
$$2 \times 90 \times \text{USD } 100 = \text{USD } 18,000$$

The dealer continues monitoring his position now at the revalued rate of 0.90 80. This only becomes a realized profit profit once the position is fully squared.

> **Note**
> This informal revaluation is repeated each night formally in the bank's books of account (using the official closing rate or central bank rate) and is the basis of the mark to market open position revaluation by which spot profit and loss is calculated (see below).

Interbank dealing amounts

In the interbank market in the majority of direct quoted currency pairings (to a US dollar base), dealers tend to deal in round amounts of US dollars and track their positions in terms of US dollars either *overbought* (long) or *oversold* (short).

With the US dollar as base currency this simplifies the tracking of open exchange positions and the calculation of average rates.

In the case of currencies quoted to a euro or sterling (or other non-USD currency) base, deals done by the dealer and the position records held will more than likely be in round amounts of euros, sterling or the other indirect quoted currency for the same reasons as above.

Keeping his position in terms of round millions of US dollars (or in the case of euro/sterling/other indirect currency round amounts of this as the base currency), and bearing in mind the value of one "point" in each currency pairing, the dealer is able to assess his overall position, risk and/or profitability accurately and quickly.

Remember, these preferences are only for deals effected in the interbank market and this does not mean that dealers will not quote calling counterparties and deal for odd amounts of US dollars, currency, or sterling.

> **Question**
>
> A typical ACI Dealing Certificate question might be:
>
> If you have sold USD 3 million against SGD at 1.75 50, bought USD 4 million at 1.75 65 and sold a further USD 5 million at 1.75 40, what is your current position and average rate (breakeven)?
>
> A: Oversold USD 4 million at 1.75 22.5
> B: Oversold USD 4 million at 1.75 65
> C: Oversold SGD 4 million at 1.75 22.5
> D: Overbought USD 4 million at 1.75 22.5
>
> **Correct answer**
> A: The average rate of your total sales of USD 8 million is 1.75 43.75 and unfortunately you have made a loss of 21.25 points on the USD 4 million bought at 1.75 65. This means that the remaining short position (oversold) of USD 4 million is at the worse average rate of 1.75 22.5 rolling in this loss.

> **Hint**
>
> *Dealers will describe their positions in respect of the base currency in any currency pair, i.e. if the dealer states his position is "3 long in Cable" it means he is overbought 3 million pounds sterling (the base currency) against US dollars.*

Official profit and loss techniques – spot exchange

Official profit and loss on open exchange positions (regardless of value date) will be struck on a daily basis in the bank's general ledger by revaluing any foreign currency balances held against local currency (or bookkeeping currency) using a bank-wide daily closing rate (in some centres this is officially fixed by the local central bank). By comparing the historic (contractual) value of foreign currency balances held on open position with the current mark to market valuation a profit or loss is computed and passed in local currency to profit and loss.

If the position at close of business is short EUR 2 million at 0.91 70 = long USD 1,834,000, and assuming the USD is the local/bookkeeping currency and the EUR/USD closing rate is 0.90 80, marking to market at the closing rate:

Position at close of business
Short EUR 2 million at 0.91 70   Long   USD 1,834,000.00
                  at 0.90 80   USD 1,816,000.00
Profit   USD   18,000.00

This is an unrealized profit which will be passed to the bank's profit and loss account according to in-house policy and procedures. Each foreign currency position will be similarly revalued against the local/bookkeeping currency. As closing rates change day to day reflecting the spot market volatility, so too will the unrealized profit and loss inherent in any dealer's open exchange position.

An exchange profit is only realized when the position is squared (here by buying in the EUR short position against USD).

With the position being carried overnight the dealer will adjust his breakeven rate to the revaluation rate used plus an adjustment depending on the cost of rolling forward the position into the new spot value date using a short date fx swap price as explained in Chapter 7.

FOR FURTHER READING

Riehl, Heinz and Rodriguez, Rita M. (1977) *Foreign Exchange and Money Markets*. McGraw-Hill.

Reuters Financial Training (1999) *An Introduction to Foreign Exchange and Money Markets*. Wiley.

Swiss Bank Corp. (1992) *Foreign Exchange and Money Market Operations*. Swiss Bank Corp. (now UBS SA).

Walmsely, Julian (1992) *The Foreign Exchange and Money Markets Guide*. Wiley.

Walmsley, Julian (1996) *International Money and Foreign Exchange Markets*. Wiley.

Topic 6 · Forward Foreign Exchange

Introduction

Forward FX transactions

Premium/discount

Forward rate quotation terminology

Forward exchange price calculations

Outright forward cross currency calculations

Corporate FX business

Interbank forward exchange operations

Other forward foreign exchange calculations

Interest arbitrage

> ### Overall objective
>
> To *explain the mechanics of trading using outrights and swaps, and to explain their use in creating synthetic currency assets and liabilities alongside the calculations involved.*
>
> At the end of this section, candidates will be able to:
>
> - explain the role of spot and interest rate differentials and the concept of arbitrage;
> - list the features of an FX outright and FX swap;
> - describe the derivation of forward rates using the basic equation for calculating points;
> - calculate broken dates through interpolation;
> - calculate complex rates such as forward crosses and forward broken dates;
> - explain the role of FX outrights and FX swaps in the money markets;
> - list the trading periods;
> - explain the use of FX outrights and FX swaps to hedge outright forwards and to create synthetic asset and liabilities;
> - list the basics of foreign exchange options.

Note

There are 15 questions on foreign exchange (spot and forward) in the ACI Dealing Certificate – 7 textual multiple choice questions out of which candidates are required to gain a minimum of 42.80 percent to pass (3 out of 7) and 8 calculation multiple choice questions out of which candidates are required to gain a minimum of 37.50 percent to pass (3 out of 8).

You will also find position keeping questions relating to forward FX included here.

INTRODUCTION

As we saw in Chapter 2 the 2001 BIS and central banks triennial surveys reported one fact louder than ever before. Wherever you are in the world's major financial centres, there is more activity these days in the forward market than in spot.

Commercial companies have become very much more sophisticated than in past years. Exchange exposure management is something which interests any enterprise with income or expenditure expressed in foreign currencies.

Topic 6 · Forward Foreign Exchange

Where these foreign currency cash flows are in the future, to neutralize the effects of fluctuating currency relationships over time the corporate treasurer seeks to close out the risks in the forward foreign exchange market.

The dealer needs to be able to calculate outright forward exchange rates, including cross rates, and also then know how best to cover these risks absorbed from his commercial customers. Quoting on an outright basis to enable his customers to cover their exposures the bank dealer seeks to eek out as much profit as he can by identifying the separate exchange and interest rate risks and then covering them individually through the spot and forward FX swap markets.

To quote outright forward prices the relationship of interest rates to currency swap points needs to be fully understood. The flexibility of being able to trade for any date when markets are open means the dealer has to be aware of relative interest rates and the calculation process to derive accurate forward rates for broken dates – not just standard forward value dates. Your ability to handle such calculations and price quotation techniques is tested in the examinations.

Interest arbitrage also features in this section. Understanding the relationship of interest rates and forward swap points permits dealers to take advantage of split-second windows of opportunity when anomalies in the markets can be exploited for profit. There will also be many occasions when liabilities in one currency can be switched into a second currency to meet a funding requirement without increasing the bank's overall balance sheet. Your grasp of the various interest arbitrage formulae (of which there are many variations) to derive one or the other interest rate or the swap points is tested in the examinations.

Forward periods available

Forward exchange rates are available from a bank in the majority of currencies for dates ranging from value tomorrow (more correctly termed an ante-spot or short date transaction) to 12 months, with the major currency pairs often able to be quoted out to five and ten years.

A typical set of standard period forward rates in the major currencies against the US dollar, euro or sterling would be:

> 1,   2,   3,   6   *and*   12 months

Forward dates

The standard period forward value dates are calculated based on the benchmark spot date and follow the same rules (including end/end) as already stated for money market (see the market conventions included in Chapter 4).

> **Question**
>
> A typical ACI Dealing Certificate question might be:
>
> If today's date is Tuesday 27 February 200X (a leap year), what would the two months maturity date from spot for forward foreign exchange dealing be?
>
> A: Wednesday 1 May 200X
> B: Tuesday 30 April 200X
> C: Monday 29 April 200X
> D: Friday 26 April 200X
>
> **Correct answer**
>
> B: If today is Tuesday 27 February then spot date will be Thursday 29 February 200X (a leap year). The standard period forward value date will normally be the same date in the appropriate forward month. But if today's spot date is the last business day in the current month for forward date calculation purposes this is deemed to be the month-end date, and all other standard period forward dates are then the last business dates in the appropriate forward months. The two months maturity date from spot date Thursday 29 February 200X (a leap year) will therefore be Tuesday 30 April 200X. This rule is termed the "end/end" rule.

Broken date forward exchange

Forward foreign exchange transactions are not, however, limited to standard period maturity dates. This is where the flexibility in the forward foreign exchange market is so apparent. Banks are prepared to quote forward exchange rates for any business day (the principal financial centre in each of the currencies to be settled has to be open for business) up to one year in the majority of currency pairings and further out in the major currencies.

Calculation methods for such broken or, in dealers' jargon, "cock date" foreign exchange forward rate quotations may be found later in this chapter.

FORWARD FX TRANSACTIONS

There are three types of forward foreign exchange contract available in the market.

- outright forward contract;
- time (or delivery) option forward contract;
- foreign exchange swap.

Outright forward contract

This is a typical corporate transaction where the customer is seeking to cover exchange exposure on a forward date rather than spot. An outright forward exchange contract is a one-way transaction to buy or sell one currency against another (like a spot transaction) except that it is for a fixed forward value date. The rate fixed on date of dealing is the current benchmark spot rate adjusted by the forward swap points for that forward period. On an outright forward transaction the bank charges the customer both the spot and the forward spread. The pricing rules applicable are explained in more detail later in this chapter. An outright forward contract is a contractual obligation on both parties.

Time (or delivery) option forward contract

Smaller customers may not have the resources to have a full-time treasury function but still want to cover their exchange exposure on a forward basis. For these customers there is a forward transaction type which permits them to cover their risk forward without tying them down to a single forward value date. This is a time or delivery option forward contract. To be accurate this is an outright forward contract in which the customer may deliver or take delivery of the currency on any date within the option period to suit his requirements (at his option). Multiple partial deliveries are possible; however, this type of transaction is *not* a performance option (see Currency options in Chapter 8) and is still a contractual obligation – meaning the contract must be completed. If for some reason the customer cannot complete the full amount of the contract it will be closed out by the bank (buying/selling at the then current spot rate) and the difference will be settled between the two parties. Alternatively it may be extended – moving the final date to a further forward date.

On a time or delivery option forward contract the bank has to cover itself for the customer completing the contract on any date or dates within the option period. Remember the bank dealer does not know when pricing the product when the customer will request delivery of funds. The price quoted by the dealer therefore will always be the most favourable to the bank of the outright forward prices for the start and end dates of the option period. The pricing rules for time or delivery option contracts are explained in more detail later in this chapter.

Forward foreign exchange business

Foreign exchange business transacted by a bank (from the bank's point of view) is shown in Figure 7.1, which illustrates the cash flows generated by an outright forward transaction dealt between a commercial customer and his bank and the outcome of covering transactions effected. (The numbers in brackets in the following paragraphs refer to this figure.)

Fig 7.1

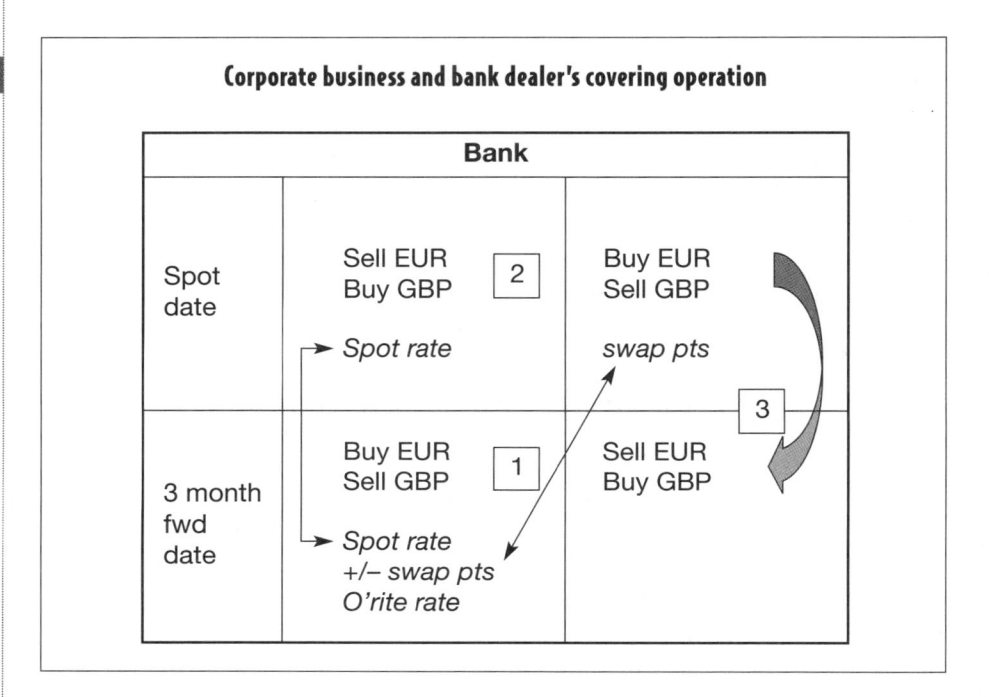

Corporate business and bank dealer's covering operation

	Bank	
Spot date	Sell EUR Buy GBP [2] → Spot rate	Buy EUR Sell GBP swap pts
3 month fwd date	Buy EUR Sell GBP [1] ↳ Spot rate +/− swap pts O'rite rate	Sell EUR Buy GBP

[3]

While banks are happy to quote their corporate customers for outright forward transactions (1) and deal on this basis, they tend *not* to deal with one another on an outright basis, preferring to cover the individual risks of the open position on the spot (2) and then manage and cover the cashflow risk separately.

To do this there are several alternatives.

1. If the dealer so chooses, he may cover the spot against forward cash flow mismatch resulting from forward purchase from the customer (1) covered by the spot sale (2) with two money market transactions – here a deposit in EUR and a loan in GBP. These operations would then of course be "on the balance sheet", and with major centre banks operating in this fashion for large amounts on a daily basis this would increase the balance sheet footings of the institution significantly merely to cover what is routine forward foreign exchange business. Such transactions can, however, be effected and they would constitute an interest arbitrage operation – discussed later in this chapter.

Topic 6 · Forward Foreign Exchange

2. The alternative for the bank dealer is to cover the cash flow mismatch with a product which has the same effect as a loan and deposit *without* impacting the balance sheet. He may elect to cover the position with a foreign exchange swap (here a spot EUR purchase against a forward EUR sale (3) swap).

    Such a swap can be dealt for exact matching dates or may be mismatched if the dealer has a particular view on the future trend of interest rates in the two currencies – or rather the differential between these interest rates.

    This sequence tends to explain why, when reviewing survey statistics, so little of the foreign exchange turnover appears to be customer related. In this example we started with an outright forward foreign exchange deal between a customer and the bank (1). The dealer effects three further deals just to square the position – meaning that in this case 25 percent of transactions are customer related. The spot deal (2) is dealt in the market with another bank and that recipient bank dealer has no corporate business, just an interbank deal. Assuming he too turns his position with another bank it is soon evident that the single customer deal with the first bank generates a number of other spot deals reducing the overall percentage of customer deals.

    The percentage is reduced still further when the forward deals are considered. A swap deal comprises two deals (spot against forward) and again the initial interbank transaction (3) will give rise to further swap deals being effected. The result of all this activity brings the percentage of customer deals overall to approximately 5 to 7 percent of all transactions in the market.

    This is the way the foreign exchange market generates its own liquidity. These sequences of transactions ensure that the next time this or another customer calls a bank the dealer will be able to find a forward price in the market and quote the customer accordingly.

3. The more sophisticated corporate customers also tend to deal on this basis preferring to choose their moment of entry into the spot market (2) and then extending the position forward using a foreign exchange swap (3).

Foreign exchange swap

A foreign exchange swap is an exchange of cash flows in the two currencies of the swap over a period ranging from one day (overnight or tom/next) to a number of months, sometimes years. It consists of two transactions reversing each other, one date against a further forward date, most frequently spot against a forward date – in Figure 7.1 a spot against three months forward foreign exchange swap. Technically, to be a swap, one of the currency amounts should be the same on both value dates though there are circumstances when this may not be the case (see Interest arbitrage later in this chapter).

Outside the dealing room the foreign exchange swap is probably the least known of the various transactions available to the dealer to cover exchange and interest rate exposure, and yet it has been around for many years and the BIS triennial survey of April 2001 showed that of all outstanding forward foreign exchange transactions 83 percent were foreign exchange swaps. The subject of foreign exchange swaps is addressed in more detail later in this chapter.

Forward foreign exchange rates

In the interbank forward market, forward rates are quoted as a two-way price in "forward swap points". These points are adjustments to be made to the spot price to achieve the forward exchange rate applicable to the dates in question.

Forward swap points differ from decimals and fractions of a cent sometimes quoted by the financial press only because they follow the quotation method of the spot rate being quoted in so many "points" or "pips". Such rate quotations are frequently referred to as being in "dealer terms".

When seeking forward rate quotations in the interbank market by telephone, typically bank dealers follow the market convention of asking for a complete set of the standard forward periods – one, two, three, six and twelve months.

These swap prices would be quoted on a rates information screen, telex, electronic dealing system or other "written" means of communication in dealer terms (points) as:

Forward GBP/USD (Cable)
21 – 19
41 – 38
63 – 58
119 – 114
214 – 194

or quoted verbally as:

Twenty-one nineteen… forty-one thirty-eight… sixty-three fifty-eight… one nineteen one fourteen… two fourteen one ninety-four

Topic 6 · Forward Foreign Exchange

Note

The description of sterling against US dollars as "Cable" is also used in forward GBP/USD points quotations i.e. "forward Cable".

PREMIUM/DISCOUNT

Forward exchange rates are quoted as swap points – price differentials by which to adjust the all-important benchmark spot exchange rate to achieve the outright forward rate.

These price differentials are termed either *premium* (pm) or *discount* (disc), identifying whether the currency being referred to is more expensive (at a premium) or cheaper (at a discount) to buy on the forward date than it is for spot value.

This comparison with the benchmark spot rate is important and gives the clue to the meaning of the premium/discount terminology.

London and international terms

Dealers in different financial centres sometimes use the terms *premium* and *discount* to relate to the differing currencies in any quote made – the base or variable (quoted) currency.

In any series of forward exchange rate quotations, if the rate for the base currency is quoted as a premium against the variable currency, then the variable currency must conversely be at a discount (against the base currency).

Sometimes it will depend in which financial centre the quote is made as to how the currency relationship is described. For example, in the UK for forward GBP/USD rate quotations, London dealers talk in terms of the *US dollar premium* (the variable currency) against sterling (the base currency) whereas in continental Europe and the United States the same rate quotations would be referred to as a *sterling discount* against the US dollar.

With two currencies involved in each and every foreign exchange transaction, the maxim "one man's premium is another man's discount" should always be borne in mind. The way the price is displayed and quoted, the meaning of the quote and all subsequent rate calculations are identical in each centre but the difference in terminology can be confusing.

Hint

When the terms premium or discount or bid and offer are used in any ACI Dealing Certificate *examination question, always re-read the question to ascertain to which currency the terms refer.*

> **Note**
>
> To avoid any confusion in describing dealing calculations for forward exchange in this book we will use only international terms referring to the base currency at a premium or discount.

> **Question**
>
> A typical ACI Dealing Certificate question might be:
>
> If USD interest rates are quoted at 6 percent in three months and the same period SGD interest rates are quoted at 5 percent, how would you expect the forward swap points to be quoted?
>
> A: At a forward SGD premium
> B: At a forward USD premium
> C: Around par
> D: Insufficient information to decide
>
> **Correct answer**
> A: In forward exchange terminology, the currency with the lower interest rate can be described as being at a forward premium. Here we are describing the variable currency SGD as being at a forward premium.

Dealer terms

When dealers quote forward swap points to each other in the interbank market they merely quote the points, without any indication of decimal point, suffix or description premium or discount. By looking at the two-way spread quoted it can easily be determined whether the base currency is at a forward premium or discount.

Base currency premium

Where the base currency in a forward foreign exchange price is described as being at a forward premium it is worth more forward than for spot value, i.e. it is more expensive to purchase forward than for spot value. The forward swap points will be quoted low–high. The currency described as being at a forward premium will always have the *lower* interest rate.

Low–high forward points are *added* to the spot exchange rate to achieve the outright forward rate – each unit of base currency costs you *more* forward than it does on the spot date. For example, the EUR/USD forwards are quoted:

Topic 6 · Forward Foreign Exchange

```
EUR/USD Spot: 0.90 50 – 60
    and forwards…
         8 – 10
        16 – 18
        25 – 27
        43 – 48
        53 – 63
```

Base currency discount

Where the base currency in a forward foreign exchange price is described as being at a forward discount it is worth less forward than for spot value, i.e. it is cheaper to purchase forward than for spot value. The forward swap points will be quoted high–low. The currency described as being at a forward discount will always have the *higher* interest rate.

High–low forward swap points are *subtracted* from the spot exchange rate to achieve the forward rate – each unit of base currency costs you *less* forward than it does on the spot date. For example, the GBP/USD forwards are quoted:

```
GBP/USD Spot: 1.50 00 – 10
    and forwards…
        21 – 19
        41 – 38
        63 – 58
       119 – 114
       214 – 194
```

FORWARD RATE QUOTATION TERMINOLOGY

As can be seen from the USD/XXX forward swap points quoted below, these can move from a base currency discount quote (5 – par) through an around par quote (–3 +2) to a base currency premium quote (par – 10) depending on the relative yield curves plotted for the interest rates in the two currencies of the pairing. The one to three months prices are quoted *high–low*, a base currency discount, ## the six months price is quoted *minus* to *plus*, around par, while the one-year price is quoted *low–high*, a

```
      USD/XXX
       5 – 0
       5 – 0
       5 – 0
    ## – 3 + 2 ##
      PAR – 10
```

base currency premium. Par can also be written as "0" or "Ø" in any printed rate quote.

A currency pair quoted in the forwards at par (or parity) means that the interest rates in the two currencies are the same and the premium/discount is equal to "zero". Therefore there is no adjustment necessary to the spot exchange rate to achieve the outright forward rate. The outright forward rate is identical to the spot rate.

Unless intentionally quoting a "choice" price a dealer will rarely quote bid and offer the same, i.e. there is typically always a spread, therefore the price quotes will look like those shown above with the base currency quoted discount to par, around par and par to premium. When quoting around par the price will always be *minus* to *plus* – no dealer ever gives away his spread!

Interest rate differential

Remember that forward exchange rates do *not* directly reflect any anticipated movements or future levels in the spot exchange market – they are directly proportionate to the interest rate differential between the two currencies for the period indicated in the eurocurrency money markets (provided both are freely convertible currencies). All forward rates quoted are arrived at arithmetically.

> **Hint**
>
> *Whether referring to base or quoted currency in examination questions remember the currency described in a forward currency pair as being at a forward discount will have a higher interest rate than the countercurrency for the period in question. Logically a currency quoted at a forward premium will have a lower interest rate than the countercurrency for the period in question.*

Bid–offer

In the last chapter we discussed how the quoting bank is prepared to deal on either side of the two-way spot price bid–offer spread for the base currency. The forward quotations are described and dealt in similar fashion, except that the bid–offer description refers to the *movement of currency on the forward date*.

> *In the interbank forward market dealers typically always refer to the bid and offer for the base currency on the forward date. Remember BOB.*

Hint

FORWARD EXCHANGE PRICE CALCULATIONS

Outright forward price (base currency premium)

To calculate the outright forward price we need to adjust the spot exchange rate by the forward points quoted for the appropriate period.

```
       EUR/USD
Spot: 0.90 50 – 60
       Forwards
        8 – 10
     ** 16 – 18 **
       25 – 27
       43 – 48
       53 – 63
```

These two-way bid–offer prices indicate the forward adjustments to be made to the spot rate for the fixed period value dates at which the bank is prepared both to buy the base currency – its forward bid for the base currency, in this instance EUR – and to sell that base currency – its forward offer for the base currency, again EUR – conversely selling and buying USD, the quoted or variable currency).

Outright forward price example

Bank as market maker (base currency premium)

As an example we will look at the two months EUR/USD outright exchange rate quotation. The two months EUR/USD swap points are quoted ** 16 – 18 **, low–high, a EUR premium:

Spot	EUR/USD:	0.90 50 – 0.90 60
Add two months	EUR/USD:	0.00 16 – 0.00 18
Outright two months	EUR/USD	0.90 66 – 0.90 78

Mastering the ACI Dealing Certificate

This means the bank dealer quoting the rate (the market maker) will:

- on the left-hand side:
  - *buy* 3 month outright EUR against USD at 0.9066
  - and conversely *sell* USD against EUR;

and will:

- on the right-hand side:
  - *sell* 3 month outright EUR against USD at 0.9078
  - and conversely *buy* USD against EUR.

Outright forward price (base currency discount)

To calculate the outright forward price we need to adjust the spot exchange rate by the forward points quoted for the appropriate period.

USD/JPY
Spot: 120.90 – 00
Forwards
48 – 45
98 – 95
*** 148 – 145 ***
300 – 295
592 – 587

These two-way bid–offer prices indicate the forward adjustments to be made to the spot rate for the fixed period value dates at which the bank is prepared both to *buy* the base currency – its forward bid for the base currency, in this instance USD – and *sell* that base currency – its forward offer for the base currency, again USD (conversely selling and buying USD, the quoted or variable currency).

Remember, the USD/JPY exchange rate is quoted to two decimal places ("big" points) – important when considering the points adjustment to achieve the outright exchange rate.

Bank as market maker (base currency discount)

As an example we will look at the three months USD/JPY outright exchange rate quotation. The three months USD/JPY swap points are quoted ** 148 – 145 **, high–low, a USD discount:

Spot	USD/JPY	120.90 – 121.00
Subtract three months	USD/JPY:	1.48 – 1.45
Outright three months	USD/JPY:	119.42 – 119.55

Topic 6 · Forward Foreign Exchange

This means the bank dealer quoting the rate (the market maker) will:
- on the left-hand side:
  – *buy* 3 month outright USD against JPY at 119.42
  – and conversely *sell* JPY against USD;

and will:
- on the right-hand side:
  – *sell* 3 month outright USD against JPY at 119.55
  – and conversely *buy* JPY against USD.

> **Question**
>
> A typical ACI Dealing Certificate question might be:
>
> If spot USD/CHF is quoted to you as 1.52 60–70 and three months forward points are quoted to you as 28–23, at what rate can you buy dollars three months outright?
>
> A: 1.5242
> B: 1.5247
> C: 1.5232
> D: 1.5237
>
> **Correct answer**
> B: The forward swap points are quoted high–low, therefore to calculate the outright USD/CHF subtract the points from the spot rate (left from left and right from right). Here we can buy USD three months outright at 1.5247 (1.5270 less 23 points).

OUTRIGHT FORWARD CROSS CURRENCY CALCULATIONS

As discussed in Chapter 6 (Spot foreign exchange rates) the method of calculation of a cross currency outright forward rate is dependent upon whether the two currencies involved are:

1. one direct (to a USD base) and one indirect (to a non-USD base) quoted currency against the US dollar: **condition 1**

   multiply the same sides

   (left-hand side by left-hand side and right-hand side by right-hand side)

2. both direct quoted currencies against the US dollar (to a USD base): **condition 2** *or*

3. both indirect quoted currencies against the US dollar (to a non-USD base): **condition 3**

   cross divide opposite sides

   (left-hand side by right-hand side and right-hand side by left-hand side).

Mastering the ACI Dealing Certificate

Three months GBP/JPY (from GBP/USD and USD/JPY): condition 1

For condition 1 the procedure noted below must be followed.
GBP/USD spot and forward rates are quoted as follows:

> GBP/USD
> Spot: 1.50 00 – 10
> Forwards
> 5 – 2
> 5 – 2
> *** 5 – 2 ***
> –3 + 2
> Par – 10

This means that in the three-month period (***) the bank dealer quoting the rates will on the *left-hand side*:

> Buy GBP and sell USD
> Spot: 1.50 00
> *less*:   0.00 05
> The bank dealer
> *Buys* GBP and *sells* USD   ———
> Outright forward 3 months at: 1.49 95

and will on the *right-hand side*:

> Sell GBP and buy USD
> Spot: 1.50 10
> *less*:   0.00 02
> The bank dealer
> *Sells* GBP and *buys* USD   ———
> Outright forward 3 months at: 1.50 08

Therefore the two-way three-month outright forward price GBP against USD is:

> 1.49 95 – 1.50 08
> US dollars
> *per* pound sterling

Topic 6 · Forward Foreign Exchange

This is *Quote No. 1* as we examine the calculations for forward cross currency quotations below.

> **Hint**
>
> *The outright forward spread is the sum of the spot spread and the forward points spread (GBP/USD outright spread (13 points) = 10 points spot + 3 points forward spread).*

USD/JPY spot and forward rates are quoted as follows:

```
        USD/JPY
   Spot: 120.90 – 00
       Forwards
        48 – 45
        98 – 95
   *** 148 – 145 ***
       300 – 295
       592 – 587
```

(Remember, USD/JPY forward points are "big points". The USD/JPY exchange rate is quoted to two decimal places.)

This means that in the three-month period (***) the bank dealer quoting the rates will on the *left-hand side*:

```
Buy USD and sell JPY
Spot:                            120.90
less:                              1.48
The bank dealer
Buys USD and sells JPY           _____
Outright forward 3 months at:    119.42
```

and will on the *right-hand side*:

```
Sell USD and buy JPY
Spot:                            121.00
less:                              1.45
The bank dealer
Sells USD and buys JPY           _____
Outright forward 3 months at:    119.55
```

Mastering the ACI Dealing Certificate

Therefore the two-way three-months outright forward price USD against JPY is:

> 119.42 – 119.55
> Japanese yen
> *per* US dollar

This is *Quote No. 2* as we examine the calculations for forward cross currency quotations below.

Hint

The outright forward USD/JPY spread (13 points) is the sum of the spot (10 points) and forward (3 points) spreads.

Outright forward cross currency calculations: Condition 1

One direct (to a USD base) and one indirect (to a non-USD base) quoted currency against the US dollar.

To calculate a GBP/JPY outright forward exchange rate quotation we have to use the sides of the two prices (GBP/USD and USD/JPY) of the outright forward prices, which will give a resultant rate to buy GBP and sell JPY and sell GBP and buy JPY in the three months.

Quote No. 1	Quote No. 2
Outright forward	Outright forward
GBP/USD	USD/JPY
1.49 95 – 08	119.42 – 55

To recap the calculation rule for Condition 1: *Multiply the same sides.* This is achieved as described for calculated spot rates in the last chapter by compensating the US dollar movements in the following simple cashflows:

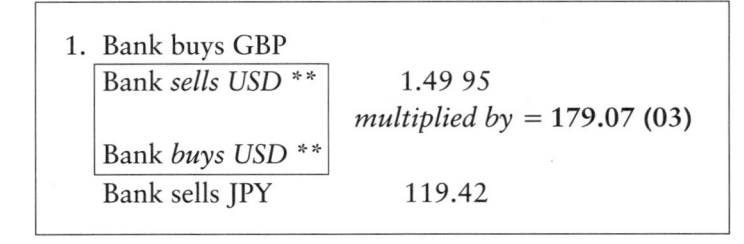

1. Bank buys GBP
   Bank *sells* USD **   1.49 95
                           multiplied by = 179.07 (03)
   Bank *buys* USD **
   Bank sells JPY   119.42

The US dollar movement (**) nets out in the above cash flow leaving us with the market maker's buying rate for GBP against JPY (conversely the selling rate for JPY against GBP).

> 2. Bank sells GBP
> | Bank *buys* USD ** | 1.50 08 |
> |---|---|
> | | *multiplied by* = 179.42 (06) |
> | Bank *sells* USD ** | |
> | Bank buys JPY | 119.55 |

The US dollar movement (**) nets out in the above cash flow leaving us with the market maker's selling rate for GBP against JPY (conversely the buying rate for JPY against GBP).

Therefore the two-way three-month outright forward price GBP against JPY is:

> **179.07 – 179.42**
> Japanese yen
> *per* pound sterling
> (rounded)

Note: The outright forward GBP/JPY is quoted (rounded) to the standard number of decimal places – here two for GBP/JPY.

Calculation rule: condition 1

As the quotes used are so many JPY per USD and so many USD per GBP we can repeat the simple rule to create any other currency rate against sterling (where that currency is quoted on a direct basis against the US dollar).

- *multiply* the two lowest rates (left-hand sides) in the original rate quotations above for the outright forward currency selling rate against sterling; and similarly
- *multiply* the two highest rates (right-hand sides) in the original quotations above for the outright forward currency buying rate against sterling.

Mastering the ACI Dealing Certificate

Hint

For the majority of foreign currency quotations against GBP the above calculation logic applies, but beware of other indirect/reciprocal currencies against the USD when calculating rates against GBP!

Forward GBP/JPY points

If asked to calculate the forward points in any so derived forward outright quotation all that is required is to compare the resultant outright with the calculated cross currency spot rate:

Spot **GBP/USD**:	1.50 00 – 1.50 10
	× ×
Spot **USD/JPY**:	120.90 – 121.00
Spot **GBP/JPY**:	181.31 – 181.62

| Outright forward GBP/JPY: | 179.07 – 179.42 |

Therefore the points in this forward outright quotation are:

| 181.31 *minus* 179.07 = 224 |
| 181.62 *minus* 179.42 = 220 |
| **GBP/JPY** swap: 224 – 220 |

The swap is quoted high–low indicating that GBP is at a discount against the JPY and the points should be subtracted from the spot to achieve the outright forward rate.

A typical ACI Dealing Certificate question might be:

Question

You are quoted the following rates: Spot USD/NOK: 7.83 50 – 60. 3 Months USD/NOK Swap: 340–380. Spot GBP/USD: 1.54 00/05. 3 Months GBP/USD Swap: 70–65. Where can you buy NOK against GBP 3 months outright?

A> 5.1330

B> 12.0787

C> 12.0632

D> 12.0708

Correct answer

C: For this cross currency forward quote you must calculate out the two 3 month outright rates and multiply out the two left hand sides (USD/NOK: 7.83 50 *plus* 340 = 7.8690 and GBP/USD:1.5400 *minus* 70 = 1.5330) to achieve the market rate at which you can buy NOK against GBP 12.0632 (GBP is the base currency of the cross currency quote).

Topic 6 · Forward Foreign Exchange

Outright forward cross currency calculations: condition 2

Both direct quoted currencies against the US dollar (both to a USD base).

As with the GBP/JPY example above we need first to calculate the outright forward exchange rates for USD/JPY (*Quote No. 2* already calculated above) and USD/CHF (*Quote No. 3* calculated below) and then use the calculation rule for Condition 2 (on page 211):

Quote No. 2	Quote No. 3
Outright forward	Outright forward
USD/JPY	**USD/CHF**
119.42 – 119.55	Calculated below

Calculation for two-way outright forward price USD/CHF (Quote No. 3)

The USD/CHF exchange rate is quoted to four decimal places.

```
        USD/CHF
   Spot: 1.42 50 – 60
        Forwards
         30 – 27
         59 – 56
     *** 88 – 85 ***
        175 – 170
        345 – 340
```

This means that in the three-month period (***) the bank dealer quoting the rates will on the *left-hand side*:

Buy USD and sell CHF	
Spot:	1.42 50
less:	0.00 88
The bank dealer	
Buys USD and *sells* CHF	
Outright forward three months at:	1.41 62

217

and will on the *right-hand side*:

Sell USD and buy CHF	
Spot:	1.42 60
less:	0.00 85
The bank dealer	
Sells USD and *buys* CHF	
Outright forward three months at:	1.41 75

Therefore the two-way outright forward price USD against CHF is:

1.4162 – 1.4175
Swiss francs
per US dollar

This is *Quote No. 3* as we examine the calculations for forward cross currency quotations below.

Hint

The outright forward USD/CHF spread (13 points) is the sum of the spot (10 points) and forward (3 points) spreads.

Outright forward rate quotes in full

Quote No. 2	Quote No. 3
Outright forward	Outright forward
USD/JPY	USD/CHF
119.42 – 119.55	1.41 62 – 1.41 75

To recap the calculation rule for Condition 2: *Cross divide opposite sides* (left-hand side by right-hand side and right-hand side by left-hand side)

Topic 6 · Forward Foreign Exchange

Outright forward cross currency calculations three months CHF/JPY from USD/CHF and USD/JPY, two direct quoted currencies (to a USD base): condition 2

```
USD/JPY      119.42 – 119.55        USD/JPY
               Quote No. 2
              ↙        ↗
            Cross divided by
              ↖        ↘
               Quote No. 3
USD/CHF      1.41 62 – 1.41 75      USD/CHF
```

Where the two currencies involved are *direct* quoted currencies against the US dollar (e.g. condition 2: both USD/CHF and USD/JPY are quoted to a USD base), the cross currency rate quotation will be the result of *cross dividing* the two USD-based rates.

Cash flows

To see this clearly look at the actual cash flows generated by the necessary USD/CHF and USD/JPY deals against the US dollar (as we did with rates against GBP earlier):

```
1. Bank sells JPY
   ┌─────────────────┐
   │ Bank buys USD **│     119.42
   └─────────────────┘     divided by = 84.24 (69)
   ┌─────────────────┐
   │ Bank sells USD **│    1.41 75
   └─────────────────┘
   Bank buys CHF
```

The US dollar movement (**) nets out in the above cash flow leaving us with the market maker's buying rate for CHF against JPY (conversely the selling rate for JPY against CHF).

```
2. Bank buys JPY
   ┌─────────────────┐
   │ Bank sells USD **│    119.55
   └─────────────────┘     divided by =  84.41 (60)
   ┌─────────────────┐
   │ Bank buys USD **│     1.41 62
   └─────────────────┘
   Bank Sells CHF
```

The US dollar movement (**) nets out in the above cash flow leaving us with the market maker's selling rate for CHF against JPY (conversely the buying rate for JPY against CHF).

Therefore the two-way price CHF against JPY is:

> 84.25 – 84.42
> Japanese yen
> *per* Swiss franc
> (rounded)

Calculation rule: condition 2

As the quotes used are so many JPY per USD and so many CHF per USD we can repeat the simple rule to create any other currency rate where both currencies are quoted on a direct basis (against the US dollar).

- *divide* the opposing sides of the prices (the left-hand side of *Quote No. 1* by the right-hand side of *Quote No. 3*) of the original rate quotations above for the cross currency buying rate for CHF against JPY; and similarly

- *divide* the opposing sides of the prices (the right-hand side of *Quote No. 1* by the left-hand side of *Quote No. 3*) of the original rate quotations above for the cross currency selling rate for CHF against JPY.

Outright forward cross currency calculations: condition 3

Both indirect quoted currencies against the US dollar (to a non-USD base).

As with the CHF/JPY example above we need first to calculate the outright forward exchange rates for GBP/USD (*Quote No. 1* already calculated above) and AUD/USD (*Quote No. 4* calculated below) and then use the calculation rule for Condition 3:

Quote No. 1	Quote No. 4
Outright forward	Outright forward
GBP/USD	AUD/USD
1.4995 – 1.5008	Calculated below

Calculation for two-way outright forward price AUD/USD (Quote No. 4)

The AUD/USD exchange rate is quoted to four decimal places.

As with the GBP/JPY example above we need first to calculate the outright forward exchange rate for AUD/USD (*Quote No. 4*) and then use the calculation rule (on page 211):

Topic 6 · Forward Foreign Exchange

> AUD/USD
> Spot 0.53 50 – 60
> 13 – 10
> 25 – 22
> *** 38 – 35 ***
> 75 – 70
> 150 – 145

Here forward Australian dollars are at a discount against the US dollar.

This means that in the three-month period (***) the bank dealer quoting the rates will on the *left-hand side*:

Buy AUD and sell USD	
Spot:	0.53 50
less:	0.00 38
The bank dealer *Buys* AUD and *sells* USD	
Outright forward 3 months at:	0.53 12

and will on the *right-hand side*:

Sell AUD and buy USD	
Spot:	0.53 60
less:	0.00 35
The bank dealer *Sells* AUD and *buys* USD	
Outright forward 3 months at:	0.53 25

Therefore the two-way outright forward price AUD against USD is:

> 0.53 12 – 0.53 25
> US dollars (¢)
> *per* Australian dollar

This is *Quote No. 4* as we examine the calculations for forward cross currency quotations below.

The outright forward AUD/USD spread (13 points) is the sum of the spot (10 points) and forward (3 points) spreads. **Hint**

Outright forward rate quotes in full

Quote No. 1	Quote No. 4
Outright forward	Outright forward
GBP/USD	AUD/USD
1.49 95 – 1.50 08	0.53 12 – 0.53 25

To recap the calculation rule for Condition 3: Cross divide opposite sides (left-hand side by right-hand side and right-hand side by left-hand side)

Outright forward cross currency calculations three months GBP/AUD from GBP/USD and AUD/USD, two indirect quoted currencies (to *non*-USD bases): condition 3

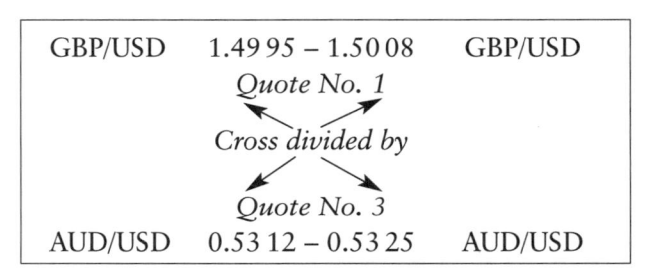

GBP/USD	1.49 95 – 1.50 08	GBP/USD
	Quote No. 1	
	Cross divided by	
	Quote No. 3	
AUD/USD	0.53 12 – 0.53 25	AUD/USD

Where the two currencies involved are both *indirect* quoted currencies against the US dollar (both GBP/USD and AUD/USD are quoted to a non-USD base) the cross currency rate quotation will be the result of cross dividing the two non-USD based rates.

Cash flows

To see the outcome clearly look at the actual cash flows generated by the necessary GBP/USD and AUD/USD deals:

> 1. Bank buys GBP
>   Bank *sells* USD **   1.49 95
>   divided by = 2.81 59 (62)
>   Bank *buys* USD **   0.53 25
>   Bank sells AUD

The US dollar movement (**) nets out in the above cash flow leaving us with the market maker's buying rate for GBP against AUD (conversely the selling rate for AUD against GBP).

Topic 6 · Forward Foreign Exchange

> 2. Bank sells GBP
> | Bank *Buys* USD ** | 1.50 08 |
> | | divided by = 2.82 53 (01) |
> | Bank *sells* USD ** | 0.53 12 |
> | Bank buys AUD | |

The US dollar movement (**) nets out in the above cash flow leaving us with the market maker's selling rate for GBP against AUD (conversely the buying rate for AUD against GBP).

Therefore the two-way price GBP against AUD is:

> 2.81 60 – 2.82 53
> Australian dollars
> *per* pounds sterling
> (rounded)

Calculation rule: condition 3

As the quotes used are so many USD per GBP and so many USD per AUD we can repeat the simple rule to create any other currency rate where both currencies are quoted on an indirect basis against the US dollar.

- *divide* the opposing sides of the prices (the left-hand side of *Quote No. 1* by the right-hand side of *Quote No. 4*) of the original rate quotations above for the cross currency buying rate for GBP against AUD; and similarly
- *divide* the opposing sides of the prices (the right-hand side of *Quote No. 1* by the left-hand side of *Quote No. 4*) of the original rate quotations above for the cross currency selling rate for GBP against AUD.

Be careful not to truncate/round up in the middle of a sequence of calculations.

Hint

Cross currency calculations

As with spot cross currency quotations, where such a forward price is required, the rate could be expressed as a changing number of Currency 1 units to a Currency 2 base or a changing number of Currency 2 units to a Currency 1 base.

When a cross rate quote is sought outside either of the countries whose currencies are involved, the rate quotation will be made according to international market conventions. These dictate a priority list of currencies and where neither the USD nor EUR nor GBP are present (ranked 1, 2 and 3) the next highest ranking currency will be taken as the base currency of the price quote.

Should the alternative quotation method be requested, however, the rate can be quoted on either basis, according to the dealing counterparties' preference. Remember the base currency should normally be written before the forward slash "/" in any currency pair description, e.g. CHF/JPY.

One is a simple mathematical reciprocal of the other, i.e. divide the rate calculated into 1 to change the quotations from one base to the other, but remember spot and forward exchange rates (on an outright basis) are always quoted low–high. The sides of the quote therefore change depending which way any of the above calculations are effected.

> **Hint**
>
> *The examiner's wording in* ACI Dealing Certificate *questions will dictate the method of quotation and base currency required.*

CORPORATE FX BUSINESS
Time or delivery option forward contract

In many countries, and the UK is an example, middle market commercial companies are keen to cover their exchange risks but perhaps do not have the time to manage these risks actively minute by minute. For such companies there is an ideal type of forward cover available.

Forward foreign exchange deals may be transacted on an option basis – to buy or sell one currency against another for a value date *within* a predetermined period in the future. These option forward contracts, used by companies with known risk exposure but unknown dates of such, are options on delivery date only and must not be confused with the risk management product *currency options* which are "true" or performance options. Currency options are the subject of Chapter 8.

A *time* or *delivery* option forward exchange contract is defined as a forward contract where the delivery date of the foreign currency is at the customer's option. The contracted amount of foreign currency must be settled in full on any date or dates (partial delivery is permitted) at the customer's option within the contractual option period. Should the full amount not be able to be settled by the final date of the option period, then a spot exchange deal reversing the initial operation must be effected to "close out" the balance of the option contract.

Periods available

Option forward contracts are quoted by banks for periods *between two specified dates, for whole calendar months* or *from spot date to a specified date in the future.*

The maximum option period a bank will quote for is typically three months, otherwise the forward premium or discount applicable makes the transaction unattractive to the customer. This three-month period can be any such period though it will probably be limited to within a 12-month horizon.

Partial take-up (delivery)

Companies which use option forward contracts frequently deal for one amount of currency which may be needed over several settlement dates within the option period. Banks are happy to provide a service whereby multiple partial deliveries against option forward contracts are permissible.

Close-out

An option forward contract is a contractual obligation on the part of the customer who must take up the full amount of currency originally dealt for. Should not all the foreign currency funds be required by the final maturity date of the option contract, the customer must buy from, or sell back to, the bank any remaining currency balance.

This transaction, termed a *close-out*, is effected at the then prevailing spot exchange rate. Any monetary difference resulting from a movement in rates between deal date and final maturity date must be settled between the customer and the bank. Such a difference could be in favour of either party.

Extensions

Option forward contracts may also be extended for a further period, should the need for the exchange deal not have arisen during the period originally anticipated by the customer. When an *extension* is requested the existing option forward contract is closed out at the spot rate, with any necessary sterling settlement taking place between the bank and the customer, and a new option forward contract is agreed based on current spot and forward premium/discount rates.

Early take-up (delivery)

Should a customer require to take up an option forward contract before the commencement date of the option period, this is possible but may result in an additional cost to the customer. What in effect the bank will do is close out the option forward contract at the forward rate applicable to the start date of the period and simultaneously do another forward contract (this time an outright) for the early delivery date requested by the customer. To a bank dealer this is the same as effecting a spot against forward or forward/forward foreign exchange swap.

Pricing of time or delivery option forward contracts

The pricing of time or delivery option forward contracts is similar in concept to that noted above for outright deals, except that as the foreign currency could be settled (delivered) on any date within the contractual period, the bank has to bear in mind that the customer may deliver on the worst possible date (as far as the market is concerned) within the contractual option period. The rate is therefore weighted accordingly.

When a bank prices an option forward contract the customer will be quoted the least favourable (to him) rate ruling during the option period. It is in the customer's interest to be as accurate as possible at estimating the required value dates of an option forward transaction – the shorter the option period the less the premium/discount will work against him.

The outright forward rates for the start and maturity dates of the option period are calculated and a comparison is made to determine the rate to be quoted to the customer. In normal market conditions this will be either the start date of the option period or the end date of the option period depending on the decision rules outlined below.

Time or delivery option forward quotation rules

The following simple rules express in a concise form the basis on which a bank will price forward exchange business on a time or delivery option basis.

Bank buys base currency (at a forward premium)

If the forward points are quoted low–high the base currency is at a forward *premium*. For the forward purchase of the base currency the bank quotes the *least* number of points (to be added to spot) of the rates applicable to the two dates in question – the start date of the option period and the end date of the option period.

Bank sells base currency (at a forward premium)

If the forward points are quoted low–high the base currency is at a forward *premium*. For the forward sale of the base currency the bank quotes the *greatest* number of points (to be added to spot) of the rates applicable to the two dates in question – the start date of the option period and the end date of the option period.

Bank buys base currency (at a forward discount)

If the forward points are quoted high–low the base currency is at a forward *discount*. For the forward purchase of the base currency the bank quotes the *greatest* number of points (to be subtracted from spot) of the rates applicable to the two dates in question – the start date of the option period and the end date of the option period.

Bank sells base currency (at a forward discount)

If the forward points are quoted high–low the base currency is at a forward *discount*. For the forward sale of the base currency the bank quotes the *least* number of points (to be subtracted from spot) of the rates applicable to the two dates in question – the start date of the option period and the end date of the option period.

> **Question**
>
> A typical ACI Dealing Certificate question might be:
>
> Which of the following is *not true* of a traditional forward exchange (time or delivery) option contract?
>
> A: No obligation to complete the contract
> B: Multiple partial deliveries are possible during the option period
> C: May be extended at maturity
> D: Must be closed out at spot if full contractual amount is not delivered
>
> **Correct answer**
> A: In a traditional forward exchange (time or delivery) option there *is* a contractual obligation to complete the contract. A traditional forward exchange option contract grants the customer the option as to date of delivery of the currency. It is *not* a true open contract like a currency option. The customer may not walk away from his obligation. The full amount of the contract must be delivered within the option period.

Pricing date

In 99 cases out of 100 the two dates in question are the *start* date and the *end* date of the option period requested by the customer.

Note

> In certain circumstances where there are other unusual dates (such as reserve dates with higher interest rate structures in one of the currencies within an option period) other dates may also enter the decision process.

INTERBANK FORWARD EXCHANGE OPERATIONS

While banks are prepared to quote outright rates to their customers and effect deals on this basis with them, they tend to deal with each other in the interbank market on a foreign exchange swap basis.

Foreign exchange swap definition

A foreign exchange swap is defined as a simultaneously dealt set of two linked exchange transactions involving the purchase and the sale of an identical amount of one currency against a countercurrency with differing maturities, most frequently spot value against a forward value date. On effecting a foreign exchange swap the banks are seeking to match cash flow requirements in the two currencies involved over various periods (between differing value dates).

Example

EUR/USD spot and forward rates are quoted.

EUR/USD
Spot: 0.89 97 – 03
Forwards
8 – 10 **16 – 18** 25 – 27 43 – 48 53 – 63

Interbank foreign exchange swaps

The bank quoting the forward points (the market maker) is happy to exchange cash flows as follows.

The left-hand side rate is the market maker's *bid* for the base currency on the forward date (the bank's forward bid for EUR). (In a foreign exchange swap the spot date cash movement will be the reverse.) On the left-hand side of the price (** above) the market maker therefore sells spot and buys two months forward EUR against US dollars.

The right-hand side rate is the market maker's offer of the base currency on the forward date (the bank's forward offer of EUR).

On the right-hand side of the price (** above) the market maker buys spot and sells forward EUR against US dollars.

> **Note**
> *As for spot in Chapter 6, the rule bid offer for the base currency (BOB) applies, but this time refers to the currency movement* **on the forward date.**

Market making/market using

As in the spot market in any interbank dealing contact it is the bank dealer initiating the call (market user) who always requests the rate(s) quotation from the bank dealer (market maker) whom he has called.

> **Note**
> Traditionally it has been the practice in interbank forward dealing conversations for the calling bank to request a full run-through of all standard periods from the market maker called. Market etiquette demands that no rate is "hit" until the full run-through has been quoted and the rates quoted are only good for one deal in one period. For any additional deals the calling bank would give the market maker the opportunity to change his prices before dealing again. Alternatively a single period quote can be sought. This has become the norm as more and more dealing conversations take place by electronic means rather than voice contact.

Interbank dealing conversation – forward foreign exchange

A direct dealing telephone call from one bank dealer (market user) to another (market maker) can be a very short conversation. The basic requirements are for the dealer initiating the call to identify his/her bank, request the forwards or single period sought, listen to the quoting bank's response and then if appropriate (i.e. if the quoted rate(s) suit the calling bank), effect the desired deal and finally agree all details. For example:

> *Calling bank*: "Hi there, High Street Bank, it's Dealing Bank London here. How's forward EUR/USD please?"
>
> *Quoting bank*: "Hello there Dealing Bank; forward EUR/USD – I make you < eight – ten, sixteen – eighteen, twenty-five – twenty-seven, forty-three – forty-eight and fifty-three – sixty-three>"
>
> *Calling bank*: "Thank you. At forty-three (points my favour) in the six months I buy and sell one million euro please."
>
> **This is frequently simplified to: "At 43 in the sixes, 1 million (please)" – the dealers appreciate that they are dealing in round amounts of euro (the base currency) in interbank forward EUR quotations.**
>
> *Quoting bank*: "OK. That's agreed*, the spot is currently 97 – 02 around the figure 0.90, we sell and buy EUR, buy and sell USD, details: value spot (date...) Dealing Bank sells EUR 1 million at 0.9000 to High Street Bank and value (date...) we buy from you EUR 1 million at 0.9043 against USD."
>
> *Calling bank*: "Yes, all agreed, thanks... My spot EUR via ELS and forward USD to my account with Citibank New York. Where for you?"
>
> *Quoting bank*: "Fine, my spot dollars to my New York office please and the forward EUR via CHAPS EURO. Thanks for the deal. Goodbye for now."
>
> *Calling bank*: "OK. Thanks for the deal and goodbye."

The duration of such a typical forward FX dealing conversation over the telephone would be as long as it takes you to read the relevant passage (possibly shorter)!

Note

> Once the quoting bank (market maker) has used any wording signifying acceptance of the deal requested that constitutes the moment of contract. My word is my bond is still the market maxim. The verbal confirmation that follows takes slightly longer and is vital for the same three reasons as in the spot conversation noted in Chapter 6.

The "base" spot rate involved

In a foreign exchange swap operation it is the forward points differential which is all important – the exchange of cash flows inherent in the swap operation (typically spot date against a forward value date) being intended to reduce or remove interest rate risk in the two currencies of the swap.

Topic 6 · Forward Foreign Exchange

However, according to the Model Code (see Chapter 11) the spot rate for all foreign exchange swap operations *must* be fixed "at or around" the current market level (here 0.9000 mid point). This spot rate will therefore be agreed between the parties immediately the foreign exchange swap operation is effected and must be "within the current spread" – using the Model Code phrase.

> **Hint**
>
> *Dealers will frequently set the spot rate on a big figure or even number to make any subsequent calculation of the forward dated rate as easy as possible, always provided the above rule is not breached, i.e. rates ending in "0" are easier to adjust up or down perhaps by an odd amount of points.*

Interbank forward foreign exchange swap

Market maker's bid

As in the above conversation, the market maker has quoted and the calling bank requests to deal in the six months at 43 points EUR premium – the left-hand side of the market maker's 43 – 48 two-way six months price:

The following transactions and value dated cash movements are involved:

- Value spot:
  - *market maker* – Dealing Bank sells EUR 1,000,000.00 @ 0.9000 and buys USD 900,000.00;
- Value six months forward:
  - *market maker* – Dealing Bank buys EUR 1,000,000.00 @ 0.9043 and sells USD 904,300.00.

In dealing terminology this is referred to as "points against me" by the market maker and "points my favour" by the market user. The USD cash flows across the two days show the market maker a "cost" and the market user a "benefit" of USD 4,300 – being the equivalent of 43 points on EUR 1 million.

Market maker's offer

Had the transaction been effected on the right-hand side of the market maker's price the following would have been the situation:

- Value spot:
  - *market maker* – Dealing Bank buys EUR 1,000,000.00 @ 0.9000 and sells USD 900,000.00;
- Value six months forward:
  - *market maker* – Dealing Bank sells EUR 1,000,000.00 @ 0.9048 and buys USD 904,800.00.

In dealing terminology this is referred to as "points my favour" by the market maker and "points against me" by the market user. This time the USD cash flows across the two value dates show the market maker a "benefit" and the market user a "cost" of USD 4,800.00 – being the equivalent of 48 points on EUR 1 million.

As noted earlier in this chapter, the forward swap points, the standard method of quotation in the forward foreign exchange market, are equivalent to the interest rate differential between the two currencies involved. The EUR swap points at a forward premium mean six months euros have a lower interest rate than US dollars at the moment. Here any euro received in exchange for US dollars given up over the life of the swap will earn the euro recipient a lower return. The points in his favour are in compensation for this cost and give both parties to the swap an accurate cost of switching such cash flows.

Corporate interest in foreign exchange swaps

Banks have always traded with each other in the "professional" market on a swap basis and these days the more sophisticated corporate treasurers see the benefits of dealing on the swap – allowing them to close the major risk of a spot rate movement as one spot transaction, and then covering any forward currency flows at their leisure. Because of their link with interest rates, forward premium/discount rates tend to be less volatile than spot rates.

Question

A typical ACI Dealing Certificate question might be:

If you are told that the forward points for six months USD/CHF are quoted at a USD discount (international terminology), how would you expect them to be displayed on a dealer's rates screen?

A: Insufficient information to decide
B: "High–low"
C: "Low–high"
D: Around par

Correct answer

B: If the base currency of a foreign exchange rate quotation (here the USD) is described as being at a forward discount then the numbers in the swap bid–offer spread are quoted and displayed "high–low" (international terminology).

OTHER FORWARD FOREIGN EXCHANGE CALCULATIONS

Broken dated forward exchange contracts

As we have seen, forward exchange rate quotations are made for the standard periods, typically 1, 2, 3, 6 and 12 months, but the foreign exchange

Topic 6 · Forward Foreign Exchange

requirements of corporate and retail customers – and of the banks themselves – do not always so readily comply with these standard calendar dates.

Exchange operations (outrights, options or swaps) for non-standard forward value dates are termed broken dated forward exchange contracts, or "cock dates" in dealers' jargon.

Naturally, if a corporate treasurer or bank dealer wants to cover a known forward exchange risk position, he will request a rate for the specific date he wants, rather than one of the standard dates available in the market. In such circumstances the quoting bank will calculate the swap points and ultimately the outright rate for the date required by interpolation from the nearest available standard dates' (either side of the required date) forward swap points.

Broken dated forward exchange example

A bank dealer quotes his customer the following set of forward GBP/USD swap points:

	GBP/USD Spot: 1.50 00 – 10	
1 month	13 – 10	31 days
2 months	24 – 21	62 days
3 months	34 – 31	92 days
6 months	70 – 65	184 days
12 months	153 – 143	365 days

A corporate treasurer wants an outright two-way price for GBP/USD for a date which is exactly $2\frac{1}{2}$ months or 77 days (62 in the two months *plus* 15 extra days) from spot date.

With the 62 days in the two months quoted 24 – 21 and the 92 days in the three months 34 – 31 the 30 days of the third month can be calculated comparing bid with bid and offer with offer (left with left and right with right) using straight-line interpolation to be worth 10 points (34 – 24 = 10 points and 31 – 21 = 10 points). There are 30 days difference between the two months (62 days) and the three months (92 days).

By dividing the base currency bid adjustment of 10 points by the 30 days difference, and dividing the base currency offer adjustment of 10 points by the 30 days, each day in the third month can be seen to be worth 0.333333 (0.33) points.

The adjustment for the extra $\frac{1}{2}$ month (15 days) can then be calculated. First, the bid adjustment $0.333333 \times 15 = 4.999$ is added to the points value of the current standard two months period bid rate of 24 giving 28.999 (24 + 4.999) points and the offer adjustment again $0.333333 \times 15 = 4.999$ is added to the points value of the current standard two months period offer rate of 21 giving 25.999 (21 + 4.999) to achieve a two-way price of 28.999 – 25.99 (29 – 26 after rounding) for the 77 days rate quotation required:

> two-way price for $2\frac{1}{2}$ months (77 days) = 29 – 26 (rounded)

Note

The above enables the swap points to be calculated which, in order to quote the outright rate requested, would then have to be used to adjust the current spot exchange rate.

Broken date outright quote

```
GBP/USD
Spot        1.50 00 – 1.50 10
less        0.00 29 – 0.00 26
            1.49 71 – 1.49 84
```

In exceptional circumstances care is required using such a straight-line interpolation process. Where there are extraordinary adjustments to be made due to reserve or make-up days in either of the currencies involved on a date in the middle of a period between the two standard periods being used in the broken date calculation, consideration has to be taken of the distortion

Question

A typical ACI Dealing Certificate question might be:

If three months USD/CHF swap is quoted 25 – 28 and six months is quoted 37 – 42, what would the five months interpolated forward swap points be quoted approximately?

A: 33 – 37
B: 37 – 42
C: 27 – 33
D: 33 – 27

Correct answer
A: Both the near date swap and the far date swap are quoted at a USD premium. The five months swap is calculated on a straight-line interpolation basis (12 points difference between the three months and six months bid means that each forward month is worth 4 points. Therefore add 8 points to the near date bid swap of 25 to achieve a price of 33 points on the left-hand side. A similar calculation for the right-hand side (9.33 points) results in a two-way price of 33 – 37 for the five months swap.

Topic 6 · Forward Foreign Exchange

caused. Also, where there is an unusually shaped yield curve for any other reasons in one or both the currencies (moving from premium to discount or an exceptionally steep curve), some form of weighting may be appropriate.

Forward/forward foreign exchange swap operations

So far in this chapter we have spoken solely about spot against forward foreign exchange swaps. In the management of his forward foreign currency cash flows a bank dealer may wish to deal on a swap basis but commencing from a forward date.

A forward/forward exchange swap is a simultaneously dealt set of two linked exchange transactions involving the purchase and sale of an identical amount of one currency against a countercurrency with differing maturities, *neither* of which is spot date.

In any unusual situation such as a forward/forward swap request, the bank dealer, before making his rate quotation, must consider how such a deal can be covered. One way to cover a forward/forward swap is to deal two opposing spot against forward foreign exchange swaps, one for maturity for the first date of the forward/forward period and the other for maturity for the final date of the forward/forward period requested.

With a forward/forward swap considered as two separate opposing spot against forward foreign exchange swaps with the spot date cash movements netting out – the same spot rate being used to compensate amounts of both currencies – the logic for calculating the rate quotation is evident.

Forward/forward foreign exchange swap example

An example of a typical forward/forward quoted period would be three months forward against six months forward, which would be described in the market as "3 against 6 months" or "3/6" or 3 × 6 – said as "threes/sixies".

> **Note**
> The numbers in the description of the period do NOT relate to the calendar months numbers but to the time gaps as described above. Here the market user seeks a forward/forward rate quotation for 3 months forward from spot date against 6 months forward from spot date.

The bank dealer (market maker) quotes the following set of GBP/USD forward swap points:

GBP/USD Spot: 1.50 00 – 10		
1 month	13 – 10	31 days
2 months	24 – 21	62 days
3 months	34 – 31	**92 days**
6 months	70 – 65	**184 days**
12 months	153 – 143	365 days

The market user may wish to buy sterling (sell US dollars) three months forward (outright) and sell sterling back six months forward (outright) but in a simultaneous forward/forward swap operation. In other words, the market user wishes to deal on the market maker's **3s v. 6s forward/forward bid** for sterling in an amount of GBP 1 million.

Let's assume that the rates above are quoted in the market (by the broker). We'll look at the two covering deals able to be effected by the market making bank:

1. the market making bank dealer (acting as market user in this covering operation) sells spot GBP against USD and buys it back three months forward at 31 points GBP discount – right-hand side of broker's price ("points his favour");

2. the market making bank dealer (acting as market user in this covering operation) buys spot GBP against USD and sells it back six months forward at 70 points GBP discount – left-hand side of broker's price ("points against him").

The net effect of these two operations is that the dealer pays away 39 points against him (70 – 31) buying and selling GBP in the threes/sixes forward/forward period and *at least* this number of points must be earned when acting as market maker to the calling bank, effectively fixing the left-hand side of the price to be quoted as market maker.

Alternatively the calling bank may wish to sell sterling (buy US dollars) three months forward (outright) and buy sterling back six months forward (outright) but in a simultaneous forward/forward swap operation.

Let's assume that the rates above are quoted in the market (by the broker). We'll look at the two covering deals effected by the market making bank:

1. the market making bank dealer (acting as market user in this covering operation) buys spot GBP against USD and sells it back three months forward at 34 points GBP discount – left-hand side of broker's price ("points against him");

2. the market making bank dealer (acting as market user in this covering operation) buys spot GBP against USD and sells it back six months forward at 65 points GBP discount – right-hand side of broker's price ("points his favour").

The net effect of these two operations is that the dealer receives 31 points his favour (65 – 34) buying and selling GBP in the threes/sixes forward/forward period and this prices the maximum number of points to be paid away when acting as market maker to the calling bank.

The two-sided forward/forward price which the dealer can quote to a calling counterparty is therefore:

> 39 – 31 points (GBP discount)

Note

Bid and offer dealing sides (BOB), as with all forward quotations, refers to the forward date movement of the base currency being described. In the case of a forward/forward swap this means the *furthest forward* date of the two involved.

The 3s v. 6s forward/forward spread will be the sum of the two standard period forward spreads used – here a spread of 8 points (three months 3 points *plus* six months spread of 5 points).

Hint

In reality, in the major traded currencies, closer two-way prices can frequently be obtained in the market, but the above is the definitive method for covering forward/forward and therefore for calculating the "worst possible case" rate quotation. This is frequently referred to in the market as "the wide outside" of the price.

Question

A typical ACI Dealing Certificate question might be:

If a three months USD/DKK swap is quoted 5 – 8 and six months is quoted 35 – 30, what is forward/forward three months against six months swap?

A: 40 – 38
B: 38 – 43
C: 43 – 35
D: 54 – 35

Correct answer

C: Here the near date swap is quoted at a USD premium and the far date swap is quoted at a USD discount against the DKK (international terminology). To calculate the forward/forward therefore, the far date bid swap points have to be added to the near date offer swap points and vice versa to achieve the correct price which becomes a bigger USD premium (the wide outside).

Fixing the spot rate

As already mentioned, as with any forward exchange transaction the Model Code (see Chapter 11) requires that all forward rates should reflect the

Mastering the ACI Dealing Certificate

current spot exchange rate. It is therefore important that in the case of forward/forward swap transactions both legs are based on the current spot rate, i.e. in this 3s v. 6s example the three months forward rate should be the spot rate at the time of dealing adjusted by the three months swap points and the six months exchange rate should be the spot rate at the time of dealing adjusted by the six months swap points.

Returning to our earlier example calculation of 39 – 31 in the threes/sixes forward/forward GBP/USD period, if the market user requests to deal for GBP 1 million at 39 points "against him" GBP discount (the left-hand side); full details of such a swap operation (from Dealing Bank's point of view) would be as shown below.

At 39 points GBP discount (the bid) on the left-hand side

At 39 points GBP discount ("points his favour") on the left-hand side, Dealing Bank sells three months forward GBP 1 million against US dollars and simultaneously buys six months forward GBP 1 million against US dollars.

The rates are fixed – the three months "forward leg" rate at or near the current spot rate adjusted by the three months forward (1.50 00 *less* 31 points GBP discount) and the six months forward rate as the current spot rate adjusted by the six months forward (1.50 00 *less* 70 points GBP discount), i.e. spot minus forward points for both dates, will be:

Current mid rate for Spot Cable is:	1.50 00
…the three months "forward leg" rate is fixed at:	**1.49 69**
(being **1.50 00** *minus* **0.0031**)	
…and the six months "forward leg" rate fixed at:	**1.49 30**
(being **1.50 00** *minus* **0.0070**)	

The difference between the two forward rates is therefore the points differential dealt at, namely 39 points GBP discount.

Transactions involved (market maker at 39 points his favour)

Value **3 month forward:**
Market maker
Dealing Bank SELLS GBP 1,000,000.00 @ **1.49 69** and Buys USD 1,496,900.00

Value **6 month forward:**
Market maker
Dealing Bank BUYS GBP 1,000,000.00 @ **1.49 30** and Sells USD 1,493,000.00

At 31 points GBP discount (the offer) on the right-hand side

At 31 points GBP discount ("points against him") on the right-hand side, the market making bank dealer buys three months forward GBP 1 million against US dollars and simultaneously sells six months forward GBP 1 million against US dollars.

The rates are fixed – the three months "forward leg" rate at or near the current spot rate adjusted by the three months forward (1.50 00 *less* 34 points GBP discount) and the six months forward rate as the current spot rate adjusted by the six months forward (1.50 00 *less* 65 points GBP discount), i.e. spot minus forward points for both dates, will be:

Current mid rate for Spot Cable is: 1.50 00

…the three months "forward leg" rate is fixed at: **1.49 66**
(being **1.50 00** *minus* **0.0034**)

…and the six months "forward leg" rate fixed at: **1.49 35**
(being **1.50 00** *minus* **0.0065**)

The difference between the two forward rates is therefore the points differential dealt at, namely 31 points GBP discount.

Transactions involved (market maker at 31 points against him)

Value **3 month forward:**
Market maker
Dealing Bank BUYS GBP 1,000,000.00 @ **1.49 66** and Sells USD 1,496,600.00

Value **6 month forward:**
Market maker
Dealing Bank SELLS GBP 1,000,000.00 @ **1.49 35** and Buys USD 1,493,500.00

Calculation rule

The calculation rule is illustrated here. This rule also works when the forward points move through par.

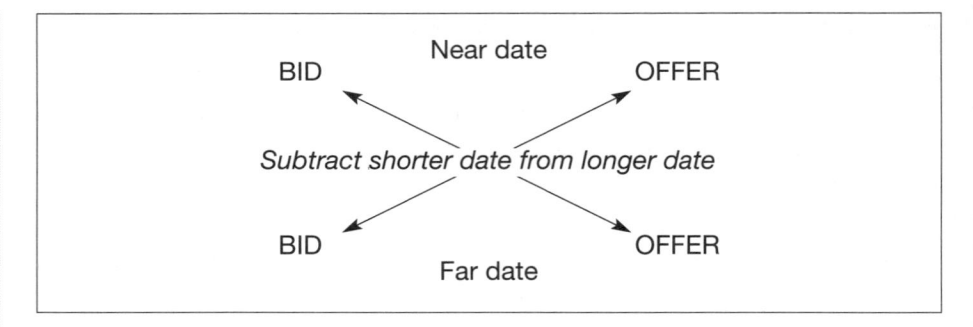

```
                    Near date
        BID                      OFFER
             ↖              ↗
           Subtract shorter date from longer date
             ↙              ↘
        BID                      OFFER
                    Far date
```

If the forwards are quoted:

```
        USD/XXX forwards
             10 – 5
              6 – 1
              2 – 7
             5 – 10
            12 – 17
```

We can see that in the one and two months the forwards are at a forward USD discount and in the three months to one year periods the forwards move through parity and are quoted on a forward USD premium. Supposing we need to calculate a forward/forward swap price 2s v. 3s. The three months is 2 – 7 low–high while the twos are quoted 6 – 1 high–low.

We can still use the rule to subtract the shorter period points from the longer period points but we must remember the move through parity changes the sign of the points. Two months high–low is actually *minus 6 minus 1* and three months low–high is actually *plus 2 plus 7*, so the calculation is:

minus 7 [*minus minus*] **6** to **plus 2** [*minus minus*] **1**

Since *minus minus* = *plus*, therefore the "wide outside" result is (7 *plus* 6) 13 – (2 *plus* 1) 3. This can be proved once again by confirming that the forward/forward spread is the sum of the two periods' spread. The two months spread is 5 and the three months spread is 5, so the forward/forward spread should be (5 *plus* 5) = 10. At 13 – 3 it is.

Short dated foreign exchange swaps

Bank dealers are responsible for squaring up the nostro cash positions of their banks in the currencies under their control. Not all foreign exchange transactions are covered deal for deal or date for date. It follows therefore that every day there will be surplus funds in one currency and a shortage of balances in the other currency of any currency pairing.

These positions can be squared in two different ways – using either money market or foreign exchange swap techniques:

- a long cash position can be lent out (asset) on a short date basis with a short cash position being squared by taking a deposit (liability) for the appropriate short date period; or
- the foreign exchange cash position can be squared by the dealer effecting a short date foreign exchange swap operation for the appropriate short date period.

Overnight and Tom/Next

The most frequently dealt short date foreign exchange swaps for these purposes are *overnight* (today against tomorrow) and *Tom/Next* (tomorrow against the next working day – which happens to be spot). In the dealing morning there are always prices available for these two periods in the market. It is these short date rates which a dealer needs before he can quote a customer for outright transactions requested for ante-spot value dates.

Other short date swaps frequently encountered are *spot/next* (spot date against the next working day) and *spot a week* (spot date against seven days forward from spot).

Outright "ante-spot" contracts

As has already been mentioned spot rate and spot date are the benchmarks on which all other rates and dates are based. Ante is the Latin word for "before". Ante-spot dates are those value dates before spot date and can only be *today* and *tomorrow*.

> It very much depends on the time zone situation whether a quote for value today can be obtained in certain currency pairings – see below.

Note

Time zone limitations

In London a value same day (value *today*) quote can be obtained for US dollars against sterling at any time up to approximately 1.00 p.m. and sometimes later. This is because it is still possible to effect the necessary physical cash payments in the two centres (London and New York). The London CHAPS payment system is still in operation (late UK payments can be effected up to around 4.00 p.m. each afternoon) and the New York clearing will not close until five or six hours afterwards (New York being those many hours behind London time).

By the same token a value *today* exchange quotation is impossible in London for USD/JPY. The requirement to pay or receive Japanese yen through the Tokyo clearing could not be met because by the time the UK market opens the Japanese yen clearing has virtually finished for the day.

Similarly for most other currency pairs, because of early morning same day value payment cut-off times, value *tomorrow* is frequently the earliest ante-spot dealing value date possible. Short date quotes are available in the market up to around 1.00 p.m. each afternoon, though the market does tend to square up the tom/next during the late morning meaning that value tomorrow deals can be effected in the morning according to short date market liquidity.

Outright value tomorrow

When pricing an outright value tomorrow, you have to ask yourself what transactions are required to cover the deal through a spot operation and a short date swap. This is best explained by way of an example:

> Spot GBP/USD: $\quad$ 1.50 00 – 10
> Tom/Next swap: $\quad$ 3 – $2\frac{1}{2}$ points
> High–low = GBP discount

Note

The tom/next swap quote of 3 – $2\frac{1}{2}$ points is in fact 0.0003 – 0.00025. Although the spot in any currency pair may only be quoted to four decimal places, short date rates can go to decimals (or fractions) of points, here to the fifth decimal place.

Example of outright value tomorrow

Our customer requests an outright exchange rate for GBP/USD for value tomorrow. The customer is a seller of GBP value tomorrow which the bank can sell in the market value spot. Let us look at the cash flows involved from the bank's point of view.

Value today	*Value tomorrow*	*Value spot*
	BUY GBP Sell USD	**SELL GBP** Buy USD
	Outright deal (customer) Rate?	Spot deal (market) 1.50 00 – 10

We must produce a rate at which we can buy GBP (sell USD) value tomorrow and cover the cash flows without cost till spot date. We know we can deal to square the position on the spot date. We can sell GBP (buy USD) value spot at the market's bid of 1.50 00.

Topic 6 · Forward Foreign Exchange

Ignoring rates for the moment, if we now buy GBP (sell USD) from the customer value tomorrow we will be long GBP (short USD) from tomorrow until spot date.

This is a Tom/Next cash position which can be squared *either* by lending the long GBP and borrowing the short USD cash positions (money market operations) or by the alternative and much more common method of dealing a Tom/Next foreign exchange swap in GBP/USD.

The short date foreign exchange swap would involve two exchange deals dealt simultaneously with another bank (assume Bank Y in the market) with the following resultant cash flow positions:

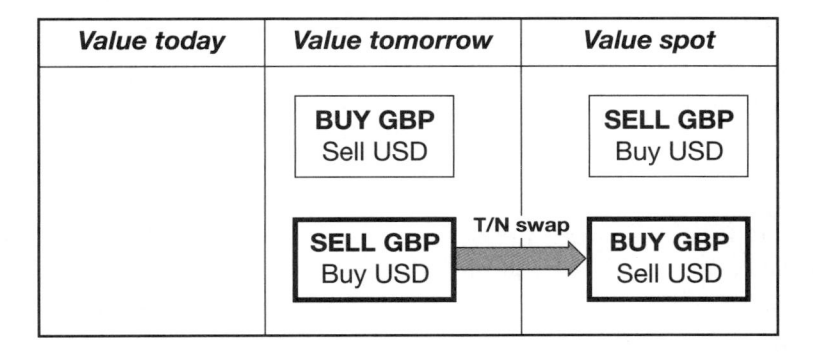

Value today	Value tomorrow	Value spot
	BUY GBP Sell USD	**SELL GBP** Buy USD
	SELL GBP Buy USD — T/N swap →	**BUY GBP** Sell USD

The highlighted deals are the two "legs" of the Tom/Next GBP/USD foreign exchange swap with Bank Y.

From the above cash flow we can see that we are able to buy GBP outright value tomorrow and cover it with a spot sale and a Tom/Next foreign exchange swap selling and buying GBP. But at what price can these transactions be done?

> **Hint**
> The ACI Dealing Certificate *examination frequently includes multiple choice questions seeking a dealing rate to buy or sell on an outright basis or an "implied" exchange rate for value today or tomorrow.*

Ante-spot pricing

Let us give these deals some values to be effected.

Customer A wants to sell GBP 1 million and buy USD value tomorrow.

Mastering the ACI Dealing Certificate

> Spot GBP/USD: 1.50 00 – 10
> Tom/Next swap: 3 – $2\frac{1}{2}$ points
> **High–low = GBP discount**

We can go to the market and sell GBP 1 million for spot value at 1.50 00 (the bid for spot sterling). We can call Bank Y and deal on his T/N offer of GBP (right-hand side of the tom/next FX swap quote of $2\frac{1}{2}$ points GBP discount (0.00025 in the rate).

The full details of the Tom/Next foreign exchange swap dealt with Bank Y are:

> Value tom we sell GBP 1 million (buy USD)   at 1.50 025
> Value spot we buy GBP 1 million (sell USD) at 1.50 000
>
> which equates to $2\frac{1}{2}$ pts our favour

With this Tom/Next swap and the spot transaction we have now effectively sold the GBP value tomorrow that Customer A wants to sell to us on that value date and at a known cost 1.50 025 (1.50 00 plus 0.00025 points earned).

As the purpose of the above transactions was to square all the cash flows (no profit no loss), the calculated rate for the outright value tomorrow purchase of GBP must therefore be 1.50025 – the spot rate of 1.50 00 adjusted by the GBP discount of $2\frac{1}{2}$ points = 0.00025. But note that we have *added* the points to the spot – the logic of subtracting the GBP discount (high–low) seems to have been reversed.

This is because the benchmark spot rate which in a forward rate calculation is the "first date rate", i.e. the starting point for the calculation, is actually the "second date rate" in this sequence. We can see that this "second date rate" is lower than the "first date rate", therefore the base currency discount dealing logic is correctly implemented.

Looking at it another way, the relationship of interest rates in sterling and US dollars in the Tom/Next period is the same as for forward periods, and the lending of GBP at the higher rate and funding of US dollars at the lower interest rate (a net gain) must be reflected in the outright exchange rate for value tomorrow.

Hint

> *Some practitioners merely state that the calculation rule for ante-spot outright rates is to reverse the dealing sides and the add/subtract logic already learned for forward rate calculations.*

Value today

If a rate for value today is required the same process must be followed but funds must be made available across the two days before spot. Both the short date swap points for overnight and Tom/Next will have to be used in the equation.

While in the interbank brokers' market the dealer might request a today/spot dealing price, it is normal to seek the overnight and Tom/Next base prices and then calculate the two-day run which will be used to adjust the spot rate to achieve outright rate value today.

Rule for pricing of outright "ante-spot" contracts

To put the above process on the same basis as the rule for forwards, a bank, to achieve a breakeven ("no profit/no loss situation"), will price ante-spot foreign exchange business on an outright basis as follows.

Base currency discount (high–low) – e.g. tom/next GBP/USD swap: $3 - 2\frac{1}{2}$

For the outright purchase on an ante-spot date of a base currency at a short date discount the market maker adjusts the left-hand side of the spot rate by adding the least base currency discount – the right-hand side. For example, to produce a buying rate for GBP against USD value tomorrow (as above); tom/next swap: $3 - 2\frac{1}{2}$:

Spot **Bid** GBP/USD:	1.50 00
plus **Offer** of	
Tom/Next swap:	0.00 025
$2\frac{1}{2}$ points	1.50 025
High – Low = GBP Discount	

For the outright sale on an ante-spot date of a base currency at a short date discount the market maker adjusts the right-hand side of the spot rate by adding the most base currency discount – the left-hand side. For example, to produce a selling rate for GBP against USD value tomorrow; tom/next swap: $3 - 2\frac{1}{2}$:

Spot **Offer** GBP/USD:	1.50 10
plus **Bid** of	
Tom/Next swap:	0.00 03
3 points	1.50 13
High – Low = GBP Discount	

Base currency premium (low–high) – e.g. tom/next EUR/USD swap: $2 - 2\frac{1}{2}$

For the outright purchase on an ante-spot date of a base currency at a short date premium the market maker adjusts the left-hand side of the spot rate

Mastering the ACI Dealing Certificate

by subtracting the most base currency premium – the right-hand side. For example, to produce a buying rate for EUR against USD value tomorrow; tom/next swap: 2 – 2½:

Spot **Bid** EUR/USD:	0.90 00
less **Offer** of Tom/Next swap:	0.00 025
2½ points	0.89 975
Low – High = EUR Premium	

For the outright sale on an ante-spot date of a base currency at a short date premium the market maker adjusts the right-hand side of the spot rate by subtracting the least base currency premium – the left-hand side. For example, to produce a selling rate for EUR against USD value tomorrow; tom/next swap: 2 – 2½:

Spot **Offer** EUR/USD:	0.90 10
less **Bid** of Tom/Next swap:	0.00 02
2 points	0.90 08
Low – High = EUR Premium	

Hint

Remember the ante-spot adjustment logic seems to be the reverse of the forward exchange rate methodology. This is because the benchmark spot rate which in a forward rate calculation is the "first date rate", i.e. the starting point for the calculation, is actually the "second date rate" in this sequence.

Question

A typical ACI Dealing Certificate question might be:

From the following rates – spot GBP/USD: 1.6656/60; T/N GBP/USD swap: 1.3/1.2 – what is the theoretical quote for GBP/USD outright value tomorrow?

A: 1.66547/1.66588
B: 1.66572/1.66613
C: 1.6669/1.6672
D: 1.66573/1.66612

Correct answer

B: For an ante-spot outright calculation as market user you must take the spot rate and adjust it for the benefit (cost) of bringing the cash flow back to tomorrow: here 1.6656 plus 1.2 points earned tom/next and 1.6660 plus 1.3 points paid away tom/next; two-way price 1.66572 – 1.66613.

INTEREST ARBITRAGE

Interest arbitrage is the link between the eurocurrency money markets via the forward exchange market. Bank dealers can enter into interest arbitrage operations for various reasons:

- **Generation of local currency.** In various financial centres overseas, the most attractive and sometimes the only means available to a foreign bank to raise scarce local currency resources is by accepting foreign currency deposits from abroad (usually US dollars) and through the medium of interest arbitrage, either as permitted by central bank regulations or in a free market situation, converting these balances to lendable resources in the desired local currency.
- **Funding foreign currency assets.** Where liabilities in the currency of asset are unavailable or expensive in comparison to a deposit and foreign exchange swap through another currency (including local currency where permitted), a dealer can raise such cover via the means of interest arbitrage.
- **Utilizing foreign currency liabilities.** Where a deposit has been accepted and the means to on-lend in that currency are limited or not as attractive as a swap operation with a view to lending the resultant countercurrency funds, the swap deal involved is an interest arbitrage operation.
- **Dealing for forward value in a currency without a well developed exchange market, or one that is predominantly deposit-based.** Interest arbitrage techniques can be used to manufacture points differentials for the purpose of quoting outright forward exchange rates in currencies where there is no developed forward market but a spot rate and associated local currency deposit market exists. In such a currency, consider the situation where a bank dealer has quoted and dealt with a corporate customer on an outright basis and subsequently covered the currency exposure by a reverse spot operation. If there are no means available to cover the resultant forward exchange time position via a foreign exchange swap transaction, or exchange controls prohibit it, the mismatched currency cash flows can be squared by a liability in one and an asset in the other currency for the period in question. The initial spot and forward outright deals must in this case be identified together as a swap and treated as interest arbitrage.
- **Trading considerations synthetic asset/liability creation.** In an active trading situation with both exchange and money market operations being effected in various currencies, opportunities may arise to deal in interest arbitrage operations, either in a package involving a deposit in one currency, a foreign exchange swap (spot against forward) and a loan in

the other currency, or by a permutation of two out of the three transactions (which must perforce include the exchange deal) to create a desired "synthetic" position to trade from in the respective currency money market.

- **Choice of market.** Sometimes, for one reason or another, a dealer may prefer to use a funding source in a different currency and/or market from that in which the asset is denominated. This could be because excessive demands for funds have already been made during the day in one particular market or that there is a known funding source through a different market in which the institution is keen to show its name. An example of this is the issuance of commercial paper denominated in US dollars by UK building societies and the swapping via interest arbitrage of the resultant balances into sterling to fund the domestic mortgage book.

Bearing in mind local exchange control and other regulations pertaining to the bank's local market presence and participation, a bank dealer is empowered to decide when he will become involved in interest arbitrage situations. What must be remembered is that the most important consideration for the dealer prior to deciding to identify any linked set of transactions as interest arbitrage is the cost of so doing and the risks ensuing.

Interest arbitrage example

For an example of interest arbitrage we will concentrate on a typical situation where a dealer is looking for funding of a EUR asset by taking a USD deposit and using the forward EUR/USD market in a "covered" interest arbitrage situation.

The funding cost in euro can be calculated by taking the US dollar liability interest cost and adjusting it by the cost or benefit of the foreign exchange swap.

We have already discussed earlier in this chapter the fact that forward swap points are equivalent to the difference in the interest rates in the two currencies concerned for the period quoted.

The following interest arbitrage example proves this concept. We will use the following spot and six months forward rates data:

EUR/USD
0.89 95 – 05
mid rate: 0.9000
6 months (180 days) EUR/USD
50 – 55

Topic 6 · Forward Foreign Exchange

These exchange rates are based on euro and US dollar money market rates of:

> six months (180 days) EUR int rate: 3.00 – 3.125%
>
> six months (180 days) USD int rate: 4.125 – 4.25%

The ACI preferred formulae below can be used to calculate the swap points or either the maximum funding rate possible or minimum asset return necessary to achieve equilibrium (the no profit no loss "breakeven" rate). In any situation involving a formula and an associated series of cash flows the latter can be used to prove the formula and this example attempts to show this.

For this worked example we need to fix the amount and rate of the EUR denominated asset we are looking to fund.

Funding requirement

Six months EUR loan: EUR 10,000,000.00
EUR loan rate: 3.125%
Six months: 180 days

EUR and USD money market interest basis both actual/360.

Note

The dealer will fund this on a foreign exchange swap basis by buying spot EUR and selling six months forward EUR (180 days) against USD.

On the six months swap price of 50 – 55 quoted to him by the market maker, the funding dealer (dealing as a market user) will enter into a foreign exchange swap at 50 points "his favour" (the market maker's bid for forward EUR) buying spot and selling forward EUR.

FX swap

With the spot rate (mid point) 0.9000 and six months forward swap of *plus* 50 points the two legs of the swap are:

spot purchase EUR 10,000,000.00 at 0.9000 sale	USD 9,000,000.00
forward sale EUR 10,000,000.00 at 0.9050 purchase	USD 9,050,000.00
swap "benefit':	USD 50,000.00

Deposit

The dealer will then fund the resultant six months USD cash requirement with a matching USD deposit. The six months (180 days) USD money market rate is currently quoted: 4.125 – 4.25 percent. The funding dealer takes a six months deposit in the amount of USD 9,000,000.00 (the spot date cash requirement) at the offered rate of 4.25 percent.

Interest arbitrage costs

- EUR interest receipt: $= \dfrac{10{,}000{,}000.00 \times 180 \times 3.125}{360 \times 100}$ = EUR 156,250.00

- USD swap "benefit" 50 points: = USD 50,000.00

- USD interest payment: $= \dfrac{9{,}000{,}000.00 \times 180 \times 4.25}{360 \times 100}$ = USD 191,250.00

The EUR interest receivable of EUR 156,250.00 must be sold outright forward for USD at 0.90 50 – the same forward rate as on the forward "leg" of the swap to achieve USD 141,406.25 which together with the swap benefit of USD 50,000.00 achieves the USD interest payable amount USD 191,406.25.

Variable currency calculation (from swap and base currency interest rate)

Using the <ACI preferred> interest arbitrage formula to calculate the USD interest expense (interest rate to be paid):

$$\text{variable currency interest rate created} = \left[\left(1 + \left(\text{base currency interest rate} \times \dfrac{\text{days}}{\text{day base for base currency}}\right)\right) \times \dfrac{\text{outright}}{\text{spot}} - 1\right] \times \dfrac{\text{day base for variable currency}}{\text{days}}$$

<ACI preferred>

In our example:

$$\left(\left(1 + \left(0.03125 \times \dfrac{180}{360}\right)\right) \times \dfrac{0.9050}{0.9000} - 1\right) \times \dfrac{360}{180} = 0.042534722$$

<ACI preferred>

We can see this is 4.2535 percent. This can be rounded to 4.25 percent and determines the maximum interest rate which can be paid for the USD deposit dealing at 50 points EUR premium on the swap to ensure the EUR funds are raised at the rate intended.

Care!

In the <ACI preferred> formula interest rates must be input as decimals, i.e. 5.00 percent is input as 0.05.

> **Note**
>
> The deposit taken is unlikely to be at exactly the rate calculated. Any USD offered rate lower than this calculated rate will result in a profit and provide additional incentive for the dealer to enter into this sequence of transactions.
>
> Most banks insist that for internal control and accounting apportionment the dealer must link the transactions as a covered interest arbitrage operation following the bank's in-house identification procedures. This is because unless all risks are clearly identified and managed by the dealer from the inception of any sequence of interest arbitrage transactions, they can turn out to be far less profitable (or even result in a loss) than first assumed or calculated.

Base currency calculation (from swap and variable currency interest rate)

Using the <ACI preferred> interest arbitrage formula to calculate the required EUR loan interest income (base currency interest rate to be achieved) we can see this is:

base currency interest rate created =

$$\left[\left(1 + \left(\text{variable currency interest rate} \times \frac{\text{days}}{\text{day base for variable currency}}\right)\right) \times \frac{\text{spot}}{\text{outright}} - 1\right] \times \frac{\text{day base for base currency}}{\text{days}}$$

<ACI preferred>

In our example:

$$\left(\left(1 + \left(0.0425 \times \frac{180}{360}\right)\right) \times \frac{0.9000}{0.9050} - 1\right) \times \frac{360}{180} = 0.031215468$$

<ACI preferred>

We can see this is 3.1215 percent. This can be rounded to 3.122 percent and determines the minimum interest rate return which must be achieved on the EUR asset dealing at 50 points EUR premium on the swap and taking the US dollars on deposit at 4.25 percent.

Swap points calculation (from base and variable currency interest rates)

Using the <ACI preferred> interest arbitrage formula to calculate the required swap points from the two interest rates (EUR = 3.125 percent and USD = 4.25 percent) we can see these are:

Mastering the ACI Dealing Certificate

$$\text{FX swap} = \text{spot} \times \frac{\left(\left(\text{variable currency interest rate} \times \frac{\text{days}}{\text{day base}}\right) - \left(\text{base currency interest rate} \times \frac{\text{days}}{\text{day base}}\right)\right)}{\left(1 + \left(\text{base currency interest rate} \times \frac{\text{days}}{\text{day base}}\right)\right)}$$

<ACI preferred>

In our example:

$$0.9000 \times \frac{\left(\left(0.0425 \times \frac{180}{360}\right) - \left(0.3125 \times \frac{180}{360}\right)\right)}{\left(1 + \left(0.03125 \times \frac{180}{360}\right)\right)} = 0.004985$$

<ACI preferred>

We can see this is 49.85 points. This can be rounded to 50 points and determines the minimum points "our favour" which must be achieved on the EUR/USD swap lending the EUR at 3.125 percent and taking the US dollars on deposit at 4.25 percent.

Hint

If the result of the swap points calculation is positive, the base currency (here EUR) = forward premium and swap will be quoted low–high. If the result of the swap points calculation is negative, the base currency = forward discount and swap will be quoted high–low.

Risk

From all the above one element stands out: the fact that the EUR interest receivable must be sold to produce sufficient US dollars (net of interest and swap points) to meet the interest payable. It can be seen that to achieve a "zero sum" from any of these interest arbitrage examples the EUR interest receivable must be sold forward at the same rate as the forward leg of the foreign exchange swap.

The calculations above only "compute" if the forward interest receivable in the asset currency is converted to the countercurrency at the same outright forward rate as the forward leg of the interest arbitrage FX swap.

Most banks have sophisticated accounting and reporting procedures to ensure that all such risk positions are identified at the time of dealing and may then be recorded accurately in the bank's accounting and management information reportage and managed by the dealer as he sees fit.

Where such outright forward interest positions are not covered, any change in the value of the currencies involved can result in reduced profit or even an overall loss.

> **Question**
>
> A typical ACI Dealing Certificate question might be:
>
> Spot EUR/USD is quoted 0.9500 (mid point). If six months (180 days) USD interest rates are quoted 5.50 percent and same period EUR are 4.50 percent, what is the approximate level of the EUR/USD forward swap points in dealer terms?
>
> A: 45 – 47
> B: 47 – 45
> C: 4.70 – 4.50
> D: 4.50 – 4.70
>
> **Correct answer**
> A: With these levels of interest rates, using the <ACI preferred> interest arbitrage formula the resultant forward swap points would be approximately 45 – 47, a EUR premium therefore low–high (0.0045 – 0.0047).

> **Hint**
>
> *Covering the exchange risk from the interest payments/receipts in differing currencies is an important element to prove the pricing formula but tends to be ignored in* ACI Dealing Certificate *examination questions.*

FOR FURTHER READING

Riehl, Heinz and Rodriguez, Rita M. (1977) *Foreign Exchange and Money Markets*. McGraw-Hill.

Reuters Financial Training (1999) *An Introduction to Foreign Exchange and Money Markets*. Wiley.

Swiss Bank Corp. (1992) *Foreign Exchange and Money Market Operations*. Swiss Bank Corp. (now UBS SA).

Walmsley, Julian (1992) *The Foreign Exchange and Money Markets Guide*. Wiley.

Walmsley, Julian (1996) *International Money and Foreign Exchange Markets*. Wiley.

Topic 4 (part) · FX Derivatives

Introduction

Currency options

Terminology and definitions

Hedging currency option positions

> **Overall objective**
>
> To *explain the derivations of forward rates, the use of interest rate protection products and the mechanics of their trading.*
>
> *At the end of this section, candidates will be able to:*
>
> • *explain the basics of options and their main characteristics;*
> • *describe the trading practices in the derivatives markets.*

Note

There are 7 questions on short-term derivatives in the ACI Dealing Certificate. Questions are chosen at random within the Prometric system, so it is impossible to say how many currency futures and/or currency options multiple choice questions under Topic 4 will be included in the examination.

INTRODUCTION

Exchange traded currency futures and options are available on the world's major exchanges such as the International Monetary Market (IMM) of the Chicago Mercantile Exchange (CME).

Short-term interest rate futures contracts and usage have already featured in Topic 4 (in Chapter 5 and while there are different currency contract specifications and pricing for currency futures, the underlying principles of trading and taking off-setting hedge positions are the same. Indeed, given the very liquid forward exchange markets (see the BIS triennial survey figures in Chapter 1), the availability and useage of currency futures in Europe is far less than in the USA. This chapter therefore assumes that the emphasis of the ACI Dealing Certificate under this topic heading is on the options product and, in the main, on the over the counter options markets.

CURRENCY OPTIONS

Definition

A currency option is a binding contract which gives the buyer (the holder) the right but not the obligation to buy or sell a specified amount of currency (the underlying currency) for another currency (the base) at an agreed rate (the strike price) for a specified period of time. Currency options can be exchange traded or over the counter (OTC).

Exchange traded options

The IMM of the CME trades currency futures and options contracts based on the future as the underlying market "options on futures", and as an example of another approach the Philadelphia Stock Exchange trades "options on physicals" (i.e. the currencies involved in any transaction are deliverable in cash on exercise).

Traded options are bought and sold on an open outcry basis in a trading pit. Contracts available are for standard quantities at current underlying market-determined strike prices. Prices for several delivery months are tracked by the exchange administration personnel and concisely and instantaneously reported via Reuters and other rates and news information vendor companies.

CME example contracts (options on futures)

Currency	Underlying	Strike prices	Premium quotation
Sterling (GBP)	One **BP** future (GBP 62,500)	USD 0.25 intervals, e.g. 1.4550, 1.4575	USD per GBP 1.0
Euro (EUR)	One **EUR** future (EUR 125,000)	USD 0.01 intervals, e.g. 87.50, 87.51	US cents per EUR

All options contracts on the CME are listed for 12 calendar months. Each option can be exercised into the quarter end currency futures contract. Therefore January, February and March options are exercisable into the March futures contract. At any point in time it is possible to trade options that expire in the next three calendar months, plus the following two quarter end expirations.

In most options traded on the CME half strikes may also be listed for the first three consecutive contract months. Trades may also be made in increments of half ticks known as *cabinets*.

Philadelphia Stock Exchange example contracts (options on physicals)

Currency option contracts on the Philadelphia Stock Exchange are quoted on the underlying spot exchange market and are deliverable in cash (nostro bank transfer) on exercise. Premium quotations are in USD per 1 unit of the currency being traded. The contracts are small with the sterling contract worth only GBP 12,500, and with limited liquidity there is seldom much opportunity to trade in wholesale marketable amounts.

Options pricing

The price of any currency option, either exchange traded or OTC, is the premium payable to purchase and not the exchange rate of the underlying (the strike price).

With traded options, as with financial futures, credit risk for either party is effectively removed by the intermediation of the clearing house which stands as buyer to every seller and seller to every buyer. It is the clearing house which guarantees performance of all options contracts traded on the exchange. While the clearing house only guarantees members' trades, all individual clients are safeguarded by legislation in all countries operating such exchanges.

Traded option buyers pay the premium to the clearing house and option writers guarantee their ability to meet the obligation if exercised via a margining system which varies from exchange to exchange. All contracts are marked to market on a daily basis in similar fashion to outstanding financial futures transactions (see Chapter 5).

OTC (over the counter) currency options

OTC options, as the name suggests, are sold over the counter by banks to their customer's exact specification. There is no central marketplace for OTC currency options and OTC options pricing may differ from market maker to market maker.

Corporate customers of banks will frequently use OTC currency options to hedge their currency exposure. In such instances the hedger will normally be the buyer of the currency option, the seller (the writer) the bank.

In OTC currency options contracts credit risk is asymmetrical. There is no credit risk for the writer of an OTC currency option once the premium has been received by him. He has this premium up front and if the contract becomes exercisable and the buyer does not exercise before expiry the writer has no further obligation or risk.

For the purchaser, however, the credit risk position is very different. Having paid the premium the buyer requires that the writer (the seller) be able to honour the contract should he (the buyer) wish to exercise his option.

Types of option

Calls and puts

A call option gives the buyer the right, but not the obligation, to *buy* (go long of) the underlying currency. For example, a euro call permits the buyer to buy EUR on exercise.

A put option, gives the buyer the right, but not the obligation, to *sell* (go short of) the underlying currency. For example, a sterling put permits the buyer to sell sterling on exercise.

American and European

The difference between these two "styles" of option is as follows.

An *American* style option can be exercised at any time up to expiry date for delivery two business days forward. It can be likened to an option on a spot exchange deal.

A *European* style option can technically be exercised at any time up to expiry date for delivery on the final delivery date *only* (although in virtually all cases this decision is left until final delivery date). It can be likened to an option on a fixed forward exchange deal.

Although currency options entered into as hedges may be either American or European, when a corporate treasurer knows the exact date of currency exposure he is more than likely going to hedge the risk with a European style currency option and leave the decision to exercise or not until final expiry date.

> **Question**
>
> A typical ACI Dealing Certificate question might be:
>
> How would you describe a European style currency option?
>
> A: An option giving the buyer the right to exercise in Europe only
> B: An option giving the buyer the right to go long of eurocurrency futures contracts
> C: An option giving the buyer the right to exercise with delivery at maturity only
> D: An option giving the buyer the right to buy a European currency only
>
> **Correct answer**
> C: A European option gives the buyer the right to exercise with delivery at maturity only. Exercise, though technically possible at any time during the life of the option, is usually only effected at maturity with delivery two days after expiry date of the option.

Uses for currency options

Any bank, financial institution or commercial company wishing to protect themselves against exchange exposure should consider using currency options almost as insurance.

Importers and exporters suffering transaction exposure, corporate treasurers running multi-currency translation exposures or companies involved in tendering for a contract (TTC) in a foreign currency are prime beneficiaries of the flexibility offered by currency options.

The buyer of a currency option

The buyer of an OTC currency option chooses the strike price to suit him. This is the "worst possible scenario" he is endeavouring to protect against.

The buyer of a currency option pays an upfront premium for the product, very similar to an insurance premium. As with life assurance, the last thing you want to do is claim (you won't be around to enjoy the proceeds), so similarly with a currency option – if it has to be exercised the worst has happened!

Rights and obligations of buyers and sellers

The *buyer* pays a premium and buys the right to exercise the option. The *seller* receives the premium and is obliged to complete the contract if exercised. In bank/customer contracts the buyer would normally be the customer, the seller (writer) the bank.

The premium (cost) of an OTC option

The price of an option will be determined by the following main factors:

1. the strike price relative to the current spot market price;
2. current interest rates for the option period in the two currencies involved;
3. the length of time the option will run;
4. market volatility;
5. supply and demand.

The most important element here is *volatility* as it is the only one which is unknown at the time of dealing. Different banks and market operators may have their own very different views on the future volatility of currencies. This data element in currency option pricing attempts to assess future volatility and is the factor upon which market makers' option prices will vary.

> **Question**
>
> A typical ACI Dealing Certificate question might be:
> A clear advantage of buying options to hedge financial risk is:
> A: Limiting downside risk
> B: Limiting upside potential
> C: Knowing with certainty the rate you will use in the future
> D: No credit risk worries on the provider of the hedge
>
> **Correct answer**
> A: By buying options you are limiting the downside risk while retaining the ability to maximize gains (minimize costs) on any movement in the underlying financial market in your favour.

Pricing

OTC currency options pricing is based on the *Black-Scholes* formula originally developed in the 1950s for stock market options and enhanced to include features specific to currencies by Professor Garman in the late 1970s.

$$\text{option premium} = \log N(X) - Kr^{-t} N(X - \sigma\sqrt{t})$$

$$\text{where } X = \frac{\log(S/Kr^{-t})}{\sigma\sqrt{t}} + \frac{1}{2}\frac{\sigma\sqrt{t}}{}$$

Key: K = strike price, σ = standard deviation of S = normal distribution function; S = market price of underlying instrument (the foreign exchange rate for the currency pair); t = time to maturity; r = one plus the current interest rate

Riskless hedge

The Black-Scholes formula is derived from the riskless hedge principle, which states that the option price must respond to variations in the underlying currency price. It follows that there must be a *perfect* hedge against changes in the value of an option.

The model assumes there is a constant risk-free interest rate for borrowing/lending from pricing date until expiry of the option. It also assumes that the price of the underlying currency will change continuously, but in a smooth fashion. This is highly unrealistic for spot foreign exchange currency rates because any number of factors such as speculation, government action and/or central bank intervention can cause large fluctuations in exchange rates.

In September 1992 this was painfully evident during the sterling crisis which ended with the currency ignominiously leaving the ERM. Leading up to, on and immediately after Black Wednesday (since which date, events having proved beneficial to the UK, some commentators have changed the alias to *White* Wednesday), the violent one-way movement in the sterling exchange rate caused serious problems in the currency options markets. Dealers fighting to maintain their delta hedge positions discovered they had little chance to hedge their exposure to sterling put currency options.

The Black-Scholes model has one other serious drawback. Volatility, perhaps the most important element in currency option pricing, is assumed to remain constant for the life of the option, something which will never happen in reality. While many have called into question the Black-Scholes model for currency option pricing, it is still (in various modified forms) the industry standard pricing model used by institutions in the pricing of OTC currency options.

Other pricing models

Another pricing formula which is favoured by exchange traded options dealers is that developed by Professors Cox, Ross and Rubenstein.

Hint

Although you may get questions on the data elements included in the various pricing models no calculations of premium requiring manipulation of the Black-Scholes formula will be set in the ACI Dealing Certificate *examination.*

Currency hedging

A currency option is an ideal hedging instrument. The protection afforded by the option can be enjoyed when required and if the hedger's opinion of market trends alters radically or the reason for the hedge disappears, the currency option can be sold back to the bank. Provided there is time left in the option period the product will still have some value.

Hedging strategies

In any situation involving currency exposure various hedging strategies are available.

- Leave all exposures to be covered only on due dates; doing nothing (except by default) can be a strategy.
- Cover everything through the forward market.
- Hedge selectively.

Topic 4 (part) · FX Derivatives

Assume:

- the customer has a requirement to buy USD 500,000 in three months' time;
- the current forward outright rate for three months GBP/USD is 1.5000;
- three months USD call (GBP put) currency option at the money forward is 1.5000;
- the GBP/USD spot exchange rate range at expiry is 1.4200–1.5600; and
- the option premium is USD 2,500.00.

Cost comparison table (payoff diagram)

Fig 8.1

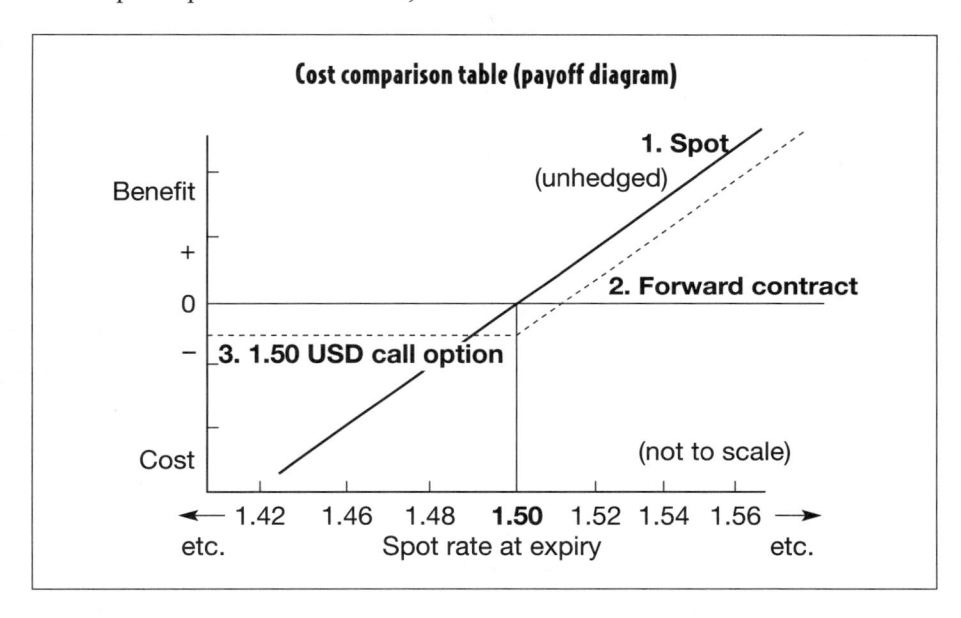

(diagram showing Benefit/Cost vs Spot rate at expiry from 1.42 to 1.56, with three strategies: 1. Spot (unhedged), 2. Forward contract, 3. 1.50 USD call option; not to scale)

Figure 8.1 graphically shows the outcome of these three strategies:

1. **Unhedged** – Doing nothing and accepting the prevailing rate at expiry of the option. This is the *unhedged* outcome. If Sterling has risen in value above the 1.5000 level the customer benefits and is able to purchase more US Dollars (the rate is higher) than he could have done initially on an outright forward basis resulting in a windfall benefit or profit. But if Sterling has fallen in value below the 1.5000 level the customer will NOT even be able to purchase as many US Dollars as he could have done on a forward outright basis thus generating a windfall cost (or loss). This outcome is a 45° angle and the important point to remember is that there is no top nor bottom.

2. **Covering** through the forward foreign exchange market. This strategy guarantees certainty, locking the customer into an outright exchange rate agreed at the time of dealing and fixes the median line (no windfall benefit or cost) in the graph. Whatever the exchange rate is at expiry (higher or lower than 1.5000) there is a contractual

obligation on both parties to the transaction and the customer is guaranteed the forward outright rate of 1.5000.

3. **Hedging** the exposure with a Currency Option. The outcomes of this strategy are a) if Sterling appreciates the customer does not exercise the option and deals in the spot market at expiry at the higher exchange rate and enjoys a benefit - he has to bear in mind however that he has paid a premium for the option thereby reducing the benefit to the dotted line slightly below the unhedged result. b) If on the other hand Sterling has gone down in value the customer exercises the option and buys USD at the strike price of 1.5000. He will achieve a slightly lower rate than the strike price again by dint of the premium originally paid for the option. In this situation the dotted line is unerringly parallel with the median line meaning regardless of exchange rate at expiry the customer's cost is limited to the premium paid.

Summary

Currency options provide additional flexibility for managing foreign currency exposure. They are particularly effective during periods of high market volatility – though in such a market scenario will necessarily be expensive – and where the nature of the exposure or its timing is uncertain.

A non-refundable fee (premium) is payable at the start of the option, which allows the cost to be quantified from the outset.

Buyers (holders) retain the right, but not the obligation, to exercise the option contract.

In an OTC option the buyer can nominate the strike price and the duration of the option (usual maximum 12 months) to suit his own specific requirements.

TERMINOLOGY AND DEFINITIONS

- *In the money (ITM)* – an option where the strike price is more advantageous than the current market price (i.e. there is immediate profit in exercise).
- *At the money (ATM)* – an option with the strike price equal to the current market price.
- *Out of the money (OTM)* – an option where the strike price is less advantageous than the current market price (i.e. the option will not be immediately exercisable).

Intrinsic value

The benefit to the holder if he were to exercise the option immediately, i.e. the amount by which an option is "in the money", is known as the *intrinsic value*.

Time value

Time value is that part of an option premium which reflects the remaining life of the option. As with car insurance – a policy will cost you more for twelve months cover than for six months as there is more chance of you having an accident in the longer period – the length of time an option has to run has on impact on its price.

As long as time remains to the expiry date of an option there will always be time value. Time value is a reflection of the opportunity for the price of the underlying to change so that there will be intrinsic value for the purchaser in the exercise of the option. At expiration there will be no time value remaining. Therefore it can be seen that time value falls away as expiry date approaches.

Time value decay

This reduction in time value in the price of an option falls away at a steady pace and reduces by approximately 50 percent until there remains approximately one month to expiry date. The remaining time value then reduces to zero more quickly in that final month. This is referred to as *time value decay* and can be plotted as shown in Figure 8.2. For this reason an option is described as a wasting asset for the purchaser/holder.

Time value decay

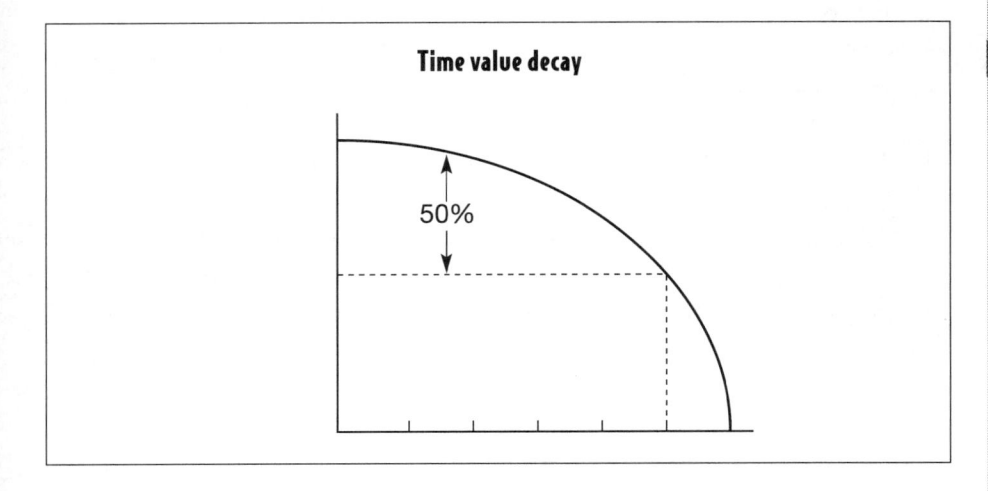

Fig 8.2

Volatility

Volatility refers to how much the value of the underlying currency is likely to change over time. The more the likelihood of change, the greater will be the effect on the status of any option (out, at and most importantly in the money). It is a measure of the amount by which the price of a currency is expected to fluctuate over a given period (the option period) and is normally measured by the annual standard deviation of daily price changes.

Volatility can be historic, current or implied. *Historic* volatility is interesting but cannot be relied upon to predict what it will be in future. It is recorded through the use of charts of daily price changes. *Current* volatility identifies market sentiment on how options are being priced in today's market, while *implied* volatility is the "big unknown" and is what is required for input into any option pricing model – i.e. what probability might there be that because of potential underlying price changes the option being valued will be exercisable at (or, in the case of American options, before) expiry.

It is this element in option valuation where option sellers/writers are most likely to differ in their pricing. In the interbank options market dealers ask each other for a two-way price in volatility in the relevant option and will buy from the offer (if the market user's view is that volatility quoted is priced too low) or sell to the bid (if the market user's view is that volatility is priced too high by the market maker).

> **Question**
>
> A typical ACI Dealing Certificate question might be:
>
> What does volatility measure in respect of currency options pricing?
>
> A: The number of times a currency option may be "in the money" during its life
>
> B: The variability but not the direction of the price of the underlying currency exchange rate
>
> C: The direction of the price of the underlying currency
>
> D: The variability and direction of the underlying currency exchange rate
>
> **Correct answer**
>
> B: Volatility (as one of the factors entered in an option pricing model) is the option writer's assessment of the future variability but not necessarily the direction of the price of the underlying currency exchange rate.

"The Greeks"

Delta

The *delta* of a currency option is the rate of change in price of an option following a change in the price of the underlying currency. For example, if a change of 1 percent in the exchange rate causes the currency option premium to change by 0.5 percent then the delta is described as being 0.5:

$$\text{delta} = \frac{\text{change in option price}}{\text{change in price of underlying}}$$

The delta represents the speed with which an option price will change relative to the underlying. It gives an idea of the probability that the option will be in the money at expiry. It can be described as the option's "payoff".

The delta, being a ratio, will always lie between 0 and 1. As a rule of thumb, an at-the-money option will have a delta of 0.5. There is a 50:50 chance of the option going into or out of the money.

If an option is deep in the money with little time value impact, its price will be virtually all a reflection of intrinsic value. The option premium and the underlying will change on an almost one for one basis and the delta will be near to 1.

A deep out of the money option will have a delta close to zero. Small changes in the price of the underlying will not alter the premium.

Gamma

Delta changes in a non-linear way. *Gamma* measures the change in the delta when a small change in the underlying occurs. If delta measures the speed with which an option price changes then gamma can be described as the measure of the acceleration in the change in the option price as the underlying changes.

Gamma will be large when an option is at the money and near to expiry. Gamma will be small, near to zero, when either an in- or out-of-the-money option is nearing expiry date. Delta does not change much when expiration is near for in-the-money options – changes in premium will be almost totally a reflection of changes in intrinsic value. Options which are out of the money have little chance of acquiring any intrinsic value as expiry date approaches, therefore there is little change in the option's premium.

Options with a high gamma ratio will be attractive to option buyers, but less attractive to option sellers. High gammas mean fast, accelerating changes in delta, thus options going in the money accelerate sellers' losses and purchasers' gains.

Theta

Theta measures an option's loss in value due to time decay. As time is constantly passing the theta is almost always a negative number. However, the premium of a deep-in-the-money European option will not fall. For an American option, on the other hand, say an option on a future, a theta of −0.05 means that it will lose 5 ticks in price for each day that passes.

Mastering the ACI Dealing Certificate

Vega (or kappa or sigma)

Vega is a measure of change in an option price brought about by a change in the level of volatility of the underlying. It is calculated as a change in option premium for a 1 percent change in implied volatility.

Volatility of the underlying can and, in the case of currencies, certainly does change frequently. This fact has caused questions to be asked regarding the Black-Scholes model used for currency options pricing.

If a currency option has a vega of 0.05 and implied volatility in the underlying is 10 percent, then if volatility were to change by 1 percent (moving up to 11 percent) the premium on the currency option would change by 0.05 percent.

> **Hint**
>
> *The* ACI Dealing Certificate *examination frequently contains questions relating to definitions of the various Greek ratios encountered in options trading.*

> **Question**
>
> A typical ACI Dealing Certificate question might be:
>
> If a currency option is described as "out of the money", the delta:
>
> A: Tends towards 1
> B: Tends towards 0.5
> C: Is equal to zero
> D: Tends towards zero
>
> **Correct answer**
> D: An "out-of-the-money" option has less probability of being exercised and the delta tends towards zero, indicating to the options trader that he needs less position in the underlying commodity to hedge his risk under these conditions.

HEDGING CURRENCY OPTION POSITIONS

As we have seen foreign exchange exposure can be hedged by using currency options. In the commercial world this type of hedge would be put in place by the corporation buying a currency option from a bank: buying a put option against GBP to protect against a future fall in value of a foreign currency receipt (or rise in value of sterling) and buying a call option to protect against a future rise in the value of a foreign currency (thereby costing more sterling).

But what about the bank dealer? Having sold the right to exercise to the customer how can he, himself, manage the risk now assumed from the customer?

First, the dealer can, if he is able, obtain a favourable price in the interbank options market and cover the option risk by himself buying an exactly matching option. He must be aware though that because of the nature of the option product the transaction must be exactly matching. Too many options dealers confess that when they first attempted to cover a sold call option they sold a put – in effect not a cover at all but a trading strategy called a straddle – or, worse still, having sold the call they purchased a put, actually doubling their potential for a cash short position in the underlying currency! As with all such learning curve errors you (hopefully) only make the same mistake once. The correct cover therefore for the initial sale of a call is the purchase of a similar call, the premium received from the original customer going to pay for the purchase in the market.

This first method of managing the options risk was in fact described as a covering operation. How can the dealer hedge his option position, i.e. still leave himself the opportunity to benefit perhaps from a further move in his favour?

Delta hedging

The most common form of hedging currency option positions is *delta hedging*. Let's look at an example of the options dealer delta hedging his sold options position (see Figure 8.3).

Currency options dealer's delta hedging

Deal no.	Option position	Strike rate	Market rate	Current delta	Cash market transaction	Delta position
1.	Sold GBP 10 mio call	1.5500	1.5500	0.5	Buy GBP 5 mio at 1.5500	Long GBP 5 mio
2.	Same	1.5500	1.5600	0.7	Buy GBP 2 mio at 1.5600	Long GBP 7 mio
3.	Same	1.5500	1.5500	0.5	Sell GBP 2 mio at 1.5500	Long GBP 5 mio

Fig 8.3

Figure 8.3 is for illustration purposes only – delta hedge requirements are not mathematically calculated.

Note

To explain Figure 8.3, a bank's options dealer has sold an at-the-money sterling call GBP 10 million with a strike price of 1.5500 (Deal No. 1). The current underlying spot market rate is 1.5500. The delta ratio of this position is calculated to be 0.5 – there is a 50:50 chance that the rate could go either way. The dealer will buy GBP 5 million in the cash market as a hedge (GBP 10 million × 0.5).

Suppose now that sterling appreciates – the rate rises to 1.5600, meaning that should the option be exercised there is an immediate profit to the buyer (the bank's counterparty). The options dealer will recalculate his delta and discover it has moved to 0.7 – there is a greater likelihood that the option will be exercised. An additional GBP 2 million is purchased (Deal No. 2 at the current market rate 1.5600) to make the cash hedge position up to GBP 7 million (GBP 10 million × 0.7). Once the dealer has operated in the cash market as dictated by the ratio his position is described as being delta neutral.

Now suppose the rate falls away again to 1.5500. Again the dealer will recalculate the delta (0.5) and he realizes he now requires only GBP 5 million cash hedge. The GBP 2 million excess is sold at the current market rate of 1.5500 (Deal No. 3) to restore the delta neutral position to 0.5 (GBP 10 million × 0.5).

Looking more closely at these operations – which are typical of a currency options dealer's delta hedging transactions – we can see that following market trends and dealing against himself (the purchase of GBP at 1.5600 was reversed by a sale at the lower rate of 1.5500) will result in a cash market dealing loss of 100 points or USD 20,000 – being USD 3,120,000 paid for the GBP 2 million minus USD 3,100,000 received – another reason why currency option premiums are expensive. The tracking of delta ratios and cash market hedging will probably always cost the dealer money and eat away at the initial premium received from the buyer of the option – the only *benefit* the option seller receives.

We have looked at a single sold currency option in this example. In reality the options dealer is managing his risks on a portfolio basis and the net sold positions and a weighted strike price are tracked almost on a minute-by-minute basis. The example above looks at two snapshots 1 cent apart – in reality many more delta hedging operations would have been effected and possibly reversed between the two points selected. The cash market transactions effected will probably be internal deals with his spot dealers meaning that the cost or benefit is actually being transferred or apportioned between dealing sections. However, at the end of the day there is a real cost to delta hedging as evidenced by the above example.

Option variations

There are many variations on the option product. Two of those encountered frequently in the Treasury environment are featured here.

Cylinder option

A cylinder option, also known as a range forward or a fence, is the currency option equivalent of an interest rate collar (see Apendix II), and is designed to reduce the cost of an option hedge to the buyer.

A cylinder option can combine a call purchase with a put sale at different strike prices or a put purchase with a call sale.

The call option buyer has to accept an exchange rate range with his upside potential restricted – the benefit being that in selling the put the premium income is used to offset the premium cost of the call purchase thereby reducing the overall cost to the hedger.

Example

A UK importer needs to purchase US dollars 1,000,000 in three months' time. He is worried that exchange rates will move against him (sterling will weaken and be worth less US dollars). The current GBP/USD exchange rate is 1.5000.

He can buy an OTC US dollar call currency option with a strike price of 1.5000 but the premium cost is, in his opinion, high at 1.00 percent = GBP 10,000. He can reduce the premium cost by entering into a cylinder option as follows:

Current market: GBP/USD 3 months fwd outright rate 1.5000

Importer buys USD call ATM fwd strike price 1.5000 premium cost	GBP 10,000.00
Importer sells USD put OTM strike price 1.6000 premium income	GBP 7,250.00
Net premium cost	GBP 2,750.00

The payoffs from this type of strategy restrict the cylinder option hedger's potential benefit from an improvement in the rate above 1.5000 up to a maximum exchange rate of 1.6000 (see Figure 8.4 overleaf).

Should the underlying spot rate be anywhere between 1.5000 and 1.6000 at expiry, both legs of the cylinder option expire worthless. Should the underlying exchange rate be below 1.5000, the hedger (the call buyer) exercises and achieves the hedged rate. Should the underlying exchange rate be anything above 1.6000, the put buyer will exercise against the hedger who will achieve a maximum exchange rate of 1.6000. This type of hedge restricts the hedger's opportunity to benefit beyond the rate obligation of the sold put but is a less expensive hedge.

Fig 8.4

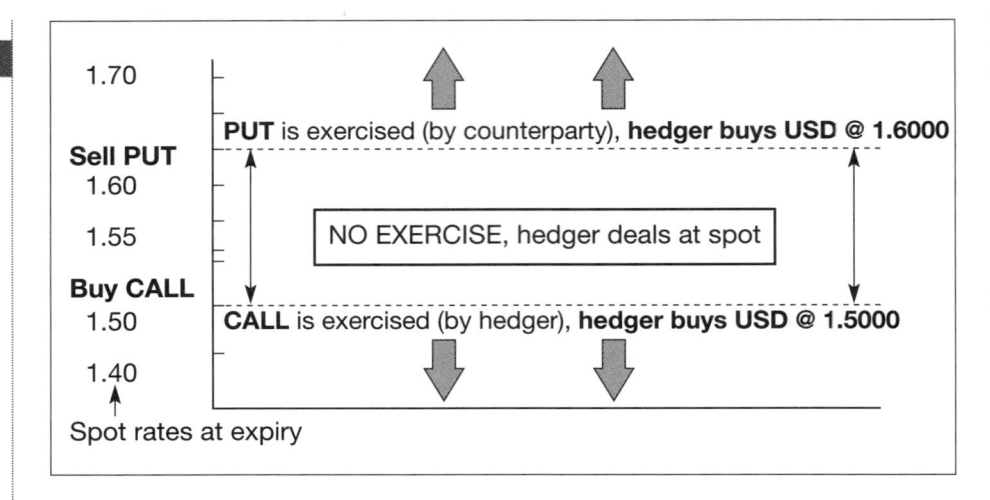

```
1.70  ─┤         ↑              ↑
       │   PUT is exercised (by counterparty), hedger buys USD @ 1.6000
Sell PUT ┌─ ─ ─ ─ ─ ─ ─ ─ ─ ─ ─ ─ ─ ─ ─ ─ ─ ─ ─ ─ ─ ─ ─ ─ ─ ─ ─ ─ ─
1.60   ─┤
       │
1.55   ─┤     ┌──────────────────────────────────────────┐
       │     │   NO EXERCISE, hedger deals at spot      │
Buy CALL     └──────────────────────────────────────────┘
1.50   ─┤   CALL is exercised (by hedger), hedger buys USD @ 1.5000
       │
1.40   ─┤         ↓              ↓
  ↑
Spot rates at expiry
```

Zero cost cylinder

It is possible to construct such a strategy at zero cost where the premium income equals the premium cost. The two strike prices will probably be very close to one another meaning the range within which the hedger can benefit is severely restricted, but of course the cost of the hedging strategy is nil – the reason for entering into the strategy.

Average rate option

Currency options as described above are an extremely flexible method of hedging exchange exposure in the corporation, but where regular in- or outflows of currency are involved a series of such options purchased would probably create more administrative problems than hedging benefits.

The average rate option has been introduced by many banks to assist corporations in their hedging strategies at a lower cost than would be the case using standard currency options while maintaining the flexibility and opportunities to benefit from favourable currency movements.

An average rate option is a currency option which enables the buyer to establish a budgeted rate of exchange, based on an average rate on certain future reference dates, at the start of any period. On the predetermined reference dates the market rate is compared to the average rate option strike price: if the market is higher (in the buyer's favour) then the buyer deals in the cash market and gets the benefit; if lower (against the buyer) the buyer still deals in the market but is reimbursed the difference between this cover and the average rate of the option. In this way the company is guaranteed from the outset to at least achieve and most likely improve on the average rate throughout the average rate option period.

The buyer may choose reference dates to suit his requirements. The reference date exchange rate used will be agreed between the parties at the outset. An independently sourced rate such as the daily Bank of England rate on Reuters is frequently used.

In practical terms the administration of an average rate option is much simpler to manage than other hedging methods. There are no forward outstandings to record and monitor. The premium for such an option is typically lower than premiums for a series of standard options and is payable upfront by the buyer. During the average rate option period all transactions entered into (preferably at or around the time of striking the reference rate on the reference dates) are standard spot exchange deals. At the end of the average rate option period any differences due to the market spot rate achieved being worse than the option strike rate are paid over to the buyer.

If the average of the reference date rates is better than the average rate option strike price no payment is due and the buyer will have benefited from the more favourable exchange rates achieved throughout the period.

Example

An exporter has income over the life of a contract of USD 500,000 per month for 12 calendar months (total USD 6,000,000.00). The treasurer has budgeted for a rate of 1.5000, meaning anticipated total receipts of GBP 4,000,000 over the year.

To protect this budgeted income the treasurer buys an average rate option for his bank giving him the right to sell a total of USD 6,000,000 against sterling at an exchange rate of 1.5000 over the one-year period. The exact dates of receipts of the remittances are unknown at this stage in the contract. The premium payable is calculated to be 1.20 percent flat – equivalent to GBP 48,000 which is payable immediately.

The agreed reference rate is to be the Bank of England sterling exchange rate index taken at 11.00 a.m. on the first day of each month. If the exact dates of the receipts of US dollars had been known the reference date could have been more accurately set.

On receipt of any US dollars these will be placed on an interest bearing currency account until the first of the next month (the next reference date) and then the treasurer will sell the US dollars in the spot market at or around 11.00 a.m. Matching the timing of the spot deal and the reference rate ensures accuracy in the overall hedge.

Outcome

If, at the end of the year, the average exchange rate calculated from the reference date rates is above 1.5000 (a worse rate for the treasurer) then the writer of the option (the bank) will pay the company compensation. This will be equal to the principal amount USD 6,000,000 valued at the average rate achieved *less* USD 6,000,000 valued at the strike rate of the average rate option. Provided the treasurer has achieved spot market rates close to the average reference date exchange rate, the net result of the average rate option will be the budgeted rate of 1.5000.

If, however, the average reference date exchange rate is lower than 1.5000 (a better rate for the treasurer) then no payment will be made and the company will have achieved a better rate than the budgeted rate. Assuming the average rate option noted here is dealt in December 0X for the 12 months period January 0Y to December 0Y and exchange rates vary between 1.4800 and 1.6000 (average 1.5500), the results shown in Figure 8.5 would be achieved (ignoring the premium originally paid by the treasurer).

Fig 8.5

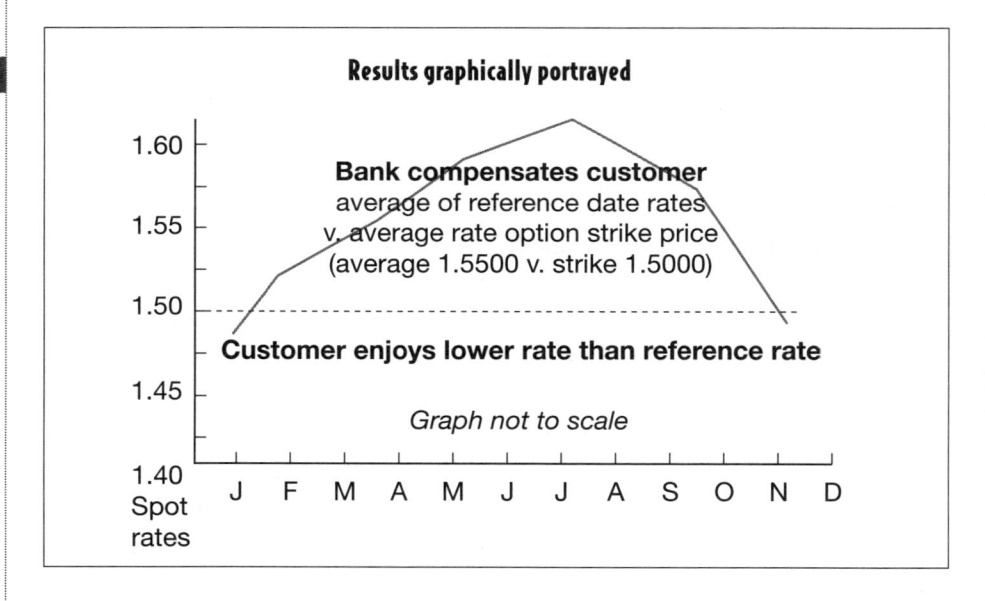

Results graphically portrayed

Bank compensates customer
average of reference date rates
v. average rate option strike price
(average 1.5500 v. strike 1.5000)

Customer enjoys lower rate than reference rate

Graph not to scale

Spot rates: J F M A M J J A S O N D (1.40–1.60)

Financial results

To complete our example above, if, as stated, in one year's time the average of the reference date rates is 1.5500 the bank will pay the company compensation of GBP 129,032.26, being:

```
USD 6,000,000   @ 1.5000   GBP 4,000,000.00
USD 6,000,000   @ 1.5500   GBP 3,870,967.74
                           GBP   129,032.26
```

Options trading strategies

The following is a list of some of the other frequently invoked option variations and trading strategies. Please note that the list is not exhaustive.

- *Barrier option.* An option which is either cancelled or activated if the underlying currency reaches a set level. Also known as a knock-in (trigger) or knock-out option. It is usually a straightforward European style option until or from the time the underlying currency reaches the barrier price. There are four major types: up-and-out, up-and-in, down-and-out and down-and-in. These terms are descriptive of the way the instruments operate. For example, with an up-and-in option there is no value at maturity unless the underlying currency rises in the interim period above the predetermined price, at which point it becomes a standard European style put or call option. On the other hand with a down-and-out the option is cancelled if the underlying currency falls below the agreed price.

- *Bear spread.* An option strategy that combines a bearish view on a market with a view on volatility. Each strategy has limited risk but also limited potential gain. There are two potential choices for the trader who feels the market is currently overpriced. The buyer of a put spread believes that implied volatility should be higher and the seller of a call spread believes that volatility is too high.

- *Binary (digital) option.* A binary option pays out a fixed amount if the underlying currency reaches a predetermined level (the strike price). The two types of binary option available are known as all-or-nothing and one-touch options. All-or-nothing options pay out a set amount if the underlying currency is above (or below) a certain point at expiry. One-touch options pay a fixed amount if at any time during the life of the option the underlying currency reaches a certain point.

- *Box.* Buying and selling mispriced exchange traded options on futures and hedging the risk again using options is described as a box. The options trader creates a synthetic short futures position by buying the put and selling the call at the same strike price. To neutralize the market risk he then sells another put and buys another call but at different strike prices.

- *Break forward.* A forward exchange contract with an inbuilt option to break before maturity if the market rate is more favourable. The premium is charged in the rate which will be a worse rate than the forward rate on deal date. Another variation on this theme is the forward with optional exit (FOX).

- *Bull spread.* An option strategy that combines a bullish view on a market with a view on volatility. Each strategy has limited risk but also limited potential gain. There are two potential choices for the trader who feels the market is currently underpriced. The buyer of a call spread believes that implied volatility should be higher and the seller of a put spread believes that volatility is too high.
- *Butterfly spread.* The simultaneous sale of an at-of-the-money straddle and a purchase of an out-of the-money strangle. The structure profits if the underlying currency remains stable, and it has limited downside risk in the event of a large movement in either direction.
- *Call spread.* A strategy which reduces the cost of buying a call option by selling another call at a higher strike price. This limits potential gain if the underlying currency goes up, but the premium received from selling the out-of-the-money call partly finances the at-the-money call purchase. A call spread may also be advantageous if the purchaser thinks there is only limited upside in the underlying currency.
- *Condor.* The simultaneous purchase (sale) of an out-of-the-money strangle and sale (purchase) of an even deeper out-of-the-money strangle. The strategy gives a limited profit/limited loss payoff and is directionally neutral.
- *Contingent option.* An option for which the buyer pays no premium unless the option is exercised. The premium cost is equal to the premium payable on a normal option divided by the option delta, hence the price increases dramatically for out-of-the-money options. Contingent options are a zero cost option strategy (unless exercised) and can be broken down into a binary option plus a conventional option.
- *Convertible option contract.* A currency option with a "trigger" price above (put) or below (call) the strike price at which it automatically converts into a standard forward exchange contract.
- *Digital option.* See Binary option.
- *Knock-in and knock-out options.* See Barrier option.
- *Lookback option.* An option that gives the buyer the right to exercise the option at the lowest (in the case of a call) or the highest (in the case of a put) price reached by the underlying currency over the life of the option, compared with a predetermined strike price. The potential benefits of such options tend to be outweighed by their cost.
- *Lookback strike option.* An option that permits the buyer to purchase or sell the underlying currency at the low or high that the underlying currency reaches over a predetermined period.

- *Naked option*. An option which is sold (bought) without an offsetting position in the underlying currency. The dealer is taking a trading (speculative) view on the underlying currency.
- *Participating forward contract*. A forward exchange contract with a guaranteed minimum rate with the ability for the customer to benefit in a share (less than 100 percent) of any profit in a favourable exchange rate move. There is no upfront premium payable, the price of the contract is reflected in the percentage share on the bank's part.
- *Put spread*. A strategy which reduces the cost of buying a put option by selling another put at a lower strike price. This limits potential gain if the underlying currency goes down, but the premium received from selling the out-of-the-money put partly finances the at-the-money put purchase. A put spread may also be advantageous if the purchaser thinks there is only limited downside in the underlying currency.
- *Range forward*. See Cylinder option (page 270).
- *Straddle*. The sale or purchase of a put option and a call option, with the same strike price, on the same underlying currency and with the same expiry. The buyer benefits in return for paying two premiums if the underlying currency moves enough either way. It is a way of taking advantage of an expected upturn in volatility. Sellers of straddles assume unlimited risk but benefit if the underlying currency does not move. Straddles are potential trading instruments.
- *Strangle*. As with a straddle the sale or purchase of a put option and a call option on the same underlying currency with the same expiry, but at strike prices equally out of the money. The strangle costs less than the straddle because both options are out of the money, but profits are only generated if the underlying currency moves dramatically and the breakeven is worse than for a straddle. Sellers of strangles make money in the range between the two strike prices, but lose if the price moves outside the breakeven range (the strike prices plus the premium received).
- *Trigger option*. See Barrier option.

FOR FURTHER READING

Reuters Financial Training (1999) *An Introduction to Derivatives*. Wiley.
Wilmott, Howson and Dewynne (1995) *The Mathematics of Financial Derivatives*. Cambridge University Press.
Winstone, David (1995) *Financial Derivatives – Hedging with Futures, Forwards, Options and Swaps*. Chapman & Hall.

WEBSITE WORTH A VISIT

Chicago Mercantile Exchange (exchange traded futures and options): www.cme.com

Topic 8 · The Role of Settlements

Introduction

The treasury division

Treasury division support functions

Mastering the ACI Dealing Certificate

> **Overall objective**
>
> *To identify the role and responsibilities of the back office and to explain the importance of timely and accurate settlement.*
>
> *At the end of this section, candidates will be able to:*
>
> - *explain the need for the separation of the dealing function from the settlement function;*
> - *explain the use of nostro accounts and reconciliation;*
> - *describe the workflow of a typical transaction and state the responsibilities of the back office;*
> - *calculate settlement amounts correctly.*

Note

As with the Background and Position Keeping topics, there is no separate Role of Settlements question basket in the ACI Dealing Certificate examination. Questions relating to settlements (back office) issues could be generated under the Risk Management and Control or the Market Conventions and Environment question baskets.

There are 4 questions on Risk Management and Control out of which candidates are required to gain a minimum of 25 percent to pass (1 out of 4) and 5 on Market Conventions and Environment out of which candidates are required to gain a minimum of 40 percent to pass (2 out of 5).

INTRODUCTION

The division of duties between dealers and processors, settlement procedures, a day in the life of a "spot" deal, nostro account management and the overall role and responsibilities of the back office feature under this "catch all" heading with calculations of FRA settlement amounts also included here.

While the main part of the ACI syllabus relates to markets and dealing techniques the overall structure of a bank and the significance of back office operations must not be overlooked. This section starts with setting the scene for an international bank in the markets and the position of the treasury division responsible for the dealing functions (see Figure 9.1). It goes on to describe the role and responsibilities of the principal settlements areas.

Each of the banking divisions is an individual business in its own right, responsible for all aspects of running its business in its chosen markets. These responsibilities include premises, personnel, systems, etc.

Depending on the bank's chosen markets there may be further subdivisions. All the divisions will report to a holding company which will set performance

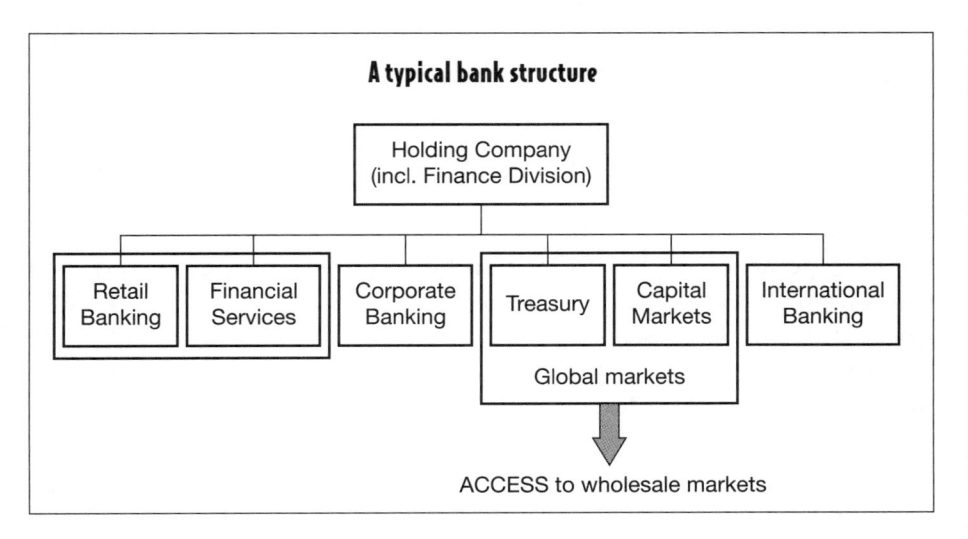

Topic 8 · The Role of Settlements

Fig 9.1

A typical bank structure

```
        Holding Company
        (incl. Finance Division)
                |
   ┌──────┬──────┬──────┬──────┬──────┬──────┐
 Retail  Financial Corporate Treasury Capital International
Banking  Services  Banking           Markets    Banking
                            └─────────────┘
                             Global markets
                                  │
                                  ▼
                   ACCESS to wholesale markets
```

criteria such as return on assets, etc. All financial data will be collected and collated by a finance division within the holding company structure.

We will consider here, a fictional but typical UK-based commercial bank operating in western Europe from its London headquarters and through a network of branches overseas. The bank is structured in such a way as best to serve the various markets in which it operates, always ensuring it is able to serve the many differing customer bases of these markets.

We will concentrate here on the dealing activities which are managed through the bank's treasury division.

THE TREASURY DIVISION

The treasury division of the bank is the operational and controlling division in respect of the bank's financial market involvement.

The bank's worldwide market involvement is centred on the three global financial centres of London, New York and Tokyo. Its branches in other financial centres, many having fully operational dealing rooms, are subordinate to these three principal dealing branches, each within the appropriate time zone.

All dealing branches are authorized to trade in the foreign exchange and international financial markets to cover customer requirements and, within limits imposed by the treasury division, London, for their own branch account as position takers. Certain types of dealing operation may be entered into with customers only after reference to the branch's nearest global centre, which may provide the cover for the branch for that business at the global centre's discretion judged on a deal-by-deal basis.

The treasury division's responsibilities include the major account relationships with the banking, institutional and corporate customers of the bank, along with the day-to-day operations in and control of the bank's involvement in the international financial markets. This is the only area of the bank with access to the London and international wholesale treasury markets.

Within the treasury division there is a corporate sales force which acts as the focal point for the bank's relationship with major UK customers, and coordinates the relationships of the bank's branches overseas with the subsidiaries of UK companies.

The treasury division acts for the bank's own account in the international markets as well as actively selling its products to the UK corporate market through a dedicated desk in the London dealing room. It also maintains a marketing support team for the retail banking branches of the bank in the United Kingdom.

Roles and responsibilities

The treasury division's principal roles are:

- to act as banker to the bank;
- to effect and control the bank's own account dealing operations in the international foreign exchange, money markets and off balance sheet/derivative markets;
- to provide a dealing service in foreign exchange and associated products to correspondent bank contacts and international branch network abroad;
- to service the UK retail and multinational corporate customers' financial market requirements through the dealing department;
- to provide operational support for the bank's involvement in the financial markets noted above;
- to provide risk assessment functions and certain other positional and credit risk controls regarding worldwide dealing involvement of the bank.

The treasury division has responsibility for:

- overall policy regarding foreign exchange and other financial market dealing;
- the size and composition of the bank's liquid assets;
- the bank's worldwide funding strategy;
- the direction of business development in foreign exchange, money market and derivative products;

- the marketing of foreign exchange, money market and risk management products and services to worldwide banking, institutional and corporate customers;
- the liaison with other business units in all matters regarding the international financial markets;
- the setting and allocation to all dealing centres of trading limits.

Objectives

The treasury division has well defined business objectives. Those noted below are specific to its involvement in the worldwide international financial markets:

- to maintain the liquidity and therefore the solvency of the bank;
- to utilize the excess funds of the bank so that they produce the highest possible return, given the constraints imposed by the first objective;
- to borrow any necessary funds for the bank at the lowest possible cost, again given the constraints imposed by the first objective;
- to give the best possible service in the financial markets to the bank's customers, be they other banks, branches, corporate or retail customers;
- to manage the bank's positions resulting from all types of market operation within policy guidelines and limits;
- to produce a profit for the bank while accomplishing the above objectives, and to maximize the profit in the conversion to local currency of any earnings in foreign currency.

As a result of the treasury division's constant presence in and involvement with the interbank foreign exchange, money markets and treasury derivative markets, there is an additional objective:

- to trade prudently and professionally in the markets to achieve the objectives already mentioned, without prejudicing either the bank's reputation or credit rating in the eyes of other market participants.

Structure

The management structure of treasury division is shown in Figure 9.2.

Fig 9.2

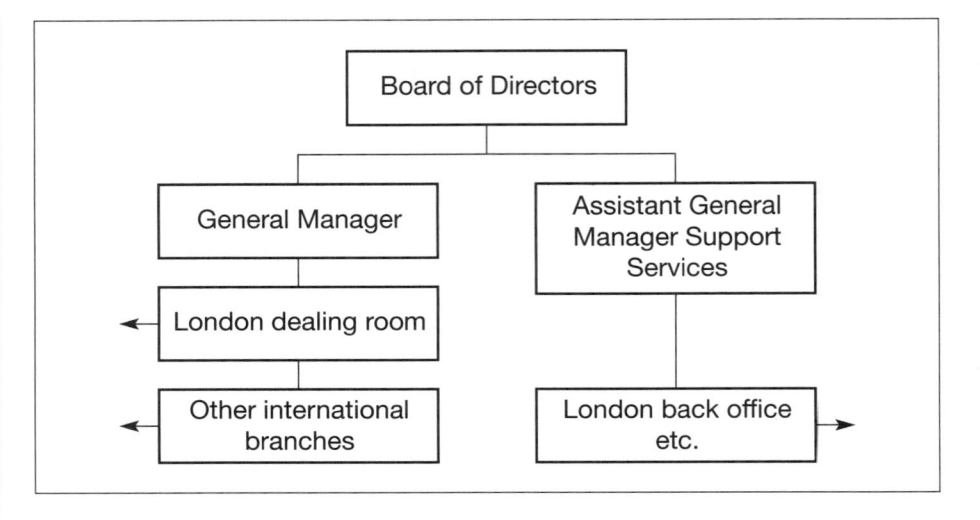

```
                    ┌──────────────────┐
                    │ Board of Directors│
                    └────────┬─────────┘
              ┌──────────────┴──────────────┐
    ┌─────────┴────────┐          ┌─────────┴────────┐
    │ General Manager  │          │ Assistant General│
    │                  │          │ Manager Support  │
    │                  │          │ Services         │
    └─────────┬────────┘          └─────────┬────────┘
    ┌─────────┴────────┐                    │
  ←─│London dealing room│                   │
    └─────────┬────────┘                    │
    ┌─────────┴────────┐          ┌─────────┴────────┐
  ←─│Other international│          │London back office│─→
    │     branches     │          │       etc.       │
    └──────────────────┘          └──────────────────┘
```

Division of duties

Under no circumstances must back office personnel come under the jurisdiction of the dealers. They must have independent reporting lines to ensure their vital separate checking function on all transactions entered into by the dealers.

TREASURY DIVISION SUPPORT FUNCTIONS

Processing/settlements departments

These include:

- the money market processing department;
- the spot and forward foreign exchange processing department;
- the treasury derivatives settlements department.

Each of these departments provides a full transactional processing service to their respective dealing operations.

The above areas report through line management to a designated main Board director *independently* of the dealing room business units. They provide services ranging from computer input and verification, confirmation despatch, inward confirmation checking and deal settlement functions (sterling payments and receipts through CHAPS, the branch network and the daily local clearing, and foreign currencies via the bank's SWIFT interface) through to any investigation functions following the identification of transaction/payment problems.

Processing department personnel responsibilities

- Processing department personnel are directly responsible to the administration management. They must not in any way report to or be influenced by the dealers or dealing management.

- Processing personnel are responsible for verifying all direct dealer input and/or deal ticket details and checking all deal (ticket) calculations.

- Processing personnel raise entry vouchers or effect computer input to this end. Where certain computer input is handled in the dealing room, processing personnel authenticate the dealers' input.

- Processing personnel prepare and despatch confirmations of deals to counterparties and are equally responsible for checking details on incoming deal confirmations from counterparties. Typically these messages will be transmitted and received via the secure SWIFT network.

- Processing personnel are authorized to prepare and issue payment instructions in respect of correctly verified deals. The payment may only be released on the authority of the appropriate level of signature. Again, these messages will be transmitted via the secure SWIFT network.

> **Question**
>
> A typical ACI Dealing Certificate question might be:
> CHIPS is the commonly used name for the domestic clearing system in:
>
> A: Hong Kong
> B: Frankfurt
> C: London
> D: New York
>
> **Correct answer**
> D: The acronym CHIPS stands for Clearing House Interbank Payment System – the electronic cash clearing system in New York.

- Processing personnel must maintain records and files to enable strict control over forward dated outstanding and non-matured contracts held in computer files and in hard copy independently of the dealing room. These forward dated outstandings can be in respect of foreign exchange, money market and/or derivative products in accordance with procedures laid down.

Brokers and brokerage

Brokerage is freely negotiable between principals and the broker companies provided that such negotiations are undertaken by senior management rather than individual dealers. (See also Chapter 11 on the Model Code.)

Brokerage

As a general rule brokerage is negotiable between senior management of broking firms and senior dealing management. Under no circumstances should such negotiations be left to the dealers themselves, particularly not on a deal-by-deal basis. Other parties should be informed but need not be directly involved with negotiations. (See also Chapter 11 on the Model Code.)

Deal ticket data elements

To enable transactions to be accurately confirmed in writing (SWIFT electronic confirmation message MT3xx series), all details in respect of each type of transaction must be appended to the deal ticket or input by the dealer to the front-end system for onwards direct interface with the processing/settlements system. These details include the following data elements which will themselves also feature on the transaction confirmation:

Date (and time*) of transaction
Dealing method (phone, telex, broker, Reuters, etc.)
Name and location of counterparty
Currency, amount
Exchange/interest rate (price)
Type of deal and dealing side
Value (effective) date
Maturity date
Any other relevant dates
Standard terms/conditions applicable (e.g. FRABBA, ISDA, etc.)
Our settlement/netting instructions (nostro account)
Their settlement/netting instructions (nostro account)
Any other significant information (e.g. interest arbitrage details)

Dealer's name   Checker/input

Useful in tracking details on telephone taping equipment after the event.

Much of the above will vary dramatically in order and content from bank to bank and system to system. However, the basic elements must be present for the transaction to be processed promptly and efficiently and ultimately settled.

Topic 8 · The Role of Settlements

Question

A typical ACI Dealing Certificate question might be:

Which of the following is *not* a vital element in data recorded on a bank's deal ticket (or direct dealer input system) recording a routine forward foreign exchange deal?

A: Dealing date
B: Value date
C: Current interest rate
D: Forward exchange rate

Correct answer
C: Dealing date and value date together with the exchange rate of a forward contract are vital elements to be recorded. The current interest rate would be superfluous to the majority of bank's recording systems on routine forward transactions.

Standard Settlement Instructions

Standard Settlement Instructions (SSI) refer to the bilateral arrangement between counterparties frequently dealing always to use the same nostro agents in settlement of foreign exchange deals.

Swapping instructions

Traditionally dealers in banks in London, when dealing direct with each other or through brokers, do not include settlement instructions in the information exchanged at the time of dealing. This is done by the back office separately and is the initial check on the validity, etc. of any deal effected.

Taping of dealing conversations

In the London Code of Conduct, the FSA recommends that "tapes should be kept for at least two months, and preferably longer". They add: "Tapes which cover any transaction which is in question should be retained until the problem has been resolved." (See also Chapter 11 The Model Code.)

Nostro accounts

Strictly speaking a nostro account (*our* account in Latin) means the account in your own bank's ledger reflecting the cash transfers over and balances on an account kept by the bank in an agent elsewhere – frequently a foreign currency account in an agent (correspondent bank) overseas.

Cash clearing and payments methods

- CHAPS is the Clearing House Automated Payments System for high-value electronic funds transfer in the UK.
- CHIPS is the Clearing House Interbank Payments System in the US.
- Euro payment systems:
  - CHAPS EURO (UK) accounts for 18 percent of payments traffic
  - ELS (Germany) accounts for 26 percent of payments traffic
  - TBF (France) accounts for 14 percent of payments traffic
  - ELLIIPS (Belgium)
  - BI-REL (Italy)
  - TOP (Netherlands)
  - SLBE (Spain)
- **SWIFT** is the Society for Worldwide Interbank Financial Telecommunications, the banks' electronic means to make international money transfers. Examples of SWIFT message types include:

100	Customer payment
103	Derivative of MT100 with optional fields
199	Free narrative version of MT100 (authenticated)
202	Interbank payment
300	Foreign exchange confirmation
340	FRA confirmation
360	Interest rate swap confirmation
361	Interest rate swap confirmation
910	Credit advice message
950	Nostro bank statement

- **TARGET** is the Trans-European Automated Real-time Gross settlement Express Transfer system, which handles inter-EU euro transfers.

Securities issue and paying agency

This area deals with all aspects of the division's business connected with the issue, transfer, safe custody and payment of money market instruments traded by the dealing room. These instruments include Gilts, Treasury bills, bills of exchange, certificates of deposit and commercial paper. Money market instruments lodged as security for short-term loans and repos are also handled by this department.

The transfer of title to many of these instruments is now processed electronically through networked systems such as the Central Gilts Office (CGO) and the Central Moneymarkets Office (CMO) administered by CrestCo.

Topic 8 · The Role of Settlements

Question

A typical ACI Dealing Certificate question might be:

Which of the following would you consider should *not* be a function of the back office (settlements department) in foreign exchange and money market operations?

A: To be subordinate and report to dealers/dealing management
B: To check, record and settle market transactions with dealing counter-parties
C: To verify deal details on incoming confirmations
D: To authorize and pay away funds

Correct answer
A: Under no circumstances should back office personnel come under the jurisdiction of the dealers. They must have independent reporting lines to ensure their vital separate checking function on all transactions entered into by the dealers.

Other support functions

- *Reconciliations* – the area responsible for reconciling receipts and payments on the division's nostro accounts with correspondent banking agents.

- *Customer static data* – the area responsible for the maintenance of customer relationship information (including the update of credit limits) and other database functions on the various divisional computer systems.

- *Filing/archiving* – the area responsible for filing and archiving deal tickets and other divisional documentation.

- *Operational services* – the area handling offline computer input, sorting and distributing telexes, confirmations, etc., answering third-party audit requests and controlling and monitoring brokerage charges.

- *Internal audit and data security* – providing an internal audit function throughout treasury, ensuring that policy guidelines for the control of risks are fully complied with, and that the bank's preferred operational procedures are followed. This area is also responsible for ensuring adequate security is in place in respect of the division's mainframe and PC databases and data-links.

- *Risk management (middle office)* – reporting directly to the Treasurer, responsible for analyzing the treasury operations of all worldwide dealing centres, controlling the effect on the bank's risk exposure and profitability, and providing instruction and guidance on all aspects of treasury business. Compliance with the Financial Services Act and the Bank of England's wholesale markets regulations is also monitored by this department.

- *Treasury systems* – reporting to the General Manager, Treasury, this area has responsibility for the development and maintenance of all computer and communications systems in use in the division. These include external information vendors' systems (Reuters or Bloomberg's), PC-based dealer rate information systems, in-house dealer decision support systems, back office mainframe processing systems, CHAPS, the SWIFT interface and other electronic settlement systems, and voice and data communications networks.
- *Financial control department* – this department provides all statutory and regulatory reporting for business booked on treasury systems. It encompasses information sent to the Bank of England, the shareholders and the tax authorities. The financial control department provides analysis of income, on a daily basis, to general management in the dealing room. It provides monthly analyses of income, costs and assets to chief management, the General Manager and the Treasurer. The department ensures that the financial records are kept in accordance with best accounting practice and that all assets and liabilities within the treasury function are properly recorded.

Bank of England recommendations following the collapse of Barings Bank

The Bank of England report in the wake of the Barings collapse made the following observations.

1. Management have a duty to understand fully the businesses they manage.
2. Responsibility for each business activity has to be clearly established and communicated.
3. Clear segregation of duties is fundamental to any effective control system.
4. Relevant internal controls, including independent risk management, have to be established for all business activities.
5. Top management and the Audit Committee have to ensure that significant weaknesses, identified to them by internal audit or otherwise, are resolved quickly.

IFEMA

IFEMA (International Foreign Exchange Master Agreement), drafted by the BBA, reflects best practices for inter-professional transactions. Many of the newer financial products have developed under master agreements over recent years. IFEMA imposes similar uniformly agreed terms and conditions on foreign exchange transactions.

Credit limits

The setting of customer credit limits would not be considered part of the bank's routine processing cycle. Credit management, often a separate entity to the dealing function, assesses and allocates credit limits for banks and other customers. See Chapter 10 for further details.

FOR FURTHER READING

BBA (1993) *The 1993 International Foreign Exchange Master Agreement (IFEMA)*. British Bankers Association (September).
BIS (2000) *A Glossary of Terms Used in Payments and Settlements Systems*. Bank for International Settlements (December).
King, Mervyn and Drummond, Gilmour (1999) *Back Office and Beyond*.
Nolan, Denis and Amos, Gordon (2000) *Mastering Treasury Office Operations*. Prentice Hall.

WEBSITES WORTH A VISIT

Bank of England, London: www.bankofengland.co.uk
Bank for International Settlements, Basel: www.bis.org
European Central Bank, Frankfurt: www.ecb.int

Topic 9 · The Risk Environment

Introduction

Risks in cash markets

Risks in financial instruments

Risks in financial futures

Risks in FRAs

Risks in interest rate swaps

Risks in spot foreign exchange

Risks in forward foreign exchange

Risks in exchange traded currency options

Risks in over the counter options

Capital adequacy

Mastering the ACI Dealing Certificate

> **Overall objective**
>
> *To identify the different types of risk in the markets, and to describe the use of limits to mitigate risks.*
>
> *At the end of this section, candidates will be able to:*
> - *price risk in currency and interest rates;*
> - *explain the difference between transaction, translation and economic risk;*
> - *explain counterparty, delivery and related risks;*
> - *describe a limit structure and how it works.*

Note

There are 4 questions on Risk Management and Control out of which candidates are required to gain a minimum of 25 percent to pass (1 out of 4).

INTRODUCTION

Everything from market risk to credit risk can be included under this topic. Candidates should be familiar with the risks, measurement methods and limits imposed by management to control exposures across the range of products and markets covered by the syllabus.

RISKS IN CASH MARKETS

Interest rate risk

In simple terms interest rate risk – the principal risk in money market operations – is when the dealer has a short (overlent) position in the fixed

Question

A typical ACI Dealing Certificate question might be:

What best defines market risk?

A: The risk involved between two different markets
B: The risk your position might change in value because of a move in the rate
C: The risk your position might be wrong
D: The risk you might choose the wrong currency pair to trade for a certain movement

Correct answer
B: Market risk is the risk your position might change in value because of a move in the rate.

periods and interest rates rise or the dealer has a long (overborrowed) position in the fixed periods and interest rates fall.

Interest rate risk results from the maintenance of mismatched maturity positions of cash market assets, liabilities, off balance sheet derivative products and outstanding commitments to lend or borrow (forward/forward) at agreed fixed rates of interest. The risk is measured per currency and on a consolidated basis with spot exchange positions and interest arbitrage operations included as money market balancing items as appropriate.

Interest rate risk also applies to money market call and notice accounts where the interest rate may be changed after a period of notice, this being determined either by the bank or the counterparty institution.

Identification

Interest rate risk is identified from analyzing outstanding assets and liabilities by maturity date or interest variation period. These must be consolidated with any derivative products expressly identified as being hedge transactions.

The interest variation date of variable interest rate operations (e.g. at two days' notice or at "prime rate") must be regarded as the next business day when a change may occur.

Mismatch maturity risk (gap) can be determined from specially constructed management information reportage showing the mismatched maturities by date and/or by maturity period.

Measurement

Such mismatched maturity positions can be evaluated by comparing historic (breakeven) and current mark to market rates of interest either from today (spot) or on a forward/forward basis. Profit and loss can be evaluated on an accrual basis and then discounted back to today's value using standard NPV techniques. Alternatively a "what-if?" style of report can be implemented.

Dealers' reportage

An accurate and timely cash flow broken down into categories of funds (foreign exchange, various cash money market instruments and hedging instruments' "pseudo" cash positions) is vital reportage for dealers and dealing management.

Additionally there should be some form of mismatch reportage available with breakeven rates compared to current mark to market valuation, with "what-if?" functionality an added bonus.

In today's highly automated front office the ideal scenario comprises dynamically updated cash flows, mismatch reports and on-screen mark to market evaluation.

In the majority of banks the information required will be available on one or more systems and may need manual intervention/consolidation to enable cross instrument and market risks to be identified accurately.

If longer-term assets are funded by shorter-term liabilities a liquidity risk arises in that there is a possibility that market funds will not be available or that marketable assets will not be able to be sold to generate the funding required. The amount that the bank may permit dealers to mismatch such liquidity risk positions could be deemed to be the bank's own internal assessment of the total available credit limits of potential market counterparties at any date in the future.

Current account funds (demand deposits) are deemed to be repayable on the next business day, but most banks take the view that there is a core of non-fugitive funds in this category which may be treated as longer-term liabilities. Certain customer fixed deposit accounts on a renewable deposit basis can similarly be categorized.

Prudential liquidity

Minimum reserve requirements

In some countries, bank liquidity is tightly controlled by the central bank/local monetary authority. Minimum reserve requirements are imposed on all banks, meaning the institutions have to place with the central bank (frequently at zero percent interest rate) balances equal to a fixed percentage of total liabilities accepted. The percentage may vary depending on the bank and/or the source of the liabilities – some deposits are considered more prone than others to be withdrawn promptly. Some central banks permit banks to meet these minimum reserve requirements on an average basis over a pre-advised reporting period, e.g. one or two weeks.

UK liquidity ratio

In other countries, notably the UK, the central bank may require that banks hold readily marketable short-term securities (the type and quality of the assets which qualify is defined by the authorities) of a value equal to a pre-agreed liquidity ratio (a percentage of eligible liabilities).

Typically, whichever method is followed, it is the responsibility of the money market dealers to ensure the required prudential liquidity levels are maintained. There will probably be a cost involved in this function, with longer-term liabilities being required to be taken in order to fund the minimum reserve deposit or purchase of short-term high-quality – therefore low-yielding – securities. This cost may be absorbed by the dealing room or sometimes passed on to lending departments in the bank as an additional margin to be included in their lending rate.

Liquidity management

Dealers also have to use the money markets to ensure that the bank's liquidity is maintained at levels commensurate with a prudent approach as required both by local regulatory authorities and good in-bank controls. Depending on the financial centre, such liquidity ratios are sometimes imposed and other times left to the individual institution's own discretion. The level of liquidity required will very much depend on the size of the institution, the nature of the bank's business, both retail and wholesale, and its principal sources of funding.

Liquidity risk

There is a further risk in trading/funding money market positions, also referred to as liquidity risk. This is the risk that, in running an overlent position, on an interim date when a funding deposit has to be repaid before the fixed asset maturity date the funding deposit will have to be replaced in the market and there is no guarantee that funds will be available to the dealer at that time.

Identification

The liquidity risk position is determined by analyzing maturities of all cash market assets and liabilities, ignoring off balance sheet derivatives. All roll-over commercial lending funded under its current or next roll-over period still constitutes a liquidity risk as there is no guarantee that it will be possible to replace current liabilities on the next and subsequent roll-over date(s).

Measurement

Liquidity risk is an absolute figure which, rather than being measured, can be compared with a preferred liquidity guideline notified by head office, which has available figures on a consolidated basis. There is no limit as such in this instance; the bank's best assessment of available credit limits in its own name among regular market counterparties is used merely as a guide to the level of short positions which may sensibly be maintained on any forward date or range of forward dates.

Credit risk and counterparty dealing limits

Credit risk is assessed and allocated by an institution per dealing counterparty to limit the risk of loss due to that counterparty's default.

Counterparty dealing limits are independently assessed, calculated and granted to dealing rooms to cover a range of cash and derivative products. This risk in money market cash transactions is relatively easy to identify. If you have lent unsecured money the risk is that the counterparty will go bankrupt before maturity date and you will not receive back the amount of your advance.

The risk is 100 percent of all monies so advanced. Some banks will permit a greater exposure to more risky counterparties in the shorter periods than they will in longer periods. Money market lending limits can therefore be tiered, but overall loans must not exceed the total limit allocated.

In a high interest rate environment this risk is sometimes assessed to be more than 100 percent to allow for the potential loss of interest in addition.

RISKS IN FINANCIAL INSTRUMENTS

Market risk

Market risk exists in all unmatched/uncovered positions in the financial instruments already discussed in respect of the cash markets in Chapter 4.

Credit risk and counterparty dealing limits

In many institutions (clean) cash advance limits are combined with other credit limits for negotiable financial instruments. The credit risk on financial instruments covered in Chapter 4 is as follows.

- *Loans*. The credit risk is in the name of the borrower of cash.
- *Repos*. The credit risk is on the issuer of the collateral (frequently government securities, therefore typically lower risk than comparator commercial collateral transactions).
- *T-bills*. The credit risk is in the name of the government issuer (typically lower risk than comparator commercial issues).
- *Eligible bills/bankers' acceptances*. The credit risk is in the name of the acceptor (guarantor).
- *CDs purchased at issue*. The credit risk is in the name of the issuer of the CD.
- *Secondary CDs purchased*. The credit risk is in the name of the issuer of the CD. In certain financial centres where physical settlement of such instruments takes place, there is also a delivery risk in the name of the seller of the CD between the date of payment and receipt of the financial instrument purchased.

- *Commercial paper.* The credit risk is in the name of the issuing company or financial institution.

> **Note**
>
> In all transactions involving exchange of cash for securities/collateral there is also a delivery risk (albeit not too long lasting) between your instructions being passed to an agent or clearing house to transfer the securities and the confirmation of receipt of cash in exchange (either through the local clearing or to your overseas nostro agent).

> **Question**
>
> A typical ACI Dealing Certificate question might be:
> Which of the following is not a limit to control market risk?
>
> B: Counterparty limit
> A: Overnight position limit
> C: Stop loss limit
> D: Forward gap limit
>
> **Correct answer**
> B: Counterparty limits control credit risks with market counterparties to transactions in the market. Market risk is controlled by the other limits listed.

RISKS IN FINANCIAL FUTURES

Market risk

Open financial futures contract positions, where the transactions are effected as trading positions, are subject to market risk in much the same way as open exchange positions. The degree of market risk depends on the price volatility of the type of contract being traded, current underlying market trends and daily volumes and volatility in the trading pit of the futures exchange involved. Risks as perceived by the exchange are reflected in differing initial margin requirements to maintain open interest positions.

Open futures contracts used either for hedging or trading also represent exposure to the extent that movements in the futures contracts may not be exactly reflected in the price of the underlying financial instrument. (Basis risk.)

Open futures contracts effected and identified as hedging transactions are one of the off balance sheet derivative products which must be consolidated into cash market reportage to assess overall interest rate risk.

Credit risk

> **Note:** Once a futures trade has been registered and matched by the exchange there is effectively no credit risk. The exchange or clearing house becomes buyer to every seller and seller to every buyer, thereby guaranteeing future performance of the contract regardless.

As a non-member of an exchange there is a risk that margin account balances, or securities pledged, effectively advanced to the execution broker, may be lost in the event of the latter's insolvency.

A futures execution broker member firm has a risk that initial and variation margins will not be paid in due time. This may result in the member having to close out contracts at current market rates, thus incurring a loss.

Because of the total lack of credit risk, financial futures are the only financial trading product which is not subject to capital adequacy requirements (see later in the chapter).

Risk management reportage

For more "bureaucratic" risk management purposes, pseudo cash flows, balance sheet nominal amounts per currency and consolidated broken down by asset/liability sector and period (ideally daily) should be available to dealer and management.

Whatever the reportage, outstandings to be assessed against any "limits" or other constraints imposed should be readily identifiable.

RISKS IN FRAS

Market risk

FRA positions, where the transactions are effected as trading positions, are subject to market risk in much the same way as open exchange positions. The degree of market risk depends on the price volatility of the currency being traded.

FRAs dealt on a hedge or trading basis either cover or create interest rate risk. Hedging FRAs are one of the off balance sheet derivative products which must be consolidated into cash market reportage to assess overall interest rate risk.

FRAs do not offset any liquidity risk (see money market cash operations risks above) as there is no commitment express or implied to enter into equivalent cash market loan or deposit transactions.

The FRA is a contract for difference, the difference being calculated on (fixing) settlement date and paid on a discounted basis at the start of any agreed FRA period once cash. There is therefore a reinvestment risk in that the LIBOR discount rate may not be achieved on reinvestment.

Credit (counterparty) risk

Credit (counterparty) risk on FRAs is the risk that the counterparty will fail before settlement of the instrument, resulting in either:

- a market replacement cost – a substitute FRA arranged at an unfavourable rate judged against the original transaction; or
- if a replacement FRA cannot be arranged, full exposure to any adverse movements in interest rates against which the original FRA was initiated.

Market replacement risk directly relates to the volatility of interest rates in the cash market and is assessed on a daily mark to market basis (a negative market to market, i.e. the bank owes the counterparty = nil risk). Some banks may still assess risk on FRAs as a flat percentage (i.e. 5 percent maximum potential interest rate swing in any period where there is an FRA outstanding).

RISKS IN INTEREST RATE SWAPS

Market risk

In general, the interest rate and currency commitments inherent in swaps should be integrated with other open positions in determining the overall interest rate risk and currency exposures of the bank.

Market risks arise when swaps are unmatched (warehoused) by traders awaiting the fixed payer client having already closed a swap with a fixed receiver. The bank is exposed to adverse movements in underlying long-term bond or other underlying markets in addition to swap spreads quoted in the interbank market. These risks are only eliminated once the unmatched position has been closed with exactly matching payment flow dates. In practice, given the nature of the swaps market and clients' bespoke requirements, swaps positions may be imperfectly matched with timing and frequency of payments differences needing to be hedged during the life of any swap.

Banks may use similar risk evaluation methods to the bond markets using duration analysis and other techniques. The use of futures markets to hedge risks has additional risks, with some of the longer-term contracts needed being the least liquid in terms of market turnover.

Liquidity risk

The degree of liquidity in the swaps market varies greatly with the type of swap and currency(ies) involved. In any secondary market dealings in swaps, movements in interest rates may result in a large premium or discount being paid when the swap is assigned. Careful consideration must be given to the investment/funding of these sums.

Documentary risk

The majority of swaps are transacted under master agreements, either the industry standard ISDA (International Swaps and Derivatives Association) or BBAIRS (British Bankers Association Interest Rate Swaps) terms.

Where the above terms are not applicable to any proposed swap, there is a documentary risk which should be cleared by reference to the bank's legal department before commitment to the conditions.

Credit (counterparty) risk

All swaps involve credit risk on the counterparty, reflecting the potential cost of replacement should the counterparty default. The cost of replacement is uncertain since it varies with market conditions.

Delivery risk

The bank is at risk in the following circumstances.

Dates of receipts and payments of fixed and floating interest flows may differ and the counterparty fails to make a payment after receiving funds from the bank.

A counterparty accepts payment to it but fails to make payment to the bank on the same day. This risk applies mainly to currency swaps since payments in the same currency on an interest rate swap are usually netted.

In respect of currency swaps the final exchange of currencies at an exchange rate agreed several years previously could lead to substantial exchange exposure.

Market replacement risk

In the event of a swap counterparty defaulting during the life of the swap, the bank will be left with an interest rate position and/or a foreign exchange position which it may only be able to cover at a loss. Swaps in such a situation would be marked to market using current rates. This must be effected on a regular (preferably daily) basis to ascertain the market replacement risk to which the bank is exposed at any time.

Other risks

Other risks to which a bank is exposed in any swap operation depend upon its role and the terms of the swap agreement, which can be complex. Where the bank is an intermediary, the counterparties to the swap are not normally aware of each other's identity, and in such circumstances the bank assumes the credit risk of each counterparty. A bank bears no credit risk where it acts merely as broker to any swap transaction.

Given the long-term nature of swaps banks must pay greater attention to increased risk the longer the period remaining to maturity of any transaction. Many banks use a sliding scale to assess credit risk on swaps based on historic analysis of movements in interest rates. Further percentage credit utilization measures may be applied where the currency(ies) involved are not traded in the major international markets.

In respect of currency (and interest rate) swaps there is also the possibility of exchange rate variation which, in absolute terms, can be much greater than interest variation, leading to a potentially higher replacement cost upon default.

There are several other factors which affect credit risk. These include:

- *the overall level of interest rates* – traditionally it is accepted that rates are more volatile when they are high, and the greater the volatility the greater the credit risk;
- *collateral* – security held against potential cost in default reduces the credit risk;
- *reset frequency* – the more frequently the swap is reset (shorter LIBOR period) the sooner a defaulting counterparty can be identified and correcting action taken;
- *the shape of the yield curve* – if currently positive then the probability is that floating rates will rise, meaning that the floating rate payer's (fixed rate receiver's) liability will increase in the future.

RISKS IN SPOT FOREIGN EXCHANGE

Foreign exchange risk

In foreign exchange there are three types of exchange exposure experienced by the corporate treasurer in commercial transactions. These all come under the heading market risk.

- *Transaction exposure.* Transaction exposure is the risk which arises from individual transactions. The import and export of goods and services invoiced in foreign currency gives rise to *transaction risk* in a commercial company. The company has three choices: to cover (sell) the risk by dealing with a bank in the traditional foreign exchange cash market; to hedge (insure against) the risk by using treasury derivatives; or to run the risk. Provided the risk has been identified and the management are happy then running the risk can be considered a risk management decision.

- *Translation exposure.* Translation exposure is the risk which arises from movements in exchange rates impacting assets and liabilities in foreign currencies but expressed in the local currency in the balance sheet of the reporting entity, which could either be a commercial company or the bank itself. *Translation risk* is more difficult to manage using cash transactions as there may be no underlying cash position at the time the risk arises. Currency options or a shrewd use of available assets and liabilities in foreign currencies is a means to manage this risk.

- *Economic exposure.* Economic exposure is the risk to which a commercial entity is exposed when operating in a highly competitive market with some competitors based and invoicing in different currencies. The commercial company has to be continuously aware of the situation from the viewpoint of its customers, who may be comparing prices in local currency against prices expressed in foreign currency but which at current exchange rate levels give an advantage to an overseas producer/supplier. *Economic risk* may be mitigated by the use of forward foreign exchange or currency options hedging strategies.

Bank exchange exposure

Unlike in the corporate treasury situation already explained above, in a bank dealing room all exchange risk is transaction based – being the result of quoting for client business and transacting a foreign exchange deal (absorbing the commercial customer's unwanted risk). Exchange risk comes down to market risk – open exchange position risk.

Market risk position limits

Banks control currency exposure by imposing trading limits that restrict their dealers' ability to maintain open exchange positions which are at risk to adverse exchange rate movements.

Central bank limits

In most financial centres banks are restricted by their local central bank regulations – the Bank of England is no exception. The maximum exposure of any bank operating in London is limited by reference to the size and market involvement of the bank and the size of its balance sheet, in particular its capital and reserves. This limit, granted by the central bank, will be operative at close of business on each day and is referred to as the overnight open exchange position limit.

Market risk limits

A bank sets market risk (trading) limits to restrict the dealers' ability to over-expose the bank. The setting and advice of trading limits to dealing functions within a bank will frequently be the responsibility of the risk management department.

The trading limits can be based on maximum exposure per market per product or sometimes per dealer.

Exchange risk

Exchange risk arises from "open exchange positions" being maintained as a trading or other position and the fact that exchange rates may fluctuate.

The open exchange position can be defined as the difference between total assets and total liabilities, regardless of value date, in any currency or pair or group of currencies. Here the bank will include assets and liabilities which are not all dealer initiated, i.e. interest accrual positions in foreign currencies.

Open exchange positions are affected by any purchase or sale of a currency, interest receivable or payable in a foreign currency, any operation or sequence of operations where the asset and liability are denominated in different currencies, interest arbitrage operations (not on the principal amounts but on the obligation to cover interest payable in one currency with interest receivable in the second in a linked set of exchange transactions), the maintenance of nostro balances in foreign currency, and in the event of counterparty failure (asset or liability in foreign currency).

A long (overbought) position in a currency which rises against the comparitor currency will result in a profit, whereas a short position in such a currency will result in a loss. There are limits used in a bank to control and monitor this risk.

Open exchange position limits

Intra-day limits

Intra-day (daylight) position limits are to limit a dealer's ability to take excessive open exchange positions during the dealing day. These are typically higher limits than overnight position limits and may be expressed as a multiple of the overnight limit.

Overnight position limits

Overnight position (close of day) limits are frequently authorized by the local central bank and will differ from bank to bank depending on balance sheet, local market size, business involvement, dealers' experience, etc.

Typically a bank's risk management department will allocate limits, sometimes expressed as being on a "net short basis", i.e. the sum of all short currency positions (this is to avoid double counting). The calculation and allocation of limits in a multi-dealing branch situation will be effected and controlled by the risk management department within the treasury division.

Limits will be granted to the international branch dealing operations for spot foreign exchange positions on the condition that outstanding positions at the close of business are advised to a branch or friendly bank in a dealing centre in the next time zone. A summary of positions held with stop loss and take profit levels to monitor while the branch is non-operational should be made available. All such positions are also frequently required to be reported to the head office risk-management function to enable a collation and consolidation to be made for the general management of the bank.

Again, while formal treasury division reportage of outstandings against limits may only be required at certain intervals, it is the local dealing room management's responsibility to ensure full compliance with trading limits at all times. Typically, all trading limits are authorized and are subject to an annual review/renewal.

Time zone risk

The foreign exchange market operates on a 24-hour basis. At any time during the day or night there is a financial centre either in the Far East, Europe or North America trading the world's major currencies. The risk on an open exchange position is not limited to "overnight" these days as, wherever you are in the world, between leaving the office in the evening and arriving at the dealing desk next morning, two or three major financial centres have been actively dealing (say two to two and a half dealing days in all).

How a bank deals with such risk depends very much on where any branch or subsidiary operations are situated in the world, and how overall exposure is controlled.

Position passing: stop loss/take profit orders

A multinational bank may have a structure which permits foreign currency exposure monitoring to be passed from centre to centre depending on who is actually open during the trading hours of the various major market centres. Others may have this ability but prefer to leave what are termed "limit orders" or "stop loss orders" with their branches or correspondent bankers in one or more financial centres.

Such a practice allows the minute-by-minute monitoring to continue even when the bank dealer is not at his desk. The bank is therefore in control of any foreign exchange risk virtually on a 24-hour basis (depending on the global services available).

Such stop loss orders are set at the level at which a bank dealer would be happy to deal. If and when not acted upon, these are advised back to the initiating bank branch at the start of business the next day for their own active monitoring to continue. At the same time, such orders from other operating branches or correspondent banks may also be advised for the UK-based dealers to similarly monitor during London market hours of trading. This topic is addressed further in Chapter 11 on the Model Code.

Credit risk

Credit (counterparty) risk on foreign exchange operations is defined under two headings, but initially for spot foreign exchange we need only concern ourselves here with the following.

Delivery risk (Herstatt risk)

The foreign exchange market is a cash market and on value date currencies involved must be physically delivered as agreed under the contract. If for some reason the bank does not receive the currency contracted to be purchased and has already paid away the countervalue in local or another foreign currency then the risk is 100 percent of the sum so paid away. The risk is assessed as being a daily risk and banks limit overall aggregate purchase and sale amounts when granting counterparty limits. Modern netting procedures (bilateral netting by novation) dramatically reduce the impact of this risk (see below).

Banks sometimes categorize the limits allocated under counterparty names by period, permitting a greater use of limit for shorter-term operations.

A typical ACI Dealing Certificate question might be:

Herstatt risk is also known as:

A: Operational risk
B: Settlement risk
C: Replacement risk
D: Translation risk

Correct answer
B: Bankhaus I. D. Herstatt was the German bank which was closed by the Bundesbank at midday (one day in 1974) giving rise to settlement risk (also known as delivery risk). No US dollars were paid by the bank (after closure) on any purchase of DEM deals value that day.

Care must be taken in some Middle Eastern currency markets where, due to the differing Islamic weekend/holiday dates, the delivery risk may be longer than 24 hours, e.g. US dollars settlement Friday, Saudi riyals Saturday.

Netting

Both as a means to reduce credit exposure and to cut processing and payment costs many banks these days are entering into netting agreements. These netting arrangements only apply to foreign exchange transactions in the same currency pairings dealt for the same value date, and the terms of all such netting are agreed bilaterally between the banks.

RISKS IN FORWARD FOREIGN EXCHANGE

Interest rate risk

Given the nature of the forward foreign exchange market it is evident that exchange exposure only really results from spot or outright foreign exchange transaction activity. Forward foreign exchange trading is effectively trading interest rate differentials "off the balance sheet".

Forward foreign exchange trading limits

Interest rate risk in forward foreign exchange dealing results from the maintenance of mismatched maturity positions of cash market spot against forward purchases and sales of foreign currency, off balance sheet derivative products and such operations effected on a forward/forward basis, all agreed at exchange rates relative to today's spot and forward rates where such forward dealing rates include the equivalent of interest rate differentials between the two currencies involved. The risk is measured per currency and on a consolidated basis with spot exchange positions and interest arbitrage operations included as money market balancing items as appropriate.

Identification

Interest rate risk emanating from forward foreign exchange trading activities is identified by analyzing outstanding forward exchange time positions by value date or forward dated period. These must be consolidated with any derivative exchange rate related products expressly identified as being hedge transactions.

Mismatch maturity risk (gap) on forward foreign exchange operations can be determined from specially constructed management information reportage showing the mismatched maturities by value date and/or by maturity period.

Interpretation (measurement)

Such mismatched maturity positions can be evaluated by comparing historic (breakeven) and current mark to market exchange rates (or forward swap points) either from today (spot) or on a forward/forward basis. Profit and loss can be evaluated and then discounted back to today's value using standard NPV techniques. Alternatively a "what-if?" style of report can be implemented.

Dealers' reportage

As already noted under the Money market heading, an accurate and timely cash flow broken down into categories of funds (here referring to foreign exchange generated balances) is vital reportage for dealers and dealing management.

Additionally there should be some form of forward foreign exchange reportage on a mismatch maturity basis with breakeven swap points prices compared to a current mark to market valuation, and some form of "what-if?" modelling functionality an added bonus. In today's highly automated front office the ideal situation is dynamically updated cash flows, mismatch reports and on-screen mark to market evaluation.

In respect of interest arbitrage operations, the principal amounts of any FX swaps transacted and identified as interest must be transferred from exchange to interest reportage and any forward interest positions generated reported under the forward value date of the FX swap.

In the majority of banks the information required will be available on one or more systems and may need manual intervention/consolidation to enable cross instrument and market risks to be identified accurately.

Risk management reportage

For more "bureaucratic" risk management purposes open exchange positions, forward exchange time positions, cash flows, balance sheets (per currency and consolidated) broken down by asset/liability sector and period (ideally daily) should be available.

Whatever the reportage, outstandings to be assessed against any "limits" or other constraints imposed should be readily identifiable.

Credit risk

Delivery risk

The foreign exchange market is a cash market and on spot and forward value dates, currencies involved must be physically delivered as agreed under the contract. If for some reason the bank does not receive the currency contracted to be purchased and has already paid away the counter-value in local or another foreign currency then the risk is 100 percent of the sum so paid away. This risk, referred to as delivery or settlement risk, is assessed as being a daily risk and banks limit overall aggregate purchase and sale amounts both spot and maturing forward exchange for all dates when granting counterparty limits.

Market replacement risk

In the event of a counterparty failure an interim movement in exchange rates could leave the bank with the additional cost of replacing a forward dated exchange deal which may not now be completed (beware of "cherry picking" in the event of counterparty liquidation). The risk is assessed per outstanding foreign exchange contract and is quantified as the cost of replacing the original contract (or contracts) at the current market rate.

Even where the exchange rate movement may seem to be in the bank's favour the risk still applies, as any deal which if not completed shows the bank a profit will not be in favour of the receivers who may apply specific performance or "cherry picking" and choose to complete those deals which suit them (i.e. showing them a profit) and drop those which do not. In such instances the risk is deemed to be zero.

This is stage one of the bank's assessment of outstandings for capital adequacy measurement and is sometimes treated in the same way with an additional calculation adding in a factor for potential future exposure (PFE).

Question

A typical ACI Dealing Certificate question might be:

Which combination of the following types of risk is associated with a forward FX deal: (1) market risk; (2) settlement risk; (3) basis risk; (4) counterparty risk?

A: (1), (2) and (4)
B: (1) and (2)
C: (1), (2) and (3)
D: (2) and (4)

Correct answer

A: A forward FX deal involves (1) market risk, (2) settlement risk and (4) counterparty risk.

FX swaps identified as interest arbitrage operations

Risks involved in interest arbitrage operations include those relating to foreign exchange operations generally, but special attention should be given to the following additional risks:

- possible default of the borrower of funds against which the interest arbitrage operation is effected, resulting in the loss of the principal and the interest element involved;
- exchange risk in respect of uncovered interest flows;
- additional mismatch risk if loan deposit and the swap identified as interest arbitrage mature on differing value dates.

RISKS IN EXCHANGE TRADED CURRENCY OPTIONS

Market risk

Market risk arises from an exchange traded option position being maintained as a trading or other position and the fact that the underlying exchange or interest rates may fluctuate, with an adverse effect on the pricing of the option contracts.

Different exchanges around the world have different margining procedures for exchange traded options.

For buyers of exchange traded options the potential loss (risk) is limited to the amount of any premium/margin paid whereas the potential profit is theoretically unlimited. For sellers (writers) of options, on the other hand, the potential loss is unlimited, with profit restricted to the amount of any premium/margin received.

A long (overbought) position in calls on a commodity, currency or interest rate where the option price (premium/margin) is rising will result in a profit, whereas a long (overbought) position in puts on the same commodity, currency or interest rate will result in a loss.

One hedging method for sold (written) options is delta hedging, with a computer model assessing the proportion of cover in the underlying cash (or security) market required given the current market position and trends (see Chapter 8). Such hedging methods may give rise to further risks (market and credit) in those underlying markets.

Credit (counterparty) risk

In similar fashion to exchange traded futures, and depending on the exchange involved, once an option has been registered and matched by the exchange there is effectively no credit risk. The exchange or clearing house becomes buyer to every seller and seller to every buyer, thereby guaranteeing future performance of the contract regardless.

As a non-member of an exchange there is a risk that margin account balances, or securities pledged, effectively advanced to the execution broker, may be lost in the event of the latter's insolvency.

A futures execution broker member firm has a risk that initial and variation margins will not be paid in due time. This may result in the member having to close out exchange traded option contracts at current market rates, thus incurring a loss.

RISKS IN OVER THE COUNTER OPTIONS

Market risk

Market risk arises from an OTC option position being maintained as a trading or other position and the fact that underlying commodity prices, exchange or interest rates and/or volatility may fluctuate with an adverse effect on the pricing of the option contracts. For buyers of OTC options the potential loss (risk) is limited to the amount of any premium paid whereas the potential profit is theoretically unlimited. For sellers (writers) of options, on the other hand, the potential loss is unlimited with profit restricted to the amount of any premium received.

A long (overbought) position in calls on a commodity, currency or interest rate where the option price (premium) is rising will result in a profit, whereas a long (overbought) position in puts on the same commodity, currency or interest rate will result in a loss.

One hedging method for sold (written) options is delta hedging, with a computer model assessing the proportion of cover in the underlying cash (or security) market required given the current market position and trends (see Chapter 8). Such hedging methods may give rise to further risks (market and credit) in those underlying markets.

Credit (counterparty) risk

The buyer (holder) of an option is exposed to the risk that the writer may be unable to fulfil his obligation within the option contract if exercised. The buyer's loss would be the market replacement cost at time of exercise. This is calculated on a daily basis (sometimes more frequently) and is akin to the similarly titled risk on forward foreign exchange outstandings.

The seller (writer) of an option has a risk between the time of agreeing the option and receipt of the premium from the buyer. Once the premium is received it is incumbent on the holder (buyer) to exercise the option within the terms and conditions of the contract. There is no obligation on the seller and therefore no risk.

OTC currency options exercise

On exercise there will be the normal risk associated with the underlying market transaction, e.g. a currency option on exercise becomes in effect a foreign exchange deal (American style = spot, European style = *possibly* forward).

The buyer of American style options has a modicum of control over the delivery dates on exercise (i.e. excess delivery risk positions can theoretically be avoided).

CAPITAL ADEQUACY

Capital adequacy requirements

All banks operating in OECD countries are subject to regulation agreed between the major central banks and formalized in the Bank for International Settlements (BIS) guidelines. Banks have to ensure that they have sufficient capital available to support all outstandings – on and off the balance sheet – on a counterparty by counterparty basis. The BIS has set risk weightings for all financial products and currently requires that banks have a minimum of 8 percent capital cover requirement.

The amount of capital required depends on the type of transaction, the domicile of the counterparty, the residual maturity and the cost of replacement, with an added percentage "just in case" for potential future exposure.

The capital adequacy requirements against each transaction will vary almost daily according to market conditions.

The Basel Accord (1988)

In 1988 the Group of Ten (G10) countries announced that international supervisory regulations governing the capital adequacy of international banks would ensure that all banks were playing "on a level playing field" by providing a minimum standard of capital cover for all risk activities. The Cooke ratio initially defined credit risks but the full ratios were only introduced in 1993.

The Basel Accord Tier 1

Tier 1 capital ("core" capital) consists of equity and disclosed reserves. General loan loss reserves constitute capital that has been earmarked to absorb future losses (a reserve for bad and doubtful debts), and when these losses occur they may be charged against the reserve account rather than to earnings. This smoothes out income over time.

The Basel Accord Tier 2

Tier 2 capital ("supplementary" capital) includes perpetual securities, undisclosed reserves, subordinated debt over five years to maturity and shares redeemable at the option of the issuer.

BIS ratio

Of the BIS ratio for capital cover of 8 percent (the Cooke ratio) at least 50 percent must be Tier 1 capital. All classes of assets are risk weighted according to asset classes and counterparty (OECD government to non-OECD non-financial counterparty). As the perceived credit risk increases so too does the risk weighting.

EU Directive 93/6/EEC

In March 1993 the Council of the European Union issued Directive 93/6/EEC in respect of the Capital Adequacy of Investment Firms and Credit Institutions, setting out the minimum standards necessary.

In 1994 the Bank of England published a consultative document on the Capital Adequacy Directive (CAD), entitled *Implementation of the CAD for UK Incorporated Institutions Authorised under the Banking Act 1987*.

> **Question**
>
> A typical ACI Dealing Certificate question might be:
>
> According to BIS Basel capital adequacy requirements, which of the following constitutes Tier 1 capital?
>
> A: Undisclosed reserves, general provisions, perpetual subordinated debt
> B: Shareholders' equity, disclosed reserves, published current year profit and loss
> C: Goodwill and other intangible assets
> D: Minority interests in permanent shareholders' equity, minority interests in Tier 2 shares
>
> **Correct answer**
>
> B: Shareholders' equity, disclosed reserves and published current year profit and loss all constitute Tier 1 capital. The other items are all Tier 2 or adjustments to be made.

The trading book concept

The CAD introduces the concept of a trading book. The trading book is based upon three broad criteria:

- that the instrument is a financial instrument; and
- that the instrument is held for trading purposes; or
- that the instrument is hedging an exposure in the trading book.

Instruments include transferable securities, money market instruments, financial futures contracts, FRAs, interest rate swaps, currency swaps and options to acquire these instruments.

Trading book definition

The trading book is defined as:

- proprietary positions in financial instruments which are held for resale and/or which are taken on by the institution with the intention of benefiting in the short term from actual and/or expected differences between their buying and selling prices or positions taken in order to hedge other elements of the trading book;
- exposures due to the unsettled transactions, free deliveries and OTC derivative instruments, exposures due to repurchase agreements (repos) and securities lending;
- those exposures in the form of fees, commission, interest, dividends and margin on exchange traded derivatives.

The UK Financial Services Authority considers that positions are held with a trading intent if:

- they are marked to market daily as part of the internal risk management process;
- the position takers have autonomy in entering into transactions within predetermined limits;
- they satisfy any other criteria which the bank applies to the composition of its trading book on a consistent basis.

Capital adequacy calculation (simplified)

There are four stages in assessing capital adequacy:

1. Determine mark to market valuation (MtM).
2. Add in factor for future volatility (PFE).
3. Sum of 1 plus 2 = credit risk equivalent (CRE).

Next:

4. The creditworthiness of the counterparty comes into consideration:

- Risk weightings:
  - OECD government = 0%
  - non-bank outside OECD = 50%
- Credit risk equivalent (CRE) multiplied by risk weighting = risk weighted asset value.

The risk weighted asset value multiplied by the capital ratio = the capital requirement, and the Basel Accord demands 8.00 percent capital cover. Capital adequacy varies dynamically with market volatility.

CAD II

CAD II is the EU Directive that allows financial institutions to use internal Value at Risk (VaR) models to calculate market risk capital requirements in line with BIS Basel standards. Banks must measure delta, gamma and vega risk when calculating capital adequacy required against written (sold) options positions. Under CAD II banks can choose to use the standard approach in calculating capital adequacy for their trading books or may seek regulatory approval to employ their own in-house VaR models.

CAD II also laid down basic standards for these in-house models. The model must express a VaR estimate to a 99 percent confidence level and must calculate losses on the basis of a ten-day holding period. In addition, all historic data used must cover at least the last 12 months.

> **Question**
>
> A typical ACI Dealing Certificate question might be:
>
> Under the BIS amendments, the risk weight category applied to aggregate net short open foreign exchange positions is:
>
> A: 8%
> B: 10%
> C: 5%
> D: 100%
>
> **Correct answer**
> D: According to the BIS guidelines on capital adequacy, the risk weight category applied to aggregate net short open foreign exchange positions is 100 percent.

FOR FURTHER READING

Risk, magazine published monthly by Risk Publications.
Basel Committee on Banking Supervision (2000). *Supervisory Guidance for Managing Settlements Risk in Foreign Exchange Transactions*. Basel Committee on Banking Supervision (September).

WEBSITES WORTH A VISIT

Bank of England, London: www.bankofengland.co.uk
Bank for International Settlements, Basel: www.bis.org
Risk Publications: www.risk.co.uk

SYLLABUS PART 2

11 Topic 10 · The Model Code

Topic 10 · The Model Code

Introduction

Chapter I – Business hours and time zone related

Chapter II – Personal conduct issues

Chapter III – Back office, payments and confirmations

Chapter IV – Disputes, differences, mediation and compliance

Chapter V – Authorization, documentation and telephone taping

Chapter VI – Brokers and brokerage

Chapter VII – Dealing practice

Chapter VIII – Dealing practice for specific transactions

Chapter IX – General risk management principles for dealing business

Chapter X – Additional guidelines for dealing with corporate/commercial clients

Chapter XI – Market terminology

Appendices 1–7

Mastering the ACI Dealing Certificate

> ### Overall objective
>
> *For candidates to have a thorough knowledge of the Model Code and market practices that regulate our markets, with particular emphasis on dispute procedures.*
>
> *At the end of this section, candidates will be able to:*
>
> - *explain the purpose of the Model Code and its application within the industry;*
> - *list the general principles of professional conduct;*
> - *explain market terminology;*
> - *explain the procedures for disputes;*
> - *list the market practices covering:*
>   - *foreign exchange*
>   - *money market*
>   - *derivatives*
>   - *securities*
>   - *dealer–broker relationships*
>   - *dealer–customer relationships.*

Note — There are 30 questions on the Model Code in the ACI Dealing Certificate. Candidates are required to gain a minimum of 50 percent to pass (15 out of 30).

INTRODUCTION

This topic within the ACI Dealing Certificate syllabus is additionally available as a separate 45 minute Level 1 examination which must be passed by any experienced candidates who have been granted an exemption from the ACI Dealing Certificate examination.

Following the release of the Model Code in June 2000 (a single global code of conduct), candidates no longer have to familiarize themselves with the five separate codes issued by regulators in the major financial market centres of London, New York, Tokyo and Singapore along with the ACI's original code. General dealing principles and market practices as outlined in the Model Code also feature in this section of the examination.

As far as revising for the examination there is nothing better than reading the Model Code. If you work in the industry, copies should be available in your institution's dealing room. If not, or if you prefer your own personal copy, you can obtain a hard copy either from your local ACI Forex Club or from the ACI

Secretariat in Paris (cost EUR 10.00). There is a printable Adobe pdf file version available for download from the website, www.aciforex.com

Most of the issues addressed in the Model Code are common sense responses to everyday financial markets situations. As with any code or rule book the Model Code has evolved over time with its origins in the "O'Brien letter" released by the Bank of England in the early 1970s following the problems experienced in Lloyds Bank International Limited's Lugano branch and other banks suffering exchange losses in the early years of floating exchange rates. The O'Brien letter grew into the Bank of England's London Code of Conduct (the Grey Book). Responsibility for this passed to the Financial Services Authority in the UK in the late 1990s, and initially a revised London Code of Conduct was issued (for principals and broking firms in the wholesale markets). This has now been replaced by the Inter-Professionals Conduct documentation. For full details see the FSA UK website at www.fsa.gov.uk

This chapter of the book takes the chapters of the Model Code one by one and where appropriate seeks to explain the rationale behind the "recommendations" for best practice contained therein. Another document well worth acquiring is the Bank of England's Non-Investment Products code (NIP), available as a downloadable Adobe pdf document from their website, www.bankofengland.co.uk

CHAPTER 1 – BUSINESS HOURS AND TIME ZONE RELATED

- After-hours/24-hour and off-premises dealing
- Monday morning trading/market opening and closing hours
- New bank holidays/special holidays/market disruption
- Stop-loss orders
- Position parking

After-hours/24-hour and off-premises dealing

One major problem for banks in today's global financial markets is the very fact that they are "global" 24-hour markets in foreign exchange, money markets and associated derivatives. Deals can be transacted after hours in your local centre with differing financial centres positioned around the world's time zones. Such deals can be concluded at any time of day or night by dealers away from their place of business – all that is needed these days is a mobile phone.

Bank management seek, to control the added risks of financial markets personnel dealing on the bank's account outside normal office hours by clearly defining policy regarding who is authorized so to deal and when and for what reasons such transactions may be effected. Obviously the policy will vary from bank to bank depending on many different issues – the size and involvement of the institution in various markets, the experience of the dealing personnel, the incidence of client dealing orders accepted by the operation and the bank's own appetite for risk (trading limits available). The Model Code recommends that written guidelines are available and that these should also include how any after-hours transactions should be advised (answer machines available for such transactions to be reported – subject to the standard security arrangements for such recording equipment), recorded in the bank's accounting records and included in reporting procedures.

This section of the Code also addresses the use of mobile phones in the dealing room, which for reasons such as the lack of independently controllable recording or caller ID facilities (as would be found on the institution's main phone systems) is not considered good practice. The Code does, however, recognize the benefits of mobile phones as a disaster contingency measure.

Monday morning trading/market opening and closing hours

With so much emphasis on the 24-hour market there is a need to formalize the official opening and closing times of the financial markets. These have been agreed by mutual consent of various market associations and local regulatory bodies as being Monday 5.00 a.m. Sydney time to Friday 5.00 p.m. New York time. Deals outside these hours (particularly in Middle Eastern markets where western weekends are normal business days) are not forbidden but the Model Code stresses these are effected in conditions "not considered to be normal market conditions or hours".

New bank holidays/special holidays/market disruption

Occasionally forward dates are altered due to national holidays in one or more centres with resultant date amendment for any transactions maturing on the previously good value date. The Model Code lays down the procedures as to how this should be effected, stressing that no bank should seek to adjust the exchange rate in FX transactions to profit out of any such date changes, and reconfirms the market practice of end/end where such dates would cross the month-end threshold.

This section also notes the practice in certain Islamic countries for split value dates – for example, USD/SAR transactions where USD are settled on a Friday (Islamic holiday) and the Saudi riyals are settled on the Saturday. In such instances it is left to the institutions involved to lay down how such transactions should be reported for trading and credit risk purposes.

Stop-loss orders

This chapter goes on to discuss the practice of market participants and corporate customers leaving stop-loss orders with their correspondent banks' dealers. Strict procedures should be laid down in banks' in-house rule books/manuals, ensuring that all details of the orders are specifically identified and confirmed at the time of acceptance and that adequate lines of communication remain open between the parties should market conditions create extreme price/rate movements leaving the market watcher unable to fulfil the client's instruction.

Banks should be aware that given the nature of the financial markets only dealers party to a transaction at a particular rate know business has actually been transacted at that level. Disputes can and do arise over whether a particular level in a market was reached and the Model Code recommends caution in this respect.

Position parking

The final section of Chapter I highlights problems which have been experienced – particularly in certain emerging markets where dealers, to get around loss limits or other trading constraints, agree with colleagues in other banks to "park" their position before close of business on one day, agreeing to take it back the following morning at the same rate or a rate showing a small profit to the position recipient. This has grave implications of position concealment, collusion in fraud, dealing at off market rates and even tax evasion, and in the words of the Model Code quite simply "should be forbidden".

A typical ACI Dealing Certificate question might be:

When you are accepting a "stop-loss" order, you must:

A: (1) Ensure that your counterparty understands the terms under which your bank accepts the order
B: (2) Ensure that the counterparty can be contacted in the event of unusual situations, events or volatile market conditions
C: Advise the customer that (1) and (2) are not practical conditions to enforce
D: Ensure both (1) and (2) are complied with

Correct answer
D: It is imperative that the counterparty fully understands all the conditions under which you are prepared to accept the stop-loss order (Model Code Chapter 1.4).

CHAPTER II – PERSONAL CONDUCT ISSUES

- Drugs and abused substances
- Entertainment and gifts
- Gambling and betting between market participants
- Money laundering
- Fraud
- Dealing for personal account
- Confidentiality
- Misinformation and rumours

Drugs and abused substances

Dealing in the financial markets is a pressure business and all banks will have detailed procedures to ensure their personnel are not exposed to too great a personal risk but of course this can only go so far. Alcohol and drugs are a real problem in today's society and, for the bank, testing prior to employment, substance abuse information dissemination, counselling and as a last resort strict procedures for offender discipline/dismissal will all be clearly defined in in-house personnel policy documents.

Entertainment and gifts

Some industries are rife with unscrupulous operators, bribery and corruption. Dealing relationships are a vital part of success in the financial markets and the financial markets have always recognized the need for such relationships within reason. This section of the Model Code lays down guidance on how management can keep track of business entertainment attended by dealing personnel as guests and frequently given as hosts to other market participants, together with the giving and acceptance of gifts.

Gambling and betting between market participants

Taking and managing risk is the dealer's job. Over the years, some individual dealers have experienced problems because they have become involved in such risks on a personal basis through gambling – sometimes with other market participants. Financial market gambling has achieved a semblance of respectability recently, being freely available from spread betting operators by phone, dealing information screens and even on the Internet. This means the potential for involvement by a dealer is sitting on his dealing screen and so management awareness of the knock-on risks is vital, with a sensible approach to the control of such activity (where not expressly forbidden) being desirable.

Money laundering

The prevention of money laundering is subject to legal requirements across the world. In the UK references to the crime can be found in the Criminal Justice Act 1988, the Prevention of Terrorism Act (Temporary Provisions) Act 1989, the Criminal Justice Act 1993 as it amends those Acts, the Drug Trafficking Act 1994, the Criminal Law (Consolidation) (Scotland) Act 1995 and the Proceeds of Crime (Northern Ireland) Order 1996.

The Money Laundering Regulations 1993, Regulation 2(3) defines money laundering and Regulation 14(d) requires the reporting of all offences of suspected money laundering.

All members of the EU are required to enact legislation and financial sector procedures in accordance with the European Money Laundering Directive. All EU countries therefore can be considered to have equivalent anti-money laundering measures. In addition, countries which belong to the Financial Action Task Force (FATF) have committed themselves to implementing the 40 FATF recommendations which in several respects are more wide ranging in nature than the provisions of the European Money Laundering Directive.

> **Hint**
>
> ACI Dealing Certificate *candidates are strongly recommended to familiarize themselves with the* Money Laundering Guidance Notes for the Financial Sector *published by the Joint Money Laundering Steering Group of the British Bankers Association (regularly updated) or their local national equivalent organization. See the website* www.bba.org.uk *or* www.mlro.net

Fraud

Fraud is of constant concern in the financial services industry. In respect of dealing operations, while a dealer may be able to cause his employing institution to suffer serious loss – even taking it into bankruptcy – it is less likely (if the appropriate segregation of duties and other controls are in place) for him to benefit personally from such fraud. The obvious exception is if the dealer is acting in collusion with bank personnel on the settlements side of the business who are able to realize the fraudulent proceeds of any transactions dealt for his or their joint benefit. Every bank will have built up rules and procedures to guard against such collusion and potential for loss.

Dealing for personal account

Where allowed, a similar management approach to that taken for gambling is appropriate to dealing for personal account. Management must, however, be well aware of any conflicts of interest which may be involved. Should such transactions be undertaken because the dealer has knowledge of market-sensitive information, the rules governing insider trading embodied in any institution's local regulatory requirements come into play.

Confidentiality

Chapter II goes on to discuss issues surrounding confidentiality – one of the mainstays of the financial markets' reputation. Both dealers and brokers have an obligation to ensure the strict standards of confidentiality are maintained. Issues regarding "squawk boxes" and open lines in dealing rooms/broking offices and the protection of confidential information prior to dealing are addressed. Brokers and dealers should only visit each others' offices with the express permission of management on both sides and no transaction must ever be effected by a dealer while on the broker's premises.

Market ethics issues such as the practice of reducing amounts dealt through a broker to close larger amounts direct once the counterparty name is known are dealt with in this section. Everyone will have heard horror stories of these and other unethical practices, such as pressurizing brokers for information they are not permitted to divulge or threatening a reduction in business if such information is not forthcoming, and all personnel should be aware of the need to report any breaches to top senior management for appropriate action.

Misinformation and rumours

Typically financial markets react dramatically on a single line of news text on an information screen often taken out of context. Being first with some news or information and reacting accordingly is very different from starting or spreading a rumour you know or suspect to be false. The Model Code stipulates that neither dealers nor brokers should relay any information which is suspect as to its veracity or which could be damaging to a third party.

Topic 10 · The Model Code

> **Question**
>
> A typical ACI Dealing Certificate question might be:
> Where dealing for personal account is allowed management must:
> A: Establish clear guidelines for such dealing
> B: Prevent insider trading with appropriate internal control
> C: All of these
> D: Ensure that adequate safeguards are set up to prevent abuse
>
> Correct answer
> C: Where personal account dealing is allowed by local regulations and in-house rules clearly state such transactions are permissible, management must be fully aware of all transactions and ensure that adequate safeguards are in place, that no conflict of interest occurs and that no possibility of insider trading is available (Model Code Chapter 2.6).

CHAPTER III – BACK OFFICE, PAYMENTS AND CONFIRMATIONS

Chapter III of the Model Code looks at back office responsibilities and associated settlement procedures:

- Back office location and segregation of duties/reporting
- Confirmation procedures (written)
- Confirmation procedures (verbal)
- Payments and settlement instructions
- Netting

All topics with the exception of verbal confirmations or oral deal checks as referred to by the FSA have already been addressed in detail in Chapter 9, The Role of Settlements.

Confirmation procedures (verbal)

In active dealing markets such as the spot foreign exchange market frequent telephone dealing counterparties and their brokers will confirm by Reuters dealing system message, fax, telex or other convenient means a list of all transactions effected between them (or via their services) by phone that day. Such messages may be sent once during the morning before lunchtime and once during the afternoon. If they are only sent once then the Model Code recommends this is undertaken towards or at the end of the trading day. The objective is to ensure that all transactions agreed by phone have been responded to by both parties. The system was introduced originally on an informal basis to identify at the earliest possible point errors, omissions and possible bogus transactions slipping into the system. This process does not impact on any other formal confirmation exchange or later settlements procedures.

> **Question**
>
> A typical ACI Dealing Certificate question might be:
>
> You have concluded a deal over the telephone at 10 a.m. this morning. You should:
>
> A: Input into the deal system and the system will take care of everything else
> B: Confirm the deal on telex or dealing system towards the end of the dealing day
> C: None of these
> D: All you need to do is to write a ticket to inform your settlements department and update your position blotter
>
> **Correct answer**
> B: It is preferred market practice that towards the end of the day a written (Reuters or telex) message is sent to counterparties confirming the details of all deals effected by telephone during the day (Model Code Chapter 3.4).

CHAPTER IV – DISPUTES, DIFFERENCES, MEDIATION AND COMPLIANCE

- Disputes and mediation
- Differences between principals
- Differences with brokers and the use of "points"
- Compliance and complaints

Candidates should note that the Model Code Syllabus Topic description (page 320) includes the following phrase: "with particular emphasis on dispute procedures".

> **Note**
>
> Appendix I of the Model Code sets out the formal rules for over the counter financial instruments dispute resolution.

Disputes and mediation

The Model Code, being a compilation of recommended best practices, contains a series of guidance notes. Sometimes disputes between market participants get to a point where there is a need for external involvement

Topic 10 · The Model Code

on an advice or arbitration basis. The ACI through its elected Committee for Professionalism is willing to give advice on professional disagreements subject to certain conditions which are laid down in this chapter.

In the introduction to the chapter we stated that there used to be five separate codes of conduct to be considered by ACI candidates. Those separate codes do still exist and this section in the Model Code suggests that parties within the same centre should be guided by their local regulatory authority and its code, while for any dispute between parties in separately regulated centres the Model Code should apply.

Differences between principals

Where differences between principals, if left unresolved until independently available assistance was obtained, would result in ongoing risks or costs to one or both parties it is eminently sensible that the parties should take appropriate action to square off or neutralize the position. Any such action, however, should not be taken as an admission of liability on either party. Also the Model Code stipulates that no party should benefit from undue enrichment due to the application of erroneously available funds.

Differences with brokers and the use of "points"

On the issue of differences with brokers the Model Code acknowledges differences of opinion within the industry and approaches by regulators. The spot FX market is a fast-moving market and although through the expertise of brokers and participants all participants endeavour to avoid "let downs" there will be times when such situations are unavoidable. In some centres (London is an example) differences are allowed to be settled by the use of "points" provided all involved are aware of the risks and that such practices are formally agreed by senior management. It is strongly recommended that candidates refer to the FSA's IPC for the full text on this issue. The Code is available as an Adobe pdf file downloadable from the FSA website, www.fsa.gov.uk

As this is a contentious issue and quite complex in its application the text of the worked example of situations giving rise to negative and positive points settlements in foreign exchange dealing is repeatedly updated here.

> **Note**
> The level of the GBP/USD exchange rate around 1.80 00 in the original example in the FSA London Code of Conduct schedule indicates how long this has been an acceptable practice in London.

"Negative" points

Suppose a broker quotes sterling at 1.45 30 – 35. Bank A hits the 30 bid for GBP 5 million. However, before the broker could let Bank A know, the price has been withdrawn by the market maker who had originally indicated to the broker a willingness to deal at the rate. The market for sterling has moved to 1.45 25 – 30.

When told that the bid price of 30 was no longer available, the trader at Bank A insists that the price is substantiated (i.e. he wants to sell GBP 5 million at 1.45 30). Suppose the broker accepts responsibility for not withdrawing the price quickly enough, or values highly his relationship with Bank A, and therefore agrees to be held to the price. He searches the market and finds Bank B (a participating bank) who is willing to help the broker by agreeing to buy from Bank A at 1.45 30 (and hopefully sell to the current bidder in the market at 1.45 25); the broker is committed to make good the 5 points difference – here a loss to Bank B of USD 2,500.00 (5 points on GBP 5 million) by doing these two transactions.

"Positive" points

The USD 2,500.00 (25 points) obligation of the broker in the above example to Bank B could obviously be settled in cash if Bank B wished. Or Bank B may be prepared to see it reduced by the broker's ability to put to Bank B other transactions that produce the desired profit to cover the USD 2,500.00 position. This might be achieved in various ways, one of which (probably the most common) is as follows.

Suppose that at some later time that day the Cable market is trading 1.45 70 – 75. This might reflect prices put into the broker as follows: Bank C bidding 1.4570, Bank D offering at 1.4575. Suppose two unrelated banks (X and Y) simultaneously have a respective need to sell/buy GBP 5 million. Bank X hits the 1.4570 bid and Bank Y takes the 1.4575 offer. The broker now has these latter two banks committed to deal in opposite directions at overlapping rates (the offer being lower than the bid in this example and equal to the market spread). The broker may, at his discretion, offer both these deals to Bank B.

The consequences of this would be:

1. Bank X has sold sterling at the market rate desired.
2. Bank Y has bought sterling at the market rate desired.
3. By being given the two deals Bank B earns an instant profit of USD 2,500.00 (the 5 point spread) and Bank B may or may not decide to reward the broker for this service in the form of offsetting these positive points against the 25 negative points the broker owes.

4. And finally the broker still has the same market spread 1.45 70 – 75 available to quote around the market (Bank C's bid of 70 and Bank D's offer at 75).

Only banks who have agreed to such practices in advance (the FSA requires brokers to obtain a formal client letter from all such market participants) will be offered this method of settlement of differences. Such banks are referred to as "participating banks". Brokers will be required by the FSA to provide them with lists of all participating banks as well as maintaining records of all situations giving rise to points differences. Where banks do accept such points settlements they must ensure they keep appropriate records while such points positions are outstanding. Also these positions should not be left outstanding for excessive periods with time limits set and monitored by senior management.

It may still be possible to settle differences with brokers by cheque after application by the bank suffering the loss to the FX Joint Standing Committee of the Bank of England.

Where a bank decides not to participate, the broker will advise the bank's management that it may no longer be able to provide a firm price service and banks will be expected to take steps to inform their dealers that the broker cannot be held to a price. None of these practices change the earlier Code sections dealing with pressurization of brokers on the part of dealers and in such circumstances any dealer attempting to "stuff" a broker will be reported to the broker's management who may raise the issue with the bank's management for them to decide on appropriate internal disciplinary measures. Also the broker has recourse to the FSA to complain.

The Model Code mentions that the ACI Committee for Professionalism states that it does not favour the practice of settlement of differences by points, but recognizes that it can be an acceptable practice in those centres where it is clearly subject to proper systems and controls.

Compliance and complaints

This chapter of the Model Code concludes with a statement that compliance with the Code is necessary to ensure that the highest standards of integrity and fair dealing continue to be observed throughout the international over the counter markets and sets out the procedures for complaints being routed to the Committee for Professionalism.

> **Question**
>
> A typical ACI Dealing Certificate question might be:
>
> What is the ACI's stance on the use by brokers of a foreign exchange points system for the settlement of differences?
>
> A: Acceptable, provided that the practice is acknowledged and properly controlled by the local regulatory authority
> B: Unacceptable under any circumstances
> C: The broker can decide whether or not to settle differences in this manner
> D: Differences can be settled in this way after application to the Committee for Professionalism
>
> **Correct answer**
>
> A: The FSA lays down the criteria for when such practices are acceptable in the London Code of Conduct and the ACI is happy to endorse the practice, provided that it is properly controlled by the local regulatory authority in all centres where it exists (Model Code Chapter 4.3).

CHAPTER V – AUTHORIZATION, DOCUMENTATION AND TELEPHONE TAPING

- Authorization, responsibility for dealing activity
- Terms and documentation
- Qualifying and preliminary dealing procedures
- Telephone taping

Authorization

The Model Code recommends that the bank's management control the activities of individuals acting as dealers on the bank's behalf in the international financial markets. Controls should include dealing policy, reporting, approved financial instruments (see the FSA London Code of Conduct, page 7, for a full list of financial markets and instruments covered in London), limits, settlement procedures and the permitted dealer/broker relationships. While there is no "licensing" as such, internally banks should have in place authorization processes recognizing the individual's aptitude, experience and training before permitting him to commit the bank to unsupervised market transactions – remembering at all times that the market's central tenet is "My word is my bond".

The Model Code states in addition that authorizations should also cover relationships with corporate customers. The FSA London Code of Conduct goes further in stating that the practice of requiring dealing mandates from commercial counterparties, while clarifying the nature of the relationship with the bank, should never be relied on in place of other more appropriate controls over dealing relationships, nor should such a mandate ever be used to pass responsibility for actions to another party.

The Model Code finishes this section with the following statement: "It is the responsibility of management to ensure that all employees are adequately trained and are aware of their own and their firm's responsibilities."

Terms and documentation

The "newer" financial instruments traded alongside the more traditionally available products tend to be governed by standard terms and conditions. The Model Code Appendix 3 lists the principal formal documentation in the markets. Whenever a transaction is subject to such a formal agreement permitting modification, this must be clearly stated and its understanding confirmed by both parties before dealing.

The Model Code stipulates that in some more complex transactions like swaps dealers should regard themselves as bound to deal at the point where the commercial terms of the transaction are agreed. Making swap transactions subject to agreement of documentation is considered bad practice and indeed the majority of banks will insist that formal documentation such as ISDA is in place, bilaterally signed prior to any such transactions being negotiated by the dealers.

This chapter goes on to discuss issues such as qualifying conditions for deals being made known clearly at the outset of any dealing conversation, and similarly any deal via a broker which may be subject to credit availability, hedging transaction execution or any other factor should also be identified before names are exchanged.

Telephone taping

This Model Code chapter covers the preferred practice when considering telephone taping in the dealing room and associated areas already discussed in Chapter 9 of this book.

> **Question**
>
> A typical ACI Dealing Certificate question might be:
>
> Tape recordings of dealers/brokers should be kept for longer than two months because:
>
> B: The longer the retention period, the higher the chances of resolving subsequent disputes satisfactorily
> A: Most disputes take longer than two months to resolve
> C: This is a standard international practice
> D: None of these
>
> **Correct answer**
> B: The Model Code recommends that tape recordings of dealers/brokers should be kept for a minimum period of two months because the longer the retention period, the higher the chances of resolving subsequent disputes satisfactorily (Model Code Chapter 5.4).

CHAPTER VI – BROKERS AND BROKERAGE

- The role of brokers and the dealer/broker relationship
- Commission/brokerage
- Electronic broking
- Passing of names by brokers
- Name substitution/switching

The role of brokers and the dealer/broker relationship

The Model Code defines the role of brokers in the OTC financial markets and strongly recommends active management involvement in monitoring dealer/broker relationships.

Brokers in the foreign exchange and money markets are intermediaries only. They are expressly forbidden to act in any discretionary fund management capacity.

The choice of brokers is the responsibility of a bank's senior management who are solely responsible for agreeing brokerage scales with the senior management of the broking companies, evidenced in writing.

Commission/brokerage

Bank management are also responsible for ongoing monitoring of broker usage, always bearing in mind most banks' emphasis on cost reduction, the discount brokerage scales negotiated together with the dealer's desire to route transactions as inexpensively as possible. Banks should settle brokerage bills as promptly as possible to avoid putting the broker at a disadvantage.

Electronic broking

With the growth in electronic brokerage services and wider and wider networks coming online the Model Code addresses the issues concerned with such screen-based matching systems. All transactions should be effected and processed in accordance with the provisions laid down in the individual system vendor's dealing rule book and any associated agreements entered into by the bank (authorized by senior management).

The major risk of unauthorized access is discussed and it is recommended that dealers should have a full comprehension of the systems involved and operational procedures.

Passing of names by brokers

The final two sections of this chapter of the Model Code harken back to the core principle of market confidentiality, describing the responsibilities of brokers and dealers in divulging/seeking counterparty names prior to dealing.

Bank dealers should provide details in advance of any credit limit restrictions that may apply to their being able to close business with certain counterparties and, equally, brokers should take full account of the best interests of their client banks and any guidance on margins expected from certain counterparties/financial instruments.

In money market transactions a bank may refuse a borrower's name for (lack of) credit limit reasons provided the dealer is aware of the obligation on him to deal once he has asked the key question "who pays?", i.e. an offer to lend (or buy) cannot be withdrawn because the initially offered counterparty is unacceptable. In respect of secondary markets in certain traded financial instruments it is the issuer's/acceptor's name which must be acceptable before the counterparty details are exchanged.

On occasions it is acceptable for a borrowing dealer to refuse to take funds from a lender. Reasons include:

- short date deposits possibly being repaid prior to confirmation of receipt of initial funds;
- the dealer has no credit line and therefore to avoid embarrassment at not being able to reciprocate will not accept deposits;
- on management instruction not to deal with the counterparty.

Name substitution/switching

This chapter of the Model Code concludes with the topic of name substitution/switching by brokers. For credit reasons banks are usually happy for a broker to find an alternative name when they either have no limit or have already utilized their limit with a particular dealing counterparty. If the dealer is himself requested to switch a name for a broker he should ensure that his management are aware of these transactions and that bank policy permits such activity. No favours should be sought by the dealer from the broker in the latter case.

Over the years name switching or rather the term "put through" has occasionally attracted bad publicity when less than honest brokers have used such transactions through a third party to generate profit for that party. Such practices are certainly not in accordance with Model Code market recommendations and should not be permitted.

Question

A typical ACI Dealing Certificate question might be:

If a rate shown by a bank to a broker is "firm subject to credit" and the name of a counterparty not acceptable to the bank is disclosed, the bank:

A: Can revise the rate according to his credit position for the counterparty
B: Should revise the rate but only with the consent of senior management
C: Should just complete the deal
D: Should not revise the rate because the identity of the counterparty has been disclosed

Correct answer

D: The broker may be able to switch a name (interpose a third-party name) should any borrower initially advised not be acceptable to the lender. For this purpose it is unethical for the market maker to immediately "change" his/her price (Model Code Chapter 6.5).

CHAPTER VII – DEALING PRACTICE

- Dealing at non-current rates – roll-overs
- Consummation of a deal
- Dealing quotations, firmness, qualification and under reference
- Dealing with unidentified principals
- Internet/online dealing

Dealing at non-current rates – rollovers

One of the first dealing losses suffered in the foreign exchange markets in the early 1970s was as a result of the dealer involved trading outright forward exchange outside his dealing authority and over his limits and then on maturity of the forward contract contacting the same bank and rolling forward the position with a swap based on the original forward outright deal rate. This meant that the two parties were able to agree to compensate the two currency amounts with no need for physical cash settlement. The dealer had successfully rolled his position without his bank management even knowing he was running one.

When the unauthorized dealing came to light the dealer admitted many millions of dollars worth of concealed forward positions and the bank suffered a loss of GBP 33 million. This was the dealing "scam" at LBI (Lloyds Bank International) Lugano mentioned briefly earlier in this book as the catalyst for the O'Brien letter. One of the first recommendations contained in this first "code" was that all foreign exchange deals regardless of value date should be based at or around the current spot market rate. The Model Code expresses this as "within the current spread, to reflect current rates at the time the transaction was done".

Failure to use current rates may result in the extension of unauthorized credit, the bank unknowingly participating in the concealment of a profit or loss and/or the perpetration of fraud.

Occasionally such practice, referred to as a historic rate rollover, is permitted with certain categories of counterparty provided prior express permission from both parties' senior management has been obtained. Cash flow implications should be taken into consideration in the pricing of such a transaction and bank policy will probably limit the number of times a transaction can be so rolled.

In all cases a clear audit trail should be provided to demonstrate that the application of non-market rates and/or prices in component(s) of a complex deal structure satisfy the legitimate requirements of counterparties to the transaction. The FSA IPC section 3.5 sets out further rules and guidance in these respects.

Consummation of a deal

With English as the international market language, appropriate training for dealers, particularly for personnel whose native language is not English, in terminology is vital. They must be totally aware of the meaning of dealing "jargon" used and the order of words in any dealing conversation. The actual moment of dealing is dictated within the market user/market maker conversation at a point when any word offering a deal (e.g. "yours" or "mine" used by the market user in conversation with a broker) or indicating acceptance of a deal ("OK", "agreed" or some other expression of acceptance by the market maker). The Model Code goes into some of this dealing jargon (really inter-professional verbal shorthand) in Chapter XI.

Dealing quotations, firmness, qualification and under reference

Some terms are explained in this section of the Model Code where it is important that a market maker makes clear on what basis any price quotation is being made. If he does not the market user may take the price quote as "firm" for at least the minimum marketable amount in that particular market. A firm price cannot then be qualified or quantified after a deal has been offered. Any such qualification must be expressed before a deal is offered.

Dealing with unidentified principals

Fund managers/investment dealers may be used to dealing under the dealing principles of different markets. Where such individuals are dealing into the foreign exchange and money markets they must identify the dealing counterparty at that moment – or certainly as soon as possible after a deal is agreed. Where this is not the case management must be aware of the increased risks and even the possibility of facilitating money laundering activities. In-house policy should adequately address all aspects of such transactions.

Internet/online trading

Many banks have developed and are offering various categories of clients online dealing facilities without the need for direct communication with the dealers. Management must ensure that the operation of these systems, many web-based and offered as margin trading facilities, are understood and that there are adequate controls in place, again particularly in respect of the potential for money laundering opportunities offered.

Topic 10 · The Model Code

Question

> A typical ACI Dealing Certificate question might be:
>
> Spot EUR/USD is 0.9050 – 55. As market user, you close a six months forward exchange deal at 100 points your favour with XYZ Bank by phone. You buy and sell EUR and XYZ Bank fixes the rates. Which of the following would be the correct exchange rates for the spot and forward deals?
>
> A: 0.9150 and 0.9250
> B: 0.9050 and 0.8950
> C: 0.8950 and 0.9050
> D: 0.9050 and 0.9150
>
> **Correct answer**
>
> D: You are buying and selling EUR (the base currency) so 100 points your favour means the EUR is at a premium and the forward rate will be higher than the spot. The Model Code requires that all exchange rates are fixed within the current spread to reflect current rates at the time of dealing – therefore the only correct answer is 0.9050 and 0.9150 (Model Code Chapter 4.1).

CHAPTER VIII – DEALING PRACTICE FOR SPECIFIC TRANSACTIONS

- Deals using a "connected broker"
- Assignments and transfers
- Repos and stock lending

Deals using a "connected broker"

To avoid any problems with conflicts of interest where a broker is offering a price on behalf of a financial institution with shareholding or other connection in/with the broking company this must be disclosed at the same time.

Assignments and transfers

In certain of the instruments covered by the Model Code assignment to a third party is permissible at a later date. Where this is the case (such as in interest rates swaps) this information must be made available at the time of negotiating the initial transaction.

Repos and stock lending

Before entering into repos in the major markets trading "classic repos" the proper legal documentation (TBMA/ISMA Global Master Repurchase Agreement) should be in place. The Model Code has no more information on such issues and candidates are advised to make themselves familiar with the GMRA agreement and the Gilt Repo Code of Best Practice (both available from the Bank of England at www.bankofengland.co.uk).

> **Question**
>
> A typical ACI Dealing Certificate question might be:
>
> Where sale and repurchase agreements or stock borrowing/lending transactions are entered into:
>
> A: Proper documentation should be in place prior to dealing
> B: Such transactions are not subject to standard terms and conditions
> C: Dealers may seek approval from management on a case by case basis
> D: None of these
>
> **Correct answer**
>
> A: Where sale and repurchase agreements or stock borrowing/lending transactions are entered into, proper documentation should be in place prior to dealing (Model Code Chapter 8.3).

CHAPTER IX – GENERAL RISK MANAGEMENT PRINCIPLES FOR DEALING BUSINESS

General risk management principles for dealing business

While Chapters I to X are supported by textual passages, this chapter of the Model Code details the basic approach required from management and all market participants in respect of the 14 core principles and is set out as a series of bullet points under the following headings:

1. Promote the highest standards of conduct and ethics
2. Ensure senior management involvement and supervision
3. Organizational structure ensuring independent risk management and controls
4. Ensure the involvement of a thoroughly professional management in all administrative processes

Topic 10 · The Model Code

5. Provide appropriate systems and operational support
6. Ensure timely and accurate risk measurement
7. Control market risk exposure by assessing maximum likely exposure under various market conditions
8. Always recognize importance of markets and cash flow liquidity
9. Consider impact of diversification and risk return trade-offs
10. Accept only the highest and most rigorous client relationship standards
11. Clients should understand transaction (see also Model Code Chapter X)
12. Risk management should be based on sound legal foundations and documentation
13. Ensure adequate expertise and human resources support trading and risk return
14. Use judgement and common sense

The final principle really summarizes those which precede it in so far as the bullet points describe "common-sense" approaches to setting up, managing and controlling financial market dealing activities.

CHAPTER X – ADDITIONAL GUIDELINES FOR DEALING WITH CORPORATE/COMMERCIAL CLIENTS

Additional guidelines for dealing with corporate/commercial clients

This chapter addresses the fact that not just "inter-professional" dealing takes place in the wholesale financial markets. A growing percentage of market turnover each year is commercially based business. These sections draw attention to aspects of the business relationships and dealing practices appropriate to corporate financial market activities as counterparty to their bankers' transactions. Further useful information on commercially based financial transactions is included in the FSA London Code of Conduct.

Mastering the ACI Dealing Certificate

Question

A typical ACI Dealing Certificate question might be:

Under guidelines for dealing with corporate/commercial clients, on the issue of complex products, instruments or strategies and the risks they entail, the Model Code stipulates the following:

A: The principal should be prepared to provide the client with whatever information the client may request pertaining to a projected transaction
B: The principal must ensure that the client fully understands the product, instrument or strategy
C: It is entirely the client's responsibility to be aware of all risks involved
D: None of these apply

Correct answer

A: Under guidelines for dealing with corporate/commercial clients, on the issue of complex products, instruments or strategies and the risks they entail, the Model Code stipulates that the principal should be prepared to provide the client with whatever information the client may request pertaining to a projected transaction (Model Code Chapter 10.3).

CHAPTER XI – MARKET TERMINOLOGY

Dealing jargon

Candidates should familiarize themselves with a wide range of market terminology (see Appendix III to this book) which could appear in the examination under a number of different question baskets within the ACI Dealing Certificate.

Question

A typical ACI Dealing Certificate question might be:

Under the Model Code guidelines, where a dealer shouts "Done" or "Yours" at the very instant the broker calls "Off":

A: Fifty percent of the deal amount must be agreed
B: The full deal must be agreed
C: No deal is done
D: None of these apply

Correct answer:

C: Under the Model Code guidelines, where a dealer shouts "Done" or "Yours" at the very instant the broker calls "Off", no deal is done (Model Code Chapter 5.4).

APPENDICES 1 – 7

Appendix 1 ACI rules for over the counter (OTC) financial instruments dispute resolution

Candidates should note that the Model Code Syllabus Topic description (page 320) includes the following phrase: "with particular emphasis on dispute procedures". Chapter IV of the Model Code has further information on disputes and mediation, differences between principals, differences with brokers and use of "points," compliance and complaints.

> A typical ACI Dealing Certificate question might be:
>
> The Chairman and members of the Committee for Professionalism are ready to assist in resolving disputes through the ACI "Expert Determination Service" in situations where:
>
> A: The amount of the deal exceeds USD 5 million
> B: The dispute cannot be resolved between the parties and where all normal channels have been exhausted
> C: Litigation has already commenced
> D: The local regulator or central bank refuse to intervene
>
> **Correct answer**
> B: The Chairman and members of the Committee for Professionalism are ready to assist in resolving disputes through the ACI "Expert Determination Service" in situations where the dispute cannot be resolved between the parties and where all normal channels have been exhausted (Model Code Chapter 4.1).

Appendix 2 Markets and instruments covered by the Model Code

All OTC financial markets and instruments on or off the balance sheet as follows:

Foreign exchange dealing – spot and forward
Foreign exchange options
Money market dealing *
Interest rate options
Forward rate agreements
Interest rate and currency swaps
Bullion and precious metals

Mastering the ACI Dealing Certificate

*Candidates should also be familiar with the UK-issued FSA London Code of Conduct (www.fsa.gov.uk), which on page 7 lists the cash and various short-term securities traded in the London money market subject to the recommendations contained therein.

> **Question**
>
> A typical ACI Dealing Certificate question might be:
>
> Products covered by the Model Code include: (1) spot and forward foreign exchange; (2) financial futures trades; (3) spot and forward gold and silver bullion; (4) public sector debt with an original maturity of more than 12 months.
>
> A: (1) and (3) only
> B: All of these
> C: (1) only
> D: (1), (2) and (3) only
>
> **Correct answer**
> A: Products noted under (1) and (3) fall within the scope of the Model Code (Model Code Appendix 2).

Appendix 3 Terms and conditions for financial instruments

This appendix includes a list of those formal documents referred to in the Model Code which govern the products and dealing processes in the financial markets.

> **Hint**
>
> *This list of market documentation is useful information to candidates and they should ensure they obtain, or at least have sight of, their contents before approaching the ACI Dealing Certificate examination.*

Appendices 4–6

These appendices contain useful information on current office holders, the other codes of conduct issued in overseas financial markets and the ACI Mission Statement and Charter.

4. Current members of ACI's Committee for Professionalism

> **Hint**
>
> *It is assumed that due to ACI elections and varying terms of office for the persons named no questions will be asked on this appendix of the Model Code.*

Topic 10 · The Model Code

5. Other published codes of conduct

> *Many of the references in the Model Code and the nature of the multiple choice question format may mean that information relating to the other codes of conduct published around the world's major financial markets could appear in examination questions.*

Hint

6. The ACI Mission statement and Charter

Topic 1 of the ACI Dealing Certificate syllabus refers to the ACI (see Chapter 3 of this book) and this Appendix could be the subject of questions asked under this heading (note, however, that there is no separate examination question basket for the Background topic).

> *This Appendix gives useful information on the ACI which may be the subject of examination questions and should be read closely.*

Hint

Appendix 7 ISO currency codes (SWIFT) for the currencies of the 60 member countries of the ACI

> *All ACI candidates must be familiar with the ISO codes used for SWIFT and other electronic input relating to currencies. Such codes can appear across any of the topic headings within the ACI Dealing Certificate syllabus and are listed at the beginning of this book.*

Hint

FOR FURTHER READING

ACI (2000) *The Model Code*. ACI – The Financial Markets Association.
Bank of England (2001) *Non-Investment Products Code*. Bank of England.
FSA (1999) *FSA London Code of Conduct*. Financial Services Authority (UK) – formerly published by the Bank of England, London
FSA (2001) *FSA Inter Professional Conduct Code*. Financial Services Authority (UK).

WEBSITES WORTH A VISIT

ACI – The Financial Markets Association: www.aciforex.com
Bank of England, London: www.bankofengland.co.uk
Financial Services Authority, London: www.fsa.gov.uk

Approaching the Examination

Preparation for the examination

The ACI Dealing Certificate examination

ACI Dealing Certificate examination techniques

Specific points to remember

PREPARATION FOR THE EXAMINATION

During your study and revision you will probably not have had the time or the opportunity to read and revise everything on the subject matter of the examination. Rather than worry about what you haven't done or read, concentrate on what you *have* done. When you finally sit the examination, that is the point when you demonstrate to the examiner what you know and will be judged on that performance on the day.

Last-minute revision may give rise to doubts in your mind. You should not allow these to detract from your understanding of the syllabus topics. Where you have been on a specific training course towards the examinations or you are relying on personal study you should refer back to what you have learnt and use your preparation for the examination to pull things together.

> **Hint**
>
> *Don't worry about what you haven't done. No one can understand everything. Concentrate on making the best use of what you have covered.*

"Honing" examination techniques

Most trainers agree that the single most useful revision activity of all is attempting old examination questions. When the ACI examinations were paper-delivered old examination papers were available from ACI Education. With the introduction of electronic examination delivery these are no longer available. There are, however, a number of sample questions and a downloadable demo of the examination screen itself (including more multiple choice questions) available on the ACI website at www.aciforex.com

There are also one or two distance learning products around such as Multimedia TradeWind Limited's WINFOREX range which replicate the Prometric examination delivery, giving you the opportunity to refine your PC-based multiple choice examination skills.

Mock examination

Should the means be available to you it is certainly well worth the discipline of attempting one (or more) mock examinations under examination conditions and, most importantly, against the clock.

Key points for revising for the ACI Dealing Certificate examination

- Study any previous examination questions and sample questions available.
- Carefully select the topics of the syllabus you intend to revise.
- Draw up a timetable for revising.

- Seek out the core elements of the syllabus topics you have chosen to revise.
- Condense the contents of your chosen topics into brief bullet points/notes.
- Practise examination techniques.
- Read the Model Code.

Final revision

Approach your final revision in a planned way. Use your time efficiently dividing it between reading and examination/dealing calculation practice. Obviously you will want to concentrate on those syllabus topics in which you feel least confident. Bear in mind the incidence of examination questions in these topics in the examination proper. For example, it would be very frustrating to spend hours revising just one topic of the "catch all" question baskets (e.g. Topic 4 derivatives) only to find that through the random selection process no questions from that topic were included in the examination. However, the reverse can be the case so a sensible background knowledge level per topic is recommended.

The Model Code topic is a difficult one to "revise". While many of the questions will be seeking a common-sense approach to the markets and the practical application of accepted practices, there may be the odd obtuse question in an area in which you are not totally familiar.

> *It is recommended that you should spend some time the evening before the examination quietly reading through the Model Code.*   **Hint**

Registration for ACI examinations

Log on to the ACI web pages at www.aciforex.com/education/registration_info.htm

Here you will find a list of Prometric test centres and registration information plus details of the regional telephone numbers for booking your examination at the most convenient local Prometric test centre.

Prometric test centre

Your ACI Dealing Certificate examination is downloaded overnight to the Prometric test centre where you have booked your examination.

On the day, if you encounter any problem concerning your examination, ask the test centre to telephone Prometric and report the problem. If the difficulty remains unresolved contact:

ACI Education: (44) 1580 754144

ACI Paris: (33) 1 42975115

ACI London: (44) 020 7731 3600

Examination demonstration

To check out the test environment you can log onto the ACI website at www.aciforex.com/education/demo-exam.htm and download a short demonstration examination and familiarize yourself with the appearance of the examination screen and the MS Windows on-screen calculator.

Permitted tools

Calculators

The ACI International Examination Board permits candidates to use any calculator of their choice in the examination. The standard MS Windows on-screen calculator is also available on the Prometric test screen as is the ACI formulae sheet (accessed via EXHIBIT button).

Dictionary

A language dictionary, e.g. English/French, is permitted.

Formulae sheet

You can obtain a copy of the formulae sheet through the following sources:

- Appendix I of this book
- your National Association or ACI education officer;
- your trainer;
- Prometric test centres will supply you with a copy;
- you can download a copy from the ACI website:
  www.aciforex.com/education/formula.htm

This final alternative is recommended to avoid any problems of non-availability at the Prometric test centre on the day.

Arrival at the Prometric test centre

On your arrival at the Prometric test centre you will be required to produce the following:

- proof of identity (including a photograph), e.g.
  – National Identity Card

Approaching the Examination

- passport
- driving licence
- *plus your* ACI candidate number.

Prometric run a number of different computer-based examination formats for very different qualifications at their various test centres. You might find yourself in an examination room with one or more candidates sitting university assessment tests and others attempting perhaps the local centre's "written" driving test. Even if there is more than one ACI Dealing Certificate candidate the nature of the overnight examination question random selection will mean that the two of you will be sitting totally different examinations.

Before the official examination time commences you are permitted 10 minutes to familiarize yourself with the PC, keyboard and mouse in the Prometric examination room. Make sure you have the ACI formulae sheet, rough paper and a pen/pencil available.

> *If the examination language is not your mother tongue you are permitted a standard language dictionary (not a business terms dictionary).* **Hint**

THE ACI DEALING CERTIFICATE EXAMINATION

Multiple choice questions (and answers)

Many people find the multiple choice format the most offputting style of examination. There are several reasons for this. One is that an answer must be right or wrong – there are no near misses or marks for "showing all workings". Another is that the examination delivery and answering processes may differ dramatically from the candidate's experience and use of the subject matter of the syllabus. A final and most significant reason is that the nature of the examination permits a large number of questions to be set meaning that questions must be answered quickly given the examination time constraints.

Examination questions are written to test your knowledge of a particular product or subject. Always read and reread the question and in the case of multiple choice questions read each choice of answer carefully. The multiple choice format of the examination means that the answer on each occasion is literally "staring you in the face". If it happens to be in a weaker topic area and you cannot immediately identify the correct answer it may all be down to a process of elimination and logic at the end of the day.

Each question may be simple in itself but, together, the 50 multiple choice questions of Part 1 aim to test your basic knowledge of the whole subject while the 30 Model Code questions are there to test your understanding of the best practice, compliance issues and market etiquette which are central to the continuing efficiency of the financial markets.

> **Hint:** *Carefully read and reread the question and each multiple choice answer offered.*

Time management

You have a total of two hours (120 minutes) to complete the ACI Dealing Certificate examination. Part 1 consists of 50 multiple choice questions on Topics 1 to 9 of the syllabus and Part 2 of 30 ACI Model Code multiple choice questions, a total of 80 questions.

- *120 minutes* – you should probably allow yourself some time at the end of the examination for an overall review of your answers. (Don't forget you can go back to any question whether answered or not and change your choice of answer – see Chapter 1 on "Mark" function and "Item review screen".) Let us assume you allow 15 minutes at the end for this purpose.
- *105 minutes remaining* – were you sitting the separate ACI Model Code examination you would have 45 minutes for the 30 questions making up Part 2 of this examination.
- *60 minutes remaining* – you have exactly one hour for the 50 questions of Part 1 (1 minute 12 seconds per question to be precise).

The way some questions are worded will mean you can almost instantly identify the correct answer while the random selection process of the Prometric system will mean that others may require more careful study (including calculations) before a final choice is made.

> **Hint:** *Most candidates do not experience any time pressures in the ACI Dealing Certificate. Provided you are well prepared you should find that the time allowed is sufficient to answer all questions and review answers.*

Calculation multiple choice questions

Don't forget there are *at least* 14 calculation questions which may necessitate the use of a calculator and/or the ACI formulae sheet. The more key strokes required for a calculation the longer the time per question. You may not be used to using the MS Windows calculator available so it is probably better to take a calculator of your choice into the examination.

ACI DEALING CERTIFICATE EXAMINATION TECHNIQUES

Order of attempting questions

Once the exam proper has started, take each question in turn, answer those you are immediately confident about and then spend time on questions which are more involved (needing careful reading and/or more than one calculation) or those you are unsure about.

Of those questions requiring further attention, many of these can be answered by a logical method of elimination of obviously wrong answers.

Who Wants To Be A Millionaire? style

The multiple choice format of the Prometric electronically delivered examination has been used in general knowledge quiz shows for many years, most recently to good effect in the TV quiz show *Who Wants To Be A Millionaire?* understanding the question and the available choice of answers is equally important in both environments.

The examination differs from the quiz in one major way. The lifelines available in the TV quiz – "Ask the audience", "50 : 50" and "Phone a friend" – are unfortunately *not* available for use by the candidate! However, an approach along similar lines to the "50 : 50" option can sometimes be invoked to good effect in the examination itself.

Process of elimination

We are talking here about a process of elimination. Of the four possible answers there is probably one which may be immediately discarded (a "red herring"). If you are lucky there may be two such answers giving you an immediate "50 : 50" option.

Just as with the TV quiz there may then be left a choice between two "obvious" answers which may be "too close to call". Unlike other examination formats multiple choice questions are often designed to lead you towards an answer including a silly error. If a question involves a calculation, no matter how simple, it is often worth using the calculator.

Bearing in mind your time management plan, if after, say, two minutes you still cannot identify the correct answer you should "Mark" the question and move on. Don't take this as a suggestion to rush through the examination in a "mad panic" but it is better to cut your losses and move on after an expensive use of time on a question which continues to puzzle you.

> **Hint**
>
> *Remember under the current ACI marking regime there is no penalty for an unanswered question or for a wrong answer. If after much deliberation you still cannot be sure of the correct answer it is worth making a guess at the correct answer without penalty and with a 1 in 4 (probably better odds because of obvious wrong answer(s)) chance to be right.*

Key points for the examination itself

- Remember your time management plan for the examination and stick to it.
- Scan through the examination identifying questions you have prepared for.
- Begin selecting answers as soon as you are confident to do so – it helps "unfreeze" you.
- As you tackle a question:
  - examine the wording carefully
  - beware of "negatives" in the question
  - in "list style" multiple choice questions be extra careful in reading the available answers
  - if the correct answer is still not evident, "Mark" the question and move on
  - make sure your time management permits all such marked question to be returned to.

SPECIFIC POINTS TO REMEMBER

The following is a list (not exhaustive) of areas where participants can make silly but expensive mistakes when reading the multiple choice questions or answer choices in respect of dealing and financial instruments/ dealing products in the ACI Dealing Certificate examination.

Loan/deposit quotations

- Some questions will be worded in London terms (i.e. offer–bid) and some in international or continental terms (i.e. bid–offer). Some may include a mix of quotation methods.

Approaching the Examination

- Remember loans/deposits and many derivatives are quoted in *basis points*. A basis point = 0.01 percent, i.e. the second decimal place.

Interest calculations

- Interest on US dollars in the international eurocurrency money markets is calculated on an *actual/360* day basis. Most currencies follow this day basis approach although some have differing day bases for international and domestic markets.
- The exceptions to this rule are sterling and typically currencies which are ex-British Empire, Commonwealth or sterling area. These exceptions must be learnt. GBP interest calculations day basis is *actual/365* for all money market cash and financial instruments.
- Government bonds (when considering repos) in the major markets of London, the EU, New York and Tokyo are quoted on *actual/actual* day basis, although coupon (dividend) payment frequencies may differ between centres, e.g. semi-annual coupon in London, New York and Tokyo government bonds while EU governments pay an annual coupon.
- Money market cash market transactions, including repos, pay interest on a simple interest basis. Loans and deposits with maturities in excess of 12 months pay interest annually and at final maturity.
- The more frequently interest is paid the higher the return, i.e. semi-annual 5 percent gives a better return than annual 5 percent.
- If the question states "use straight-line interpolation" it is a simple average price along a straight (upwards or downwards sloping) yield curve or graph line.
- Discount rates will always give a higher yield than the discount rate quoted (i.e. 5 percent discount for 90 days = yield of 5.0633 percent).

Interest rate derivatives

- On FRA fixing date, FRA rates are compared with LIBOR cash following common practice for the currency involved. For example, sterling fixing date = settlement date as GBP is a same day value currency; USD and other eurocurrencies fixing = settlement *minus* two working days, i.e. currencies are rated from value spot.

- FRA settlement (the payment of the "difference" between the parties following the fixing procedure) takes place on settlement date.

Care!
> The exam questions have been known to refer to settlement date when the FRA rate is compared with LIBOR. It is of course on the *fixing* date when this comparison is made. For sterling FRAs, however, being a value same day market fixing date = settlement date.

Spot FX quotations

- Spot is always quoted low–high and typically referred to as Bid–Offer for the base currency: BOB – bid–offer for base.

Forward FX quotations

- Forward quotes are swap points and are typically referred to as Bid–Offer for the base currency (currency movement on the *forward* date): BOB – bid–offer for base.

Base currency discount

- Forward points quoted high–low means that you should *subtract* those points from the spot rate to achieve the outright forward rate.
- The base currency at a discount will have a *higher interest rate* than the variable currency (countercurrency), e.g. USD at a discount against the Japanese yen = USD interest rate is higher than JPY.

Note
> In *London terms* dealers may refer to high–low as a forward premium because traditionally London dealers refer to the countercurrency (quoted currency), i.e. in GBP/USD dealings in London a dealer may refer to a forward premium (meaning a USD premium) whereas a dealer in Paris will refer to a forward discount (meaning a GBP discount). It is the description only which differs, the arithmetic is unchanged.

Base currency premium

- Forward points quoted low–high means that you should *add* the points to the spot rate to achieve the outright forward rate. The base currency at a

Approaching the Examination

premium will have a *lower interest rate* than the variable currency (countercurrency), e.g. USD at a premium against Singapore dollars = USD interest rate is lower than SGD.

> **Note**
>
> In *London terms* dealers may refer to low–high as a forward discount because traditionally London dealers refer to the countercurrency (quoted currency), i.e. in GBP/USD dealings in London a dealer may refer to a forward discount (meaning a USD discount) whereas a dealer in Paris will refer to a forward premium (meaning a GBP premium). Once again, it is the description only which differs, the arithmetic is unchanged.

Dealing periods money market and foreign exchange

- *Overnight* in both FX and money markets refers to a swap price or money market price for the period today against tomorrow.
- *Tom/next* (US markets = rollover) refers to tomorrow against the next day (spot date).
- *Spot/next* refers to spot date against the day after spot.
- *Spot a week* (also referred to as week fixed) refers to spot date for seven days fixed.
- *Short date* transactions tend to refer to market deals dealt for periods up to one month.

Days and dates

- Money market fixed date quotations and forward FX swap points (two-way spreads) are quoted from one month. A typical run-through from a broker would be 1, 2, 3, 6 and 12 months prices. Sometimes there are only four periods (1 to 6 months) in less liquid markets. If there are six periods quoted then a 9 months has been added (1, 2, 3, 6, 9 and 12). Make sure you are familiar with "end/end" principles for forward value dates towards the end of a month (see Chapter 4).
- Most questions will indicate the actual number of days in any period (for inclusion in formulae in the calculation multiple choice questions) or state the assumption you are to follow, e.g. assume 30-day months. Always make sure you calculate the correct number of days – in this latter case one month = 30, three months = 90, six months = 180.

Loans and deposits

- Do not confuse loans and deposits. A *loan* in banking terminology is an advance to a customer (counterparty); an *asset* is a debit balance on a loan account in the bank's books, sometimes described as a "deposit placed", placing or money out on effective date. To create a loan, you lend cash. Having lent cash you are short (cash).
- As market maker you lend on your offer (the higher interest rate). As a market user the opposite applies: you have to lend to the bid (the lower interest rate quoted to you).
- A *deposit* in banking terminology is an acceptance from a customer (counterparty); a *liability* is a credit in a deposit account in the bank's books, sometimes described as a "deposit accepted" or money in on effective date. To take a deposit, you borrow cash. Having borrowed cash you are long (cash).
- As market maker you borrow cash on your bid (the lower interest rate). As a market user the opposite applies: you have to take from the offer (the higher interest rate quoted to you). In all questions, ask yourself "Am I market maker or market user?" Remember there is a big difference between the English "You quote" and "You are quoted". If the question is worded "You quote", you are the *market maker*.
- If the question is worded "You are quoted", you are the *market user*. If rates quoted are "market rates" or quoted by a broker you must always assume that you are the market user, i.e. that is the cost to you to cover. If the question is worded "the market quotes", then you are the market user.

Calculations

- Where there is a choice of formulae and you are initially uncertain that you have used the correct one, if you have time, you can usually check your choice via a different formula or by looking at the cash flows generated by the sequence of transactions suggested by the question under consideration.
- Before starting any lengthy calculations always convert all fractions into decimals and use them in full, i.e. do *not* round $\frac{15}{32}$ percent but use 0.46875. This will avoid silly errors like using or identifying as a correct answer 5.14 (decimal) instead of the 5.25 ($5\frac{1}{4}$) decimal equivalent of a pure fraction.

Approaching the Examination

- Do *not* round or truncate figures in the middle of a sequence of calculations. Only round as instructed in the exam question or at the very end of a sequence of calculations, and then only if you are asked to in the examination question.

APPENDICES

I   ACI Formulae Sheets

II   Glossary of Terms and Dealing Jargon

Appendix I · ACI Formulae Sheets

Interest rate conversions

Money market calculations

Forward/forward and Forward Rate Agreements

Foreign exchange calculations

INTEREST RATE CONVERSIONS

Bond v. money market basis

$$\text{interest rate on bond basis} = \text{rate on money market basis} \times \frac{\text{days on money market basis}}{\text{money market year basis}} \times \frac{\text{bond year basis}}{\text{days on bond basis}}$$

$$\text{interest rate on money market basis} = \text{rate on bond basis} \times \frac{\text{days on bond basis}}{\text{bond year basis}} \times \frac{\text{money market year basis}}{\text{days on money market basis}}$$

Converting between annual and semi-annual interest rates

$$\text{annual rate} = \left(1 + \left(\frac{\text{semi-annual rate}}{2}\right)\right)^2 - 1$$

$$\text{semi-annual rate} = \left(\sqrt{(1 + \text{annual rate})} - 1\right) \times 2$$

These conversions between annual and semi-annual yields strictly apply only to a 365-day ("bond") basis, not a 360-day ("money-market") basis.

MONEY MARKET CALCULATIONS

Certificates of Deposit

$$\text{maturity proceeds} = \text{face value} \times \left(1 + \left(\text{coupon rate} \times \frac{\text{days from issue to maturity}}{\text{day base}}\right)\right)$$

$$\text{secondary market proceeds} = \frac{\text{maturity proceeds}}{\left(1 + \left(\text{yield} \times \frac{\text{days left to maturity}}{\text{day base}}\right)\right)}$$

Discount instrument quoted on a true yield

$$\text{secondary market proceeds} = \frac{\text{face value}}{\left(1 + \left(\text{yield} \times \frac{\text{days left to maturity}}{\text{day base}}\right)\right)}$$

Discount instrument quoted on a discount rate

$$\text{amount of discount} = \text{face value} \times \text{discount rate} \times \frac{\text{days}}{\text{day base}}$$

$$\text{secondary market proceeds} = \text{face value} \times \left(1 - \left(\text{discount rate} \times \frac{\text{days}}{\text{day base}}\right)\right)$$

$$\text{true yield} = \frac{\text{discount rate}}{\left(1 - \left(\text{discount rate} \times \frac{\text{days}}{\text{day base}}\right)\right)}$$

FORWARD/FORWARD AND FORWARD RATE AGREEMENTS
(for periods up to one year)

Forward/forward interest rate

$$\text{forward/forward rate} = \left[\frac{1 + \left(\text{interest rate for longer period} \times \frac{\text{days in longer period}}{\text{day base}}\right)}{1 + \left(\text{interest rate for shorter period} \times \frac{\text{days in shorter period}}{\text{day base}}\right)} - 1\right] \times \frac{\text{day base}}{\text{days difference}}$$

FRA settlement

$$\text{FRA settlement amount} = \text{principal} \times \frac{\left(\text{FRA rate} - \text{fixing rate}\right) \times \frac{\text{days in FRA period}}{\text{day base}}}{1 + \left(\text{fixing rate} \times \frac{\text{days in FRA period}}{\text{day base}}\right)}$$

FOREIGN EXCHANGE CALCULATIONS

FX swap points

$$\text{FX swap} = \text{spot} \times \frac{\left(\left(\text{variable currency interest rate} \times \frac{\text{days}}{\text{day base}}\right) - \left(\text{base currency interest rate} \times \frac{\text{days}}{\text{day base}}\right)\right)}{\left(1 + \left(\text{base currency interest rate} \times \frac{\text{days}}{\text{day base}}\right)\right)}$$

Covered interest arbitrage

variable currency interest rate created =
$$\left[\left(1 + \left(\text{base currency interest rate} \times \frac{\text{days}}{\text{day base for base currency}}\right)\right) \times \frac{\text{outright}}{\text{spot}} - 1\right] \times \frac{\text{day base for variable currency}}{\text{days}}$$

base currency interest rate created =
$$\left[\left(1 + \left(\text{variable currency interest rate} \times \frac{\text{days}}{\text{day base for variable currency}}\right)\right) \times \frac{\text{spot}}{\text{outright}} - 1\right] \times \frac{\text{day base for base currency}}{\text{days}}$$

Where, in an interbank USD/JPY quotation for example, USD is the base currency and JPY is the variable currency.

Appendix II · Glossary of Terms and Dealing Jargon

This glossary of terms (not exhaustive) has been collated from various sources and is included here to assist ACI Dealing Certificate candidates in the understanding of some of the day-to-day "jargon" and other terminology used in the treasury dealing environment and frequently the subject matter of multiple choice questions in the ACI Dealing Certificate examination. Further terms may be found in the Model Code Chapter VII.

Ante-spot Value dates in the short dates before the spot date, e.g. today and tomorrow. Rules for calculating outright exchange rates are reversed to achieve the desired ante-spot rate.

Appreciation Describes a currency strengthening in response to market demand.

Arbitrage Buying a currency, a futures contract or other commodity in one centre or market, and selling it in another to take advantage of temporary rate discrepancies. Necessarily the two transactions should take place simultaneously. Arbitrage transactions can take place over many centres and through many currency contracts or commodities before being brought (hopefully) to a satisfactorily profitable conclusion.

Around par Used in forward quotations. The two currencies' interest rates are equal (bearing in mind the bid–offer interest rate spread in both currencies), meaning that the forward price is quoted "around par", either side of parity with the spot rate. Around par will always be negative to positive – discount to premium (international terminology) – never the reverse.

(At) your risk Quoted rates by a bank or broker are subject to change.

Bankers' acceptance Commercial bill of exchange or draft that becomes a money market instrument when accepted (endorsed and guaranteed) by a bank. In the UK, once accepted, provided it meets certain criteria, the bill becomes "eligible for re-discount at the Bank of England". Such eligible bills are readily marketable instruments attracting the finest rates in the market.

Base currency The reference currency in an exchange rate quotation, i.e. in a GBP/USD rate quotation sterling is the base currency and the rate is quoted as so many US units to 1 pound sterling (e.g. 1.45 00 – 1.45 05 USD per GBP 1).

Base rate The managed rate used by commercial banks and other financial institutions as the benchmark for calculation of rates offered to depositors and charged to borrowers. Base rates are influenced by the Bank of England in accordance with the requirements of monetary policy.

Basis In financial futures terminology, the cash price minus the futures price.

Basis point The decimal format of quoting interest rates (to two decimal places) on money market instruments, interest rate swaps, etc. One basis point equals 0.01 per cent.

Bear A speculator who sells a currency short in the expectation that a devaluation or depreciation will take place before he has to buy back the currency.

Bear squeeze Any official action in the market or through regulations which makes it costly or difficult for short positions to be maintained.

Best order A firm order to deal left with another counterparty with no rate limit stipulated. The recipient of such an order is considered trustworthy.

Bid (foreign exchange quote) The currency in question is appreciating, or in demand and buyers of the currency predominate.

Bid (money market quote) There are indications that the interest rate in the currency and period in question may be rising; there are more borrowers (takers) than lenders in the market.

Bid rate (repo) The bid rate in the repo market is the bid for the security – the rate at which the reverse repoing party is prepared to borrow the securities and lend the cash.

Big figure In an exchange rate quotation the first three digits, or even only the last one or two of these, e.g. in a GBP/USD quote 1.45 00 – 05, "1.45" is the big figure, sometimes shortened to "45" or even "5" depending on how stable the market is at that time.

Black-Scholes A stock option pricing model developed by Black and Scholes in 1973 that is synonymous with option pricing and which has been adopted by the major market participants in the currency options market.

Bobl German government bond (*Bundesobligation*).

Bond basis 30/360 or 30E/360 (the method used in the eurobond market). To calculate interest on the bond basis every month is assumed to comprise 30 days with a full year (12 × 30 day months) = 360/360.

Broken date A value date in the future which is not a standard fixed period (forward) date.

Broker Intermediary who negotiates foreign exchange or money market deals between banks but who never acts as principal nor as intermediary between the banks and commercial users of the market.

Brokerage The fee charged by a broker for his services. In some countries, this fee is referred to as "commission". Brokerage charges can vary depending on currency amount and maturity of the foreign exchange, the money market or treasury product contract and levels of discount freely negotiated between bank senior management and broking companies.

BTP Italian government treasury bond (*Buono del Tesoro Poliennale*).

Bull A speculator who buys a currency in the hope that it will revalue or appreciate, enabling him to make a profit on resale.

Bund German government bond (*Bund*).

Business day Also banking day, clear day, market day and open day. Day on which foreign exchange contracts can be settled, e.g. a foreign exchange contract covering the sale of US dollars against sterling can be completed only on a day when both New York and London are open for normal banking business (of course, other cities in the US and UK are suitable for payment, but only if they are acceptable to both parties to a transaction). For the euro a business day is any day when the TARGET settlement system is operational.

Buy back The accounting procedure used to revalue forward exchange outstandings by "marking them to market" using current mid-market closing rates. This method of evaluation ensures that profit and loss is assessed regularly against an assumed market price at which such profit or loss could indeed be realized.

Cable Dealers' "jargon" for the sterling v. US dollar exchange rate, e.g. spot Cable or forward Cable.

Call option An option contract giving the buyer (holder) the right (but not the obligation) to buy the currency specified. For example, to acquire the right to buy euros (and sell US dollars), a euro call option must be purchased.

Cap (see also *Floor* and *Collar*) A sequence (strip) of interest rate options dealt with the intention of providing the buyer of the options with protection against an increase in interest rates, i.e. fixing a maximum (cap) interest rate payable.

Capital adequacy The Bank for International Settlements in Basel in agreement with national central banks has implemented minimum levels of capital adequacy to ensure that banks worldwide have sufficient capital in support of their lending and other risk assets.

Cash and carry arbitrage Cash and carry arbitrage is a round trip buying the bond, repoing the bond to finance the original purchase and selling the future to achieve a profit.

Cash driven trade According to the Bank of England Repo Code of Best Practice, where the principal reason for entering into a repo transaction is to generate cash balances then this is described as a "cash driven trade" and typically no margin or haircut is involved.

Central Gilts Office (CGO) The electronic registration, settlement and transfer system for government securities and other Bank of England registered stocks denominated in sterling and euros. The system includes an assured payments system. The CGO was set up by the Bank of England but responsibility for its operation has now passed to CrestCo. and is linked into Clearstream and Cedel to facilitate international dealing in gilts.

Central Moneymarkets Office (CMO) The CMO set up by the Bank of England but like the CGO now the responsibility of CrestCo. acts as a central depository for UK money market instruments and provides an electronic registration, settlement and transfer system for such instruments as Treasury bills, CDs, local authority bills, eligible bank bills and commercial paper.

Certificate of deposit (CD) A deposit receipt payable to bearer, issued by a bank, with a maturity that is generally less than a year. A secondary market exists in most major currencies (in which CDs are issued) for such money market instruments.

Change Quoted rate is no longer firm...the price has changed.

CHAPS Acronym for the Clearing House Automated Payments System – the electronic system for interbank sterling payments in London.

Charting Technical analysis that aims to predict price movements by identifying recurrent patterns as they take shape. Examples of such charting formations are double top, double bottom, flag, head and shoulders.

Chart point Psychologically important price level within a pattern identified by chartists who maintain that future price behaviour can be determined by whether or not the rate moves through the chart point.

Cheapest to deliver (CTD) The expression "cheapest to deliver" refers to the bonds closest to the notional underlying bond in a deliverable futures contract.

CHIPS Acronym for the Clearing House Interbank Payments System. Based in New York, this is an electronic network for settling deals that handles the transfer of the majority of US dollar funds in interbank transactions.

Classic repo According to the Bank of England Gilt Repo Code of Best Practice, bilaterally agreed documentation (TBMA/ISMA) should be in place before the parties enter into repo transactions.

Appendix II

Clean float When an exchange rate reflects only normal supply and demand pressures, with little of no official intervention.

Clean price This is the market quoted price of a bond – the sum of the net present values of the future coupon (dividend) payments plus redemption value.

Close-out A deal which will in effect cancel the remaining balance of an option (traditional time or delivery definition) by buying back the unwanted foreign currency originally sold to the customer, or selling the foreign currency which now cannot be delivered by the customer. Such close-out deals are effected at the current market spot rate and frequently involve a settlement of the difference due to exchange rate fluctuation in favour of one of the counterparties.

Close-out netting The legal arrangement under an IFEMA agreement to mark to market and settle between the parties the net difference of a series of foreign exchange transactions in the event of bankruptcy of one party.

CLS Continuous linked settlement, the multi-lateral netting process for settlement of foreign exchange transactions following the methodology of the Financial Futures Clearing House.

Collar (see also *Cap* and *Floor*) A collar is the combination of a cap and a floor. The normal reason for purchasing a collar is to reduce the premium cost of a cap. The buyer benefits from fixing a ceiling on interest rate costs but gives up any advantage from rates falling below the floor.

Collateral An asset pledged by a borrower to a lender making a secured loan.

Commercial paper (CP) Unsecured promissory notes issued by corporations at a discount to par to provide short-term financing. Such issues are managed by a bank which will also undertake to repurchase the paper at prevailing rates, thus providing liquidity to investors.

Compound interest The process of capitalization of interest. Interest is added to existing capital at the end of each compounding period so that the subsequent periods' interest payable is calculated on an accumulating capital amount.

Confirmation After transacting a foreign exchange deal over the telephone or other means, the parties to the deal send to each other written confirmations giving full details of the transaction.

Continental (international) terms Forward exchange prices may be quoted in either London terms or Continental terms. London dealers tend to use the "quoted currency" and the descriptive term premium or discount relating to the "quoted currency", e.g. in a GBP/USD forward quotation, London dealers would refer to a quote of 100 – 90 as a USD *premium* (the quoted currency, the USD, at a premium) whereas dealers in other markets abroad would use the descriptive term GBP *discount* for such a price referring to a sterling discount – the base currency at a discount. Unless both currencies are at parity (*par*), one currency at a premium in an exchange rate quotation means that the other currency must be at a discount.

Contingent exposure An exposure which may result from an uncertain future event.

Convergence In financial futures terminology, the process by which cash and future prices converge to one price as delivery approaches. (See also *Basis*.)

Convertible currency A currency which can be freely exchanged for other currencies (and sometimes gold) without special authorization from the appropriate central bank.

Correspondent bank A bank located in one financial centre with whom a bank in another financial centre frequently transacts international business – foreign exchange, trade finance, etc. – and, for this reason, with whom the first mentioned bank maintains an account relationship. This relationship can be in either the home currency of the first bank or that of the second. For example, in the books of a bank in London, a correspondent bank's account in sterling would be termed a vostro account, and the London bank's own account with that correspondent bank in the correspondent's home currency would be termed a nostro account.

Counterparty The customer (including banks) with whom an exchange or money market deal has been effected.

Coupon payment (Classic repo) In a classic repo any coupon or dividend payment during the life of the trade is paid to the original beneficial owner (the repoer).

Coupon payment (sell/buy back) In a sell/buy back, any coupon payment during the lifetime of the trade is paid to the new owner of the bond, who has no obligation to return it to the original owner although this may be factored into the buy back price.

Cover A foreign exchange deal which protects the value of a foreign currency risk position (or exposure) against exchange rate fluctuations.

CrestCo. The real time settlement system for UK and international shares, now incorporating the CGO (Central Gilts Office) and CMO (Central Moneymarkets Office), providing settlement for UK government bonds and other securities. For gilts through the CGO, CrestCo. offers an assured payments system – effectively delivery versus payment (DVP) settlement.

Cross currency repo A cross currency repo is a repo where the cash loan and collateral are denominated in different currencies.

Cross deal An exchange transaction which does not involve either the US dollar or sterling.

Cross rate The exchange rate between the two foreign currencies involved in a cross deal.

Currency option A currency option contract is a contract which gives the buyer the right but not the obligation to buy or sell a specified amount of currency at an agreed price (strike price) at or before a specified future date. Currency options can either be "exchange traded" or "over the counter".

Currency swap A currency swap is an off balance sheet interest rate swap involving two currencies which enables the counterparties to exchange fixed interest payment obligations in respect of borrowings in these different currencies. Currency swaps involve the physical transfer of the capital amount at maturity and frequently also at inception. The rate for such transactions is fixed for the forward value (sometimes several years ahead) at the same level as the exchange rate used for the start date exchange.

Deal date The date on which a foreign exchange, money market or other treasury product transaction is agreed.

Deal ticket An original source document recording a deal (exchange, money market or treasury product) written and signed by the dealer responsible.

Dealer (trader) Specialist in a bank or commercial company authorized to effect foreign exchange, money market or treasury product transactions in the market and who is authorized to take speculative positions within specific dealing limits.

Delivery Settlement of a futures or options contract via a cash commodity or bond transfer.

Delivery risk In counterparty credit limits terminology delivery risk is deemed to be the maximum exposure on any day, or in any assessment period, and is equivalent to the aggregate total of all exchange operations for that date (or dates) where the risk is that the bank will have to pay away amounts of currencies sold without prior confirmation that counterly currency amounts purchased have been duly received.

Delors Plan The EU plan for Economic and Monetary Union (EMU) named after its sponsor, the European Commissioner, Jacques Delors.

Delta The ratio by which the price of an option moves relative to movements in the price of the underlying currency, financial instrument or futures contract.

Delta hedging The method of hedging written (sold) currency options used by options traders to anticipate the potential exercise of outstanding contracts against them.

Depreciation Currency which loses in value against one or more other currencies, especially if this happens in response to natural supply and demand rather than by an official devaluation.

Details Information a dealer requires from a broker following the completion of a transaction, i.e. rates, dates, payment instructions, etc.

Devaluation An official act of a government of a country to reduce the value of its national currency in terms of another single reference currency (frequently the US dollar) or basket of currencies.

Direct quotation A foreign exchange rate is said to be a direct quotation when variable amounts of domestic currency are quoted against a fixed amount (frequently 1 unit) of foreign currency – the base currency. A direct quotation usually has the US dollar as the base currency. An example of a direct quotation is the USD/JPY rate which is expressed in terms of Japanese yen (the quoted currency) per 1 US dollar (the base currency). (See also *Indirect quotation*.)

Dirty price A bond's dirty price is the clean price plus accrued interest to the calculation date or transaction date (including repos).

Discount Used in connection with the quotation of forward rates – a currency which is less expensive (cheaper) to purchase forward than for spot delivery.

Care!

> London dealers and those based overseas use the terms premium and discount differently. See London terms/Continental (international) terms.

Discount house Historically, a financial institution unique to the City of London. The now disbanded nine discount houses (members of the LDMA) were providers of short-term liquidity to the sterling money market. They were primary dealers in Treasury bills, eligible bills and other financial instruments. It used to be through the discount market that the Bank of England effected its daily market operations.

Discount rate (pure discount) A discount rate quoted on a per annum basis is applied to the face value of a financial instrument and that instrument is then traded at a price which is the face value less the discount amount, e.g. T-bills. (See <ACI preferred> formula.)

Discount rate (by reference to a yield) A discount rate quoted on a per annum basis which is applied to the price paid for a financial instrument and that instrument is then traded at that price which is the face value less the discount amount based on a yield rate, e.g. LIBOR used in UK-issued CP. (See <ACI preferred> formula.)

Appendix II

Dollar repo A repo where the collateral repaid at maturity can differ from that originally delivered at the start date is described as a dollar repo.

Double indemnity (repo) A classic repo is described as having unique "double indemnity" status because of counterparty credit considerations and the fact that it is supported by a standard legal agreement.

Duration Technique for evaluating the price sensitivity of interest rate swaps by calculating the average period to yield adjusted cash flows.

EDSP (exchange delivery settlement price) All LIFFE short-term interest rate (STIR) futures contracts held to delivery become "contracts for difference" and are cash settled against the EDSP, which is based on LIBOR at 11.00 a.m. on final trading date.

Either-way price An either-way price (sometimes called a choice price) is when an exchange rate or interest rate is quoted by a bank or broker without any spread between offer and bid, i.e. a counterparty may deal to buy or sell or borrow or lend at the single price quoted.

Eligible bills Bills of exchange in sterling issued for a tenor of up to 187 days by a corporate company in respect of a self-liquidating trade transaction and accepted payable by a bank whose name appears on the Bank of England's list of eligible acceptors. This makes the bills "eligible for rediscount at the Bank of England", meaning they may be used as primary liquidity by banks and ensuring the finest pricing.

Elliott wave theory Popular technical analysis (charting) technique formulated in 1938 by Ralph Elliott.

EMS Acronym for the European Monetary System, introduced in 1979 as a precursor to EU moves towards Economic and Monetary Union.

EMU Acronym for Economic (*not* European) and Monetary Union (the Delors Plan leading to the introduction of the euro).

End/end Forward FX swaps or currency deposits with a spot delivery on the last working day of the current month should be described as "end/end" if it is intended that they should mature on the last working day of the appropriate future month. (See also *Forward*).

Equivalent securities If as a repo buyer you are required to return "equivalent securities" at maturity, you must deliver the same security as you took initially but not the same sequentially numbered securities (ISIN) as originally delivered to you.

ERM (Exchange Rate Mechanism) EU countries within the EMS operated within a fixed exchange rate environment leading up the introduction of the euro in January 1999. Rates were pegged against their central value against the ECU (now replaced by the euro). Agreed intervention points were acted upon to correct divergences as central banks bought and sold ERM currencies reacting to undue fluctuations in values and smoothing market trends.

EURIBOR The Euro Interbank Offered Rate – a market "benchmark" for euro (EUR) interest rates. This is the rate at which principal market makers will lend/offer euros to similar banking counterparties. Do not confuse with BBA *Euro LIBOR*.

Euro The EU common currency (ISO code: EUR) introduced as Phase 3 of EMU on 1 January 1999. Twelve countries participate – Germany, Netherlands, France, Belgium, Luxembourg, Italy, Spain, Portugal, Austria, Finland and Ireland, with Greece having joined in January 2001.

Euro LIBOR The Euro London Interbank Offered Rate is a market "benchmark" for euro (EUR) interest rates fixed daily for a range of periods via the British Bankers Association. This is the rate at which principal market makers will lend money to similar banking counterparties and is the rate preferred as comparitor for a number of London-based derivative markets (FRAs, LIFFE futures, EDSP, ISDA interest rate swap floating rates, cap and floor comparitor rates) denominated in EUR.

Eurocurrency The prefix euro denotes that the currency involved is currently in the possession of a bank or other counterparty not a resident of the country of the currency. This bank or counterparty does not necessarily have to be a resident of Europe. The funds involved never physically leave the clearing system of the country concerned. (See also *Xeno-currency*.)

Eurodollar The first developed and most liquid example of a eurocurrency market is the eurodollar market – US dollar balances held by non-residents of the United States of America.

Exotic currencies Currencies in which there is no active exchange market. Most of the currencies of the under-developed world would fall within this category.

Expiry date The last available date on which an option can be exercised. Options are wasting assets, that is they are either used or expire worthless after the agreed option period. The cost of purchasing an option (the premium) is, among other things, related to the length of this period.

Exposure Used to describe the net position in a currency. A formal definition incorporates the concept of risk to describe the maximum possible loss from a given position.

Extension Used in respect of an foreign exchange option contract (traditional time or delivery definition) where the foreign currency delivery has not been possible during the initial option period and the customer wishes to, in effect, renew the option. Bank of England procedures require that the original option contract is closed out (see definition above) and a new option contract agreed based on the current spot exchange rate, adjusted by any premium/discount applicable to the period in question.

Fed (federal) funds The short-term funds market in the USA where funds are lent by banks with excess reserves to others with financing needs, both banks being member banks of the Federal Reserve System.

Fibonacci retracement A reversal in the trend anticipated based on the calculations of Fibonacci, a twelfth-century Italian monk and mathematician. There are various ratios which occur in nature and which are replicated in the movements of markets.

Figures Regularly published economic statistics followed by the foreign exchange and money markets to give a yardstick on a country's economic performance. The market reaction to figures will vary according to how optimistic or pessimistic is sentiment, and on how the figures accord with the predictions of economic forecasters.

Financial futures A financial futures contract is a legal agreement to buy or sell a standard quantity of a specific currency, financial instrument or commodity at a predetermined future date and at an agreed price. Financial futures can only be dealt at recognized exchanges (the London International Financial Futures Exchange – LIFFE – is an example) and trading takes place under strictly controlled conditions. Many exchanges, including LIFFE, have now migrated onto electronic trading platforms.

Firm A dealer making an offer or bid on a "firm" basis commits the bank but he would be advised to put some restriction on at the same time (e.g. "firm for one minute" or "firm for one million only").

Fixed exchange rate Official rate of exchange set by monetary authorities or currency board for one or more currencies. In most instances, even fixed exchange rates are allowed to fluctuate between definite upper and lower intervention points.

Fixed (period) date The market quotes rates for standard periods for foreign exchange and money market operations. These standard periods are termed fixed dates. As an example, a bank or broker asked for a "run through" of the fixed dates will quote 1, 2, 3, 6 and 12 months prices.

Fixing (bourse) Certain European financial centres used to have a daily "fixing" session, usually held at the stock exchange. The principal function of such sessions was to fix for the day the official spot exchange rate for the domestic currency against various foreign currencies.

Fixing date (FRA) The date upon which the contracted rate on a forward rate agreement is compared with the appropriate benchmark reference rate (LIBOR under FRABBA terms) to ascertain the settlement amount due and to whom this amount is payable (on settlement date). In most currencies fixing date is two days before the start date of the notional period of the contracted FRA. Sterling is the exception, being a value same day currency, and fixing date equals settlement date – the actual start date of the notional period.

Flat basis According to the Bank of England Gilt Repo Code of Best Practice, a repo on which the initial margin is zero is described as being on a "flat basis".

Flex repo A flex repo is a repo with a pre-agreed repayment schedule across the life of the repo.

Floating exchange rate When the value of a currency is decided by market supply and demand only.

Floor (see also *Cap* and *Collar*) A sequence (strip) of interest rate options dealt with the intention of providing the buyer of the options with protection against a decrease in interest rates, i.e. fixing a minimum interest rate receivable.

For indication (only)/For information (only) Quotations which are not firm and are intended as an indication of unwillingness or inability to deal.

Foreign exchange The buying and selling of currencies. The conversion of one currency into another.

Foreign exchange (market) The foreign exchange market handles all transactions involving the purchase or sale of currency. This can be on a spot, forward or FX swap basis.

Foreign exchange option The traditional time or delivery option forward exchange contract whereby the rate is fixed but the counterparty has the option to take delivery on any day between two specified dates. Such contracts must be delivered in full by final maturity date. They should not be confused with a *currency option* (see definition above).

Forward All exchange deals over seven working or business days from spot, fixed at the time of dealing. Where maturity falls on a non-trading day, settlement takes place on the following working day *but* where the forward deal is arranged for a fixed period on a day for which spot delivery occurs on the last working day of the month, it matures on the last working day of the appropriate month in the future (see also *End/end*).

Forward contract Exchange agreement between a bank and a commercial counterparty to deliver one currency in exchange for another at a forward or future date at a fixed exchange rate agreed in advance. Also known as an *outright* forward contract.

Forward exchange time position Various net exposures for forward maturities which a bank has incurred by deliberate policies or as a result of dealing activities.

Forward/forward A money market operation (deposit or loan) or an FX swap where the value dates are not effective immediately. For example, a deposit commencing three months from spot date and maturing six months from spot date would be termed a "forward/forward" operation in the market. The aim of such an operation is to even out the "lumps and bumps" in any forward dated currency cash flow brought about by previously dealing on a mismatched basis.

Forward Rate Agreement (FRA) A forward rate agreement (sometimes referred to as a future rate agreement) is an agreement between two parties, frequently banks, developed to protect the parties against a future move in interest rates over a notional deposit period. An FRA is like an over the counter financial futures contract and is totally flexible as to amount, rate and dates. No initial or variation margin is payable and the transaction (a contract for differences in Bank of England terms) is settled at the start date of the notional deposit period by a discounted payment from one party to the other following comparison of the original contract rate against the current market rate (LIBOR under FRABBA terms).

FRABBA Forward Rate Agreements British Bankers Association standard terms and conditions for FRAs – also included in ISDA (see below) terms and conditions.

Fraption A single-period interest rate option contract, also referred to as an interest rate guarantee.

Front office A commonly used term referring to the dealing room, including the dealers and support staff involved.

Fungibility With a small number of exceptions the exact terms of a financial futures contract are specific to a particular exchange. Where more than one exchange across different time zones quote identical contract specifications, they frequently offer fungibility, i.e. positions opened in one time zone (e.g. Simex) can be closed in another (e.g. Chicago). This means that initial margins paid to the first clearing house do not have to be duplicated to the second and the original position is considered squared by the second transaction.

Futures See *Financial futures*.

Gamma Gamma is a ratio used by options traders to measure the change in the delta when a change in the underlying occurs.

Gap structure The maturity profile of money market or forward exchange time positions. Gap mismatches determine the sensitivity of positions to changes in a currency's yield curve shape, or the interest differential between the two currencies in a forward exchange time position.

General collateral (GC) According to the Bank of England Gilt Repo Code of Best Practice, a general collateral repo trade is one whose principal aim is the borrowing or lending of money secured against most issues of gilts.

Gilt edged stock (Gilts) In the UK describes medium and long-term debt issued by the UK government.

Gilt repo If you deal a single currency repo in which the collateral is a Gilt (Gilt edged security), then you have dealt a classic repo where the collateral is a UK government bond (gilt).

Haircut The term "haircut" (or initial margin) refers to the excess of either cash over the value of securities or the value of securities over cash in a repo transaction at the time it is executed and, subsequently, after margin calls.

> **Care!** In other markets, the term "haircut" may be used differently.

Hedging Dealing in various markets or products (frequently off balance sheet) with the intention of offsetting known risk positions in underlying or parallel markets to protect against adverse rate movements in market prices or interest rates. A hedge is frequently referred to as "a temporary substitute for a known future requirement".

HIC (hold in custody) An HIC repo is where the security remains with the custodian who is arranging repos on instructions from the owner.

Hot money Short-term international capital flows. These are driven by interest rates and investors' perception of the relative value of currencies. The huge volume of such funds makes them a powerful determinant of short-term foreign exchange rate and interest rate price movements.

Icing This is the practice of holding gilts in reserve at the request of other parties who expect to need them in repo operations. This is subject to "open challenge" by other third parties who may also want the securities.

Implied repo rate The implied repo rate is the breakeven rate at which it is possible to buy a bond, repo it out and sell a futures contract (cash and carry arbitrage).

Indication (indication rate) When a dealer states "for indication" or "indication rate", this means that he does not want to transact business at the given rate or rates. The use of this expression can lead to confusion and it is preferable to substitute the less ambiguous term "for information only".

Indirect (reciprocal) quotation A foreign exchange rate is said to be an indirect quotation when variable amounts of foreign currency are quoted against a fixed amount (frequently 1 unit) of local currency. An example of an indirect quotation is the GBP/USD (Cable) rate which is expressed in terms of US dollars (the quoted currency) per 1 pound sterling (the base currency). The euro is also quoted on this basis against all other currencies in the wholesale markets.

Interest accrual The apportionment of the interest receivable/received or payable/paid on a money market or other interest related treasury transaction during the contract period of that transaction. This is to take into profit and loss account such interest only in proportion to that part of the contract period which has elapsed. Accruals are struck in the currency of the transaction and where this is a foreign currency these may be immediately converted to local currency by taking them into consideration as part of the bank's open exchange position and passing entries over the general ledger at a bank's official closing rate for the accounting period in question.

Interest arbitrage The term used to describe a linked set of two exchange operations (usually a spot purchase/sale against a forward operation in reverse) dealt with the specific intention of producing or utilizing funds in one currency (creating synthetic liabilities or assets) where the corresponding liability or asset is in the countercurrency of the foreign exchange swap. Sometimes the description "synthetic asset/liability" may be used to describe the positions so created.

Interest rate guarantee A single period interest rate option contract also referred to as a fraption.

Interest rate option An interest rate option contract is a contract which gives the buyer the right but not the obligation to buy or sell a specified interest rated financial instrument at an agreed rate (strike price) at or before a specified future date. A series of such interest rate options is termed a *cap*, *floor* or *collar* (see the various definitions elsewhere in this glossary).

Interest rate swap (IRS) An interest rate swap involves the counterparties undertaking to exchange interest flows (payments) in respect of an agreed underlying notional principal amount of a single currency, but calculated on differing rate bases (frequently a fixed rate basis against a floating rate basis). There is no exchange of principal either at inception or maturity, and the transaction is off balance sheet.

Intervention The practice of central banks entering the foreign exchange market to support (buy) a currency (frequently their own national currency) is termed intervention. An additional method of support can also be the central bank's intervention in the short date deposit markets – restricting the supply of currency funds when the market is speculatively short of balances.

Intra-day position Overall limit of foreign exchange exposure in one or more currencies a dealing room is allowed to run during the dealing day – to be reduced or closed at a later time during the day.

ISDA International Swaps and Derivatives Association.

ISDA terms The financial markets' industry standard terms and conditions for derivatives such as interest rate swaps bilaterally signed by counterparties transacting such business.

ISMA International Securities Market Association.

Leads and lags The term "leads and lags" in the foreign exchange market is used to describe the practice of exporting customers holding on to their foreign currency earnings until the last moment before conversion to local currency in the expectation of a deterioration in the exchange rate for the local currency, and importing customers buying foreign currency in advance of requirements for the same reason. In a situation where the local currency is expected to appreciate in value the converse applies.

Leverage Achieving the potential for profit and loss several times greater than the original investment. Examples of treasury-related products with high leverage are financial futures – for the payment of a small percentage of "margin" cover for risks in a much larger amount is guaranteed.

LIBID The London Interbank bid rate at which principal market making banks are prepared to accept deposits.

LIBOR The London Interbank Offered Rate – a standard benchmark for domestic sterling and the eurocurrency markets. This is the average of rates at which eight principal market makers will lend money to similar banking counterparties (16 offered rates are obtained and the four highest and lowest are discarded with the remaining eight averaged). Official LIBOR in various currencies and for various time periods is fixed daily at 11.00 a.m. and broadcast by the popular information vendors (Reuters, Bloomberg). Commercial loans are usually rated at a margin over LIBOR, and many of the treasury derivative products use this benchmark rate in their calculations, or settlement procedures. (See also *Euro LIBOR* and *EURIBOR*.)

LIMEAN The median or mean rate between LIBOR and LIBID sometimes used for transfer pricing and other rate comparisons.

Limit Maximum authorized dealing amount that is designed to control banks' credit and trading risk profiles. Limits may be agreed by currency, sector, instrument or counterparty.

Appendix II

Limit order An instruction to deal (stop-loss order) left by a customer or bank with another bank or broker to be executed should the given rate level or set of circumstances be achieved. Limit orders are left at close of business in one centre to ensure 24-hour monitoring of risk positions during other global market opening hours.

Liquidity (market) A cash market such as the foreign exchange or money market is deemed to be liquid when there are constantly available prices and counterparties to any transactions proffered by banks or other market participants. The level of liquidity is frequently measured by the narrowness of the bid–offer spread and market makers' willingness to deal in large amounts.

Liquidity (prudential) All banks are required by their local regulatory authorities to maintain reasonable levels of liquidity – ensuring that a percentage of their monetary assets are held on a short-term basis in support of liabilities which themselves may be withdrawn under similar notice periods, e.g. current accounts (demand deposits).

Local authority bill A bill of exchange issued by a local authority in the UK. These bills are issued by the top 20–25 local authorities as and when funding is required. The bills are issued on a tender basis either direct or through money brokers in the City of London.

London Discount Market Association (LDMA) The association to which the nine member institutions who operated in the sterling discount market used to belong.

London terms Forward exchange prices may be quoted in either London terms or Continental terms. London dealers tend to use the "quoted currency" and the descriptive term premium or discount relating to the "quoted currency", e.g. in a GBP/USD forward quotation, London dealers would refer to a quote of 100 – 90 as a *premium* (a US dollar premium – the quoted currency at a premium) whereas dealers in other markets abroad would use the descriptive term *discount* for such a price, referring to a sterling discount – the base currency at a discount. Unless both currencies are at parity (*par*), one currency at a premium in an exchange rate quotation means that the other currency must be at a discount.

Long bond The 30-year maturity US government issued security – the benchmark bond for longer-term interest rates.

Long (exchange) Excess of purchases over sales (overbought).

Long (money market) Excess of liabilities over assets (i.e. long of cash).

Managed float When the monetary authorities intervene regularly in the market to stabilize the rates or to aim the exchange rate in a direction.

Manufactured dividend A manufactured dividend is a coupon payment repaid by the repo buyer to the repo seller.

Margin (commercial loans) The expression used in eurocurrency loans to determine the amount of interest charged to the borrower over and above the rate of interest which is fixed at the commencement of each drawdown or roll-period, e.g. margin of x percent p.a. above LIBOR (London Interbank Offered Rate).

Margin (financial futures) The initial payment required by the exchange (or the clearing member) on opening a position in any financial futures contract. This initial margin is refundable on closing such futures position. (See also *Variation margin*.)

Margin (spread) Difference between the buying and selling rates, but also used to indicate the discounts or premiums between spot and forward.

Margin or haircut (repos) According to the Bank of England Gilt Repo Code of Best Practice, the excess of value of securities (collateral) over the loan or additional money pledged as margin against the value of Gilts changing during the life of a classic repo transaction is described as a haircut.

Mark to market The process whereby trading positions are revalued using current market prices in order to determine the current profit and loss situation.

Mark to market (classic repo) When a repo is marked to market, the calculation takes into consideration accrued interest on the cash loan and accrued coupon on the collateral. Such mark to market may be done daily or even intra-day during periods of high volatility. Variation margin may be called when the difference in pricing following a fall in collateral value is "material" – defined within the master agreement.

Market maker A bank or other financial institution which is prepared to make a two-way price to most comers for a given currency, financial instrument or commodity.

Market user A bank or other financial institution who calls a market maker seeking their price or rate quotation for a given currency, financial instrument or commodity.

Matched book trading Matched book trading means that the repo trader makes two-way prices for repo transactions as a market maker.

Matched sales In open market operations repo transactions, although initiated by the central bank, are always considered and described from the commercial banks' point of view. When the Federal Reserve Bank does matched sales (or system reverse repos) this means the central bank is selling and buying securities to drain excess liquidity from the market implying that interest rates are too low.

Appendix II

Matching Ensuring that: (a) forward purchases and sales and/or (b) placings (loans) and deposits are in equilibrium by maturity date/period.

Maturity date Due date of an exchange or money market contract, that is the day that the settlement between the contracting parties will have to be effected.

Mine Expression sometimes used to indicate that the contracting party is willing to buy or borrow at the rate offered by the quoting bank. As the term can lead to misunderstandings, it is better to use "I buy" or "I take" rather than "mine" and qualify the statement with an amount to be dealt.

Mismatch (gap) Offsetting money market or forward exchange time positions that do not exactly correspond to each other.

Money market(s) The money markets – both domestic and foreign currency – handle all transactions involving the loan or deposit of currency. This can be on an unsecured loan (time deposit) or secured basis (CDs, repos, etc.) and either short dated (including call and notice accounts) or for fixed date periods.

Moving average In charting terminology, the average rate or price over a specified recent period, which is rolled forward daily. This is used to iron out fluctuations and identify trends, e.g. 30-minute, seven-day, 30-day.

Negotiable instrument A security or other promissory note that may be bought and sold on the secondary market.

Net present value (NPV) The accounting treatment for future cash flows giving each the equivalent value in terms of funds required to invest today at current interest rates to produce the desired amount on the future date.

Non-convertible currency A currency which cannot be exchanged for other currencies, either because this is forbidden by local foreign exchange regulations or because there are no buyers who wish to acquire the currency.

Nostro Foreign currency account maintained at a correspondent bank abroad to make and receive payments in that currency.

Novation Legal method for transferring ownership of an asset by the payment of a cash differential amount.

OAT A French government treasury bond (*Obligation Assimible du Trésor*).

Offer rate (repo) The offer rate in the repo market is the offer of the security – the rate at which the repoing party is prepared to lend the securities and borrow the cash.

Offered (foreign exchange quote) The currency in question is depreciating and sellers of the currency predominate.

Offered (money market) There are indications that the interest rate in the currency and period in question may be falling; there are more lenders (givers) than borrowers in the market.

Open interest In financial futures terminology, the number of outstanding long and short positions for a particular option or futures contract. This is a good indicator of future liquidity in that market.

Open position The difference between total spot and forward purchases and sales in a currency on which an exchange risk is run (exposure), or the difference between the totals of foreign currency assets and liabilities.

Open repo An open repo is the same as a day-to-day repo.

Opportunity cost The risk that by buying a particular financial strategy, a market participant may not be able to take advantage of an alternative that may prove more remunerative. Opportunity cost pricing describes the mathematical relationships that underlie the interdependence of financial markets and for the links that are used by risk managers and arbitrageurs.

Outright The purchase or sale of a currency for delivery on any date other than spot and not forming part of a swap operation.

Over the counter (OTC) Over the counter instruments are traded by individual banks. They are tailored to the individual needs of customers, giving greater flexibility. However, the lack of any formal secondary market for many tailored instruments can sometimes pose liquidity problems.

Overnight (O/N) The shortest period for a money market operation or a foreign exchange swap – a deal with value dates of today against tomorrow.

Par or parity In a forward quote, meaning the outright forward price is identical to the spot, i.e. the swap price = 0.

Point (or pip) In currencies whose exchange rate against the US dollar is quoted to four decimal places 1/10,000 of the currency unit. Where an exchange rate is quoted to only two decimal places 1/100 of the currency unit.

Premium (used in connection with currency or interest rate options) The price paid by the buyer of an option contract to the writer (seller).

Premium (used in connection with the quotation of forward rates) A currency which is more expensive (dearer) to purchase forward than for spot delivery.

> **Care!** London dealers and those based overseas use the terms premium and discount differently. See *London terms/Continental terms*.

Prime rate A preferential lending rate granted by US commercial banks to their most creditworthy customers. Prime rates are sometimes used as benchmark rates for other US dollar rate fixings.

PSA Public Securities Association (now known as The Bond Market Association – TBMA).

Put option An option contract giving the buyer (holder) the right (but not the obligation) to sell the currency specified. For example, to acquire the right to sell euros (and buy US dollars) a euro put option must be purchased.

Quoted currency The currency in which the base currency is "valued" in an exchange rate quotation, i.e. in a GBP/USD rate quotation the US dollar is the quoted currency, there being so many US units to 1 pound sterling (e.g. 1.63 00 – 05 = USD 1.6300 – 1.6305 per GBP 1).

Real Time Gross Settlement (RTGS) The method used by operators of financial centre payments systems (e.g. CHAPS) to reduce the possibility of systemic risk (financial meltdown) by requiring all member institutions to collateralize their maximum daylight exposure to default risk, thereby creating guaranteed (cleared) payments.

Repo A repo is an agreement to enter into a "sale and repurchase" of securities. As an example a short cash position can be covered by means of a repo of bonds (sale and repurchase agreement).

Repo rate The simple interest rate at which a repo is agreed. The repo interest is payable on the cash amount which changes hands in a repo transaction. Typically this will be at a lower interest rate than the cash market as there is collateral involved. The repoer – the cash borrower – pays the interest at maturity of the transaction.

Repurchase agreement (repo) The sale and commitment to repurchase securities at a fixed price at a later date. This mechanism is used by securities traders as a form of collateralized financing. Under 1996 Bank of England regulations, gilt repos have now become one of the major funding vehicles for banks in the short-term London money market.

Rescheduling Mechanism for prolonging an existing debt by rolling over capital (frequently including capitalization of interest payments due on the loan) to a later maturity under new terms and conditions.

Resistance point A chart point which technical analysts predict will be the upper or lower limit of a rate or price movement.

Revaluation An official act of a government of a country to increase the value of its national currency in terms of another single reference currency (frequently the US dollar) or basket of currencies.

Reverse repo The purchase and resale of security at a fixed price at a later date, used by securities dealers as a form of collateralized lending (a repo looked at from the point of view of a lender of funds).

Roll-over The term used to describe the practice in the eurocurrency loan market where the interest rate is variable and fixed only at certain specified intervals, i.e. five-year loan on six months roll-over (periods).

Secondary market Two-way market for securities and other negotiable instruments that have already been issued.

Sell/buy back A repo not governed by the TBMA/ISMA master repurchase agreement – thereby not enjoying the same legal status as a classic repo.

Settlement date The date on which cash settlement of a transaction is effected.

Settlement date (FRA) The date, the start date of the notional period hedged by the original FRA transaction, on which the settlement amount (calculated on fixing date two days before) is paid between the two parties to an FRA. Sterling is the exception: being a value same day currency, fixing date equals settlement date – the actual start date of the notional period.

Shade To narrow or close up or otherwise alter a rate quotation to reflect an interest to deal one way in preference to the other. This may be either on an exchange rate quotation or a money market rate quote.

Short date Money market or exchange swap operations where both the start date and maturity date fall between deal date and the one month fixed date maturity date. Typical dealing periods in the short dates are overnight, tom/next, spot/next and spot a week.

Short (foreign exchange) Excess of sales over purchases (oversold).

Short (money market) Excess of assets over liabilities (i.e. short of cash).

Special collateral When a bond goes "special" it means that demand for bonds in the repo market exceeds supply. Typically the cheapest to deliver (CTD) bond against a bond futures contract will attract this status in reverse repo transactions.

Speculator Someone who trades in financial markets and is willing to accept a measure of risk in return for the prospect of capital gain.

Spot Cash settlement two working or business days from deal date. (Exceptions to the rule may occur either due to differing local market practices or mutual agreement between the counterparties.)

Spot a week A short date operation for either a money market operation or a foreign exchange swap – a deal with value dates of spot date against seven days from spot date (if such a day is a good business day).

Spot/next A short date operation for either a money market operation or a foreign exchange swap – a deal with value dates of the spot date against the day after (spot date plus 1).

Spread The difference (in points) between the buying and selling rates of a foreign exchange quotation or between the offered (lending) and bid (borrowing) rates in money market transactions (expressed in this instance in fractions of a percentage point).

Square (position) Purchases and sales, or foreign currency assets and liabilities, are equal, i.e. no open or mismatch maturity position exists, or there is no further interest in dealing.

Squawk box Voice communications provided by brokers to dealing rooms and used to signal bids and offers to the market participants.

STIR (short term interest rate) Contracts traded on various financial futures exchanges, typically based on three months notional deposits which eventually settle against LIBOR (or equivalent benchmark rate).

Stop-loss order Order given to ensure that should a currency weaken by a certain percentage or other measurement, a short position will be covered even though this involves taking a loss. "Take profit orders" are less common.

Stuffed Being put into a position due to market making which immediately goes wrong.

Substitution In repo terminology "substitution" is when the seller substitutes one type of collateral for another.

Support level When an exchange rate depreciates to a level where the monetary authorities usually intervene to stop any further up or downward movement.

Swap (foreign exchange swap) A simultaneously dealt set of two linked exchange transactions involving the purchase and the sale of an identical amount of one currency against a countercurrency with differing maturities, most frequently spot value against a forward value date.

Swaption (swap option) A swaption provides the buyer (holder) with the right but not the obligation to enter into an interest rate swap involving all the deal details of the swaption with the writer.

SWIFT Society for Worldwide Interbank Financial Telecommunications – an electronic inter-bank communications system which facilitates the sending of currency payment instructions in an efficient and secure fashion, as well as providing member banks with the means to send numerous other types of computer readable communications including foreign exchange confirmations, nostro statements, etc.

System repo If the Federal Reserve Bank New York wants to add liquidity to the US money market it will do system repos. Repos describe the transaction from the commercial banks' point of view.

System reverse repo In open market operations repo transactions, although initiated by the central bank, are always considered and described from the commercial banks' point of view. When the Federal Reserve Bank does system reverse repos (or matched sales) this means the central bank is selling and buying securities to drain excess liquidity from the market, implying that interest rates are too low.

TARGET Trans European Automated Real Time Gross Settlement Express Transfer System – the system operated by central banks in the euro area to facilitate inter-country payments in euros. The Bank of England has a link into the TARGET system and as CHAPS is also linked to the Bank, payments intended to be made through TARGET may be passed over CHAPS Euro.

TBMA The Bond Market Association (formerly known as the Public Securities Association (PSA)).

Technical analysis What a chartist does. An important factor in futures markets.

Term repo According to the Bank of England Gilt Repo Code of Best Practice, a term repo is a repo trade (of a maturity over one day) with a fixed end or maturity date.

Theta Theta measures an option's loss in value due to time decay.

Tom/next (tomorrow/next) A short date operation for either a money market operation or a foreign exchange swap – a deal with value dates of tomorrow against the next day (spot date).

Trading A risk position to take advantage of anticipated short-term rate movements – sometimes only a matter of minutes or hours – is termed a trading position. Examples are spot currency open exchange positions, financial futures and forward rate agreement (FRA) positions. All such trading positions are marked to market for profit and loss assessment purposes.

Treasury bill (T-bill) A short-term US or UK government security with very liquid secondary markets.

Treasury bond (T-bond) A US government security issued for maturities in excess of ten years.

Treasury note (T-note) A medium-term US government security issued for maturities between two and ten years. US T-notes and T-bonds are collectively referred to as "Treasurys".

Two-way price Standard market terminology for the money market or exchange rate quotation made in a currency/period by a market maker.

The price quoted defines the lending/borrowing or selling/buying rates at which the market maker is prepared to deal – always subject to counter-party limits.

Under reference A deal cannot be finalized without reference to the bank which placed the order with a broker, whose name should not be mentioned until reference has been made to that bank.

Underlying The ultimate deliverable instrument or currency on a futures or options contract.

Value date The value date of an exchange transaction is the contracted delivery date on which the payments will be exchanged with the counterparty. For a money market transaction, the value date is the date on which the agreement becomes effective, i.e. the date from which a deposit/loan runs.

Value today or value tomorrow Ante spot value dates in the short dates before the spot date, meaning exactly what they say. Rules for calculating outright exchange rates are reversed to achieve the desired value today or value tomorrow ante spot rates.

Variation margin All financial futures positions are marked to market on a daily basis. Where such procedures result in a net profit or loss situation per futures contract position, settlement between the ultimate position holding member or client and the clearing house takes place in the form of payments which in this case is termed variation margin.

Vega (kappa or sigma) In options trading, volatility in the underlying can and, in the case of currencies, certainly does change frequently. Vega is the measure of change in an option price brought about by a change in the level of volatility in the underlying.

Volatility Measurement of instability in the markets. It is usually quoted on an annualized basis. Volatility is probably the major element in the pricing of options.

Vostro Domestic currency account maintained by a correspondent bank in a foreign financial centre to make and receive payments in that centre, e.g. sterling vostros held by correspondent banks with Blair Bank plc London banks.

Writer (Seller) Guarantor of option who receives the premium in return for guaranteeing the agreed rate of exchange or interest rate to the buyer for the specified period of the option.

Xeno-currency The prefix xeno, coined by Sir Edward George, Governor of the Bank of England (on the introduction of the euro as the EMU common currency), denotes that the currency involved is currently in the possession of a bank or other counterparty not a resident of the country of the currency. The funds involved never physically leave the clearing system of the currency concerned. (See also *Eurocurrency*.)

Yard Dealer's slang to describe one billion (1,000,000,000) units of a currency – from the term "milliard" meaning one thousand million. Most commonly used when quoting yen.

Yield Measurement of value of interest bearing instrument. It combines income and capital gain to show the total return on an investment.

Yield curve The term structure of interest rates over a range of different maturities.

Yours Expression sometimes used to indicate that the contracting party is willing to sell or lend at the rate bid by the quoting bank. As the term can lead to misunderstandings, it is better to use "I sell" or "I give" rather than "yours" and qualify the statement with an amount to be dealt.

Zero coupon In bond dealing terminology, a bond that has no coupons. It is issued at a deep discount and is redeemed at par. The discount depends on the period to maturity and current market yields. A zero coupon bond is frequently used in comparative calculations for interest rate swap operations.

INDEX

accounting
  deal date accounting entries 66
  profit and loss 66, 123, 126–7,
    189–92, 194–5
accreting swaps 153
accrued interest 93–4
ACI (The Financial Markets Association)
  charter 36–7, 345
  mission statement 36, 345
  see also examination; Model Code
actual/360 day count basis 49
actual/365 day count basis 49
actual/actual day count basis 49
after-hours dealing 321–2
Allfirst Maryland 35
Allied Irish Banks 35
American style options 259
amortizing swaps 153
annual/semi-annual conversion formula
  53–5, 364
answer selection button 6
ante-spot contracts 161, 241, 243–6
Arab-Israeli War 30
arbitrage 108
  futures/FRA arbitrage 117, 139–40
  interest arbitrage 199, 247–53, 310–11,
    367
Asia-dollar market 13
asset-based swaps 154
assignments to third parties 339
at the money (ATM) options 264
audits 289
authorization for dealing 332–3
average rate options 272–4
averaging foreign exchange positions
  192–3

averaging money market positions 65

back-to-back loans 145
balance sheets, off balance sheet products
  13, 19, 100
bankers' acceptances 71
Bankhaus I.D. Herstatt 31
banks
  balance sheet constraints 100
  capital adequacy requirements 313–16
  central banks 12, 15, 304–5
  collapses/closures 28, 30, 35
  commercial lending 58–9
  core capital 313
  current account funds 296
  minimum reserve requirements 296
  organizational structure 280–1
  participation in markets 15–16
  position limits 304–6
  prudential liquidity 296–7
  supplementary capital 313
  US banking legislation 28
  use of forward rate agreements 137
  see also treasury divisions
Barings Bank 35
barrier options 275
base currency 15, 169–70
Basel Accord 313–14
basis risk 117
basis swaps 153
BBA (British Bankers Association) 57
BBA Euro LIBOR 57
BBA LIBOR 57, 58
bear spreads 275
betting between market participants
  324–5

Index

bid-offer quotations 20–1
  see also quotation rules
"big figure" 165–6
bills of exchange *see* commercial bills of exchange
binary option 275
BIS survey 13–14, 17–18, 128, 142, 187
Black Wednesday 34, 262
Black-Scholes formula 261–2
bond futures 113–16
bond markets
  bond/money market interest conversion 51–3, 364
  clean prices 93
  dirty prices 93, 94
  interest day count basis 50
  see also government debt
box option strategy 275
break forward option strategy 275
Bretton Woods agreement 27–8
British Bankers Association (BBA) 57
broken dates
  forward foreign exchange 200, 232–5
  interest rate swaps 146–7
  interest rates 62–4, 103
brokerage 110, 286, 334–6
brokers 17, 334–6
  confidentiality standards 326, 335
  connected brokers 339
  disputes with 329–31
  name switching 336
  spot foreign exchange transactions 187
bull spread 276
business entertainment 324
butterfly spread 276

calculators 4, 7, 350
calendar spread trading *see* spread trading
call account money 42–3
call options 258
call spread 276
capital adequacy requirements 313–16
cash clearing and payments methods 288

cash market 41–57
  call account money 42–3
  end/end rule 47
  fixed date loans/deposits 44, 46–8, 357
  interest payment 43, 44
  maturity dates 44, 46–8
  notice deposits 42–3
  retail transactions 42
  risk management 294–8
  wholesale transactions 42
  see also interest rates; money markets
cashflow risk management 202–3
central banks 12, 15, 304–5
Central Moneymarkets Office (CMO) 84
certain (base) currency 15, 169–70
certificates of deposit 78–84, 365
  coupon rate 81
  credit risk 298
  discount calculations 79
  discount CDs 79
  formula 81–2
  issuance 79
  purchasing liquidity 79
  quotations 80
  secondary market trading 79–84
  simple interest bearing 79
  UK market 78
  US market 78
  yield prior to maturity 83–4
  yield to maturity 82–3
changing answers 7
CHAPS payment system 241, 288
Charter of the ACI 36–7, 345
Chicago Mercantile Exchange (CME) 105, 117
CHIPS payment system 61–2
circus swaps 153
classic repos 90, 91–4
clean prices 93
clearing house funds 61–2
clearing houses 108, 258
closing hours 322

Index

Code of Conduct *see* Model Code
comments on the examination 9–10
commercial banks 16
commercial bills of exchange 71–8
  bankers' acceptances 71
  credit risk 298
  discount calculations 73–8
  eligible bills 71–8
commercial lending 58–9
commercial paper 84–7
  credit risk 299
  dealer banks 85
  discount calculations 85–7
  issuance 84
  UK market 84–6
  US market 86–7
commission (brokerage) 110, 286, 334–6
compliance 331
condor 276
confidentiality 326, 335
confirmation procedures 327–8
connected brokers 339
consummation of a deal 337–8
contingent option 276
contract strips 118–19
contracts for difference 132
convertibility of banknotes 27, 29
convertible option contracts 276
Cooke ratio 313, 314
core capital 313
corporate business, forward foreign exchange 201–3, 224–8, 232
corporate treasurers 137–8
corporate/commercial client transactions 341–2
counterparty dealing limits 291, 297–9, 335
counterparty risk *see* credit risk
credit limits 291, 297–9, 335
credit risk
  cash markets 298–8
  currency options 258, 311–12
  financial futures 300
  forward foreign exchange 309–10
  forward rate agreements 301
  interest rate swaps 302
  negotiable financial instruments 298–9
  spot foreign exchange 307–8
cross currency calculations 162, 174–84, 211–24
  one direct one indirect currency pair 174–7
  two direct currencies 178–81
  two indirect currencies 181–4
currency codes xxi–xxii, 14–15, 345
currency futures 256, 257
see also financial futures
currency options 19
  American 259
  at the money (ATM) 264
  average rate 272–4
  calls 258
  credit risk 258
  cylinder option 270–2
  definition 256
  delta 266–7, 269–70
  European 259
  exchange traded 257, 311–12
  gamma 267
  hedging strategies 262–4, 268–70
  intrinsic value 265
  in the money (ITM) 264
  options on futures 257
  options on physicals 257
  OTC (Over The Counter) options 258, 312–13
  out of the money (OTM) 264
  pricing premium payments 258, 260–2
  puts 259
  rights and obligations 260
  risk management 311–13
  theta 267
  time value 265
  trading strategies 275–7
  uses 259–60
  vega 268
  volatility 260, 266
  zero cost cylinder option 272

Index

currency pairs 15, 159
currency swaps 150–3
current account funds 296
customer repos 91
cylinder option 270–2

data security 289
day count basis 49–50
  bond/money market conversion 51–3, 364
deal date accounting entries 66
deal ticket data elements 286–7
dealing jargon 342
dealing limits 291, 297–9, 335
dealing for personal account 326
deferred swaps 153
delivery option forward contracts 201–3, 224–8
delivery risk 302, 307–8, 309–10
delivery and settlement
  bond futures 115–16
  delivery dates 107
  Exchange Delivery Settlement Price 115
  forward rate agreements 131–2, 134–6
  processing/settlements departments 284–5
  repo markets 92
  STIR contracts 115
Delors Plan 34
delta 266–7, 269–70
depositor protection schemes 42
deposits 43, 44, 46–8, 296, 354–5, 357, 358
Deutsche Termine Bourse (DTB) 57
devaluations 28, 29
dictionaries 4, 350
digital option 275
direct quoted currencies 164, 167
Directives *see* EU Directives
dirty prices 93, 94
discount calculations 365
  certificates of deposit 79
  commercial bills of exchange 73–8

commercial paper 85–7
discount rates 55
  equivalent yield from discount rates 76–8
  Treasury Bills 69–71
discount certificates of deposit 79
discount houses 72
disputes 328–32, 343
documentary risk 302
documentation agreement 333
domestic currency money markets 12
drug abuse 324

EBA (European Banking Association) 57–8
economic exposure risk 304
Economic and Monetary Union (EMU) 34–5
Edge Act 28
EEC (European Economic Community) 28, 31, 33, 34
electronic deal-matching systems 17, 106, 187, 335
eligible bills 71–8
emerging markets 18
EMS (European Monetary System) 32, 162
EMU (Economic and Monetary Union) 34–5
end/end rule 47
entertainment *see* business entertainment
equivalent securities 93
ERM (Exchange Rate Mechanism) 32, 33–4, 162
EU Directives
  93/6/EEC 314
  CAD II 316
EURIBOR 57–8
euro 168, 172–4
eurobond markets 50
eurocurrency markets 12–13, 46
eurodollar futures contract 107
EURONEXT 105

Index

European Banking Association (EBA) 57–8
European currency revaluations 28
European Economic Community (EEC) 28, 31, 33, 34
European Monetary System (EMS) 32, 162
European style options 259
European Union *see* EU Directives
examination xv–xvi, 3–10
   checking calculations 358–9
   multiple choice questions 6–8, 351–3
   permitted tools 350–1
   preparation 348–9
   registration for 349
   revision 348, 349
   time management 352
exchange controls 30, 32
Exchange Delivery Settlement Price 115
Exchange Rate Mechanism (ERM) 32, 33–4, 162
exchange risk 305
exchange traded options 257, 311–12
exchangeability of banknotes 27, 29
extendable swaps 153
extraordinary days 61–2

fair value 117
federal funds 61–2
Federal Reserve 32, 91
financial futures 105–27
   bond futures 113–16
   contract specifications 110–11
   dealing commission 110
   delivery and settlement *see* delivery and settlement
   eurodollar futures contract 107
   evolution of 105–7
   fair value 117
   fungibility 110
   futures equivalent run 117
   futures/FRA arbitrage 117, 139–40
   hedging with STIR contracts 116–23
   margin payments 109, 114

position keeping 126–7
pricing 111–14
profit and loss accounting 123, 126–7
quotations 112
risk management 299–300
spread trading 123–6
tick size 113
uses of 107–8
Financial Services Act (1986) 42
Financial Services Authority (FSA) 321
fixed date loans/deposits 44, 46–8, 357
flat yield curves 60–1
floating exchange rates 29, 30
foreign exchange markets 14–15
   currency codes xxi–xxii, 14–15, 345
   evolution of xiii, 26–35
   floating exchange rates 29, 30
   quotation methods 20
   US crisis programme 29
   volumes and values traded 14, 18
   see also forward foreign exchange; spot foreign exchange
foreign exchange swaps 19, 203–4, 228–32, 367
   forward/forward foreign exchange swaps 235–40
   short dated foreign exchange swaps 240–6
formulae sheets 4, 7, 350, 364–7
forward foreign exchange 198–253
   broken date 200, 232–5
   cashflow risk management 202–3
   corporate business 201–3, 224–8, 232
   cross currency calculations 211–24
   discount to benchmark swap rates 205–7, 356
   forward swap points 204
   interbank transactions 228–32
   and interest arbitrage 199, 247–53, 310–11, 367
   and interest rate differential 208
   outright forward contracts 201, 202, 209–24

Index

forward foreign exchange *Continued*
  periods available 199
  premium to benchmark swap rates
    205–7, 356–7
  quotation of forward rates 20, 204,
    356–7
    bid-offer spreads 208–9
    option forward contracts 226–7
    premiums/discounts 205–7, 356–7
    terminology 207–9
  risk management 308–11
  time (delivery) option forward contracts
    201–3, 224–8
  value dates 200
forward rate agreements (FRAs) 14,
  127–41, 355–6, 366
  benefits 138
  buy/sell logic 128
  FRABBA terms and conditions 127–8
  futures/FRA arbitrage 117, 139–40
  market growth 128
  market participants 137–8
  position keeping 141
  quotations 129, 130–1
  risk management 300–1
  settlement 131–2, 134–6
  spread trading 140
  trading in 132–6
  unwinding positions 136–7
forward swap points 204
forward/forward foreign exchange swaps
  235–40
forward/forward interest rates 101–4,
  366
FRABBA terms and conditions 127–8
fraud 325–6
fungibility 110
future value (FV) 55, 56–7
futures contracts *see* financial futures
futures equivalent run 117
futures/FRA arbitrage 117, 139–40

gambling between market participants
  324–5

gamma 267
gap positions 65–6
gifts 324
gilts 87–8, 90, 92
Global Master Repurchase Agreement
  (GMRA) 91
GMRA (Global Master Repurchase
  Agreement) 91
gold price 27, 33
Gold Standard 27
government debt
  gilts 87–8, 90, 92
  Treasury bills 67–71, 298
  Treasury bonds 88
  Treasury notes 88
  see also repo market
Gresham's Law 26
Grey Book 321

"haircut" 92
hedge funds 17
hedge ratios 117–18, 269–70
hedging 108, 116–23
  basis risk 117
  contract strips 118–19
  with currency options 262–4, 268–70
  delta hedging 269–70
  and forward/forward interest rates
    104
  futures/FRA hedging 117, 139–40
  hedge ratios 117–18, 269–70
  IMM dates 117
  long hedges 116
  profit and loss accounting 123, 126–7
  recording positions 126
  rolling hedges 119–20
  short hedges 116
  stack hedges 119–20
  stubs 121
  tails 121–2
Help button 7–8
Herstatt risk 307–8
humped yield curves 61

Index

IMF (International Monetary Fund) 27–8
IMM dates 117
in the money (ITM) options 264
index-linked gilts 88
indirect quoted currencies 167–8, 172–4
initial margin 109
interbank market
  call and notice deposits 42–3
  forward foreign exchange 228–32
  spot foreign exchange 184–6, 193–4
interest arbitrage 199, 247–53, 367
  risk management 310–11
interest day basis *see* day count basis
interest rate futures *see* STIR (short-term interest rate) futures
interest rate swaps 14, 141–54
  and back-to-back loans 145
  broken date 146–7
  evolution of 142
  fixing of rates 147, 150
  interest calculation bases 146–7
  market size 142
  master agreements 146
  netting 149
  plain vanilla interest rate swaps 143–6
  quotations 143–4
  risk management 301–3
  terms and conditions 142–3, 145
  uses 148, 152
  variants 153–4
  see also swaps
interest rates
  accrued interest 93–4
  annual/semi-annual conversion formula 53–5, 364
  benchmarks 57–8
  bond/money market conversion 51–3, 364
  broken date 62–4, 103
  day count basis 49–50
  equivalent yield from discount rates 76–8
  future value (FV) 55, 56–7

LIBOR 57–8
  on non-standard periods 62–4
  on nostro balances 32
  payment on deposits 43, 44
  position average rates 65
  present value (PV) 55, 56
  risk management 294–6, 308–9
  on roll-over loans 58–9
  selection of best rates 45
  simple interest formula 48–9
  time value of money 55–7
  in the US 32
  see also discount calculations; yield curves
internal audits 289
International Monetary Fund (IMF) 27–8
International Monetary Market (IMM) 105, 117
international trading companies 16
Internet 189, 338
interpolation *see* broken dates
intra-day position limits 305
intrinsic value 265
investment banks 16
Irish punt 32
Islamic weekend 160, 322
ISMA (International Securities Market Association) 91
ISO (International Standards Organization) codes xxi–xxii, 14–15, 345
Item Review screen 6, 7, 8

Joint Standing Committee 331

kappa 268
knock-in options 275

Leeson, Nick 35
lender of last resort 12, 13
LIBOR 57–8
LIFFE 57, 58, 105–7
LIFFE Connect 106–7
limit orders 306–7

401

Index

liquidity risk 296–7, 302
Lloyds Bank International 31, 321, 337
loans 43, 44, 46–8, 296, 354–5, 357, 358
  back-to-back loans 145
London Clearing House (LCH) 108
London Code of Conduct 321
  see also Model Code
long hedges 116
lookback option 276
lookback strike option 276
Louvre Accord 33
LTOM (London Traded Options Market) 105

Maastricht Treaty 34–5
Major, John 33
margin payments 92, 109, 114
  initial margin 109
  SPAN (Standard Portfolio Analysis of Risk) 109
  variation margin 109, 114
market centres 13, 18
market making 19–20
market opening and closing hours 322
market participants 15–17
market replacement risk 302–3, 310
market risk
  currency options 311–12
  financial futures 299
  financial instruments 298
  forward rate agreements 300–1
  interest rate swaps 301
Marking questions 7, 8
matched sales 91
mediation 328–9
merchant banks 16
Middle Eastern currencies 160, 322
minimum reserve requirements 296
misinformation 326
mismatch positions 65–6, 295
mission statement 36, 345
mobile phones 322

Model Code 3, 37, 320–45
  assignments to third parties 339
  authorization for dealing 332–3
  brokers and brokerage 334–6
  compliance 331
  confirmation procedures 327–8
  connected brokers 339
  corporate/commercial client transactions 341–2
  dealing practice 336–9
  disputes 328–32, 343
  documentation 333
  fixing spot rates 231, 237–8
  instruments covered 343–4
  market terminology 342
  markets covered 343–4
  mobile phones 322
  personal conduct 324–7
  position parking 323
  repo market 340
  risk management 340–1
  stock lending 340
  stop-loss orders 323
  telephone taping 287, 333
  trading hours/days 321–2
money laundering 325
money market derivatives 13, 14, 100–55
  financial futures 105–27
  forward rate agreements 127–41, 355–6, 366
  forward/forward interest rates 101–4, 366
  interest rate swaps 141–54
money markets 12, 40–97
  cash market 41–57
  day count basis 49–50
  deal date accounting entries 66
  dealing periods 357
  evolution of xiii, 26–35
  interbank market 42–3
  money market/bond market interest conversion 51–3, 364
  negotiable financial instruments 66–87

Index

position keeping 64–6
profit and loss calculation 66
quotation methods 21, 44–5, 48
risk management 294–8
see also interest rates; repo market
multinational corporations 16
multiple choice questions 6–8, 351–3

naked option 277
name switching 336
national holidays 322
negative yield curves 60
negotiable financial instruments 66–87
  certificates of deposit 78–84, 365
  commercial bills of exchange 71–8
  commercial paper 84–7
  Treasury Bills 67–71
netting agreements 149, 307, 308
Next question button 6
nostro accounts 32, 287
notice deposits 42–3

O'Brien letter 31, 321
off balance sheet products 13, 19, 100
off-premises dealing 321–2
oil price 30
online trading 338
open exchange positions 305–6
open outcry trading 106, 108
opening and closing hours 322
option forward contracts 201–3, 224–8
  close-out transactions 225
  early take-up 226
  extensions 225
  partial take-up 225
  periods available 225
  pricing 226
  pricing date 228
  quotation rules 224–7
OTC (over the counter) products 19, 258, 312–13
out of the money (OTM) options 264
outright forward contracts 201, 202, 209–24

outright value tomorrow 242–3
overnight position limits 306

participating forward contracts 277
pass marks 3, 4
perpetual gilts 88
personal account dealing 326
personal conduct 324–7
Philadelphia Stock Exchange 257
plain vanilla interest rate swaps 143–6
Plaza Accord 33
position keeping
  averaging foreign exchange positions 192–3
  averaging money market positions 65
  describing forward/forward positions 104
  financial futures 126–7
  forward rate agreements 141
  mismatch positions 65–6, 295
  money markets 64–6
  spot foreign exchange 189–95
position limits 304–6
  central bank regulations 304–5
  intra-day limits 305
  market risk limits 305
  open exchange positions 305–6
  overnight limits 306
position parking 323
positive yield curves 59–60
present value (PV) 55, 56
private clients 17
processing/settlements departments 284–5
profit and loss accounting
  financial futures 123, 126–7
  money markets 66
  spot foreign exchange 189–92, 194–5
  see also position keeping
Prometric electronic delivery examination 5–10
Prometric test centre 349–50, 350–1
prudential liquidity 296–7

403

Index

put options 259
put spread 277
putable swaps 154

quotation rules
  certificates of deposit 80
  change in quoted rates 188
  declining to quote 186
  eligible bills 72
  euro 168, 172–4
  financial futures 112
  forward foreign exchange 20, 204–9, 226–7, 356–7
  forward rate agreements 129, 130–1
  information/indication quotes 188
  interest rate swaps 143–4
  loans/deposits 354–5
  and the Model Code 338
  money markets 21, 44–5, 48
  option forward contracts 224–7
  repo market 89–90
  spot foreign exchange 20, 162–74, 186, 188, 356
  Treasury Bills 68

rate capped swaps 154
recording positions 126
registration for ACI examination 349
Regulation Q 28
repo market 41, 87–96, 340
  classic repos 90, 91–4
  coupon payments 92
  credit risk 298
  customer repos 91
  equivalent securities 93
  gilts 87–8, 90, 92
  Global Master Repurchase Agreement (GMRA) 91
  initial consideration 94
  interest accruing 92
  legal title 91–2
  margin payments (haircut) 92
  matched sales 91

quotations 89–90
reverse repos 88–9, 91
sale and repurchase agreements 88–9
system repos 91
terminology 94–5
Treasury bonds 88
Treasury notes 88
US markets 90–1
repo rates 90
reportage 9, 295–6, 300, 309
  deal ticket data elements 286–7
  see also position keeping; profit and loss accounting
Reprint Report button 9
Results screen 8–9
Reuters 112–13, 188–9
revaluation of currencies 28
reverse repos 88–9, 91
Review Item boxes 8
revision for ACI examination 348, 349
risk management
  capital adequacy requirements 313–16
  cash markets 294–8
  cashflow 202–3
  credit limits 291, 297–9, 335
  currency options 311–13
  delivery risk 302, 307–8, 309–10
  documentary risk 302
  financial futures 107, 299–300
  financial instruments 298–9
  forward foreign exchange 308–11
  forward rate agreements 300–1
  Herstatt risk 307–8
  interest arbitrage operations 310–11
  interest rate risk 294–6, 308–9
  interest rate swaps 301–3
  liquidity risk 296–7, 302
  market replacement risk 302–3, 310
  market risk position limits 305
  Model Code 340–1
  netting agreements 307, 308
  in spot foreign exchange 303–8
  time zone risk 306

404

Index

Value at Risk (VaR) models 316
  see also position limits
riskless hedge principle 261–2
roll-over loans 58–9
roller coaster swaps 153
rolling hedges 119–20
rollover positions 337
rumours 326

sale and repurchase agreements 88–9
screen-based trading 17, 106, 187, 335
Section Scores button 9
seigneurage 27
semi-annual/annual conversion formula 53–5, 364
settlement see delivery and settlement
short dated foreign exchange swaps 240–6
  ante-spot contracts 241, 243–6
  outright value tomorrow 242–3
  time zone limitations 241–2
short hedges 116
short sterling contracts see STIR
SIBOR 58
sigma 268
simple interest formula 48–9
Smithsonian Agreement 29
Snake 30
SPAN (Standard Portfolio Analysis of Risk) 109
spiked yield curves 61
spot foreign exchange 158–95
  ante-spot dates 161
  base currency 169–70
  "big figure" 165–6
  broker transactions 187
  choice of best rates 169–71
  cross currency calculations 162, 174–84
  direct quoted currencies 164, 167
  electronic deal-matching systems 187
  indirect quoted currencies 167–8, 172–4

information on rates 188–9
interbank transactions 184–6, 193–4
limit orders 306–7
low value unit currencies 191–2
market makers 163
market users 163, 169–71
measure of value 162–3
"my word is my bond" 188
"points" or "pips" 166–7
position keeping 189–95, 304–6
processing time 160
profit and loss accounting 189–92, 194–5
quotations 20, 162–74, 356
  change in quoted rates 188
  declining to quote 186
  euro 168, 172–4
  information/indication quotes 188
risk management 303–8
short date transactions 161–2
spot value date 159–60
spreads 164–5
stop loss orders 306–7
variable currency 170–1
see also foreign exchange markets
spot value date 159–60
spread trading 123–6, 140
squawk boxes 326
stack hedges 119–20
Standard Settlement Instructions (SSI) 287
sterling devaluations 28, 29
sterling/euro foreign exchange quotations 172–4
STIR (short-term interest rate) futures 111–13, 115, 116–23
  see also financial futures
stock lending 340
stop-loss orders 306–7, 323
straddle 277
strangle 277
strips 118–19
stubs 121

405

Index

substance abuse 324
supplementary capital 313
survey input screen 5
swaps 19, 58
  asset-based 154
  benchmark rates 205–7, 356–7
  currency 150–3
  documentation agreement 333
  foreign exchange 19, 203–4, 228–32, 367
  forward/forward foreign exchange 235–40
  short dated foreign exchange 240–6
  variants 153–4
  see also interest rate swaps
SWIFT 15, 288
Swiss franc 32, 62
Swiss National Bank 32
system repos 91

TAG (Trainers Action Group) 9
tails 121–2
taping dealing conversations 287, 333
TARGET system 57, 160–1, 288
TBMA (The Bond Market Association) 91
telephone taping 287, 333
theta 267
Thursday/Friday anomaly 61–2
TIBOR 58
tick size 113
time (delivery) option forward contracts 201–3, 224–8
time management 7, 352
time value of money 55–7
time value of options 265
time zone risk 241–2, 306
trading banks 16
trading books 314–15
Trading Host 106–7
trading hours/days 61–2, 321–2
  Islamic weekend 160, 322

time zone risk 241–2, 306
training companies 5
transaction exposure risk 304
translation exposure risk 304
Treasury bills 67–71, 298
Treasury bonds 88
treasury divisions 137–8, 281–91
  Bank of England recommendations 290
  best practice 290–1
  brokerage negotiations 286
  cash clearing and payments methods 288
  and credit limits 291, 297–8
  deal tickets 286–7
  division of duties 284
  management structure 283–4
  nostro accounts 287
  objectives 283
  processing/settlements departments 284–5
  roles and responsibilities 282–3, 285
  securities issue 288
  Standard Settlement Instructions (SSI) 287
  support functions 289–90
  taping dealing conversations 287, 333
Treasury notes 88
trigger options 275
two-tier currencies 30

uncertain (quoted) currency 15, 164, 167–8, 172–4
unidentified principles 338
unwinding forward rate agreements 136–7

Value at Risk (VaR) models 316
value dates 159–60, 200
  ante-spot dates 161, 241, 243–6
value of one point rule 190–1
value same day 47–8

Index

value tomorrow 242–3
variable currency 170–1
variation margin 109, 114
vega 268
voice brokers *see* brokers
volatility 260, 266
Volker, Paul 32
volumes and values traded
  derivatives 14, 18, 19
  foreign exchange markets 14, 18

WI (When Issued) market 69
World Bank 27–8

yield curves 59–62, 101–2, 117
  spread trading 123–5

zero cost cylinder option 272
zero coupon swaps 153

MARKET EDITIONS:
From the heat of the markets

Everyone knows that in the financial markets stakes are high. But when you're on the frontline or at the heart of decision making, gaps in your understanding and application could cost millions.

Market Editions is a series of professional finance books designed to keep your head above water. Covering cutting-edge topics and essential fundamentals within a host of financial areas, they enable you to pick up the concepts and theories fast and apply them with maximum success and minimum effort.

Also available:

- **Mastering Foreign Exchange and Money Markets**
- **Mastering Foreign Exchange and Currency Options**
- **Mastering Credit Derivatives**
- **Mastering Repo Markets**

Visit our websites at
www.business-minds.com
www.financialminds.com

LYWOOD DAVID INTERNATIONAL LIMITED

presents a range of specialised open training courses on a regular basis in London and other financial centres

Courses include:
Introduction to treasury Dealing operations
Introduction to Capital markets operations
Asset and Liability management – a practical course on cashflow/interest rate risk management
Accounting for Treasury transactions, risks and profits
Auditing the Dealing room – Demystifying Treasury and Capital markets operations
and the ever popular **ACI CLINIC** covering training towards
ACI Settlements Certificate / **ACI Dealing Certificate** / ACI Model Code / ACI Diploma

Multimedia TradeWind Limited

Lywood David International Limited's sister company **Multimedia TradeWind Limited** designs and develops PC based distance learning software. The company offers the **WINDEAL** range of dealing simulation products and **WINFOREX** - the unique PC based study aid (replicating Prometric electronic examination delivery) available in four modules for **ACI Education candidates** either for individual candidate purchase or on a site licence basis for financial institutions training departments / open learning centres.

Please see the websites: www.lywood-david.co.uk and www.acitraining.co.uk
or contact the companies by Phone: +44 1732 463014, Fax: +44 1732 463015
or e-mail: training@lywood-david.co.uk for further information